Leo Wiener

The History of Yiddish Literature in the nineteenth Century

Leo Wiener

The History of Yiddish Literature in the nineteenth Century

ISBN/EAN: 9783337205959

Printed in Europe, USA, Canada, Australia, Japan

Cover: Foto ©ninafisch / pixelio.de

More available books at **www.hansebooks.com**

To My Mother

PREFACE

A SUGGESTION to write the present book reached me in the spring of 1898. At that time my library contained several hundreds of volumes of the best Judeo-German (Yiddish) literature, which had been brought together by dint of continued attention and, frequently, by mere chance, for the transitoriness of its works, the absence of any and all bibliographies, the almost absolute absence of a guide into its literature, and the whimsicalness of its book trade made a systematic selection of such a library a difficult problem to solve. Not satisfied with the meagre details which could be gleaned from internal testimonies in the works of the Judeo-German writers, I resolved to visit the Slavic countries for the sake of gathering data, both literary and biographical, from which anything like a trustworthy history of its literature could be constructed. A recital of my journey will serve as a means of orientation to the future investigator in this or related fields, and will at the same time indicate my obligations to the men and the books that made my sketch possible.

From Liverpool, my place of landing, I proceeded at once to Oxford, where I familiarized myself with the superb Oppenheim collection of Judeo-German books of the older period, stored in the Bodleian Library; it does not contain, however, anything bearing on the nineteenth century. In London the British Museum furnished me with a few modern works which are now difficult to procure, especially the periodical *Kolmewasser* and *Warschauer Jüdische Zeitung*. Unfortunately my time was limited, and I was unable to make thorough bibliographical notes from these rare publications; besides, I then hoped to be able to discover sets of them in Russia. In this I was disappointed — hence the meagreness of my references to them. The Rosenthaliana in Amsterdam and the Imperial Library in Berlin added nothing material to my information. Warsaw was my first objective point as regards facts and books. The latter I obtained in large numbers by rummaging the bookstores of Scheinfinkel and Morgenstern. In a dark and damp cellar, in which Morgenstern kept part of his store, many rare books were picked up. In Warsaw I received many valuable data from Perez, Dienesohn, Spektor, Freid, Levinsohn, both as to the activity which they themselves have developed and as to what they knew of some of their *confrères*. In Bialystok I called on the venerable poet, Gottlober; he is very advanced in years, being above ninety, is blind, and no longer in possession of his mental faculties, but his daughter gave me some interesting information about her father. Wilna presented nothing noteworthy, except that in a store a few early prints were found.

In St. Petersburg I had hoped to spend usefully a week investigating the rich collections of Judeo-German in the Asiatic Museum and the Imperial Library. The museum was, however, closed for the summer, and the restrictions placed on the investigator in the library made it impossible to inspect even one-tenth of the three or four thousand books contained there. When

about to abandon that part of my work the assistant
librarian, Professor Harkavy, under whose charge the
collection is, most generously presented me with one
thousand volumes out of his own private library. In
Kiev I had a long conference with S. Rabinowitsch
and with A. Schulmann; the latter informed me that
he is now at work on a history of Judeo-German
literature previous to the nineteenth century; the
specimen of his work which he published a few years
ago in the *Jüdische Volksbibliothēk* gives hope that it
will entirely supersede the feeble productions of M.
Grünbaum. In Odessa I learned many important facts
from conversations with S. J. Abramowitsch, J. J. Linetzki, J. J. Lerner, P. Samostschin, and depleted the
bookstores, especially that of Rivkin, of their rarer
books. Jassy in Roumania and Lemberg in Galicia
offered little of interest, but in Cracow Faust's book-
store furnished some needed data by its excellent
choice of modern works.

Thus I succeeded in seeing nearly all the living
writers of any note, and in purchasing or inspecting
books in all the larger stores and libraries that contained such material. In spite of all that, the present
work is of necessity fragmentary; it is to be hoped
that by coöperation of several men it will be possible
to save whatever matter there may still be in existence
from oblivion ere it be too late. The greatest difficulty
I encountered in the pursuit of my work was the identification of pseudonyms and the settlement of bibliographical data. As many of the first as could be
ascertained, in one way or other, are given in an
appendix; but the bibliography has remained quite
imperfect in spite of my efforts to get at facts. A
complete bibliography can probably never be written,

on account of the peculiar conditions prevailing in the Imperial Library, from which by theft and otherwise many books have disappeared; but even under these conditions it would not be a hard matter to furnish four or five thousand names of works for this century. This task must be left to some one resident in St. Petersburg who can get access to the libraries.

This history being intended for the general public, and not for the linguistic scholar, there was no choice left for the transliteration of Judeo-German words but to give it in the modified orthography of the German language; for uniformity's sake such words occurring in the body of the English text are left in their German form. All Hebrew and Slavic words are given phonetically as heard in the mouths of Lithuanian Jews; that dialect was chosen as being least distant from the literary German; for the same reason the texts in the Chrestomathy are normalized in the same variety of the vernacular. The consonants are read as in German, and *ž* is like French *j*. The vowels are nearly all short, so that *ü, ie, i* are equal to German *i*; similarly *ä, ö, eh, ee* are like German short *e*. The German long *e* is represented by *ē, oe, ae*, and in Slavic and Hebrew words also by *ee*. *Ei* and *eu* are pronounced like German *ei* in *mein*, while *ēi* is equal to German *ee*; *ā* and *o* are German short *o*; *au* sounds more like German *ou*, and *äu* and *ō* resemble German *öi*; *aü* is equal to German *ai*.

The collection of data on the writers in America has been even more difficult than in Russia, and has been crowned with less success. Most of the periodicals published here have been of an ephemeral nature, and the newspapers, of which there have been more than forty at one time or other, can no longer be procured;

and yet they have contained the bulk of the literary productions written in this country. It is to be hoped that those who have been active in creating a Judeo-German literature will set about to write down their reminiscences from which at a later day a just picture may be given of the ferment which preceded the absorption of the Russian Jews by the American nation.

The purpose of this work will be attained if it throws some light on the mental attitude of a people whose literature is less known to the world than that of the Gypsy, the Malay, or the North American Indian.

CAMBRIDGE, MASS.,
    December, 1898.

CONTENTS

xiii

CHRESTOMATHY

THE HISTORY OF YIDDISH LITERATURE IN THE NINETEENTH CENTURY·

I. INTRODUCTION

THE literatures of the early Middle Ages were bilingual. The Catholic religion had brought with it the use of the Latin language for religious and ethical purposes, and in proportion as the influence of the clergy was exerted on worldly matters, even profane learning found its expression through the foreign tongue. Only by degrees did the native dialects manage to establish themselves independently, and it has been but a few centuries since they succeeded in emancipating themselves entirely and in ousting the Latin from the domain of secular knowledge. As long as the Jews have not been arrested in their natural development by external pressure, they have fallen into line with the conditions prevalent in their permanent homes and have added their mite towards the evolution of the vernaculars of their respective countries. It would be idle to adduce here proofs of this; suffice it only to mention Spain, whose literature would be incomplete without including in the list of its early writers the names of some illustrious Jews active there before the expulsion of the Jews in the fifteenth century. But the matter everywhere stood quite differently in regard to the Latin language. That being the language of the Catholic clergy, it could not be cultivated by the Jews

without compromising their own faith ; the example of
the bilingualism was, however, too strong not to affect
them, and hence they had recourse to the tongue of their
own sacred scriptures for purposes corresponding to those
of the Catholic Church.   The stronger the influence of
the latter was in the country, the more did the Jews cling
to the Hebrew and the Jargon of the Talmud for literary
purposes.   It need not, then, surprise us to find the Jewish literature of the centuries preceding the invention
of printing almost exclusively in the ancient tongue.

As long as the German Jews were living in Germany,
and the Sephardic Jews in Spain, there was no urgent
necessity to create a special vernacular literature for
them : they spoke the language of their Christian fellow-citizens, shared with them the same conception of
life, the same popular customs, except such as touched
upon their religious convictions, and the works current
among their Gentile neighbors were quite intelligible,
and fully acceptable to them.   The extent of common
intellectual pleasures was much greater than one would
be inclined to admit without examination.   In Germany
we have the testimony of the first Judeo-German or
Yiddish works printed in the sixteenth century that
even at that late time the Jews were deriving pleasure
from the stories belonging to the cycle of King Arthur
and similar romances.   In 1602 a pious Jew, in order to
offset these older stories, as he himself mentions in his
introduction,[1] issued the ' Maasebuch,' which is a collection of Jewish folklore.   It is equally impossible, however,

---

[1] " Drum ir liben Mannen un' Frauen, leient ir oft daraus so wert
ir drinnen behäuen um nit zu leienen aus dem Bicher von Kühen un'
von Ditrich von Bern un' Meister Hildabrant sollt ir ach euch nit tun
müen, nun es sein wärlich eitel Schmitz, sie geben euch nit Warem
noch Hitz, ach sein sie nit gettlich darbei." (*Serapeum*, Vol. XXVII.
p. 3.)

to discover from early German songs preserved by the Jews that they in any way differed from those recited and sung by the Gentiles, and they have to be classed among the relics of German literature, which has actually been done by a scholar who subjected them to a close scrutiny.[1] On the other hand, the Jews who were active in German literature, like Süsskind, only accidentally betray their Jewish origin. Had they not chosen to make special mention of the fact in their own works, it would not be possible by any criterion to separate them from the host of authors of their own time.

Had there been no disturbing element introduced in the national life of the German Jews, there would not have developed with them a specifically Judeo-German literature, even though they may have used the Hebrew characters in the transliteration of German books. Unfortunately, in the beginning of the sixteenth century, a large number of Jews, mainly from the region of the Middle Rhine, had become permanently settled in Bohemia, Poland, and Russia. Here they formed compact colonies in towns and cities, having been admitted to these countries primarily to create the nucleus of a town population, as the agricultural Slavs had been averse to town life. They had brought with them their patrimony of the German language, their German intellectual atmosphere and mode of life; and their very compactness precluded their amalgamation with their Slavic neighbors. Their numerical strength and spiritual superiority obliterated even the last trace of those Jews who had been resident in those regions before them and had spoken the Slavic dialects as their mother-tongues. Separated from their mother-country, they

[1] F. Rosenberg, *Ueber eine Sammlung deutscher Volks- und Gesellschafts-lieder in hebräischen Lettern*, Berlin, 1888.

craved the intellectual food to which they had been accustomed there; but their relations with it were entirely broken, and they no longer took part in the mental life of their German contemporaries. The Reformation with its literary awakening could not exert any influence on them; they only turned back for reminiscences of ages gone by, and hungered after stories with which their ancestors had whiled away their hours of leisure in the cities along the Rhine. And so it happened that when the legendary lore of the Nibe-lungen, of Siegfried, of Dietrich of Bern, of Wigalois, of King Arthur, had begun to fade away even from the folk books of Germany, it lived on in the Slavic coun-tries and continued to evoke pleasure and admiration.

These chapbooks, embodying the folklore of past generations, were almost the first printed Judeo-German books, as they certainly were the most popular. That the early Judeo-German literature was intended mainly for readers in the east of Europe is amply evidenced by specific mention in the works themselves, as for example in the 'Maasebuch,' where the compiler, or author, urges the German women to buy quickly his book, lest it be all too fast sold in Bohemia, Poland, and Russia.[1] In fact, the patron of the 'Maasebuch,' or the author of the same, for it is not quite clear whether they are not one and the same person, was himself a native of Mese-ritz in Lithuania. Only after these story books had created a taste for reading, and in order to counteract the effects of the non-Jewish lore, the Rabbis began to

---

[1] "Drum ir liben Frauen kauft ir sie behend, e sie werden kummen in fremden Länd, in Pehm un' in Reussen un' in Polen, aso wert man sie ach tun weidlich holen, un' andern Ländern mer, drum kauft ir sie ser, dernoch werd ir sagen, warum hab ich keins gekauft, da sie sein gewesen in Land." (*Serapeum*, Vol. XXVII. p. 3.)

substitute the more Jewish legends of the 'Maasebuch' and the 'Zeena Ureena,' and the ethical treatises which were intended to instruct the people in the tenets of their fathers. In this manner the Judeo-German literature was made possible. Its preservation for four centuries was mainly due to the isolation of the German Jews in Russia and Poland, where the German medievalism became ossified and was preserved intact to within half a century ago, when under favorable conditions the Russianization of the Jews began. Had these conditions prevailed but a short time longer, Judeo-German literature would have been a thing of the past and of interest only to the linguist and the historian. But very soon various causes combined to resuscitate the dialect literature. In the short time that the Jews had enjoyed the privileges of a Russian culture, then German medievalism was completely dispelled, and the modern period which, in its incipient stage, reaches back into the first quarter of this century, presents a distinct phase which in no way resembles the literature of the three hundred years that preceded it. It is not a continuation of its older form, but has developed on an entirely new basis.

The medieval period of Judeo-German literature was by no means confined to the Slavic countries. It reacted on the Jews who had remained in Germany, who, in their narrow Ghetto life, were excluded from an active participation in the German literature of their country. This reaction was not due alone to the fact that the specifically Jewish literature appealed in an equal degree to those who had been left behind in their old homes, but in a larger measure to the superior intellectual activity of the emigrants and their descendants who kept alive the spark of Jewish learning when it had become weakened at home and found no food for its replenish-

ment within its own communities. They had to turn
to the Slavic lands for their teachers and Rabbis, who
brought with them not only their Hebrew learning,
but also their Judeo-German language and literature.
Up to the middle of the eighteenth century there was no
division of the Jews of the west and the east of Europe;
they took equal part in the common Judeo-German literature, however scanty its scope. What was produced
in Russia was read with the same pleasure in Germany,
and *vice versa*, even though the spoken form of the vernacular in Slavic countries was more and more departing from that of Germany.

Even Mendelssohn's teacher was a Galician Jew.
But with Mendelssohn a new era had dawned in the
history of the German Jews. By his example the dialect was at once abandoned for the literary language,
and the Jews were once more brought back into the
fold of the German nation. The separation of the two
branches of the German Jews was complete, and the
inhabitants of the Slavic countries were left to shift for
themselves. For nearly one hundred years they had to
miss the beneficent effects of an intellectual intercourse
with the West, and in the beginning of our century the
contrast between the two could not have been greater:
the German Jews were rapidly becoming identified with
the spiritual pursuits of their Gentile fellow-citizens,
the Slavic Jews persevered in the medievalism into
which they had been thrown centuries before. Only
by slow degrees did the Mendelssohnian Reform find
its way into Poland and Russia; and even when its
influence was at its highest, it was not possible for it
to affect those lands in the same way that it affected
the districts that were more or less under German
influence. The German language could not become

the medium of instruction for the masses, whose homely dialects had so far departed from their mother-tongue as to make the latter unintelligible to them. In Russia it was a long time before the native literature could make itself felt, or before Russian education came to take the place of the German culture ; so in the meanwhile the Judeo-German language was left to its own evolution, and a new literature had its rise.

In arriving at its present stage, Judeo-German literature of the nineteenth century has passed through several phases. At first, up to the sixties, it was used as a weapon by the few enlightened men who were anxious to extend the benefits of the Mendelssohnian Reform to the masses at large. It is an outgrowth of the Hebrew literature of the same period, which had its rise from the same causes, but which could appeal only to a small number of men who were well versed in Hebrew lore. Since these apostles of the new learning had themselves received their impetus through the Hebrew, it was natural for them to be active both in the Hebrew and the Judeo-German field. We consequently find here the names of Gottlober and J. L. Gordon, who belong equally to both literatures. Those who devoted themselves exclusively to creating a Judeo-German literature, like the other Mendelssohnian disciples, took the German literature as the guide for their efforts, and even dreamed of approaching the literary language of Germany in the final amalgamation with the Mendelssohnian Reform. In the meanwhile, in the sixties and still more in the seventies, the Jews were becoming Russianized in the schools which had been thrown open to their youths. In the sixties, the Judeo-German literature, having received its impetus in the preceding generation, reached its highest development

as a literature of Reform, but it appealed only to
those who had not had the benefits of the Russian
schools.   In the seventies it became reminiscent, and
was in danger of rapid extinction.   In the eighties, the
persecutions and riots against the Jews led many of
those who had availed themselves of the Russian culture
to devote themselves to the service of their less fortunate brethren ; and many new forces, that otherwise
would have found their way into Russian letters, were
exerted entirely in the evolution of Judeo-German.
In this new stage, the Mendelssohnian Reform, with its
concomitant German language, was lost sight of.   The
element of instruction was still an important one in this
late period, but this instruction was along universal lines,
and no longer purely Jewish ; above all else, this literature became an art.

Poetry was the first to be developed, as it lent itself
more readily to didactic purposes ; it has also, until
lately, remained in closer contact with the popular poetry,
which, in its turn, is an evolution of the poetry of the
preceding centuries.   The theatre was the latest to de-
tach itself from prose, to which it is organically related.
These facts have influenced the separate treatment of
the three divisions of literature in the present work.
It was deemed indispensable to add to these a chapter
on the Judeo-German folklore, as the reading of Judeo-
German works would frequently be unintelligible without some knowledge of the creations of the popular
mind.   Here the relation to medievalism is even more
apparent than in the popular poetry ; in fact, the greater
part of the printed books of that class owe their origin
to past ages ; they are frequently nothing more than
modernizations of old books, as is, for example, the case
with ' Bevys of Hamptoun,' which, but for the lan-

guage, is identical with its prototype in the beginning of the sixteenth century.

In its popular form, Judeo-German is certainly not inferior to many of the literary languages which have been fortunate enough to attract the attention of the linguist and student of comparative literature. In its *belleslettres* it compares favorably with those of countries like Bulgaria, which had their regeneration at about the same time; nay, it may appear to the unbiassed observer that it even surpasses them in that respect. And yet, in spite of it all, Judeo-German has remained practically a sealed book to the world. The few who have given reports of it display an astounding amount of ignorance on the subject. Karpeles devotes, in his history of Jewish literature, almost thirty pages to the medieval form of it, but to the rich modern development of it only *two lines!*[1] Steinschneider knows by hearsay only Dick, and denies the practical value of modern Judeo-German.[2] But the acme of complacent ignorance, not to use a stronger word, is reached by Grünbaum,[3] who dishes up, as specimens of literature, newspaper advertisements and extracts of Schaikewitsch, not mentioning even by name a single one of the first-class writers. It is painful to look into the pages of his work, which, apart from endless linguistic blunders of a most senseless character, has probably done

---

[1] G. Karpeles, *Geschichte der jüdischen Literatur*, Berlin, 1886, 1029 pp.

[2] M. Steinschneider, *Die italienische Litteratur der Juden*, in *Monatschrift für Geschichte und Wissenschaft des Judenthums*, Vol. XLII. pp. 74–79.

[3] M. Grünbaum, *Die jüdisch-deutsche Litteratur in Deutschland, Polen und Amerika* (Abdruck aus Winter und Wünsche, *Die jüdische Litteratur seit Abschluss des Kanons*, Bd. III. s. 531 ff.), Trier, 1894, 8vo, 91 pp.

more than anything else to divert attention from this interesting literature.

Much more sympathetic are the few pages which Berenson devotes to it in an article in the *Andover Review;*[1] though abounding in errors, it is fair and unbiassed, and at least displays a familiarity with the originals. Still better are the remarks of the Polish author Klemens Junosza in the introductions to his translations of the works of Abramowitsch into Polish; the translations themselves are masterpieces, considering the extreme quaintness of Abramowitsch's style. There are, indeed, a few sketches on the Judeo-German literature written in the dialect itself,[2] but none of them attest a philosophical grasp of the subject, or even betray a thorough familiarity with the literature. A number of good reviews on various productions have appeared in the Russian periodical *Voschod*, from the pen of one signing himself "Criticus."[3] To one of these reviews he has attached a discussion of the literature in general; this, however short, is the best that has yet been written on the subject.

It is hard to foretell the future of Judeo-German. In America it is certainly doomed to extinction.[4] Its

---

[1] B. Berenson, *Contemporary Jewish Fiction*, in *Andover Review*, Vol. X. pp. 598–602.

[2] J. Dienesohn, *Die jüdische Sprache un' ihre Schreiber*, in *Hausfreund*, Vol. I. pp. 1–20; N. Solotkov, *A Maisse wegen Maisses; oder A Blick über die žargonische Literatur*, in *Städt-anzeiger*, No. I. pp. 11–16, No. II. pp. 17–22; J. Goido, *Die žargonische Literatur in America*, in *Amerikanischer Volkskalender*, Vol. III. pp. 73–77; Americanus, *Die jüdisch-deutsche Literatur in America*, in *Neuer Geist*, No. VI. pp. 352–355.

[3] *Novosti žargonnoj literatury*, in *Voschod*, Vol. IX. No. 7, pp. 19–37; see also *Sistematičeskij ukazatel'*, pp. 285–287, Nos. 4651–4683.

[4] Cf. Ph. Wiernik, *Wie lang wet unser Literatur blühen?* in *Neuer Geist*, No. VI.

lease of life is commensurate with the last large immigration to the new world. In the countries of Europe it will last as long as there are any disabilities for the Jews, as long as they are secluded in Ghettos and driven into Pales.[1] It would be idle to speculate when these persecutions will cease.

[1] The Pale of Jewish settlement is confined to the western provinces, coinciding almost exactly with the old kingdoms of Poland and Lithuania.

II. THE JUDEO–GERMAN LANGUAGE

THERE is probably no other language in existence on which so much opprobrium has been heaped as on the Judeo-German.[1]   Philologists have neglected its study, Germanic scholars have until lately been loath to admit it as a branch of the German language, and even now it has to beg for recognition.   German writers look upon it with contempt and as something to be shunned; and for over half a century the Russian and Polish Jews, whose mother-tongue it is, have been replete with apologies whenever they have had recourse to it for literary purposes.[2]   Such a bias can be explained only as a manifestation of a general prejudice against

---

[1] To cite one example out of many: In the *Journal of American Folklore*, Vol. VII. pp. 72–74, there appeared a short appeal, by F. S. Krauss, to the folklorists of America, to collect whatsoever of Jewish lore may be found here ere the German Jews become entirely Americanized.   It seems that Krauss had in mind the German language; but, for some reason, R. Andree, editor of the Globus, thought of Judeo-German, whereupon he made a violent attack upon it in an article, *Sprachwechsel der Juden in Nord-America*, in Vol. LXV. of his periodical, p. 363.   Lenz, in his *Eindringlinge im Wörter- und Zitaten-schatz der deutschen Sprache* (Münster, 1895, 8vo, 28 pp.), caps, however, the climax in his antipathy for the Jargon by making it the subject of antisemitic propaganda !

[2] Even Frug, who is a master of the dialect, and who wields it with more vigor than the Russian language, thought it necessary to devote a whole series of poems to the reluctant defence of his vernacular, in *Lieder vun dem jüdischen Žargon*, in *Jüdisches Volksblatt*, Vol. VIII. (Beilage) pp. 881–896; also reprinted in his *Lieder un' Gedanken.* Cf. p. 108 of the present work.

everything Jewish, for passions have been at play to such an extent as to blind the scientific vision to the most obvious and common linguistic phenomena. Unfortunately, this interesting evolution of a German dialect has found its most violent opponents in the German Jews, who, since the day of Mendelssohn, have come to look upon it as an arbitrary and vicious corruption of the language. of their country.[1] This attack upon

[1] Witness the frequent dogmatic statements and attacks on it by the historian Grätz. These finally brought forth a rejoinder by J. Dienesohn in the *Jüd. Volksblatt*, Vol. VIII. (Beilage), pp. 33–43, entitled *Professor Grätz un' der jüdischer Žargon, oder Wer mit wās darf sich schämen?* and this was followed by a similar article (*ibid.* pp. 65–68, 129–133) from the editor of the *Volksblatt*, in which Grätz's dogmatism is put in no enviable light. Even Steinschneider has no love for it; although he has written so much and so well on its literature, he knows nothing of its nineteenth-century development, and nearly all his quotations of Judeo-German words that in any way differ from the German form are preposterously wrong. Karpeles, writing the history of its literature, confessedly knows nothing of the language. M. Grünbaum, in his *Jüdisch-deutsche Chrestomathie* and *Die Jüdisch-deutsche Litteratur*, displays an ignorance of the dialect which would put to shame a sophomoric newspaper reporter of a scientific lecture. What wonder, then, that D. Philipson, devoting a chapter to *The Ghetto in Literature* (pp. 220–255 in *Old European Jewries*, Philadelphia, 1894), should not even suspect the existence of an extensive and highly interesting literature of the subject in the language of the Ghetto itself! Among the few memorable exceptions among German scholars are Güdemann and Strack, who approach Judeo-German in a fair and scholarly manner. See M. Güdemann, *Quellenschriften zur Geschichte des Unterrichts und der Erziehung bei den deutschen Juden,* etc., Berlin, 1891, pp. xxii, xxiii, and, by the same author, *Geschichte des Erziehungswesens und der Cultur der Juden in Frankreich und Deutschland*, Vol. I. note iii. pp. 273–287, and Vol. III. note vii. pp. 280–297. Still fewer are those who have subjected Judeo-German to a thorough philological investigation. All efforts in that direction will be found catalogued by A. Landau, *Bibliographie des Jüdisch-deutschen*, in *Deutsche Mundarten, Zeitschrift für Bearbeitung des mundartlichen Materials*, herausgegeben von Dr. Johann Willibald Nagl, Vienna, 1896, Heft II. pp. 126–132. To those men-

it, while justifiable in so far as it affects its survival in Germany, loses all reasonableness when transferred to the Jews of Russia, former Poland and Roumania, where it forms a comparatively uniform medium of intercourse of between five and six millions of people, of whom the majority know no other language. It cannot be maintained that it is desirable to preserve the Judeo-German, and to give it a place of honor among the sisterhood of languages; but that has nothing to do with the historic fact of its existence. The many millions of people who use it from the day of their birth cannot be held responsible for any intentional neglect of grammatical rules, and its widespread dissemination is sufficient reason for subjecting it to a thorough investigation. A few timid attempts have been made in that direction, but they are far from being exhaustive, and touch but a small part of the very rich material at hand. Nor is this the place in which a complete discussion of the matter is to be looked for. This chapter presents only such of the data as must be well understood for a correct appreciation of the dialectic varieties current in the extensive Judeo-German literature of the last fifty years.

All languages are subject to a continuous change, not only from within, through natural growth and decay, but also from without, through the influence of foreign languages as carriers of new ideas. The languages of Europe, one and all, owe their Latin elements to the

tioned by him must be added A. Schulmann's *Die Geschichte vun der Žargon-literatur*, in *Jüdisches Volksblatt*, Vol. II. pp. 115–134, which is very rich in data, and A. Landau's *Das Deminutivum der galizisch-jüdischen Mundart, Ein Kapitel aus der jüdischen Grammatik*, in *Deutsche Mundarten*, Vol. I. pp. 46–58. This is, outside of Şaineanu's work (mentioned in Landau's *Bibliographie*), the best grammatical disquisition on Judeo-German that has so far appeared.

universality of the Roman dominion, and, later, of the
Catholic Church. With the Renaissance, and lately
through the sciences, much Greek has been added to
their vocabularies. When two nations have come into
a close intellectual contact, the result has always been
a mixture of languages. In the case of English, the
original Germanic tongue has become almost unrecognizable under the heavy burden of foreign words. But
more interesting than these cases, and more resembling
the formation of the Judeo-German, are those non-
Semitic languages that have come under the sway
of Mohammedanism. Their religious literature being
always written in the Arabic of the Koran, they were
continually, for a long period of centuries, brought
under the same influences, and these have caused them
to borrow, not only many words, but even whole turns
and sentences, from their religious lore. The Arabic
has frequently become completely transformed under
the pronunciation and grammatical treatment of the
borrowing language, but nevertheless a thorough knowledge of such tongues as Turkish and Persian is not
possible without a fair understanding of Arabic. The
case is still more interesting with Hindustani, spoken
by more than one hundred millions of people, where
more than five-eighths of the language is not of Indian
origin, but Persian and Arabic. With these preliminary
facts it will not be difficult to see what has taken place
in Judeo-German.

Previous to the sixteenth century the Jews in Germany spoke the dialects of their immediate surroundings; there is no evidence to prove any introduction
of Hebrew words at that early period, although it must
be supposed that words relating purely to the Mosaic
ritual may have found their way into the spoken lan-

guage even then. The sixteenth century finds a large number of German Jews resident in Bohemia, Poland, and Lithuania. As is frequently the case with immigrants, the Jews in those distant countries developed a greater intellectual activity than their brethren at home, and this is indicated by the prominence of the printing offices at Prague and Cracow, and the large number of natives of those countries who figure as authors of Judeo-German works up to the nineteenth century. But torn away from a vivifying intercourse with their mother-country, their vocabulary could not be increased from the living source of the language alone, for their interests began to diverge. Religious instruction being given entirely in Hebrew, it was natural for them to make use of all such Hebrew words as they thus became familiar with. Their close study of the Talmud furnished them from that source with a large number of words of argumentation, while the native Slavic languages naturally added their mite toward making the Judeo-German more and more unlike the mother-tongue. Since books printed in Bohemia were equally current in Poland, and *vice versa*, and Jews perused a great number of books, there was always a lively interchange of thoughts going on in these countries, causing some Bohemian words to migrate to Poland, and Polish words back to Bohemia. These books printed in Slavic countries were received with open hands also in Germany, and their preponderance over similar books at home was so great that the foreign corruption affected the spoken language of the German Jews, and they accepted also a number of Slavic words together with the Semitic infection. This was still further aided by the many Polish teachers who, in the seventeenth and eighteenth centuries, were almost the only instructors of Hebrew in Germany.[1]

We have, then, here an analogous case to the formation of Osmanli out of the Turkish, and Modern Persian out of the Old by means of the Arabic, and if the word Jargon is used to describe the condition of Judeo-German in the past three centuries, then Gibberish would be the only word that would fit as a designation of the corresponding compounds of the beautiful languages of Turkey, Persia, and India. A Jargon is the chaotic state of a speech-mixture at the moment when the foreign elements first enter into it. That mixture can never be entirely arbitrary, for it is subject to the spirit of one fundamental language which does not lose its identity. All the Romance elements in English have not stifled its Germanic basis, and Hindustani is neither Persian nor Arabic, in spite of the overwhelming foreign element in it, but an Indian language. Similarly Judeo-German has remained essentially a German dialect group.

Had the Judeo-German had for its basis some dialect which widely differs from the literary norm, such as Low German or Swiss, it would have long ago been claimed as a precious survival by German philologists. But it happens to follow so closely the structure of High German that its deviations have struck the superficial observer as a kind of careless corruption of the German. A closer scrutiny, however, convinces one that in its many dialectic variations it closely follows the High German dialects of the Middle Rhine with Frankfurt for its centre. There is not a peculiarity

---

[1] Cf. Zunz, *Die gottesdienstlichen Vorträge der Juden, historisch entwickelt*, Frankfurt a. M., 1892, pp. 452–463, and Güdemann, as above.

in its grammatical forms, in the changes of its vocalism, for which exact parallels are not found within a
small radius of the old imperial city, the great centre
of Jewish learning and life in the Middle Ages.   No
doubt, the emigration into Russia came mainly from
the region of the Rhine.   At any rate those who arrived
from there brought with them traditions which were
laid as the foundation of their written literature,
whose influence has been very great on the Jews
of the later Middle Ages.   While men received their
religious literature directly through the Hebrew, women
could get their ethical instruction only by means of
Judeo-German books.   No house was without them,
and through them a certain contact was kept up with
the literary German towards which the authors have
never ceased to lean.   In the meanwhile the language
could not remain uniform over the wide extent of the
Slavic countries, and many distinct groups have developed there.   The various subdialects of Poland differ
considerably from the group which includes the northwest of Russia, while they resemble somewhat more
closely the southern variety.   But nothing of that
appears in the printed literature previous to the beginning of this century.   There a great uniformity
prevails, and by giving the Hebrew vowels, or the
consonants that are used as such, the values that
they have in the mouths of German Jews, we obtain,
in fact, what appears to be an apocopated, corrupted
form of literary German.   The spelling has remained
more or less traditional, and though it becomes finally
phonetic, it seems to ascribe to the vowels the values
nearest to those of the mother-language and current
in certain varieties of the Lithuanian group.   From
this it may be assumed that the Polish and southern

Russian varieties have developed from the Lithuanian, which probably bears some relation to the historical migrations into those parts of the quondam Polish kingdom, and this is made the more plausible from the fact that the vowel changes are frequently in exact correspondence with the changes in the White Russian, Polish, and Little Russian. Such a phenomenon of parallelism is found also in other languages, and in our case may be explained by the unconscious changes of the Germanic vowels simultaneously with those in the Slavic words which, having been naturalized in Judeo-German, were heard and used differently in the new surroundings.

However it may be, the language of the Judeo-German books in the sixteenth, seventeenth, and eighteenth centuries is subject to but slight variations. It is true, the Blitz Bible printed in Amsterdam in 1676 seems to deviate greatly from other similar works, and the uncouth compound which is found there does, indeed, have all appearances of a Jargon. It owes its origin to the Polish Jews who but a few years before had been exiled from more than two hundred and fifty towns [1] and who, having settled in Holland, began to modify their Judeo-German by introducing Dutch into it. Although the Bible was intended for Polish Jews, as is evident by the letters-patent granted by John the Third of Poland, yet it has never exerted any influence on the dialects in Russia and Poland, for not one word of Dutch origin can be found in them. This older stage of the language is even now familiar to the Russian Jewish women through the

---

[1] Cf. M. Steinschneider, *Die italienische Litteratur der Juden*, in *Monatschrift für Geschichte und Wissenschaft des Judenthums*, Vol. XLII. p. 74.

' Zeena Ureena,' the prayer book, and the special prayers which they recite in Judeo-German, and Jewish writers have recourse to it whenever they wish to express a prayer, as, for example, in Abramowitsch's 'Hymns' and 'Saturday Prayers.' This older stage is known under the name of *Iwre-teutsch, Korben-ssider-teutsch, Tchines-teutsch*, thus indicating its proper sphere in lithurgical works. This form of the language is comparatively free from Hebrew words.[1] On the other hand, Cabbalistic works become almost unreadable on account of the prevalence of Semitic over German words.[2]

In the beginning of the nineteenth century a Galician, Minchas Mendel Lefin, laid the foundation for the use of the vernacular for literary purposes.[3] This example was soon followed by the writers in Russia who became acquainted with German culture through the followers of the Mendelssohnian School at Lemberg, who comprise nearly all the authors from Ettinger to Abram-

[1] Naturally, words belonging to that stage of the language have survived in the *cheeder* (school), where the *melamed* (teacher) is frequently compelled to fall back on the old commentaries for translations. Abramowitsch has, in his *Dās klēine Menschele*, the following passage (p. 49) bearing upon this point : " Die Talmudtōre hāt mir äuch gegeben a Bissel Deutsch vun die Teutschwörter in Chumesch, wie a Stēiger (for example): *wealoto* un' a Nepel, *wesaadu libchem* un' lehent unter euer Harz, *jereechi* mein dich, *machschof* entpleckt, *boochu* auf'n Gemeesachz, *been hamischpessoim* die Gemarken, *wetcha-lelo* un' du hāst sie verschwächt, *kōmmijōs* hofferlich, uchdōme noch asōlche Teutschen."

[2] An example of this style is given by Linetzki, in *Dās chsidische Jüngel*, p. 32 : " a Stēiger wie er hāt mit mir geteutscht : *ischo* an Ische, *ki sitmo* as sie wet tome weren, *wessakriw* un' sie wet makriw sein, *korbon* a Korben, *wehikriw* soll makriw sein, *hakōhen* der Kōhen, *al hamisbeach* zum Misbeach, *beōhel mōed* in'm Ōhel-mōed."

[3] Cf. A. B. Gottlober, *Sichrōnes über žargonische Schreiber*, in *Jüd. Volksbib.*, Vol. I. pp. 250-259.

owitsch, most of whom wrote in some southern dialect. The language of these abounds in a large number of idiomatic expressions for which one would in vain look in the older writings; words of Slavic origin that were familiar in everyday life were freely introduced, and an entirely new diction superseded that of the past century. At first their spelling was quite phonetic. But soon their leaning towards German literature led them into the unfortunate mistake of introducing German orthography for their dialect, so that it now is frequently impossible to tell from the form of a word how it may have been pronounced. Add to this the historical spelling of the Hebrew and the phonetic of the Slavic words, and one can easily imagine the chaos that prevails in the written language. And yet it must not be supposed that Judeo-German stands alone in this. The same difficulty and confusion arises in all those tongues in which the historical continuity has been broken. Thus Modern Greek is spelled as though it were Ancient Greek, with which it has hardly any resemblance in sound, while Bulgarian is still wavering between a phonetic, a Russian, and an Old Slavic orthography. Similar causes have produced similar results in Judeo-German.

There is no linguistic norm in the language as now used for literary purposes. The greater number of the best authors write in slightly varying dialects of Volhynia; but the Lithuanian variety is also well represented, and of late Perez has begun to write in his Polish vernacular.[1] German influence began to show itself early, and it affected not only the spelling, but

---

[1] On the various dialects and styles, see *Die jüdische Sprache*, in *Hausfreund*, Vol. V. pp. 60–64; cf. also Rabnizki, *Hebräisch un' Jüdisch*, in *Hausfreund*, Vol. V. pp. 38–48.

also the vocabulary of the early writers in Lithuania. Dick looked upon Judeo-German only as a means to lead his people to German culture, and his stories are written in a curious mixture in which German at times predominates. This evil practice, which in Dick may be excused on the ground that it served him only as a means to an end, has come to be a mannerism in writers of the lower kind, such as Schaikewitsch, Seiffert, and their like. The scribblers of that class have not only corrupted the literature but also the language of the Jews.

Various means have been suggested by the writers for the enrichment of the Judeo-German vocabulary. Some lovers of Hebrew have had the bad taste to propose the formation of all new words on a Semitic basis, and have actually brought forth literary productions in that hybrid language. Others again have advised the introduction of all foreign words commonly in use among other nations. But the classical writers, among whom Abramowitsch is foremost, have not stopped to consider what would be the best expedient, but have coined words in conformity with the spirit of their dialect, steering a middle course between the extremes suggested by others. In America, where the majority of the writers knew more of German than their native vernacular, the literary dialect has come to resemble the literary German, and the English environment has caused the infusion of a number of English terms for familiar objects. But on the whole the language of the better writers differs in America but little from that of their former home. There is, naturally, a large divergence to be found in the language, which ranges from the almost pure German of the prayers and, in modern times, of the poems of Winchevsky, to the language abounding in Russicisms of Dlugatsch, and in Hebraisms of Linetzki, from the pure dialects of the best writers to the corrupt forms of Dick and Meisach, and the even worse Jargon of Seiffert, but in all these there is no greater variety than is to be found in all newly formed languages.[1] The most recent example of such variety is furnished by the Bulgarian, where the writers of the last fifty years have wavered between the native dialects with their large elements of Turkish and Greek origin, a purified form of the same, from which the foreign infection has been eliminated, approaches to the Old Slavic of a thousand years ago, and, within the last few years, a curious mixture with the literary Russian. Judeo-German not only does not suffer by such a comparison, but really gains by it, for all the best writers have uniformly based their diction on their native dialects.

In former days Judeo-German was known only by the name of *Iwre-teutsch*, or *Jüdisch-teutsch*. Frequently such words were used as *Mame-loschen* (Mother-tongue), or *Prost-jüdisch* (Simple Yiddish), but through the efforts of the disciples of the Haskala (Reform), the designation of *Jargon* has been forced upon it; and that appellation has been adopted by later writers in Russia, so that now one generally finds only this latter form as the name of the language used by the writers in Russia. The people, however, speak of their vernacular as *Jüdisch*, and this has given rise in England and America to the word *Yiddish* for both the spoken and written form. It is interesting to note that originally the name had been merely *Teutsch* for the language of the Jews, for they were conscious of their participation

---

[1] An excellent satire on the widely different styles of Judeo-German in vogue by their writers is given by S. Rabinowitsch, in his *Kolmewasser* (q.v.), under the title of *Korrespondenzies* (cols. 26–31).

with the Germans in a common inheritance. Reminiscences of that old designation are left in such words as *verteutschen*, 'to translate,' *i.e.* to do into German, and *steutsch*, 'how do you mean it?' contracted from *is teutsch?* 'how is that in German?'

The main differences between Judeo-German[1] and the mother-tongue are these: its vocalism has undergone considerable change, varying from locality to locality; the German unaccented final *e* has, as in other dialects of German, disappeared; in declensional forms, the genitive has almost entirely disappeared, while in the Lithuanian group the dative has also coincided with the accusative; in the verb, Judeo-German has lost almost entirely the imperfect tense; the order of words is more like the English than the German. These are all developments for which parallels can be adduced from the region of Frankfurt. Judeo-German is, consequently, not an anomaly, but a natural development.

---

[1] For a complete discussion of the subject, see L. Şaineanu, *Studiu dialectologic asupra graiului evreo-german*, Bucureşti, 1889, 8vo, 78 pp.

III. FOLKLORE

THERE can be no doubt that the Jews were the most, potent factors in the dissemination of folk-literature in the Middle Ages.[1] Various causes united to make them the natural carriers of folklore from the East to the West, and from the West back again to the East. They never became so completely localized as to break away from the community of their brethren in distant lands, and to develop distinct national characteristics. The Jews of Spain stood in direct relations with the Khazars of Russia, and it was a Jew whom Charlemagne sent as ambassador to Bagdad. The Jewish merchant did not limit his sphere of action by geographical lines of demarkation, and the Jewish scholar was as much at home in Italy and Germany as he was in Russia or Egypt. Again and again, in reading the biographies of Jewish worthies, we are confronted with men who have had their temporary homes in three continents. In fact, the stay-at-homes were the exception rather than the rule in the Middle Ages. In this manner not only a lively intercourse was kept up among the Jews of the diaspora, but they unwittingly became also the mediators of the intellectual life of the most remote lands: they not only enriched the literatures of the various nations by new kinds of compositions, but also brought with them the substratum of that intellectual

[1] Read, on this subject, Joseph Jacobs, *Jewish Diffusion of Folk Tales*, in *Jewish Ideals and Other Essays*, London, 1896, pp. 135–161.

life which finds its expression in the creations of the popular literature.

The Jews have always possessed an innate love for story telling which was only sharpened by their travels. The religious and semi-religious stories were far from sufficient to satisfy their curiosity, and in spite of the discussions by the Rabbis of the permissibility of reading foreign books of adventure, they proceeded to create and multiply an apocryphal and profane folk-literature which baffles the investigator with its variety. Most addicted to these stories were the women, who received but little learning in the language of their religious lore, and who knew just enough of their Hebrew characters to read in the vernacular books specially prepared for them. Times changed, and the education of the men varied with the progress of the Hebrew and the native literatures; but the times hardly made an impression on the female sex. The same minimum of ethical instruction was given them in the eighteenth century that they had received in the fourteenth, and they were left to shift for themselves in the selection of their profane reading matter. The men who condescended to write stories for them had no special interest to direct the taste of their public, and preferred to supply the demand rather than create it; nor did the publishers have any more urgent reason why they should trouble themselves about the production of new works as long as the old ones satisfied the women. Consequently, although now and then a 'new' story book saw daylight, the old ones were just as eagerly received by the feminine readers. And thus it happens that what was read with pleasure at its first appearance is accepted as eagerly to-day, and the books that were issued from the printing presses of the sixteenth century may be found in almost unchanged hundredth editions, except as to the language, printed in 1898 in Wilna or Warsaw.

Time and space are entirely annihilated in the folklore of the Russian Jews. Here one finds side by side the quaint stories of the Talmud of Babylonian, Persian, Egyptian origin, with the Polyphemus myth of the Greeks, the English ' Bevys of Hamptoun,' the Arabic 'Thousand and One Nights.' Stories in which half a dozen motives from various separate tales have been moulded into one harmonious whole jostle with those that show unmistakable signs of venerable antiquity. Nowhere else can such a variety of tales be found as in Judeo-German; nor is there any need, as in other literatures, to have recourse to collections of the diligent searcher; one will find hundreds of them, nay thousands, told without any conscious purpose in the chapbooks that are annually issued at Wilna, Lemberg, Lublin, and other places. Add to these the many unwritten tales that involve the superstitions and beliefs of a more local character, in which the Slavic element has been superadded to the Germanic base, and the wealth of this long-neglected literature will at once become apparent to the most superficial observer.[1]

[1] The following books and essays treat on Judeo-German folklore in general : Herman Lotze, *Zur jüdisch-deutschen Litteratur*, in Gosche's *Archiv für Litteraturgeschichte*, Vol. I., Leipsic, 1870, pp. 90–101 ; M. Steinschneider, *Über die Volkslitteratur der Juden*, ibid., Vol. II. pp. 1–21 ; S. Gelbhaus, *Mittelhochdeutsche Dichtung in ihrer Beziehung zur biblisch-rabbinischen Litteratur*, Frankfurt a. M., 1893, IV. Heft, pp. 59 ff.; Brüll, *Beiträge zur jüdischen Sagen- und Sprachkunde im Mittelalter*, in *Jahrbücher für jüdische Geschichte und Litteratur*, IX. *Jahrgang*, Frankfurt a. M., 1889, pp. 1–71 ; J. Jacobs, *Jewish Diffusion of Folk Tales*, a paper read before the Jews' College Literary Society, in *The Jewish Chronicle*, London, June 1, 1888 (also published separately in *Jewish Ideals and Other Essays*, as above);

These stories have dominated and still dominate the minds of the women and children among the Russian, Roumanian, and Galician Jews. For them there exists a whole fantastic world, with its objects of fear and admiration. There is not an act they perform that is not followed by endless superstitious rites, in which the beliefs of Chaldea are inextricably mixed with French, Germanic, or Slavic ceremonies. To pierce the dense cloud of superstition that has involved the Mosaic Law, to disentangle the ancient religion from the rank growth of the ages, to open the eyes of the Jews to the realities of this world, and to break down the timeless and space-less sphere of their imaginings — that has been the task of the followers of the Mendelssohnian Reform for the last one hundred years. In the pages of the Judeo-German works that they have produced to take the place of the story books of long ago, one meets continually with lists of superstitions that they are laboring to combat, with the names of books that they would fain put in an index expurgatorius.

M. Gaster, *Jewish Folk Lore in the Middle Ages*, in papers read before the Jews' College Literary Society during the Session 1886–87, London, 1887, pp. 39–51 (also published separately by *The Jewish Chronicle*, 1887, 8vo); G. Levi, *Christiani ed Ebrei nel Medio Evo, Quadro di costumi con un appendice di recordi e leggende giudaiche della medesima epocha*, Florence, 1866, 16mo (pp. 307–406); A. M. Tendlau, *Das Buch der Sagen und Legenden jüdischer Vorzeit* (2te Auflage), Stuttgart, 1845, 8vo, 335 pp.; the same, *Fellmeiers Abende, Mährchen und Geschichten aus grauer Vorzeit*, Frankfurt a. M., 1856, 16mo, 200 pp.; Israel Lévi, *Contes juifs*, in *Revue des Études Juives*, Vol. XI. pp. 209–234; Is. Loeb, *Le folklore juif dans la chronique du Schébet Jehuda d'Ibn Verga*, in *Revue des Études Juives*, Vol. XXIV. pp. 1–29. For general ethnographic sketches of the Russian Jews, containing a great deal of material of a folklore nature, see *Sistematičeskij ukazatel' literatury o evrejach na russkom jazykě so vremeni vvedenija graždanskago šrifta (1708 g.) po dekabr' 1889 g.*, St. Petersburg, 1893, Part V. pp. 198–204 and 206–207; of the works mentioned there, Nos. 2831 and 2912 are especially important.

It is not difficult to discern a number of distinct
strata in the many folk-tales that are current now, even
though the motives from various periods may be found
hopelessly intertwined in one and the same story.   The
oldest of these may be conveniently called the Talmudical substratum, as in those older writings the prototypes
of them can be found.   Of course, these in their turn are
of a composite nature themselves, but that need not dis-
concert us in our present investigation as long as the
resemblance is greater to the stories in the Talmud than
to the originals from which that collection has itself
drawn its information.   There is a large variety of subjects that must be classified in that category.   Here
belong a number of animal fables, of stories of strange
beasts, much imaginary geography, but especially a vast
number of apocryphal Bible stories.[1]   One of the most

[1] For stories of that period, cf. A. S. Isaacs, *Stories from the
Rabbis*, London, Osgood (and New York, Webster), 1893, 8vo, 202 pp.;
M. Gaster, *Beiträge zur vergleichenden Sagen- und Märchenkunde*,
Bukarest, 1883, 8vo.   Dr. B. Königsberger, *Aus dem Reiche der
altjüdischen Fabel*, in *Zeitschrift des Vereins für Volkskunde*, Vol. VI.,
1896, pp. 140–161 ; F. Baethgen, *Salomo in der jüdischen Sage*, in
Allgemeine Zeitung, Nos. 151, 152, 181, 182 (Beilage).   Other shorter
articles on the same subject will be found in the *Urquell*, Vol. II.
p. 209 ; Vol. IV. p. 76 ; Neue Folge, Vol. I. pp. 13, 14 ; Z. d. V. f. V.,
Vol. IV. p. 209; J. Trubnik, *Talmudische Legenden*, in *Jüd. Volksbib.*,
Vol. I. pp. 264–279.   Of special interest are the discussions of Talmudical legends and fables with their western developments or imitations, by L. Dukes, *Übersicht der neuhebräischen Literatur weltlichen
Inhalts in Prosa und Versen*, in *Israelitische Annalen* (edited by Jost),
1839, No. 13, pp. 100 ff.; No. 17, pp. 131 ff.; No. 25, pp. 196 ff.; No. 31,
pp. 244 ; No. 52, pp. 415 ff.   Eisenmenger's *Entdecktes Judenthum*,
Königsberg, 1711 (or Dresden, 1893), in spite of its bias, may be consulted for the legends; better than that is the English form of the
same, *The Tradition of the Jews; or, The Doctrine of Expositions
Contained in the Talmud*, etc., London, 8vo, (64) and 337 and 363 pp.,
the appendix of which has a *Translation, by Way of Abridgement, of
Buxtorf's Latin Account of the Religious Customs and Ceremonies of*

interesting series of that class is the one that comprises
tales of the river Sambation.[1] This river has rarely
been discovered by poor mortals, although it has been
the object of their lifelong quest. During the week it
throws large rocks heavenwards, and the noise of the
roaring waters is deafening. On the Sabbath the river
rests from its turmoil, to resume again its activity at its
expiration. Behind the Sambation lives the tribe of the
Red Jews.

The best story of that cycle is told by·Meisach. An
inquisitive tailor sets out in search of the Sambation
River. Of all the Jews that he meets he inquires
the direction that he is to take thitherward; and he
makes public announcements of his urgent business at
all the synagogues that he visits. But all in vain.
Three times he has already traversed the length and
the breadth of this earth, but never did he get nearer
his destination. Undaunted, he starts out once more
to reach the tribe of the Red Jews. Suddenly he
arrives near that awful river. Overwhelmed by its
din, terrified at its eruptions, he falls down on the

---

the Jews (Vol. II. pp. 225–363). See also G. G. Bredow, *Rabbinische
Mythen, Erzählungen und Lügen, nebst zwei Balladen der christli-
chen Mythologie im Mittelalter* (2te Auflage), Weilburg, 1833, 16mo,
136 pp.; also C. Krafft, *Jüdische Sagen und Dichtungen nach den
Talmuden und Midraschen, nebst einigen Makamen aus dem Divan
des Alcharisi*, Ansbach, 1839, 16mo, 212 pp.

[1] The Sambation is mentioned in *Eldad ha-Dani aus dem Stamme
Dan;* see for this Steinschneider's *Jüdisch-deutsche Litteratur*, in
Serapeum, Vol. IX. (1848), p. 319, No. 13. See also *Jüdische Litteratur*, by· Steinschneider, in *Ersch und Gruber*, § X, A. 2. Other
essays and stories are : D. Kaufmann's *Le Sambation*, in *Revue des
Études Juives*, Vol. XXII. pp. 285–287, and *Der˙ Sambation, eine ety-
mologische Sage*, in *Allgemeine Zeitung des Judenthums*, 1893, May
20, p. 247 ; Meisach, *Sambation*, in *Jüd. Volksblatt*, Vol. VIII. (Beilage), p. 53, and (the same story) in his *Nissim we-Nifloes, q.v.*

ground and prays to the all-merciful God. It happened to be a few minutes before the time that the river was to go to rest. The clock strikes, and, as if by magic, the scene is changed. The tailor finds a ford, passes on the other side, and, exhausted from his wandering, he lies down to sleep in the grass. The tribe of men that live there are a race of giants. One of them, noticing the intruder, takes him to be a new species of a grasshopper, picks him up, and slips him in his spacious coat pocket. He proceeds to the bath-house to take his ablution, and thence to the synagogue, leaving the tailor all the while in his pocket. The giants begin to pray. At the end, while a pause ensues, the pious tailor unconsciously exclaims 'Amen!' Astonished to hear that mysterious voice, the giant brings the tailor to light and showers many signs of respect upon him, for even the giants know how to honor a pious man. The tailor liked it there so much that he never returned to his native home.

Abramowitsch has made fine use of this story in his Jewish 'Don Quixote.' The hero of that novel has so long pondered about the Sambation River and the mysterious race of men that live beyond it, that he loses his reason, and starts out to find them. But he does not get beyond Berdichev. Another very fruitful class of stories belonging to that category is the one in which the prophet Elijah plays an important part.[1] According to the popular belief, Elijah did not die; he even

[1] In A. S. Isaac's *Stories from the Rabbis* (see above), there is a chapter on *Elijah in the Legends* (pp. 92–103). Other stories of Elijah: D. Cassel, *Elia in der Legende*, in *Allgemeine Zeitung des Judenthums*, 1892, Feb. 26, p. 104, and March 6, p. 115; *Urquell*, Vol. IV. pp. 11–14, 42–45, 120, 121; Z. d. V. f. V., Vol. IV. p. 209. An older story is mentioned in Steinschneider's *Catalogue, Serapeum*, Vol. IX. (1848), p. 384, No. 174. See also B. W. Segel, *Materyaly*

now frequently comes to visit men, to help them in some dire necessity. His presence is surmised only when he has disappeared, generally leaving behind him a vapory cloud. So rooted is this belief in the visitation of Elijah, that during the ceremony of the circumcision a chair is left unoccupied for the good prophet. Elijah is not the only one that may be seen nowadays. Moses and David occasionally leave their heavenly abodes to aid their devotees or to exhort those that are about to depart from the road of righteousness. King David presides over the repast at the conclusion of the Sabbath, for it is then that a song in which his name is mentioned is recited. There are some who regard it as a devout act to celebrate that occasion with unswerving accuracy. To those who have made the vow of 'Mlawe-Malke,' as the repast is called, King David is wont to appear when they are particularly unfortunate. Unlike Elijah, he makes his presence known by his company of courtiers and musicians, and he himself holds a harp in his hands; and unlike him, he resorts to supernatural means to aid his *protégés*.

Most of the medieval legends cluster around the Rabbis of Central Europe who have in one way or another become famous. The cities of Amsterdam, Frankfurt, Worms, Prague, Cracow, have all their special circle of wonderful tales about the supernatural powers of the worthies of long ago. But the king of that cycle of miracle workers is Rambam, as Maimonides is called.[1]

do etnografii żydów wschodnio-galicyjskich, in *Zbiór wiadomości do antropologii krajowej*, Cracow, Vol. XVII. pp. 296–298.

[1] Stories of Maimonides are contained in *Maasebuch* (or, rather in addition *Maase Adonai*), according to Steinschneider, *Serapeum*, Vol. XXVII. (1866), p. 5, No. 7. For other stories, see Bibliography.

His profound learning and great piety, his renowned art of medicine, his extensive travels, have naturally lent themselves to imaginative transformations. He has undergone the same transmogrification that befell Vergil. Like the latter, he is no longer the great scholar and physician, but a wizard who knows the hidden properties of plants and stones, who by will power can transfer himself in space, and who can read dreams and reveal their future significance. His whole life was semi-miraculous. When he had arrived at the proper age to enter an academy of medicine, he applied to a school where only deaf-mutes were accepted as disciples of Æsculapius. This precaution was necessary, lest the secrets of the art be disseminated, to the disadvantage of the craft. Rambam pretended to have neither hearing nor speech. His progress was remarkable, and in a short time he surpassed his teachers in the delicate art of surgery. Once there came to the school a man who asked to be cured of a worm that was gnawing at his brain. The learned doctors held a consultation, and resolved to trepan the skull and extract the worm. This was at once executed, and Rambam was given permission to be present at the operation. With trembling and fear he perceived the mistake of his teachers and colleagues, for he knew full well that the man would have to die as soon as the seventh membrane under the *dura mater* was cut away. With bated breath, he stood the pang of anxiety until the sixth covering had been removed. Already the doctors were applying the lancet to the seventh, when his patience and caution gave way, and he exclaimed, 'Stop; you are killing him!' His surprised colleagues promised to forgive his deceit if he would extract the worm without injury to the membrane. This Rambam carried out in a very simple manner. He placed a cabbage leaf on the small opening in the seventh covering, and the worm, attracted by the odor of the leaf, came out to taste of the fresh food, whereupon it was ousted.[1]

Of such a character are nearly all of his cures. The supernatural element of the later period, where everything is fantastic, is still absent from the Rabbi legends. There is always an attempt made to combine the wonderful with the real, or rather to transfer the real into the realm of the miraculous. The later stories of miracle-working pursue the opposite course : they engraft the most extraordinary impossibilities on the experiences of everyday life. Rambam's travels have also given rise to a large number of semi-mythical journeys. One of the legends tells of his sojourn in Algiers, where he incurred the hatred of the Mussulmans for having decided that an oil-vat had become impure because a Mohammedan had touched it, whereas another vat into which a weed had fallen was pronounced by him to be ritually pure. Knowing that his life was in danger, he escaped to Egypt, making the voyage in less than half an hour by means of a miraculous document that he took with him and that had the power of destroying space. In Cairo he became the chief adviser of the king, and he later managed to save the country from the visitation of the Algerian minister, who had come there ostensibly to pursue the fugitive Rambam, but in reality to lay Egypt waste by his magical arts.

The most interesting stories that still belong to that cycle are those that have developed in Slavic countries. Out of the large material that was furnished them by the German cities, in conjunction with the new matter

[1] Nearly the same story is in Gaster's *Jewish Folk Lore*, etc.

with which they became familiar in their new homes,
they have moulded many new stories in endless variety.
The number of local legends is unlimited. There is
hardly an inn on the highways and byways of Western
Russia and Galicia that has not its own circle of wonderful tales. Every town possesses its remarkable
Rabbi whose memory lives in the deeds that he is
supposed to have performed. But none, except the
town of Mesiboz, the birthplace of Bal-schem-tow, the
founder of the sect of the Khassidim, can boast of such a
complete set of legendary tales as the cities of Wilna
and Cracow. In Wilna they will still tell the curious stranger many reminiscences of those glorious days
when their Rabbis could arrest the workings of natural
laws, and when their sentence was binding on ghosts as
well as men. They will take him to the synagogue and
show him a large dark spot in the cupola, and they will
tell him that during an insurrection a cannon-ball struck
the building, and that it would have proceeded on its
murderous journey but for the command of the Rabbi
to be lodged in the wall. They will take him to a
street where the spooks used to contend with humankind
for the possession of the houses in which they lived : —
the contention was finally referred to the Gaon of Wilna.
After careful inquiry into the justice of the contending
parties he gave his decision, which is worthy of the wisdom of Solomon : he adjudicated the upper parts of the
houses, as much of them as there was above ground, to
the mortals, while the cellars and other underground
structures were left in perpetuity to the shadowy inhabitants of the lower regions.[1] One of the Gaons at
Wilna was possessed of the miraculous power to create

---

[1] A similar story, also of a local character, is told by Dick in
Alte jüdische Sagen oder Ssipurim, p. 42, where he mentions a Polish

a Golem, a homunculus. It was a vivified clay man
who had to do the bidding of him who had given him
temporary life. Whenever his mission was fulfilled
he was turned back into an unrecognizable mass of
clay.[1]

A special class of legends that have been evolved in
Slavic countries are those that tell of the Lamed-wow-
niks. According to an old belief the world is supported
by the piety of thirty-six saints (Lamed-wow is the numerical representation of that number). If it were not
for them, the sins of men would have long ago worked
the destruction of the universe. Out of this basal belief
have sprung up the stories that relate the deeds of the
'hidden' saints. They are called 'hidden' because it
is the very essence of those worthies not to carry their
sanctity for show : they are humble artisans, generally
tailors or shoemakers, who ply their humble vocations
unostentatiously, and to all intents and purposes are
common people, poor and rather mentally undeveloped.
No one even dreams of their hidden powers, and no one
ever sees them studying the Law. When by some accident their identity is made apparent, they vigorously
deny that they belong to the chosen Thirty-six, and
only admit the fact when the evidence is overwhelm-
ingly against them. Then they are ready to perform
some act by which a calamity can be averted from the

work, *Przechadzki po Wilnie i jego okolicach* przez Jana ze Śliwnia
(A. Kirkor), Wilna, 1859, that contains many Jewish tales.

[1] Also told of a Rabbi of Prague, in *Sippurim, Sammlung jüdischer
Volkssagen, Erzählungen, Mythen, Chroniken, Denkwürdigkeiten und
Biographien berühmter Juden aller Jahrhunderte, besonders des Mit-
telalters* (*Jüdische Universalbibliothek*), Prague, 1895. These *Sippurim* have no great folklore value, as they show too much the hand
of the literary worker. Of similar value is H. Iliowizi's *In the Pale;
Stories and Legends of the Russian Jews*, Philadelphia, 1897.

Jews collectively, and after their successful undertaking they return to their humble work in some other town where there is no chance of their being recognized and importuned.

One of the most perfect stories of that kind is told of a hidden saint who lived in Cracow in the days of Rabbenu Moses Isserls. The Polish king had listened to the representations of his minister that as descendant of the Persian king he was entitled to the sum of money which Haman had promised to him but which he evidently had not paid, having been robbed of it by the Jews. He ordered the Jews of Cracow to pay forthwith the enormous sum upon pain of being subjected to a cruel persecution. After long fasting Rabbenu Isserls told his congregation to go to Chaim the tailor who was living in the outskirts of the town and to ask him to use his supernatural powers in averting the impending calamity. After the customary denials, Chaim promised to be the spokesman of the Jews before the king. On the next morning he went to the palace. He passed unnoticed by the guards into the cabinet of his majesty and asked him to sign a document revoking his order. In anger, the king went to the door to chide the guards for having admitted a ragged Jew to his presence. As he opened it, he stepped into space, and found himself in a desert. He wandered about for a whole day and only in the evening he met a poor man who offered him a piece of dry bread and showed him a place of shelter in a cave. The poor man advised him not to tell of his being a king to any one that he might meet, lest he be robbed or killed. He gave him a beggar's garments, and supplied him with a meal of dry bread every day. At the expiration of a year, the poor man offered him work as a woodcutter with an improvement in his fare if he would first sign a document. The king was only too happy to change his monotonous condition, and without looking at it signed the paper presented to him. His trials lasted two years more, after which he became a sailor, was shipwrecked and carried back to Cracow. Just then he awoke to discover that his three years' experience had only lasted fifteen minutes by the clock. He abided by his agreement in the document which he had signed in his dream, and thus the great misfortune was once more warded off by the piety of a Lamed-wow-nik. The minister, the story continues, escaped to Italy and hence to Amsterdam, where he became a convert to Judaism. In his old age he returned to Cracow to make pilgrimages to the graves of Rabbenu Isserls and Chaim, the saint.

All the previous stories and legends pale into insignificance by the side of the endless miracles spun out by the Khassidim and ascribed to the founder of the sect and his disciples.[1] Nothing is too absurd for them. There seems to be a conscious desire in these stories to outdo all previous records, in order to throw the largest halo on their Bal-schem-tow, or Bescht, as he

---

[1] On the Khassidim, read M. Sachor-Masoch, *Sectes juives de la Galicie*, in *Actes et Conférances de la Société des Études Juives*, 1889, pp. cxli–clxiii, and S. Schechter, *Studies in Judaism*, pp. 1–45 and 341. For the Russian sources on the Khassidim, see *Sistematičeskij ukazatel' literatury o evrejach*, pp. 177–179 (Nos. 2424–2476). Stories of Adam Balschem are mentioned by Steinschneider, as *Geschichte des R. Adam Baal Schem*, and *Geschichte des R. Adam mit dem Kaiser*, in *Serapeum*, Vol. X. (1849), p. 9, No. 183. See also *Urquell*, Vol. V. p. 266, and Vol. VI. p. 33. B. W. Segel's *Jüdische Wundermänner*, in *Globus*, Vol. LXII. pp. 312–314, 331–334, 343–345, are merely translations from the *Sseefer Ssipuree Maisses* (*Khal Chsidim*); of similar origin is his *O chasydach i chasydyzmie*, in *Wisła*, Vol. VIII. pp. 304–312, 509–521, 677–690; other stories by him are in his *Materyały do etnografii żydów*, as above.

is called by his initials. Bal-schem-tow was neither
the miracle-worker that his adherents would have him,
nor the impostor that his opponents imagine him to
have been. He was a truly pious man who sought
a refuge in mysticism against the verbalism of the
Jews of his days, in the middle of the eighteenth
century. His followers, unfortunately mistaking the
accidental in his teachings for the essentials of the
new doctrine, have raised the Cabbalistic lucubrations
of his disciples to the dignity of religious books, and
have opened wide the doors for superstitions of all
kinds. The realities of this world hardly exist for
them, or are at best the temporal reflexes of that mystic sphere in which all their thoughts soar. Their
rabbis are all workers of miracles, and Bescht is adored
by them more than Moses and the Biblical saints. His
life and acts have been so surrounded by a legendary
atmosphere that it is now, only one hundred and fifty
years after his life, not possible to disentangle truth
from fiction and to reconstruct the real man. A large
number of books relate the various miraculous incidents in his life, but the one entitled 'Khal Chsidim'
surpasses them all in variety, and attempts to give as
it were a chronological sequence of his acts.

In that book his grandfather and father are represented as foreshadowing the greatness of their descendant. His grandfather is a minister to a king, and
Elijah announces to him that at the age of one hundred years his wife will bear him a son who will be
a shining light. His father is a wizard and a scholar,
and enjoins his son before his death to study with a
hidden saint in the town of Ukop. After his studies
were completed he became a teacher in Brody, and a
judge. He marries the sister of Rabbi Gerschon, who

takes him for a simpleton, and in vain tries to instruct him. No one knows of the sanctity of Bescht. He goes into the mountains accompanied by his wife, and there meditates a long while. At one time he was about to step from a mountain into empty space, when the neighboring mountain inclined its summit and received the erring foot of Bescht. After seven years of solitary life he returns to Brody to become a servant in Gerschon's household. Later his career of miracle-working begins: he heals the sick, exorcises evil spirits, brings down rain by prayers, breaks spells, conquers wizards, predicts the future, punishes the unbelievers, rewards the faithful by endowing them with various powers, and does sundry other not less wonderful things. When he prays, the earth trembles, and no one can hear his voice for loudness. He sleeps but two hours at night and prays the rest of the time, while a nimbus of fire surrounds him.

Not less marvellous are the deeds of his disciples as related in the 'Sseefer Maisse Zadikim' and other similar productions that are issued in penny sheets in Lemberg to impress the believers with the greatness of their faith. Many of these have sprung up from the desire to instill the necessity of observing certain religious rites, and this the authors think they can accomplish best by connecting a moral with some miraculous tale. For every imaginable vow there is a special story telling of the blissfulness that the devotee has reached or the misery that the lax follower of Khassidism has had occasion to rue. Every good deed according to them creates its own protecting spirits, while every crime produces a corresponding monstrous beast that pursues the sinner and leads him to destruction. Interesting also are those cases

when a man has been as prone to sin as he has been
to perform virtuous acts, for then the struggle between
the beings of his creation leads to amusing results in
which all depends on the preponderance of one kind
of deeds over the other. The worst of men is not excluded from the benefits of mercy if he makes amends for
his crimes by an earnest repentance which is followed
by a long penance.

Of the latter class, the following is a typical story.
Chaim has brought many misfortunes to Jewish families by denouncing and blackmailing them to the Polish
magnate, the chief authority of the district. Once
while on his way to the magnate he sees a half-starved
beggar in the road, and he divides with him his bread
and carries him to his house and takes care of him
until he is well enough to proceed on his journey.
Chaim has occasion after several years to denounce
some one to the magnate. He goes to the cupboard
to fill his wallet for the journey, when he sees a dead
person in it. After he has collected himself from his
fright, he steps up once more to the cupboard. The
dead person tells him that he is ·the beggar that he
saved from starvation some time ago, that he had
heard in heaven that Chaim was to be given his last
chance in life, and that he had come to warn him to
repent his misdeeds. Chaim takes his advice to heart,
and for seven years stays uninterruptedly in the synagogue, perfecting himself in his knowledge of the religious lore. On the eve of the Passover he allows
himself to be tempted by Satan in the shape of a
scholar, to eat leavened bread at a time when the Law
prohibits it. As he steps out to the brook to wash
his hands before tasting of the bread, the dead person
once more appears to him and tells him that Satan

has been sent to him to tempt him, because it was
thought that his seven years' penance alone was not
sufficient to atone for his many evil deeds ; that all
his labors have been in vain, and that he will have
to do penance another seven years. This Chaim is
only too ready to undergo, and he applies himself with
even more ardor than before to get a remission of his
sins. At the expiration of the allotted time Chaim
dies and is at once taken to heaven.

The legends and folk-tales so far considered are of a
strictly Jewish character, whatever their origin. They
are in one way or another connected with the inner life
of the Jewish community. They deal with the acts of
their worthies and inculcate religious truths. But
these are far from forming the bulk of all the stories
that are current to-day among the German Jews in
Slavic countries. Among the printed books of a popular character there are many that not only are of Gentile
origin, but that have not been transformed in the light
of the Mosaic faith ; they have been reprinted without
change of contents for the last four centuries, furnish-
ing an example of long survival unequalled probably
in any other literature.[1] Many of the stories that

[1] The older literature of that class is briefly discussed by Steinschneider in his articles in the *Serapeum* under the following numbers
(for the years 1848, 1849, 1864, 1866, 1869): 392, *Kalilah we-Dimnah ;*
393, *Barlaam and Josaphat ;* 59, 399, *Diocletianus ;* 266 b, *Octavi-
anus ;* 22, *Bevys of Hamptoun ;* 51, *Ritter Sigmund und Magdalena ;*
266, *König Artus ;* 13, *Eldad ha-Dani ;* 156–198, 410–413, 420, various
stories ; 212, 213, fables (*Kuhbuch*) ; 167, *Maase Nissim ;* 156–158,
Maasebuch. But the latter has been superseded by his *Jüdisch-
deutsche Litteratur und Jüdisch-deutsch, mit besonderer Rücksicht
auf Avé-Lallemant ;* 2. *Artikel : Das Maase-Buch, Serapeum,* Vol.
XXVII. (1866), No. 1. This *Maasebuch* is extremely rare now, but
in its day it was enormously popular, having been used for regular
religious readings on the Sabbath. Wagenseil and Buxtorf mention

had been current in Germany long before the time of printing were among the first to be issued from Jewish printing presses. Stories of the court of King Arthur in verse, of Dietrich of Bern, of the 'Constant Love of Floris and Blanchefleur,' of 'Thousand and One Nights,' had been common in the sixteenth and seventeenth centuries, and many of them may be found in editions of this century ; but none of them has been so popular as the 'Bovo-maisse,' the latest edition of which is known to me from the year 1895. It is identical` with the English 'Bevys of Hamptoun' and was done into Judeo-German by Elia Levita in Venice in the year 1501. It is, no doubt, related to some one of the many Italian versions in which Bevys is turned into Bovo. The popularity of this book has been second only to the 'Zeena-Ureena' which contains a very large number of folk-tales interwoven in a popular exposition

this fact, while Helwich thought it of sufficient importance to translate the book into German and supply it with critical notes. Helwich's book seems to have escaped the attention of all who have dealt on the *Maasebuch*, Steinschneider included ; and yet without it a study of the Jewish folklore is very difficult, as the *Maasebuch* can hardly be procured. The title of the book is : *Erster Theil jüdischer Historien oder Thalmudischer Rabbinischer wunderlicher Legenden*, so von Juden als wahrhafftige und heylige Geschicht an ihren Sabbathen und Festtagen gelesen werden. Darausz dieses verstockten Volcks Aberglauben und Fabelwerck zu ersehen. Ausz ihren eigenen Büchern in Truck Teutsch verfertigt, von neuem übersehen und corrigiert durch Christophorum Helvicum, der H. Schrift und Hebräischen Sprach Professorem in der Universitet zu Giessen, Giessen, bey Caspar Chemlein, Im Jahre 1612, 16mo, 222 pp. Second part with slightly different title. After gelesen werden follows : Sampt beygefügten Glossen und Widerlegung, 16mo, 207 pp. See also Is. Lévi, *Cinq contes juifs*, in *Mélusine*, Vol. II. col. 569-574. On the *König Artus*, cf. Schröder, *Mitteilungen über ein deutsches Wigaloisepos aus dem 17. Jahrhunderte, M. Hanau B. V. Hess. G.* Some of these stories are discussed in Jacobs's *Jewish Diffusion of Folk Tales* (as above).

of the Bible. There are also books that contain stories
of 'Sinbad the Sailor,' or what seem to be versions of Sir
John Maundeville's 'Travels,' and other similar fantastic
tales. These stories, having once been committed to writing
and printing, have remained intact up to our times,
except that they have undergone linguistic modernizations. But there is also an unlimited number of fairy
tales and fables in circulation which have never been
written down, which have therefore been more or less
subjected to local influences ; in these Hebrew, German,
and Slavic elements meet most freely, causing the stories
to be moulded in new forms.[1] It may be asserted without fear of contradiction that among the Russian Jews
the investigator will find the best, most complete versions
of most, if not all, the stories contained in Grimm's or
Andersen's collections. The reason for it is to be
sought in the inordinate love of story-telling that the
Jews possess. They are fond of staying up late in the

[1] A few scattered stories may be found in the following publications : M. Schwarzfeld, *Basmul cu Pantoful la Evrei, la Români şi la
alte Popoare, Studiu folkloristic*, Bucureşti, 1893, 8vo, 27 pp. (*Extras
din Anuarul pentru Israeliţi*, Vol. XV. pp. 138–165); by the same,
Scrisoare către Dumnezeu, Cercetare folcloristică (*Anuarul pentru Israeliţi*, Vol. XV. pp. 191–198); R. T. Kaindl, *Eine jüdische Sage über
die Entstehung des Erdbebens, Zeitschrift für Ethnologie*, Vol. XXV.
p. 370 ; B. W. Segel, *Jüdische Volksmärchen*, in *Globus*, Vol. LX.
pp. 283 ff., 296–298, 313–315. The largest collection of folk-tales by
the same author are given in *Zbiór wiadomości do antropologii krajowej*, Vol. XVII., Cracow, 1893, under the title, *Materyały do etnografii żydów wschodnio-galicyjskich*, pp. 261–332 ; a review of this
important work, in German, is given in the *Urquell*, Vol. V. pp. 183–
186. Scattered through the *Urquell* there are many interesting tales,
mainly on *gilgulim, leezim, meessim ;* cf. Vol. IV., pp. 96, 97, 257;
Neue Folge, Vol. I. pp. 80, 81, 121, 122, 344, 345, 351 ; see also Z. d.
V. f. V., Vol. IV. p. 210. See also the bibliography of the legends,
etc., in *Sistematičeskij ukazatel*, p. 211 (Nos. 3133–3136).

night, particularly in the winter, and whiling away the time with an endless series of stories. The stranger who is a good raconteur is sure of a kind reception wherever he may chance to stay; but his nights will be curtailed by the extent of his fund of stories, for his audience will not budge as long as they suspect that the stranger has not spent all the arrows from his quiver. The wandering beggar-students and tailors have the reputation for story-telling; it was by one of the latter that a large number of fairy tales were related to me. I choose for illustration one that is known in a great variety of versions.

The Fool is Wiser than the Wise

"Once upon a time there lived a rich man who had three sons : two of them were wise, while one was a fool. After his death the brothers proceeded to divide the property, which consisted mainly of cattle. The two wise brothers suggested that the herd be divided into three equal parts, and that lots be cast for each ; but the fool insisted that corrals be built near the house of each and that each be allowed to keep the cattle that would stray into his corral. The wise brothers agreed to this, and to entice the oxen and cows they placed fresh hay in their enclosures; but the fool did not take measures to gain possession of cattle by unfair means. The animals were attracted by the odor of the new-mown hay, and only one calf strolled into the fool's enclosure. The fool kept his calf for eight days, and forgot to give it fodder during that time ; so it died. He took off its hide, and placed it in the sun to get dry. There it lay until it shrivelled up. Then he took the hide to Warsaw to sell it, but no one wanted to buy it, for it was all dried up.

"He started for home and came to an inn where he wanted to stay over night. He found there twelve men eating, and drinking good wine. He asked the landlady whether he could stay there over night. She told him she would not keep him in the house for all the money in the world, and she asked him to leave the house at once. He did not like her hasty manner, and he hid himself behind the door where no one could see him. There he overheard the landlady saying to the men: 'Before my husband gets home you must go down in the cellar and hide behind the wine-casks. In the night, when he will be asleep, you must come up and kill him. Then I shall be satisfied with you!' After a short while her husband returned from the distillery with some brandy, and the men hurried down into the cellar. He unloaded the brandy-casks, and went into the house. He asked his wife for something to eat; but she said there was nothing in the house. Just then the fool stepped in and asked the innkeeper whether he could not stay there over night. The landlady got angry at him and said: 'I told you before that there was no bed here for you!' But the innkeeper said: 'He will stay here over night!' and the innkeeper's word was law. He told the fool to sit down at the table with him, and they started a conversation. The fool accidentally placed his hand on the hide, which being dry began to crackle. The innkeeper asked him: 'What makes the hide crackle that way?' and the fool answered: 'It is talking to me!' 'What does it say?' 'It says that you are hungry, and that your wife says that there is nothing in the house, but that if you will look into the oven you will find some dishes.' He went up to the oven and found there enough for himself and the fool to eat. Then the hide crackled again, and the innkeeper asked again: 'What does it say?' 'It says that you should start a big fire in the oven!' 'What is the fire for?' 'I do not know, but you must obey the hide.' So he went and made a big fire in the oven. Then the hide crackled again. Says he: 'What does the hide say now?' 'It tells to heat kettles of water.' When the water got hot, the hide crackled again. Then he asked: 'What does the hide say now?' 'It says that you should take some strong men with you to the cellar and pour the water behind the wine-casks.' And so he did. The robbers were all scalded, and they ran away. Then he came upstairs, and the hide crackled again. Said he: 'Why does it crackle now?' 'The twelve robbers wanted to kill you at night, because your wife ordered them to do so.' When the wife heard that, she also ran away. Then the innkeeper said: 'Sell me your hide!' The fool answered: 'It costs much money.' 'No matter how much it costs, I shall pay for it, for it has saved my life.' 'It costs one thousand roubles.' So he gave him one thousand roubles. The fool went home, and when the brothers heard that he had sold his hide for one thousand roubles, they killed all their cattle, and took their hides to Warsaw to sell. They figured that if their brother's calf brought one thousand roubles, the hides of their oxen ought to fetch them at least two thousand roubles apiece. When they asked two thousand roubles apiece, people laughed and offered them a rouble for each. When they heard that, they went home and upbraided their brother for having cheated them. But he insisted that he had received one thousand roubles for his hide, and the brothers left him alone.

" After a while the fool's wife died. The undertakers wanted one thousand roubles for her interment. But

the fool would not pay that sum. He placed his wife
in a wagon and took her to Warsaw. There he filled
the wagon with fine apples and put the dead body at
the head of the wagon all dressed up. He himself stood
at some distance and watched what would happen.
There rode by a Polish count, and as he noticed the
fine apples, he sent his servant to buy some. The servant asked the woman several times at what price she
sold the apples ; but as she did not answer him, he hit
her in the face. Then the fool ran up and cried, saying
that they had killed his wife. The count descended
from his carriage, and when he had convinced himself
that the woman was really dead, he asked the fool what
he could do to satisfy him. The fool asked five thousand
roubles, and the count paid him. The fool paid the
undertaker in Warsaw a few roubles, and he buried his
wife. He returned home and told his brothers of his
having received five thousand roubles for his dead wife.
Upon hearing that, they killed their wives and children
and took the dead bodies to Warsaw to sell. When
they arrived in Warsaw, they were asked what they
had in their wagons. They said: 'Dead bodies for
sale.' The people began to laugh, and said that dead
bodies had to be taken to the cemetery. There was
nothing left for the brothers to do but to take them to
the cemetery and have them buried.

"They wept bitterly, and swore that they would take
revenge on their brother. And so they did. When
they arrived home, they told him that they wished to
make him a prince. They enticed him for that purpose
into a bag, and wanted to throw him into the water.
They went away to find a place where they could throw
him in without being noticed. In the meanwhile the
fool kept on crying in the bag that he did not care to

be a prince, that he wished to get out of the bag. Just then a rich Polish merchant drove by. When he heard the cries in the bag, he stepped down from his carriage and asked the fool why he was crying so. He said: 'I do not want to be a prince!' So he untied him and said: 'Let me get into the bag and be made a prince! I shall make you a present of my horses and my carriage, if you will let me be a prince.' The rich man crept into the bag, and the fool tied it fast. He went into the carriage and drove away. The brothers came, picked up the bag, and threw it into the water. The fool watched their doings from a distance. The brothers were sure they had drowned the fool and returned home. The next morning they were astonished to see their brother driving around town in a fine carriage. They asked him: 'Where did you get that?' He answered: 'In the water.' 'Are there more of them left?' 'There are finer ones down there.' So they went down to the water's edge, and they agreed that one of them should leap in and see if there were any carriages left there, and if he should find any, he was to make a noise in the water, when the other one would follow him. One of them leaped in, and beginning to drown, began to splash the water. The other, thinking his brother was calling him, also jumped in, and they were both drowned. The fool became the sole heir of all their property; he married again, and is now living quite happily."

Corresponding to the diffusion of folklore among the Jews, their store of popular beliefs, superstitions, and medicine is unlimited. Their mysterious world is peopled with the imaginary beings of the Talmud, the creatures of German mythology, and the creations of

the Slavic popular mind. These exist for them, however, not as separate entities, but as transfused into an
organic whole in which the belief of Babylonia and
Assyria has much of the outward form of the superstition of Russia, just as the spirits of Poland and Germany
are made to be brothers to those of Chaldea and Egypt.
To their minds the transmigrated souls of the *Gilgulim*,
the scoffing *Leezim*, the living dead bodies of the *Meessim*, the possessing *Dibukim*, the grewsome *Scheedim*,
are as real as the *Riesen* and *Schraetele* of Germany
and the *Nischtgute* (niedobry), *Wukodlaki* (werewolf),
Zlidne, *Upior* (vampyre), and *Domowoj* of Russia. The
beast *Reem* of the Talmud, the *Pipernätter* (Lindwurm)
of Germany are not less known to them than the fabled
animals of Russian fairy tales. In case of sickness they
consult with equal success the miracle-working Rabbi
with his lore derived from Talmud and Cabbala, as the
Tartar medicine man (znachar), or get some old woman
to recite the ancient German formula for warding off
the evil eye. There is not an incident in their lives,
from their births unto their deaths, that is not accompanied by its own circle of superstitious rites and prac-
tices.[1]

---

[1] On the customs, beliefs, superstitions, etc., of the Jews, see A. P.
Bender, *Beliefs, Rites, and Customs of the Jews Connected with Death,
Burial, and Mourning*, in *Jewish Quarterly Review*, Vol. VI. pp. 317–
347, 664–671, and Vol. VII. pp. 101–118; Dan, *Volksglauben und
Gebräuche der Juden in der Bukowina*, in *Zeitschrift für österreich-
ische Volkskunde*, Vol. II. Nos. 2, 3; Hedvige Heinicke, *Le carnaval
des juifs galiciens*, in *Revue des Traditions populaires*, Vol. VI. p. 118;
I. Buchbinder, *Jüdische Sabobones*, in *Hausfreund*, Vol. II. pp. 167–
170; Steinschneider mentions books dealing on superstitions in his
catalogue in the *Serapeum*, under the numbers 219 and 421. This subject is treated extensively in the *Urquell*, Vol. II. pp. 5–7, 34–36, 112,
165, 166, 181–183; Vol. III. pp. 18, 19, 286–288; Vol. IV. pp. 73–75,
94–96, 118, 119, 141, 142, 170, 171, 187–189, 210, 211, 272–274; Vol.

Their literature, both oral and printed, is also full of
evidences of that popular creative spirit which finds its
expression in the form of maxims and proverbs. One
can hardly turn the pages of a novel or comedy without
finding some interesting specimens of this class. But
little has been done to classify them, or even to collect
them. The printed collections of Tendlau and Bernstein contain less than three thousand proverbs, while
the seven thousand saws on which Schwarzfeld bases
his generalizations in a Roumanian periodical (*Anuarul
pentru Israeliți*) have not yet been published by him.[1]

V. pp. 19, 81, 170, 171, 225–228, 290, 291; Neue Folge, Vol. I. pp. 9,
46–49, 270, 271; Vol. II. pp. 33, 34, 46, 108–110. See also Segel,
Materyały do etnografii żydów, etc., pp. 319–328; S. Abramowitsch,
Dās kléine Menschele, pp. 76–77; Linetzki, *Dās chsidische Jüngel*,
pp. 29–31, 114. For a general work on Jewish superstitions, see
M. Schuhl, *Superstitions et coutumes populaires du Judaisme con-
temporain*, Paris, 1882, 4to, 42 pp. The most important contribution
on the beliefs of the German Jews in the early Middle Ages is given
by Güdemann, *Geschichte des Erziehungswesen und der Cultur der
Juden*, etc., Vol. I. Chap. VII. pp. 199–228, under the title *Der
jüdische Aber-, Zauber- und Hexen-glaube in Frankreich und Deutschland im 12. und 13. Jahrhunderte*. See also the bibliography of the
subject in the *Sistematičeskij ukazatel'*, pp. 211, 212 (Nos. 3137–
3159). A large number of superstitions, beliefs, etc., are scattered
throughout the Judeo-German literature: probably the most important of such works is Schatzkes' *Der jüdischer Var-Peessach* (*q.v.*).

[1] For proverbs and the discussion of the same, see: M. Spektor,
Jüdische Volkswörtlich, in *Jüdisches Volksblatt*, Vol. VI. pp. 63, 95,
112, 128, 191, 304, 423, 488; I. Bernstein, *Sprichwörter*, in *Hausfreund*,
Vol. I. pp. 89–112, and Vol. II. pp. 1–49 (second part); S. Adelberg,
Przysłowia żydowskie, in *Wisła*, Vol. IV. pp. 166–187; M. Schwarzfeld,
Literatura populară Israelită ca element etnico-psichologic, in *Anuarul
pentru Israeliți*, Vol. XII. pp. 41–52; the same, *Evreii în Literatura
lor populară sau Cum se judecă evreii însuși*, *Studiu etnico-psichologic*,
Bucuresti, 1898, 8vo, 37 pp. (*Anuarul pentru Israeliți*, Vol. XIX.
pp. 1–37). In connection with the last two, though not strictly on
Jewish proverbs, see his *Evreii în Literatura populară Romană*, *Studiu
de psichologie populară*, — Anex, *Evreii în literatura populară univer-*

Equally rich would prove the harvest of popular anecdotes, either as told of separate individuals, as Herschele Ostropoler, Motke Chabad, Jössef Loksch, the wise man of Chelm, and the like, or as applied to the inhabitants of certain Abderitic towns.[1] Many such collections are mentioned in the appendix, but they do not by any means exhaust the stories that are current among the people. Though they generally are of the same character as those told of Schildburg and Till Eulenspiegel, and are even borrowings from those German stories, yet they contain so much original matter, and have been welded into such new forms, that they deserve the attention of the student of folklore. They also bear excellent witness to that pungent wit for which the Jews are so justly famous.

sală, *Tablou comparativ*, Bucureşti, 1892, 8vo, 78 pp. (*Extras din Anuarul pentru Israeliţi*, Vol. XIV. pp. 97–172). A large number of proverbs from various Slavic localities are given in the *Urquell:* Vol. II. pp. 26, 27, 66, 112, 131, 163, 178, 196; Vol. IV. pp. 75, 76, 194, 212, 215, 256, 257; Vol. VI. pp. 33, 34, 69, 119–121; Neue Folge, Vol. I. pp. 14, 15, 119–121, 172–175, 271–270; Vol. II. pp. 221, 222, 311–313, 338–340. For the proverbs of the German Jews, see A. Tendlau, *Sprichwörter und Redensarten deutsch-jüdischer Vorzeit, als Beitrag zur Volks-, Sprach- und Sprichwörter-kunde, aufgezeichnet aus dem Munde des Volkes und nach Wort und Sinn erläutert*, Frankfurt a. M. (1860).

[1] The older books on Eulenspiegel are given by Steinschneider in the *Serapeum*, under Nos. 10, 288, and 388; in the *Urquell*, there are a few stories on *Chelm* in Vol. III. pp. 27–29, and Neue Folge, Vol. I. pp. 345, 346. A large number is given by Segel in his collection in the *Zbiór wiadomości do antropologii krajowej*, pp. 303–306.

IV. THE FOLKSONG

The Jews have been preëminently inhabitants of towns ; their very admission into Poland was based on the supposition that they would be instrumental in creating towns and cities, from which the agricultural Slavs kept aloof. Centuries of city life have incapacitated them for any other occupation than commerce and artisanship, and have entirely estranged them from nature. On the other hand, their civil disabilities and oppression have led them to cling more closely to the Bible and their religious lore than was customary among their coreligionists in other lands. It was in these Slavic countries that the Talmud was rediscovered and that it was introduced to the rest of Judaism. All these circumstances developed in them a strong retrospective spirit, so that in the centre of their intellectual horizon stands man in all his varying moods and vicissitudes of fortune. Consequently all their folksongs[1] have more or less of a lyrical tinge, and·

---

[1] In a general way the Judeo-German folksong was treated by I. G. Oršanskij, in his *Evrei v Rossii, Očerki ekonomičeskago i obščestvennago byta russkich evreev*, St. Petersburg, 1877, 8vo, on pp. 391–402 ; more specially by J. J. Lerner, *Die jüdische Muse*, in *Hausfreund*, Vol. II. pp. 182–198, from which a few songs are quoted here. The most of the songs given here are from my manuscript collection made in Boston and New York among the Russian Jews. In the *Urquell* folksongs are given in Vol. IV. pp. 119, 120 ; Vol. V. p. 106 ; Vol. VI. pp. 43, 158 ; Neue Folge, Vol. I. pp. 45, 50, 82, 83, 175, 230–242 ; Vol. II. pp. 27–29, 39, 40. Cf. B. W. Segel, *Materyały do etnografii żydów wschodnio-galicyjskich*, in *Zbiór wiadomości do antropologii krajowej*, Vol. XVII. pp. 306–319.

the consideration of nature is almost entirely absent
from them; occasionally a flower, a natural phenomenon, finds a passing mention in them, but these are never
used for their own intrinsic interest. Outside of himself, the Jew knows only his duties to God and his
duties to man, as flowing from his duties to God. Not
feeling himself as a constituent part of a nation, having
no other union with his fellow-men except that of religion, he could never rise to the appreciation and formation of an epic poem, although the material for such a
one was present in the very popular legend of the one-
day king, Saul Wahl.[1]

The cradle songs reflect this spirit.[2] While babies
of Gentiles hear meaningless nursery rhymes or comical ditties, Jewish infants are early made acquainted
with the serious aspects of life. They are told of the
ideal of their future occupation, which is commerce,
they are spurred on to 'Tōre,' which is learning, mainly
religious, and they are reminded that they must remain
an 'ehrlicher,' *i.e.* an orthodox, Jew. The following
poem is, probably, the most popular song in Judeo-
German, as it is sung from Galicia to Siberia, and
from the Baltic provinces to Roumania:

Hinter Jankeles Wiegele
Stēht a klār-weiss Ziegele:

---

[1] The legend has been admirably treated by the historian, S. A.
Beršadskij, in *Evrej korol' polskij*, in the *Voschod*, Vol. IX. Nos. 1-5.

[2] The *Urquell* (see above) gives some children's songs. See also
L. Wiener, *Aus der russisch-jüdischen Kinderstube*, in *Mitteilungen
der Gesellschaft für jüdische Volkskunde, herausgegeben von M. Grun-
wald*, Hamburg, 1898, Heft II, pp. 40–49; R. F. Kaindl, *Lieder, Neck-
reime, Abzählverse, Spiele, Geheimsprachen und allerlei Kunterbuntes
aus der Kinderwelt, in der Bukowina und 'in Galizien gesammelt*, in
Z. d. V. f. V., Vol. VII. pp. 146, 147. In Linetzki's *Dās chsidische
Jüngel*, p. 23, a number of children's songs are mentioned by title.

Ziegele is' gefähren handlen
Rožinkelach mit Mandlen.
•Rožinkelach mit Mandlen
Sanen die beste S-chŏre, —
Jankele wet lernen Tŏre,
Tŏre wet er lernen,
Briewelach wet er schreiben,
Un' an ehrlicher Jüd'
Wet er af tomid verbleiben.

Behind Jacob's cradle there stands a clear white goat : the goat has gone a-bartering raisins and almonds. Raisins and almonds are the best wares, — Jacob will study the Law, the Law he will study, letters he will write, and an honest Jew he will forever remain.

But commerce and learning are not for girls. They are generally incapacitated for the first by their onerous duties of home; and learning, at least a knowledge of the Sacred language and its lore, has never been regarded as a requisite of woman. She received her religious instruction and ethical training by means of Judeo-German books which owe their very origin to the necessity of educating her. The name of the script in which all these books of the past three centuries are printed is *Weiberdeutsch*, indicating at once the use to which it was put. The title-pages of the works generally tell that they are 'gar hübsch bescheidlich far frumme Weiber un' Maidlich,' or that 'die Weiber un' Meidlich di Weil damit vertreiben die heiligen Täg.' The Biblical injunction 'fructify and multiply yourself' invests family life with a special sacredness, throws a gloom over the childless home, and leads this people to regard motherhood as the ideal state of the Jewish woman. All these sentiments find frequent expressions in their songs, and while the infant boy is lulled to sleep with a recitation of his future manly virtues, the baby girl hears in her cradle, 'In the month of Tamuz, my little lady, you will become a mother !'

Childhood alone claims exemption from oppressing thoughts and gloom : childhood must have its merriments, its pranks, its wantonness, no matter how serious life is to become later, or how soon it is to be ended. With the Jew youth, indeed, lasts but 'an hour,' and in after-life he has many an occasion to regret its short duration :

> Jāhren klēine, Jāhren schoene,
> Wās sent ihr asō wēnig dā?
> Ihr sent nor gekummen,
> Me hāt euch schoen aufgenummen,
> Un' sent nor gewe'n bei uns ēin Scho?

> Jāhren junge, Jāhren g'ringe,
> Wās sent ihr asō gich aweg?
> Es seht euch nit kēin Äugel,
> Es derjāgen euch nit die Voegel,
> Ihr sent aweg gār ohn' ein Eck'!

Little years, beautiful years, why are there so few of you? You had scarcely come, you were well received, and you stayed but an hour with us! — Young years, light years, why have you passed so quickly? Not an eye can see you, not a bird can fly as swiftly, you have passed without return!

The number of ditties sung by children is very great. They do not in general differ from similar popular productions of other nations, either in form or content ; some are evidently identical with German songs, while a few are Slavic borrowings.

But there are two classes of songs peculiarly Jewish : the mnemonic lines for the study of Hebrew words, and those that depict the ideal course of a boy's life. To the second belongs :

> A klēine Weile wöllen mir spielen,
> Dem Kind in Cheeder wöllen mir führen,

Wet er lernen a Päar Schures,
Wöllen mir hören gute Pschures,
Gute Pschures mit viel Mailes,
Zu der Chupe paskenen Schailes.
's 'et sein gefällen der ganzer Welt,
Chossen-kale — a vulle Geld,
A vulle Geld mit Masel-broche,
Chossen-kale — a schoene Mischpoche,
Schoene Mischpoche mit schoenem Trest,
Abgestellt auf drei Jähr Köst.

A little while we shall play, we shall lead the child to school; there he will learn a few lines, and we shall get good reports, good reports with many good things, and he will settle religious disputes upon his wedding day. The whole world will be satisfied, — bridegroom and bride — a purse full of money; full of money, may it bring blessings; bridegroom and bride — a fine family; a fine family with fine apparel, and at their house you'll stay three years.

The man's career used to run in just such a stereotyped manner: at a tender age, when children have not yet learned to properly articulate their speech, he was sent to the Cheeder, the elementary Jewish school; long before the romantic feeling has its rise in youth, he was betrothed and married; but unable to earn a livelihood for the family with which he prayed to be blessed, he had to stay for a number of years with his parents or parents-in-law, eating ' Köst,' or board; this time he generally passed in the Talmud school, perfecting himself in the casuistry of religious discussion, while the woman at once began to care for her everincreasing family. Under such conditions love could not flourish, at least not that romantic love of which the young Gentiles dream and which finds its utterance in their popular poetry. The word ' love' does not exist in the Judeo-German dictionary, and wherever that feeling, with which they have become acquainted

only since the middle of this century, is to be named,
the Jews have to use the German word 'Liebe.' The
man's hope was to marry into some 'schoene Mischpoche,' a good and respected family, while the girl's
dream was to get a husband who was well versed in
'rabonische Tŏre,' *i.e.* Jewish lore. While the boy, by
his occupation with the Bible and the Talmud, was
taught to look on marriage as on an act pleasing to
God, the girl was freer to allow her fancy to roam in
the realms bordering on the sensations of love :

> Schoen bin ich, schoen, un' schoen is' mein Nāmen :
> Redt män mir Schiduchim vun grösse Rabonim.
> Rabonische Tŏre is' sēhr grŏss,
> Un' ich bei mein Mamen a züchtige Rŏs'.
> A Rŏs' is' auf'n Dach,
> A lichtige Nacht,
> Wasser is' in Stub, Holz is' in Haus,
> Welchen Bocher hāb' ich feind, treib' ich ihm araus !
> Fischelach in Wasser, Kräppelach in Puter,
> Welchen Bocher hāt mich feind, a Ruch in sein Mutter !

Pretty I am, pretty, and pretty is my name; they talk of great
rabbis as matches for me.   Rabbi's learning is very great, but I
am a treasured rose of my mother's.   A rose upon the roof, a clear
night; water is in the room, wood is in the house, — If I love not
a boy, I drive him away !   Fish in the water, fritters in butter, —
If a boy love me not, cursed be his mother !

But such an exultation of free choice could be only
passing, as the match was made without consulting her
feelings in the matter; her greatest concern was that
she might be left an old maid, while her companions
passed into the ordained state of matrimony.   Songs
embodying this fear are quite common; the following
is one of them :

> Sitz' ich mir auf'n Stēin,
> Nemmt mir ān a grŏss Gewēin :

Alle Maedlach häben Chassene,
Nor ich bleib' allēin.
Oi wēh, Morgenstern!
Wenn well ich a Kale wer'n,
Zi heunt, zi morgen?
A schoene Maedel bin ich doch
Un' a reichen Taten häb' ich doch!

I sit upon a stone, and am seized by great weeping: all girls get married, but I remain single. Woe to me, morning star! When shall I become a bride, to-day or to-morrow? I surely am a pretty girl, and I have a rich father!

In the more modern songs in which the word 'love' is used, that word represents the legitimate inclination for the opposite sex which culminates in marriage.

Now that love and love matches are not uncommon, it is again woman who is the strongest advocate of them; love songs addressed by men to women are rare, and they may be recited with equal propriety by the latter. The chief characteristic of woman's love, as expressed in them, is constancy and depth of feeling.

Schwarz bist du, schwarz, asō wie a Zigeuner,
Ich häb' gemēint, as du we'st sein meiner;
Schwarz bist du, āber mit Cheen,
Für wemen du bist mies, für mir bist du schoen;
Schoen bist du wie Silber, wie Gold, —
Wer 's hät dich feind un' ich häb' dich hold.
Vun alle Fehlern känn a Doktor äbhēilen,
Die Liebe vun mein Herzen känn ich var Kēinem nit derzaehlen.

Black you are, black as a Gypsy, I thought you would always be mine; black you are, but with grace, — for others you may be homely, but for me you are handsome; handsome you are, like silver, like gold, — let others dislike you, but I love you. Of all troubles a doctor can cure, the love in my heart I can tell to no one.

Many are the songs of pining for the distant lover; they show all the melancholy touches of similar Slavic

love ditties, and are the most poetical of all the Jewish
songs.   They range from the soft regrets of the lover's
temporary absence to the deep and gloomy despair of
the betrothed one's death, though the latter is always
tempered by a resignation which comes from implicit
faith in the ways of Heaven.   Here are a few of them
in illustration of the various forms which this pining
assumes :

> Bei 'm Breg Wasser thu' ich stēhn
> Un' känn zu dir nit kummen,
> Oi, vun weiten rufst du mich,
> Ich känn āber nit schwimmen !

At the water's edge I do stand, and I cannot get to you. Oh,
you call me from afar, but I cannot swim !

> Finster is' mein' Welt,
> Mein' Jugend is' schwarz,
> Mein Glück is' verstellt,
> Es fault mir mein Harz.
>
> Es zittert mir jetwider Eewer,
> Es kühlt mir dās Blut,
> Mit dir in ēin Keewer
> Wet mir sein gut.
>
> Ach, wās willst du, Mutter, hāben,
> Wās mutschest du dein Kind ?
> Wās willst du mir begrāben ?
> Für wässere Sünd' ?
>
> Ich hāb' kēin Nachas geha't,
> Nor Leiden un' Kummer,
> Ich welk' wie ein Blatt,
> Wie ein Blum' Ssof Summer.
>
> Wu nemm' ich mein' Freund
> Chotsch auf ēin Scho ?
> Alle hāben mir feind
> Un' du bist nit dā !

Dark is my world ; my youth is black, my fortune is veiled, my
heart is decaying. — Every limb of mine is trembling ; my blood

grows cold; I should feel well with you in one grave. — Oh, what do you want of me, mother? Why do you vex your child? Why do you wish to bury me? For what sins of mine? — I have had no joy, only suffering and sorrow. I am fading like a leaf, like a flower at the end of summer. — Where shall I find my friend but for one hour? No one loves me, and you are not here.

With the same feeling that prompts the Jewish woman to repeat the prayer, ' O Lord, I thank Thee that Thou hast. created me according to Thy will ! ' while the man prays, ' I thank Thee that Thou hast created me a man,' she regards her disappointments in love as perfectly natural; and the inconstancy of man, which forms the subject of all songs of unhappy love, does not call forth recriminations and curses, which one would expect, but only regrets at her own credulity.

One would imagine that the wedding day must appear as the happiest in the life of the woman, but such is not the case. With it begin all the tribulations for which she is singled out; and the jest-maker, who is always present at the ceremony of uniting the pair, addresses the bride with the words:

Bride, bride, weep! The bridegroom will send you a pot full of horseradish, and that will make you snivel unto your very teeth,

inviting her to weep instead of smiling, and he follows this doggerel with a discussion of the. vanities of life and the sadness of woman's lot. Even if her marital happiness should be unmarred by any unfaithfulness of her husband, — and Jewish men for the greater part are good husbands and fathers, — there are the cares of earning the daily bread, which frequently fall on the woman, while the stronger vessel is brooding over some Talmudical subtleties ; there are the eternal worries over the babies, and, worst of all, the proverbial mother-in-

law, if the wife chances to board with her for the first
few years after marriage.   The ideal of the Jewess is
but a passing dream, and no one can escape the awakening to a horrible reality:

A Maedele werd a Kale
In ēin Rege, in ēin Minut,
Mit ihr freuen sich Alle
Die Freud' is' nor zu ihr.

Der Chossen schickt Presenten,
Sie werd gār neu geboren,
Wenn sie thut sich ān,
Wünscht sie ihm lange Jāhren.

Sie gēht mit 'n Chossen spazieren
Un' thut in Spiegele a Kuck,
Stēhen Ōlem Menschen
Un' seinen mekane dem Glück.

Ot führt män sie zu der Chupe,
Un' ot führt män sie zurück,
Stēhen a Kupe Maedlach
Un' seinen mekane dem Glück.

Auf morgen nāch der Chupe,
Die Freimut is' noch in Ganzen:
Der Chossen sitzt wie a Meelach
Un' die Kale gēht sich tanzen.

Drei Jāhr nāch der Chupe
Der Freimut is schōn arāb:
Die junge Weibel gēht arum
Mit a zudrēhter Kopp.

*   *   *   *   *

"Oi wēh, Mutter, Mutter,
Ich will vun dir nit hören,
Ich wollt' schōn besser wöllen
Zurück a Maedel wer'n!"

A girl is made a bride in a moment, in a minute, — all rejoice
with her, with her alone. — The groom sends presents, she feels all
new-born; when she attires herself, she wishes him long years. —

She gets ready to walk with the bridegroom, and looks into the mirror, — there stands a crowd of people who envy her her good luck. — Now she is led to the baldachin, now she is led back again, — there stands a bevy of girls who envy her her luck. — The next day after the marriage, — the joy is still with them: the bridegroom sits like a king, the bride is a-dancing. — Three years after the marriage, — the joy has left them: the young woman walks around with a troubled head. . . . 'Woe to me, mother, mother, I do not want to hear of you, — I should like, indeed, to be a young girl again.'

Pathetic are the recitals of suffering at the house of her husband's parents, where she is treated worse than a menial, where she is without the love of a mother to whom she is attached more than to any one else, and where she ends miserably her young years:[1]

> Mein' Tochter, wu bist du gewesen?
> Bei 'm Schwieger un' Schwähr,
> Wās brummt wie a Bär,
> Mutter du liebe, du meine!

> Mein Tochterl, awu häst du dorten gesessen?
> Auf a Bank,
> Kēinmāl nit geramt,
> Mutter du liebe, du meine!

> Mein' Tochter, awu häst du dorten geschlāfen?
> Auf der Erd,
> Kēinmāl nit gekehrt, etc.

> Tochterulu, wās hāt män dir gegeben zu Koppen?
> A Säckele Hēu,
> In Harzen is' wēh, etc.

> Tochterulu, in wās hāt män dir geführt?
> In kowanem Wāgen,
> Mit Eisen beschlāgen, etc.

[1] See the prototype of this song in K. Francke, *Social Forces in German Literature*, p. 120.

Tochterl, über wās hāt män dir geführt?
Über a Brück',
Kēinmāl nit zurück, etc.

Tochterulu, mit wās hāt män dir geführt?
Mit a Ferd,
Jung in der Erd',
Mutter du liebe, du meine!

My daughter, where have you been? — At mother-in-law's and
father-in-law's, who growls like a bear, mother dear, mother mine!
— My daughter, where did you sit there? — Upon a bench never
cleaned, mother dear, mother mine! — My daughter, where did
you sleep there? — Upon the ground, never swept, etc. — Daughter
dear, what did they lay under your head? — A bag of hay, in my
heart there is a pain, etc. — Daughter dear, in what did they drive
you? — In a wagon covered with iron bands, etc. — Daughter
dear, over what did they lead you? — Over a bridge, never back,
etc. — Daughter dear, with what did they drive you? — With a
horse, young into the earth, mother dear, mother mine!

Equally pathetic are the songs that sing of widow-
hood. This is a far more common occurrence among
Jews than among other people and causes much greater
inconveniences to the helpless woman. It is caused
either by the natural occurrences of death or by self-
assumed exile to escape military service which is naturally not to the tastes of the Jew, as we shall see later,
or frequently by ruthless abandonment. This latter
case is the result of early marriages in which the contracting parties are not considered as to their tastes;
often the young man finds awakening in himself an
inclination for higher, Gentile, culture, but he finds his
path impeded by the ties of family and the gross interests of his consort. If he can, he gets a divorce from
her, but more frequently he leaves her without further
ado, escaping to Germany or America to pursue his
studies. His wife is made an *Agune*, a grass-widow,

who, according to the Mosaic law, may not marry again until his death has been duly certified to :

Auf'n Barg stēht a Taübele,
Sie thut mit ihr Pāar brummen,
Ich hāb' geha't a guten Freund
Un' känn zu ihm nit kummen.

Bächen Trähren thuen sich
Vun meine Äugen rinnen,
Ich bin geblieben wie a Spündele
Auf dem Wasser schwimmen.

Gār die Welt is auf mir gefallen,
Seit ich bin geblieben allēin,
Sitz' ich doch Tāg un' Nacht
Jāmmerlich un' wēin'.

Teichen Trähren thuen sich
Rinnen vun meine Äugen,
Ich soll hāben Fliegelach,
Wollt' ich zu ihm geflögen.

Lēgt sich, Kinderlach, alle arum mir,
Euer Tate is' vun euch vertrieben.
Klēine Jessomim sent ihr doch
Un' ich bin ein Almone geblieben.

On the mountain stands a dove ; she is cooing to her brood : I have had a good friend, and I cannot get to him. — Brooks of tears flow out of my eyes ; I am left like a piece of wood swimming on the water. — The whole world has fallen upon me since I am left alone ; I sit day and night and weep bitterly. — Rivers of tears pour forth from my eyes. If I had wings I should fly to him. — Lie down, children, all around me ! Your father has been taken away from you : You are now young orphans, and I am left a widow.

As sad as the widow's is the lot of the orphan. Fatherless and motherless, he seems to be in everybody's way, and no matter what he does, he is not appreciated by those he comes in contact with. There are many songs of the dying mother who finds her last

moments embittered by the thought that her children
will suffer privations and oppression from their stepmother and from other unkind people.   There are also
beggar's songs which tell that the singers were driven
to beggary through loss of parents.   The following
verses, touching in their simplicity, recite the sad
plight of an orphan :

> Wasser schaumt, Wasser schaumt,
> Thut män ganz weit hören, —
> Wenn es starbt der Väter-Mutter,
> Giesst der Jossem mit Trähren.
>
> Der Jossem gēht, der Jossem gēht,
> Der Jossem thut gār umsüst, —
> Leut' schatzen, Leut' sāgen,
> As der Jossem täug' gār nischt.
>
> Der Jossem gēht, der Jossem gēht,
> Un' in Zar un' in Pein, —
> Leut' schatzen, Leut' sāgen,
> As der Jossem is' schicker vun Wein.
>
> Bei meine Freund', bei meine Freund'
> Wachst Weiz un' Körner, —
> Bei mir Jossem, bei mir Jossem
> Wachst doch Grās un' Dörner.
>
> Gottunju, Gottunju,
> Gottunju du mein,
> Wās häst du mich nit beschaffen
> Mit dem Masel wie meine Freund?

Water foams, water foams, one can hear afar.   When father
and mother die the orphan sheds tears. — The orphan goes, the
orphan goes, the orphan does all in vain.   People judge, people say
that the orphan is good for nothing. — The orphan goes, the orphan
goes, in pain and in sorrow.   People judge, people say that the
orphan is drunk with wine. — With my friends, with my friends
there grows wheat and grain.   With me, orphan, with me, orphan,
there grow but grass and thorns. — Dear God, dear God, dear God
of mine!   Why have you not created me with the same luck as my
friends have?

The tender feelings of love, replete with sorrows and despair, are left almost entirely to women; men are too busy to sing of love, or less romantic in their natures. But they are not entirely devoid of the poetic sentiment, and they join the weaker sex in rhythmic utterance, whenever they are stirred to it by unusual incidents that break in on their favorite attitude of contemplation and peaceful occupations. Such are military service, the *pogroms*, or mob violence, and riots periodically instituted against the Jewish population, expatriation, and the awful days of Atonement. On these occasions they rise to all the height of feeling that we have found in the other productions, and the expression of their attachment to their parents, wives, and children is just as tender and pathetic. The Russian Jew is naturally averse to the profession of war. He is not at all a coward, as was demonstrated in the Russo-Turkish War, in which he performed many a deed of bravery; but what can be his interest to fight for a country which hardly recognizes him as a citizen and in which he cannot rise above the lowest ranks in civil offices or in the army, although he is called to shed his blood on an equal footing with his Christian or Tartar fellow-soldier? Before the reign of Nicholas he was regarded beyond the pale of the country's attention and below contempt as a warrior; he was expected to pay toward the support of the country, but was not allowed to be its defender in times of war. He easily acquiesced in this state of affairs, and learned to regard the payment of taxes as a necessary evil and the exemption from enlistment as a privilege. Things all of a sudden changed with the ukase of Emperor Nicholas, by which not only military service was imposed on all the Jews of the realm, but the most atrocious regime was inaugurated to seize the persons who might elude the vigilance of the authorities. A whole regiment of *Chapers*, or catchers, were busy searching out the whereabouts of men of military age, tearing violently men from wives, fathers from infant children, minors from their parents. The terror was still increased by the order of 'cantonment,' by which young children of tender age were stolen from their mothers to be sent into distant provinces to be farmed out to peasants, where it was hoped they would forget their Hebrew origin and would be easily led into the folds of the Greek-Catholic Church.[1]

This sad state of affairs is described in a long poem, a kind of a rhymed chronicle of the event; it lies at the foundation of many later lyrical expressions dealing with the aversion to military service, even at a time when it was divested of the horrors of Nicholas' regime. Under the best conditions, the time spent in the service of the Czar might have been more profitably used for the study of the Bible and commentaries to the same, is the conclusion of several of such poems :

Ich gēh' arauf auf'n Gass'
Derlangt män a Geschrēi : " A Pass, a Pass ! "
A Pass, a Pass hāb' ich gethān verlieren,
Thut män mir in Prijom areinführen.
Führt män mir arein in ersten Cheeder,
Thut män mir aus mein' Mutters Kleider.
  Och un' wēh is' mir nischt geschehn,
  Wās ich hāb' mir nit arumgesehn !

Führt män mir arein in andern Cheeder,
Thut män mir ān soldatske Klēider.
  Och un' wēh is' mir nit geschehn, etc.

---

[1] See p. 142 ff. ; add to these A. M. Dick, *Der soldatske Syn*. Wilna, 1876, 16mo, 108 pp., which gives a graphic description of the career of a cantonist.

Führt män mir arein in Schul' schwören,
Giesst sich vun mir Teichen Trähren.
Och un' wēh is mir nit geschehn, etc.

Ehder zu trāgen dem Kēissers Hütel,
Besser zu lernen dem Kapitel,
Och un' wēh is' mir nit geschehn, etc.

Ehder zu essen dem Kēissers Kasche,
Besser zu lernen Chumesch mit Rasche.
Och un' wēh is mir nit geschehn,
Wās ich hāb' mir nit arumgesehn!

I walk in the street,—they cry: "A passport, a passport!"
The passport, the passport I have lost. They take me to the en-
listing office. They lead me into the first room. They take off the
clothes my mother made me. Woe unto me that I have not be-
thought myself in time!—They lead me into the second room;
they put on me a soldier's uniform. Woe unto me, etc.—They
lead me into the synagogue to take my oath, and rivers of tears
roll down my face. Woe unto me, etc.—Rather than wear the cap
of the Czar—to study a chapter of religious lore. Woe unto me,
etc.—Rather than eat the Czar's buckwheat mush—to study the
Bible with its commentaries. Woe unto me that I have not be-
thought myself in time!

Other soldier songs begin with a detailed farewell
to parents, brothers, sisters, and friends, after which
follows a recital of the many privations to which the
Jewish soldier will be subjected; in all of these, the
forced absence from wife or bride is regarded as the
greatest evil.

The cup of bitterness has never been empty for the
Jews that inhabit the present Russian Empire; they
had been persecuted by Poland, massacred by the
Cossacks, and are now exiled from the central provinces of Russia. Each massacre, each 'pogrom,' has
given rise to several poems, in which God is invoked
to save them from their cruel tormentors, or in which

there are given graphic descriptions of the atrocities perpetrated on the unwary. Like the soldier songs, they vary in form from the chronicle in rhymes to the metrical lyric of modern times. The oldest recorded rhymed chronicle of this kind is the one that tells of the blood bath instituted in the Ukraine in the middle of last century. The simple, unadorned recital of inhumanities concocted by the fertile imagination of a Gonto, a Silo, a Maxim Zhelezniak, produces a more awful effect than any studied poem could do.[1]

It is no wonder, then, that the Jew takes a gloomy view of life, and that whenever he rises to any generalizations, he gives utterance to the blackest pessimism. One such poem depicts the vanities of human life, into which one is born as into a prison, from which one is freed at best at the Biblical age of three score and ten, to leave all the gold and silver to the surviving orphans. There is but one consolation in life, and that is, that *Tōre*, ' learning,' will do one as much good in the other world as it does in this. And yet, under all these distressing circumstances, the Jew finds pleasure in wholehearted laughter. His comical ditties may be divided into two classes, — those in which he laughs at his own weaknesses, and those in which he ridicules the weaknesses of the Khassidim, the fanatical sect, among whom the Rabbis are worshipped as saints and are supposed to work miracles. This sect is very numerous in Poland and South Russia, is very ignorant, and has opposed progress longer than the Misnagdim, to which sect the other German Jews in Russia belong. As an example of the first class may serve a poem in which poverty is made light of:

[1] Cf. Dr. Sokolowski, *Die Gseere vun Gonto in Uman un' Ukraine,* in *Volksbibliothēk*, Vol. II. pp. 53–60.

Ferd' hāb' ich vun Paris:
Drei ohn' Köpp', zwēi ohn' Füss'.
Ladrizem bam, ladrizem bam.

A Rock hāb' ich vun guten Tuch,
Ich hāb' vun ihm kein Bröckel Duch.
Ladrizem, etc.

Stiewel hāb' ich vun guten Leder,
Ich hāb' vun see kein Bröckel Feder.
Ladrizem, etc.

Kinder hāb' ich a drei Tuz',
Ich hāb' vun see kein Bröckel Nutz.
Ladrizem, etc.

Jetzt hāb' ich sich arumgetracht
Un' hāb' vun see a Barg Asch' gemacht.
Ladrizem bam, ladrizem bam.

Horses I have from Paris, three without heads, and two without feet, — ladrizem bam, etc. — A coat I have of good cloth, — I have not a trace left of it. — Boots I have of good leather, not a feather's weight have I left of them. — Children I have some three dozen, — I get no good out of them. — So I fell a-thinking and made a heap of ashes of them.

The sensuality, intemperance, and profound ignorance and superstition of the *Rebe*, or Rabbi, of the Khassidim, and the credulity and lightheartedness of his followers, form, perhaps, the subject of the most poems in the Judeo-German language, as they also form the main subject of attack in the written literature of the last forty years.

V. PRINTED POPULAR POETRY

THE author of a recent work on the history of culture among the Galician Jews [1] has pointed out how at the end of the last century the Mendelssohnian Reform, and with it worldly education, took its course through Austria into Galicia, to appear half a century later in Russia. This quicker awakening in the South was not due to geographical position alone, but in a higher degree to political and social causes as well. The language of enlightenment was at first naturally enough a modernized form of the Hebrew, for the literary German was not easily accessible to the Jews of Galicia in the period immediately following the division of Poland. Besides, although books had been printed in Judeo-German for the use of women and 'less knowing' men, the people with higher culture, to whom alone the Mendelssohnian Reform could appeal, looked with disdain on the profane dialect of daily intercourse. When, however, the time had come to carry the new instruction to the masses, the latter had become sufficiently familiar with the German language to be able to dispense with the intermediary native Jargon.[2] Consequently little opportunity was offered here for the development of a dialect literature.

---

[1] Max Weissberg, *Die neuhebräische Aufklärungs-literatur in Galizien. Eine literar-historische Charakteristik.* Leipzig und Wien, 1898, 8vo, 88 pp.

[2] The first two weeklies of Galicia, the *Zeitung* and *Die jüdische Post*, published in 1848 and 1849 respectively, are not in the vernacular, but in a slightly corrupt German.

While the Jews of the newly acquired provinces were becoming more and more identified with their coreligionists of German Austria, their Russian and Polish brethren in the Russian Empire were by force of circumstances departing gradually from all but the religious union with them, and were drifting into entirely new channels. Previous to the reign of Nicholas I., their civil disabilities barred them from a closer contact in language and feeling with their Gentile fellow-citizens, while their distance from Germany excluded all intellectual relations with that country. The masses were too downtrodden and ignorant to develop out of themselves any other forms of literature than the one of ethical instruction and stories current in the previous century. In the meanwhile the Haskala, as the German school was called, had found its way into Russia through Galicia, and such men as J. B. Levinsohn, A. B. Gottlober, M. Gordon, Dr. S. Ettinger, had become its warmest advocates. They threw themselves with all the ardor of their natures upon the new doctrine, and tried to correct the neglected education of their childhood by a thorough study of German culture. It was but natural for them to pass by the opportunities offered in their country's language and to seek enlightenment abroad : the Jews were a foreign nation at home, without privileges or duties, except those of paying taxes, while from Germany, their former abiding-place, there shone forth the promise of a salvation from obscurantism and spiritual death. Henceforth the word ' German ' became in Russia the synonym of ' civilized,' and a ' German ' was tantamount to ' reformed ' and ' apostate ' with the masses, for to them culture could appear only as the opposite of their narrow Ghetto lives and gross superstition.

The inauguration of the military regime by Nicholas was in reality only meant as a first step in giving civil rights to the Jews of his realm ; this reform was later followed by the establishment of Rabbinical schools at Wilna and Zhitomir, and the permission to enter the Gymnasia and other institutions of learning. The Jews were, however, slow in taking advantage of their new rights, as they had become accustomed to look with contempt and fear on Gentile culture, and as they looked with suspicion on the Danaid gifts of the government. The enlightened minority of the Haskala, anxious to lead their brethren out of their crass ignorance and stubborn opposition to the cultural efforts of the Czar, began to address them in the native dialects of their immediate surroundings and to elicit their attention almost against their will. Knowing the weakness of the Jews for tunable songs, they began to supply them with such in the popular vein, now composing one with the mere intention to amuse, now to direct them to some new truth.[1] These poems, like the

---

[1] The love for songs is very old with the German Jews. Steinschneider's catalogue in the *Serapeum* mentions a very large number of songs. See also L. Löwenstein, *Jüdische und jüdisch-deutsche Lieder*, in *Jubelschrift zu Ehren des Dr. Hildesheimer*, Berlin, 1890, pp. 126 ff., and under the same title, in *Monatschrift für Geschichte und Wissenschaft des Judenthums*, Vol. XXXVIII. pp. 78–89; A. Neubauer, *Jüdisch-deutsches Weingedicht*, in *Israelit Letterbode*, Vol. XII. 1. pp. 13 f. But the most thorough work is by F. Rosenberg, *Ueber eine Sammlung deutscher Volks- und Gesellschafts-lieder in hebräischen Lettern*, Berlin, 1888, 8vo, 84 pp. That the modern songs are set to music is generally indicated in the title-pages or the introductions to the printed collections, as, for example, Lieder zu singen mit sehr schoene Melodien ; Schoen zum Singen un' zum Lesen ; Mit sehr schoene Melodien. In one of his books Zunser (see pp. 90 ff.) informs us :

Ob ihr lejent in Büchel meine Lieder,
Un' die Melodie hät män euch nit übergegeben,

dramas and prose writings by this school of writers previous to the sixties, were not written down, but passed orally or in manuscript form from town to town, from one end of Russia to the other, often changing their verses and forming the basis for new popular creations. The poet's name generally became dissociated from each particular poem; nay, in the lapse of time the authors themselves found it difficult to identify their spiritual children. An amusing incident occurred some time ago when the venerable and highly reputed poet, J. L. Gordon, had incorporated a parody of Heine's 'Two Grenadiers' among his collection of popular poems, for a plain case was made out against him by the real parodist. Gordon at once publicly apologized for his unwitting theft by explaining how he had found it in manuscript among his papers and had naturally assumed it to be his own production.[1] Another similar mistake was made by Gottlober's daughter, who named to me a dozen of current songs

> Is' däs wie a photographische Bild, liebe Brüder, —
> Dacht sich, Alles richtig, nor es fehlt Leben.
>
> INTRODUCTION TO HAMNAGEEN.

While another, B. Z. Rabinowitsch (in *Disput vun a Schüler mit a Klausnik*), thinks he must offer an apology for not having composed a tune for his poem:

> Mit wäs far a Melodie ihr wet spielen,
> Wöllen die Wörter gewiss nächtanzen!

Zunser, who did not scruple to make use of other people's property (see p. 92), objects, in *Kol-rina*, to the people's appropriation of his songs in the following words:

> Wie me hät mich gehört a Mäl zu zwéi,
> Is' schön gewe'n auf morgen geschrieben bei see:
> Es hät mir vardrossen sejer Müh', 'chleben,
> Un' häb' see besser a fartigen, a gedruckten gegeben.

[1] *Voschod*, 1886, No. 5.

which she said belonged to her father, having received
that information from himself, but which on close
examination were all but one easily proven as belonging
to other poets.[1]

Most difficult of identification are now Gottlober's
poems,[2] he having never brought out himself a collective volume of his verses, although he certainly must
have written a great number of them as early as the
thirties when he published his comedy ' Dās Decktuch.'
Those that have been printed later in the periodicals
are either translations or remodellings of well-known
poems in German, Russian, and Hebrew; but even they
have promptly been caught by the popular ear. The
one beginning ' Ich lach' sich vun euere Traten aus,' in
which are depicted humorously the joys of the Jewish
recluse, has been pointed out by Katzenellenbogen as a
remodelling of a poem that appeared in a Vienna periodical;[3] the sources of some of the others he mentions
himself, while the introductory poem in his comedy is
a translation of Schiller's ' Der Jüngling am Bache.'
From these facts it is probably fair to assume that
most, if not all, of his other poems are borrowings from
other literatures, preëminently German. This is also
true of his other productions, which will be mentioned

[1] The only collection of Judeo-German poetry accessible to those
who do not read the Hebrew type is G. H. Dalman's *Jüdisch-deutsche
Volkslieder aus Galizien und Russland*, Zweite Auflage, Berlin, 1891,
8vo, 74 pp.; unfortunately there are a number of errors in it that
destroy the sense of some lines. See also L. Wiener, *Popular Poetry
of the Russian Jews*, in *Americana Germanica*, Vol. II. No. 2 (1898),
pp. 33–59, on which the present chapter is based.

[2] His poems have been printed in the following periodicals: *Kol-
mewasser*, Vol. I. Nos. 4, 5, 6 (*Dās Gräber-lied*) et seq.; *Warschauer
jüdische Zeitung; Jisrulik*, No. 13; *Jüd. Volksblatt*, Vol. II. No. 10;
Wecker, pp. 26–29 ; *Jüd. Volksbibliothēk*, pp. 148–153.

[3] Katzenellenbogen, *Jüdische Melodien* (*q.v.*), p. 55, note.

in another place. Nevertheless he deserves an honorable place among the popular poets, as his verses are written in a pure dialect of the Southern variety, — he is a native of Constantin in the Government of Volhynia, — and as they have been very widely disseminated.

No one has exercised a greater influence on the succeeding generation of bards than the Galician Wolf Ehrenkranz, better known as Welwel Zbarżer, *i.e.* from Zbaraż, who half a century ago delighted small audiences in Southern Russia with his large repertoire. There are still current stories among those who used to know him then, of how they would entice him to their houses and treat him to wine and more wine, of which he was inordinately fond, how when his tongue was unloosened he would pour forth improvised songs in endless succession, while some of his hearers would write them down for Ehrenkranz's filing and finishing when he returned to his sober moods. These he published later in five volumes, beginning in the year 1865 and ending in 1878. While there had previously appeared poems in Judeo-German in Russia, he did not dare to publish them in Galicia except with a Hebrew translation, and this method was even later, in the eighties, adopted by his countrymen Apotheker and Schafir. Ehrenkranz has employed every variety of folksong known to Judeo-German literature except historical and allegorical subjects. Prominent among them are the songs of reflection. Such, for example, is 'The Nightingale,' in which the bird complains of the cruelty of men who expect him to sing sweetly to them while they enslave him in a cage , but the nightingale is the poet who in spite of his aspiration to fly heavenwards must sing to the crowd's taste, in order to earn a living. In a similar way 'The Russian Tea-machine,' 'The

Mirror,' 'The Theatre,' and many others serve him only as excuses to meditate on the vanity of life, the inconstancy of fortune, and so forth.

'The Gold Watch' is one of a very common type of songs of dispute that have been known to various literatures in previous times and that are used up to the present by Jewish bards. They range in length from the short folksong consisting of but one question and answer to a long series of stanzas, or they may become the subject of long discussions covering whole books. In 'The Gold Watch' the author accuses the watch of being unjust in complaining and in allowing its heart to beat so incessantly, since it enjoys the privilege of being worn by fine ladies and gentlemen, of never growing old, of being clad in gold and precious stones. Each stanza of the question ends with the words :

Wās fehlt dir, wās klapt dir dās Herz ?

The watch's answer is that it must incessantly work, that it is everybody's slave, that it is thrown away as useless as soon as it stops. So, too, is man. Upon this follows what is generally known as a *Zuspiel*, a byplay, a song treating the contrary of the previous matter or serving as a conclusion to the same. The *Zuspiel* to 'The Gold Watch' is entitled ' 'Tis Best to Live without Worrying.' There is a series of songs in his collection which might be respectively entitled 'Memento mori' and 'Memento vivere.' Such are 'The Tombstone' and 'The Contented,' 'The Tombstone-cutter' and 'The Precentor,' 'The Cemetery,' and 'While you Live, you Must not Think of Death.' The cemetery, the gravedigger, the funeral, are themes which have a special fascination for the Jewish popular singers, who nearly all of them have written songs of the same character.

Another kind of popular poetry is that which deals with some important event, such as 'The Cholera in the Year 1866,' or noteworthy occurrence, as 'The Leipsic Fair,' which, however, like the previously mentioned poems, serves only as a background for reflections. There are also, oddly enough, a few verses of a purely lyrical nature in which praises are sung to love and the beloved object. These would be entirely out of place in a Jewish songbook of the middle of this century had they been meant solely as lyrical utterances; but they are used by Ehrenkranz only as precedents for his 'Zuspiele,' in which he makes a Khassid contrast the un-Jewish love of the reformed Jew with his own blind adoration of his miracle-working Rabbi. These latter, and the large number of Khassid songs scattered through the five volumes, form a class for themselves. The lightheartedness, ignorance, superstitions, and intemperance of these fanatics form the butt of ridicule of all who have written in Judeo-German in the last fifty years, but no one has so masterfully handled the subject as Ehrenkranz, for he has treated it so deftly by putting the songs in the mouth of a Khassid that half the time one is not quite sure but that he is in earnest and the poems are meant as glorifications of Khassidic blissfulness. It is only when one reads the fine humor displayed in 'The Rabbi on the Ocean' that one is inclined to believe that the extravagant miracles performed by the Rabbi were ascribed to him in jest only. Owing to this quality of light raillery, the songs have delighted not only the scoffers, but it is not at all unusual to hear them recited by Khassidim themselves.

Ehrenkranz also has some songs in which are described the sorrows of various occupations, — a kind of poetry more specially cultivated by Berel Broder. Of the latter little is known except that he composed his songs probably at a time anterior to those just mentioned, that he had lived at Brody, hence his name, and that he had never published them. They were collected by some one after his death and published several times; however, it is likely that several of them are of other authorship, as is certainly the case with 'The Wanderer,' which belongs to Ehrenkranz. As has been said above, he prefers to dwell on the many troubles that beset the various occupations of his countrymen, of the shepherd, the gravedigger, the wagon-driver, the school teacher, the go-between, the usurer, the precentor, the smuggler. They are all arranged according to the same scheme, and begin with such lines as: ' I, poor shepherd,' 'I, lame beadle,' 'I, miserable driver,' 'I, wretched school teacher,' and so forth. The best of these, and one of the most popular of the kind, is probably the 'Song of the Gravedigger.' Of the two songs of dispute, 'Day and Night' and 'Shoemaker and Tailor,' the first is remarkable in that each praises the other, instead of the more common discussions in which the contending parties try to outrival one another in the display of their virtues.

The style of these two Galicians and their very subject-matter were soon appropriated by a very large class of folksingers in Russia who amuse guests at wedding feasts. Before passing over to the writers in Russia we shall mention the two other Galicians who, writing at a later time, have remained unknown beyond their own country, but one of whom at least deserves to be known to a larger circle of readers. The one, David Apotheker, in his collection ' Die Leier,' pursues just such aims as his Polish or Russian fellow-bards and is entirely without any local coloring. The poems are written in a pure dialect, without any admixture of German words, but their poetic value is small, as they are much too didactic. Of far higher importance and literary worth are the productions of his contemporary, Bajrach Benedikt Schafir. Being well versed in German and Polish literature, he generally imitates the form of the best poems in those languages and often paraphrases them for his humble audiences. His language is now almost the literary German, now his native dialect, according as he sings of high matters or in the lighter vein. In the introduction to one of his earlier pamphlets written in a pure German, he says that in Germanizing his native dialect it has been his purpose so to purify the Jargon that it should become intelligible even to German Jews. The most of his songs were collected in 'Melodies from the Country near the River San.' These he divided into four parts : Jewish national songs, songs of commemoration, songs of feeling, and comical songs, — the first three, with an elegy on the death of Moses Montefiore, forming the first part, the comical songs the second part, of the collection.

The most of the comical songs are in the form of dialogues in which a German, *i.e.* a Jew of the reformed church, discusses with a Khassid the advantage of education ; in others he describes the ignorance of the latter. Many of them do not rise above the character of theatre couplets, but in the lyrical part the tone is better, and in some of his songs he rivals the best folksingers of Russia. His 'Midnight Prayer' and 'Greeting to Zion' are touching expressions of longing for the ancient home, just as ' Przemysl, You my Dear Cradle,' and ' Homesickness,' are full of yearning for his native country. Of the four songs of commemoration, two deal on the famous accusation, in 1883, of the use of

Gentile blood by the Jews in the Passover ceremony, one describes the fire in the Vienna Ring theatre, while another narrates a similar catastrophe in the town of Sheniava.

As early as 1863[1] there was printed in Kiev a volume of songs under the name of 'The Evil-tongued Wedding-jester,' by Izchak Joel Linetzki. Before me lies a somewhat later edition of the book: it is published in a form of rare attractiveness for those days and bears on the title-page a picture of two men, one in European dress, the other in the garments of a Khassid, in the attitude of discussion. This illustration has appeared on all the subsequent editions of the same work; it expresses the author's purpose, which becomes even more patent in his prose works, to instruct the Khassidim in the advantages of culture, however, the few poems in the book devoted to this differ from the usual unconditional praise of reform, in that they point out that the servile imitator of the Gentiles is no better than the stubborn advocate of the old regime. Two of the poems are versified versions of the Psalms, and there are also the usual songs of reflection, and a song of dispute between the mirror and the clock. Two of the poems sing of the joys of May, presenting the rare example of pure lyrics at that early time. These alone will hold a comparison with the best of Ehrenkranz's songs; the others are somewhat weak in diction and loose in execution.

Few poets have been so popular in Russia as Michel Gordon and S. Berenstein were in the past generation, the first singing in the Lithuanian variety of the lan-

---

[1] This I merely surmise, from the statement in the *Sseefer Sikorōn*, that he wrote it in 1863, in Kiev, though it is probable that he did not print it before 1869. For biography of Linetzki, see pp. 161 ff.

guage, the second in a southern dialect. Both published
their collections in Zhitomir in 1869, and Gordon wrote
an introductory poem for the book of his friend Berenstein. In this he indicates the marked contrast that
exists in the productions of the two. While the first
writes to chide superstition and ignorance, the other
sings out of pity for his suffering race; while the one
sounds the battle-cry of progress, the other consoles his
brothers in their misery; the one, fearing prosecution
from the fanatic Khassidim whom he attacks, sent his
poems out into the world anonymously, the other signed
his name to them. And yet, however unlike in form
and content, they were both pervaded by a warm love
for their people whom they were trying to succor, each
one in his own way.

Gordon's [1] poems are of a militant order: [2] he is not
satisfied with indicating the right road to culture, he
also sounds the battle-cry of advance. The keynote is
struck in his famous ' Arise, my People ! ' ' Arise, my
people, you have slept long enough ! Arise, and open
your eyes ! Why has such a misfortune befallen you
alone, that you are asleep until the midday hour ? The
sun has now long been out upon the world ; he has put
all men upon their feet, but you alone lie crouching and
bent and keep your eyes tightly closed.' In this poem
he preaches to his race that they should assimilate
themselves in manners and culture to the ruling people,
that they should abandon their old-fashioned garments

---

[1] For short notices of Gordon and his work, see B. Woloderski, *A
kurze Biographie vun Michel Gordon*, in *Hausfreund*, Vol. II. pp. 147–
149, and necrology in *Hausfreund*, Vol. III. p. 312.

[2] Other poems by M. Gordon than those contained in his collective
volume are to be found in *Jüd. Volksblatt*, Vol. VIII. (Beilage) pp.
93, 94, 362, 363; Vol. IX. No. 16; *Hausfreund*, Vol. I. pp. 39–43;
Vol. II. pp. 73–75, 261–264; *Familienfreund*, Vol. I. pp. 3–6.

and distinguishing characteristics of long beard and forelock, and that they should exchange even the language in which he sings to them for the literary language of the country.

Assimilation was the cry of all the earnest men among the Russian Jews before the eighties, when the course of events put a damper on the sanguine expectations from such a procedure. Many of his other poems are of a humorous nature and have been enormously popular. In 'The Beard,' a woman laments the loss of that hirsute appendage of her husband, who, by shaving it off, had come to look like a despised 'German.' 'The Turnip Soup' and 'I Cannot Understand' are excellent pictures of the ignorance and superstitious awe of the Khassidim before their equally ignorant and hypocritical Rabbis ; other poems deal with the stupidity of the teachers of children, and the undue use of spirituous drinks on all occasions of life.

Two of his earliest poems are devoted to decrying the evil custom of early marriages, in which the tastes of the contracting parties are not at all considered. In the one entitled 'From the Marriage Baldachin,' he paints in vivid colors the course of the married life of a Jew from the wedding feast through the worries of an ever-increasing family, and the helplessness of the father to provide for his children, with the consequent breaking up of the family ties. The catching tune to which the poem is sung, and all folksongs are naturally set to music, generally by the authors themselves, and the lifelike picture which it portrays, have done a great deal to diminish the practice ; while the other, 'My Advice,' addressed to a girl, advising her to exercise her own free will and reasonable choice of her life's companion, has helped to eliminate misery and to introduce the element of love in the marital stage.

In his advocacy of reform, Gordon had in mind the clearing of the Jewish religion from the accumulated superstitions of the ages which had almost stifled its virgin simplicity, not an abandonment of any of its fundamental principles in the ardent desire for assimilation. True culture is, according to him, compatible with true piety, and a surface culture, with its accompanying slackness of religious life, is reprehensible. When he saw that so many had misunderstood the precepts of those who taught a closer union with the Gentiles in that they adopted the mere appearances of the foreign civilization and overthrew the essential virtues of their own faith, he expressed his indignation in 'The True Education and the False Education,' of which the final stanza is :

> True culture makes good and mild,
> False culture makes bad and wild.
> The truly-cultured is a fine man,
> The falsely-cultured is a charlatan.

Gordon has also written a ballad, 'The Stepmother,' which has given rise to a large number of popular imitations. In this he tells of a mother whose rest in the grave is disturbed by the tears of her child. Upon learning that the child has been maltreated by his stepmother, she sends up her voice to God, interceding in her son's behalf, and then addresses herself to her weeping child, assuring him that God has heard her prayer.

Berenstein was no less cultured a man than Gordon. His acquaintance with German literature is evidenced by his motto from Körner, an occasional quotation from Schiller, and his several epigrams which he frankly acknowledges as translations or adaptations of German originals. Thus it happens that Schiller's 'Hoffnung' has been popularized among the Russian Jews in the form of a stanza of a long poem, 'The False Hope.' Except for these literary allusions, Berenstein wrote in the true popular vein. His 'The Cradle,' in which he makes use of the well-known verses, 'Hinter Jankeles Wiegele,' has become as universal as the oral cradle song. Its last stanza enjoins the child to sleep well in order to gather strength for the sufferings of the next day, and this pessimistic view of life becomes ever after the prevailing tone in the many cradle songs that have been written by younger men.[1] 'The Sleep' is a variation on the motto from Körner's 'Tony,' which is put at the head of it : 'Der Schlummer ist ja ein Friedenhauch vom Himmel — Schlummern kann nur ein spiegelreines Herz.' 'Young Tears' is one of the very few love lyrics that appeared in print before the second half of the eighties. In 'The Bar of Soap' Gordon shows that with soap one cannot wash off the blot from his brow, the sorrow from his heart. 'The Empty Bottle' describes the loneliness of him who has lost his wealth, and with it his friends. As a 'byplay' to it follows a pretty lyric, 'Consolation.' A 'byplay' bearing the same name follows an elegy upon the death of an only son. Several of the poems are devoted to the praise

[1] In this conjunction a few of the very many cradle songs will be mentioned here as an offset to the statement, frequently heard, that the Jews have no songs of that character ; in the chapter on the traditional folksongs there have been mentioned a few such ; add to these the one given in *Mitteilungen der Gesellschaft für jüdische Volkskunde*, Heft II. p. 49. Of the literary cradle songs, the best are Abramowitsch's *Alululu, bidne Kind, Weh is' der Mame, wēh und wünd* (in *Dās klēine Menschele*, p. 121) ; Linetzki's *Varschliess schön deine Äugen* (in *Der bœser Marschelik*, p. 66); Goldfaden's *Schläf' in Freuden, Du wēisst kēin Leiden* (in *Die Jüdene*, p. 6); S. Rabinowitsch's *Schläf', mein Kind* (with music, in his *Kol-mewasser*, col. 25, 26).

of the Sabbath, and only two are given to sarcastic
attacks on the Khassidim. In the latter, the words
are put in the mouth of a Khassid, who prays to God
that he may send again darkness instead of the victorious light in order that his kind may the more securely
shear their sheep.

Another very popular poet of the sixties was Abraham Goldfaden,[1] who, in 1876, became the founder of
the Jewish theatre. His literary activity may be
roughly divided into the period before, and the period
after, the establishment of the theatre. The first only
is the subject of our present discussion. Like the other
two, he published his works in Zhitomir, which, on account of the Rabbinical school opened there in the
forties, had come to be the rallying ground of all those
who were advocating a progressive Judaism. As the
title of his first collection, 'The Jew,' indicates, his
poems are all devoted to strictly Jewish matters. Although he occasionally has recourse to the method of
Ehrenkranz, or, foreshadowing his future career, even
descends to the use of theatre couplets, yet the most
of his poems have an individual character, differing
from all of his predecessors. He treats with great
success, and in a large variety of rhymes, the allegorical
and the historical song, sometimes as separate themes,
more often by combining them.

One of the best allegorical poems is the triad, 'The
Aristocratic Marriage.' In the first part, 'The Be-
trothal,' he tells us how the humble Egyptian slave,

---

[1] Some of Goldfaden's poems may be found in: *Kol-mewasser;*
Jisrulik; *Wecker,* pp. 7–15, 56–62; *Der jüdischer Handelskalender,*
pp. 114–118; *Familienfreund,* Vol. I. pp. 27–35, Vol. II. pp. 57–59;
Hausfreund, Vol. II. pp. 5–7; *Volksbibliothēk,* Vol. II. pp. 188, 247,
267, 268; *Dās hēilige Land,* pp. 25–29; *New Yorker Illustrirte
Zeitung.*

Israel, was betrothed to his aristocratic bride on Mount
Sinai. God was the father who gave away the Law to
his son, and Moses was the *Schadchen*, the go-between,
the never-failing concomitant of a Jewish marriage.
The second part describes a typical Jewish wedding—
Israel's entrance into Jerusalem; while the third shows
how Israel has misused his opportunity while living in
the house of his wife's father during the years that immediately follow the marriage. He committed adultery
with idolatry, and God drove him out of his home, but
out of regard for his pious ancestry He allowed him
to take his wife along with him on his wanderings,
and promised him that after ages of repentance He
would send him the Messiah to restore him to his former
home.

A similar triad, but of a historical nature, is his well-
known 'That Little Trace of a Jew,' in which he successively portrays the virtues, the sufferings, and the
vices of his race. The last part is identical in sentiment with Gordon's 'Arise, my People,' and inculcates
tolerance for the various religious parties of the Jews
and love of worldly learning. 'The Firebrand' relates
the destruction of the Temple; 'Rebecca's Death' gives
a Talmudical version of the event; and 'Cain' tells of
his wanderings over the face of the earth after his killing of his brother, and his vain search of death. The
latter is the most popular of his Biblical songs. Among
the other poems, many of which are of sterling worth,
there must be mentioned his lullaby, whose widespread
dissemination is only second to Berenstein's cradle song.

The poems which Goldfaden has written during his
lifetime would fill several large volumes; they can be
found scattered through various periodicals which have
appeared in the last thirty years, and in the greater

part of the dramas which he has composed for the
stage which he has created. Most of these are mere
street ballads, but there are some of a serious nature;
of these mention will be made in the chapter on the
theatre. To the best productions of his first, the most
original period of his poetical activity, belong the poems
touching women, contained in the volume entitled 'The
Jewess.' From the contents we learn that one of them
is a translation from Béranger, the other from the Russian. It is also characteristic of the history of Jewish
folk-music that one of the songs, as we are informed in
the same place, is to be sung to the tune of a well-known
Russian lullaby, the other with a Little-Russian melody,
while for a third, is mentioned one of M. Gordon's songs.

All the above-mentioned poets belong to what might
be termed the German school. These men were more
or less intimately acquainted with German literature,
and frequently borrowed their subject-matter from that
source. They all were active at a time when the conflict between the old religious life of the Russian Jews
and the modern tendencies was at the highest. They
looked for a solution in the reform which, since the days
of Mendelssohn, has become the watchword of progress
in Germany. They hoped finally to substitute even the
German language for the Judeo-German, which they
regarded as a corrupted form of German, and, therefore,
named Jargon, an appellation that has stuck to it ever
since. In the meanwhile, the better classes were receiving their instruction in Russian schools that alienated
them alike from the German influence and from a closer
contact with their humble coreligionists. Even such
men as had begun in the forties and fifties as folk-poets,
were abandoning their homely dialect for the literary
language of the country. Jehuda Loeb Gordon, the

Hebrew scholar and poet, had given promise of becoming the greatest of popular singers. Yet, in the seventies, he wrote only in Hebrew and Russian, and it was only in the eighties, when the riots and expatriations of the Jews had destroyed all hopes that had been placed in assimilation, that he returned to compose songs for the consolation of his humble and unfortunate brothers.[1] J. L. Gordon has written but few Judeo-German poems, and, of these, not more than nine or ten are folksongs ; but they represent the highest perfection of the older school of the popular bards. He has not been surpassed by any of them in simplicity of diction, warmth of feeling, and purity of language. Two of his oldest poems, ' A Mother's Parting,' and 'A Story of Long-Ago,' relate, the first, the hardships of a Jewish soldier in the forties ; the second, the horrors of the regime of *Chapers*, the dishonesty and inhumanity of the *Kahal*, the representative body of the Jewish community. The newer poems are all of a humoristic nature, except the one devoted to the praise of ' The Law Written on Parchment' that has been the consolation of the Jews during their many wanderings and persecutions.

Parallel with the German school, now overlapping its territory, now pursuing its own course, ran the class of poetry that had for its authors the *Badchens* or *Marschaliks*[2] — the wedding jesters. In medieval times

[1] A song expressive of this sentiment, under the title *Unsere liebe Schwester un' Brüder*, appeared in *Jüd. Volksblatt*, Vol. I. (1881), No. 2. Other poems were printed in the same year in Nos. 1 and 5 ; another poem was printed in *Jüd. Volksbibliothēk*, Vol. I. pp. 295, 296. A review of his collected poems is given in *Voschod*, Vol. VI. (1886), Part. II. pp. 26-31. For necrology see *Hausfreund*, Vol. III. p. 312.

[2] Cf. Abrahams, *Jewish Life in the Middle Ages*, pp. 198 ff. It is not uncommon in Judeo-German literature to meet with the descrip-

the jester's function was to amuse the guests at the wedding, while the more serious discourses were delivered by the Rabbi and the bridegroom. In Russia he had come to usurp all these functions. He improvised verses upon the various stages of the marriage ceremony, delivered the solemn discourses to bridegroom and bride, and furnished the wit during the banquet. His improvisations were replete with Biblical and Talmudical allusions, and cabbalistic combinations of the Hebrew letters of the names of the married couple. His verses were mere rhyming lines, without form or rhythm, and his jests were often of a low order and even coarse. The name of 'badchen' came to be the byname of a coarse, uncultured jester. A change for the better was made in the second half of the fifties by Eliokum Zunser,[1] then but in his teens, who had conceived the idea of making the badchen a singer of songs, rather than a merry person. He was, no doubt, led to make this innovation through the many new folksongs, by Gordon, Ehrenkranz, and Berel Broder, that were then current among the people, and that were

tion of the old-fashioned badchen and his craft, but probably the best illustrations of his performances are to be found in the following works: Linetzki, *Dās chsidische Jüngel*, pp. 94 ff. ; Gottlober, *Dās Decktuch*, pp. 43 ff. (2d act, 2d scene); *Der krummer Maschelik mit a blind Äug'*, Es is' sēhr schoen zu lejenen die Lieder, wās der Marschelik hāt gesungen, un' wie er hāt Chossen-kale besungen, un' see sennen noch kēin Mal nit gedruckt gewor'en: Kukariku ! Der Marschelik is' dā, Warsaw, 1875 ; U. Kalmus, *Geschichte vun a seltenem Bris un' a genarrte Chassene, Theater in vier Akten*, Warsaw, 1882, pp. 65–72.

[1] In addition to the large number of collective books of poetry, Zunser has published his poems in: *Jüd. Volksblatt*, Vol. V. pp. 51, 67 ; *Wecker*, pp. 74–88; *Familienfreund*, Vol. I. pp. 6–27 ; *Hausfreund*, Vol. II. pp. 99–108; Spektor's *Familienkalender*, Vol. IV. pp. 94–103 ; *Jüd. Volksbib.*, Vol. I. pp. 273, 274 ; *Dās hēil. Land*, pp. 134–141.

received with so much acclamation, both on account of their pleasing contents and the excellent tunes to which they had been set. In 1861, he published eight of his songs which he had been singing at weddings. One of these, at least, 'The Watch,' is merely a differently versified form of Ehrenkranz's 'The Gold Watch,' which must have reached him in its oral form, as it was printed only in 1865. Zunser possessed an excellent voice, and had received a good musical training, and his songs and tunes spread with astonishing rapidity throughout the whole length and breadth of Russia, wherever Jews lived, and became also popular in Galicia and Roumania. This innovation came to stay, and, within a short time, the host of badchens throughout the country began to sing songs at wedding feasts. Whoever could, composed songs of his own; whoever was not gifted with the power of versification, sang the songs of others. These badchens were the most potent factors in the dissemination of the songs of the above-mentioned poets, long before they were accessible in a printed form.

Since it was the badchen's business to amuse, it was natural for Zunser to adopt the manner of Ehrenkranz and Berel Broder, rather than that of his countrymen, Gordon and Goldfaden. But to the Russian Jew, that is amusing which gives him food for reflection, and nature and its manifestations are interesting to him only in so far as they interpret man in all his aspects of life and vicissitudes of fortune. It is this facile power of dissolving external facts in the alembic of his introspective imagination, that has brought Zunser so near to the people, and that has made him so popular. He does not possess the poetical instincts of his contemporaries, Gordon and Ehrenkranz; and many of his poems are mere plagiarisms from other singers. Yet they have become better known in the form in which he has sung them than in their original verses.

All the characteristics of the poets whom he imitates are repeated in Zunser: we have the dispute in ' The Countryman and the Townsman,' ' The Old World and the New,' ' Song of Summer and Winter.' The best of his songs of reflection is ' The Flower,' in which the Jew is compared with a neglected flower; other poems of the same category are ' The Railroad,' ' The Ferry,' ' The Iron Safe,' ' The Clock,' ' The Bird.' There are also songs in which he scourges the hypocrite, the usurer, the inordinate love of innovations and fashion, and some give good pictures of various incidents in the life of a Russian Jew.

Zunser has had many imitators, and their name is legion; few of them have been so versatile or have become so popular as he. They delight in their vocation of badchen, and take pains to mention their profession on the title-pages of the pamphlets which they publish, and frequently they try to make their publications more attractive by giving them the title of ' The Lame Marschalik,' ' The Marschalik with One Eye,' and so forth. Many of the improvisations of the badchen never see daylight, but pass in manuscript form to their brothers in the profession. Although, in the eighties, there has arisen a new class of singers who sing in the manner of the poets of the literary languages, yet the badchens still recite in the old style, frequently, however, reflecting the new conditions of life in their poems. A strange departure has taken place in the badchen's profession in America, where, under more favorable conditions of existence and increased well being, there has come to be a greater demand for amusement; the wedding day is no longer the one day of joy, but the 'jester' is now invited to entertain companies at any and all pleasurable meetings. He is now no longer required to create new poems, but to sing well the current couplets of the day.

VI. OTHER ASPECTS OF POETRY BEFORE THE EIGHTIES

THE popular poem, *i.e.* the tunable song, had only two purposes, to. amuse and to prepare a way for the Reform. But these did not exhaust all the possibilities of poetic compositions and, in fact, were not the only ones to task the powers of the Judeo-German versifiers. An opportunity for more extended themes was given the badchens in their songs of contemplation, in which the moralizing tendency needed only to be developed at the expense of the allegory, in order to change the song into a rhymed sermon. Nor was the public unprepared for serious matters, for the greater part of all Judeo-German literature had been merely treatises of an ethical character in which the element of sadness caused by centuries of suffering predominated. The perfection of art is to the mind of a Jew its ability to move to tears. It is expected of the violinist that he shall play the saddest tunes in the minor key, such as will make his hearers weep like 'beavers'; the precentor's reputation depends on his powers to crush his audience, to call forth contrition of spirit, to make the hearts bleed; and the author who can make his reader dissolve in tears, no matter how absurd the story, is sure to become popular with a Jewish public. We have seen how the badchen at the marriage ceremony bade the bride to weep, and it has also been mentioned that he delivered the more serious discourses upon that occasion. It was then that he would spin out hundreds of

stanzas upon such subjects as 'The Unhappy Man,'
'Pity,' 'Dialogue of the New-born Soul with the Angel
of Life,' 'Sorrow,' and the like.

In the meanwhile, the old rhymed moral treatises
continued in force and gave rise to compositions of a
more regular structure. Two authors must here be
specially mentioned, S. Sobel and Elieser Zwi Zweifel.
The first published, in 1874, a book under the title of
'Destiny, or Discussions for Pleasant Pastime,' in which
he makes use of the popular method of disputes between
various objects in order to inculcate a series of moral
truths. He excels in the use of a vigorous, idiomatic
language, while Zweifel has shown what strength there
lies in the employment of the simplest words for a similar kind of literature. Zweifel's[1] older productions,
only two in number, are, one, a translation from
the Hebrew, the other probably an imitation of a
foreign model. The first contains a series of aphorisms,
while the other teaches the wisdom of life in the testament of a dying father. These verses, like his prose
works, belong among the most cherished writings of
the Russian Jews and have been reprinted in a large
number of editions. After his death another one of
his poems was published which differs from its predecessors in that it is somewhat more elaborate and is
entirely original.

Considering the love of verse on the one hand and the
great demand on the other for a Judeo-German prayer-
book for women, which has never ceased to be a necessity, the book-firm Eisenstadt and Schapiro had the

---

[1] Other works by Zweifel than those given in the Bibliography are :
Hausfreund, Vol. I. pp. 73–78, Vol. II. pp. 143–145 ; Spektor's *Fami-
lienkalender*, Vol. II. pp. 82–87 ; *Jüd. Volksbibl.*, Vol. I. pp. 48–61,
Vol. II. pp. 132–135.

happy idea to ask the then famous author Abramo-witsch[1] to make a trial translation of a part of the Psalms in verse. This appeared to them so successful that they had him proceed with the Sabbath-prayers and the hymns, which were then printed in 1875 at Zhitomir. By the machinations of the great firm of Romm, in Wilna, who were afraid that such an excellent transla-tion might seriously interfere with their sale of their old, stereotyped form of the prayer-book, Abramowitsch was made to desist from finishing the meritorious task that he had begun, and even the two books printed were for a long time kept out of circulation. The Sabbath-prayers he gave not merely in a versified form, but the most prosaic passages, by slight additions and remodellings, he so changed that they resemble the songs in a Gentile hymn-book. Still greater has been the work that he had to perform in making poetry out of the laconic hymns, for that could be accomplished only by amplifying them to ten and twenty times their original size. For this purpose he has availed himself of the current commentaries to the hymns, and this he has done in such a way that the hymns, in their origi-nal form, occur as conclusions to the poems. Except for a certain monotony of the masculine rhymes which are employed in them, they are masterpieces of religious poetry, and it is only a pity that the author has not published yet a translation of the Psalms, which cer-tainly lend themselves more easily to poetic diction.

While these sacred poems were being printed in Zhitomir, there appeared in Warsaw another poetical production by the same author, in its way the most remarkable work in the whole range of Judeo-German literature. It bears the title of 'Judel, a Poem in

[1] For note on Abramowitsch, see pp. 148 ff.

Rhymes,' and in about four thousand verses tells the
unfortunate course of the life of Judel, — the Jew.
When examining it closely, one discovers that, like
Goldfaden's 'The Aristocratic Marriage,' it is an allegorical story of the historical vicissitudes in the development of Judaism and of the sufferings of the Jew through
the centuries. Not only is the story told unobtrusively,
so that one does not at all suspect the allegory, but the
wonderment increases when upon a second and third
perusal one becomes aware of the wealth of Biblical
allusions upon which alone the whole plot is based.
The future commentator of this classic will, when it
shall be fully appreciated, find his task made much
easier by the many references to Biblical passages which
Abramowitsch has himself made in footnotes. The
value of this gem is still more enhanced by the refined
language used in it, — a characteristic of all of Abramowitsch's works.

Ten years later Goldfaden returned to the allegory
of his 'Aristocratic Marriage,' completing it, after the
example of Abramowitsch, in a poem of about six hundred lines, entitled 'Schabssiel, a Poem in Ten Chapters (Thoughts after the Riots in Russia).' The
master's influence on this poem is not to be mistaken,
for it serves as a pendant to the previous work; it is
as it were a continuation of it. Abramowitsch's
poem ends with the futile attempt of Mephistopheles
to tempt Judel to a course of vice, when he discovers
Judel's wife, *i.e.* the Law, faithfully by his side. In
Schabssiel, the sufferings of the Jew are ascribed to his
having departed from the Law, to his having desecrated
the Sabbath. Though somewhat fantastic in its plot,
and far from reaching his predecessor's philosophic
grasp of the Jew's history, his work is full of fine pas-

sages and may be counted among the best of his productions. At about the same time, another young writer, M. Lew, made use of the form of 'Judel' in a poem whose title 'Hudel' seems to indicate its obligation to the prototype. There is in this even less of a philosophical background than in the verses just mentioned, and by its subject-matter it clearly belongs to the following period, for it describes not a purely Jewish theme, but one of a more general character, namely the fall of an orphan who is left to shift for herself in the world. It is, however, given in this place as being, at least in outward form, a direct descendant of Abramowitsch's 'Judel.' While not of the highest poetic value, it is written in a good style and gives promise of better things should the author choose to proceed in his poetic career. Mention must here also be made of a versified story, 'Lemech, the Miracle Worker,' by M. Epstein, to which we shall return later.

Like the allegory, the fable has been a favorite subject of imitation among the writers from the beginning of this century. We possess such, partly translations or adaptations, partly original, from Suchostawer, Dr. Ettinger, Gottlober, Reichersohn, Katzenellenbogen. Of Suchostawer's, only one, a translation of one of Krylov's fables, 'The Cat and the Mice,'[1] has come down to us. It was written in 1829, and, like the fables by Ettinger, circulated in the thirties and forties, is far superior to any translation from Krylov that has appeared before 1880. The most original production is that by Gottlober called 'The Parliament,' a poem of more than one thousand lines, in which he gives an explanation why the lion had been chosen king of all

---

[1] Mordechai Suchostawer, *Der wöler Eeze-geber*, in *Jüd. Volksblatt*, Vol. V. p. 310.

the animals.   While some of the matter contained in it
is unquestionably borrowed from other sources, yet the
whole is moulded in so novel a form, with such a pronounced Jewish setting and biting wit, that it occupies
a place by itself in the history of fables.   After the
candidacy of all the beasts, from the donkey to the
wolf, had been rejected as incompatible with the highest
security of the rest, the lion appears on the scene, and
by his majestic presence at once silences the contending parties ; and he is at once and unanimously chosen
to his high post.   "He rules in fairness, does no wrong,
not a sigh is heaved by any of the animals against him ;
the forest is ruled as of yore : the weak lie still, the
strong go free, the great are great, the humble are
humble : well to him who has sharp teeth ! It has
been so of old, and you cannot change the course of
things.   But no one need complain of the lion as
long as he feels no hunger in his stomach, for then
he is all peace and rest, — God grant there be many
such ! "

The whole of Krylov was translated into Judeo-German, though with but moderate success, in 1879 by Zwi
Hirsch Reichersohn, and more weakly still in 1890 by
Israel Singer.   Two of the fables have been admirably
rendered by Katzenellenbogen, who has also produced a
number of excellent poems in the popular style which
surpass those of Goldfaden in regularity of structure.
He has also translated a few poems from the Russian
and Hebrew, all with the same degree of care displayed in the renderings from Krylov.   His songs
have not been disseminated among the people, the
most of them not having been published until quite
lately.

The most unique person in Judeo-German literature

of the first half of this century is Dr. Ettinger.[1]   All
that is known about him is given in the scanty literary
recollections by Gottlober.   He there says that Dr.
Ettinger had studied medicine at Lemberg, where he
became acquainted with the Judeo-German writings
of Mendel Lefin, who is regarded as the first man of
modern times to use the dialect of everyday life for
literary purposes.   He then settled in Zamoszcz, which
had been a seat of Hebrew learning of the Haskala.
Being prohibited to practise medicine with his foreign
diploma, he became a colonist in the newly formed
Jewish colonies of the South, but not being successful
there, he finally settled in Odessa.   This is all that is
given of his biography.   It is further known that he
wrote his comedy ' Serkele' in the twenties and that
he composed a large number of poems, a few of which
were published in the *Kol-mewasser* in the sixties, a
few in the *Volksblatt* in the eighties.   In 1889 his
family issued a volume of his poetical works which
forms the basis of our discussion.   In this book are
contained sixty fables, a number of poems of various
character, and epigrams.   About one-half of the collection consists of translations from the German; among
these are fables and epigrams by Lessing, ballads and
poems by Schiller, Blumauer, and others.   The other
half is made up of original compositions.   All are of
equal excellence both as to the language used in them
and the more mechanical structure of the verses.

In all these poems there is nothing specifically Jewish

---

[1] Several of the poems contained in the volume of his poetry had
appeared before: *Jüd. Volksblatt*, Vol. I. No. 12, Vol. V. pp. 239, 357,
Vol. VI. pp. 83, 717 ff.; *Familienfreund*, Vol. I. pp. 86-93.   The
Astor Library of New York possesses a manuscript of Ettinger's
fables.

except the language, and they might as well have been
written in any other language without losing the least
part of their significance. Dr. Ettinger is thus an
exceptional phenomenon among his confreres, but exceptional only in appearance, as the cause for it is not
far to seek. From the few data of his life we have
learned that he received his training in the beginning of
this century in Galicia, where at that time the influence
of the Mendelssohnian school was most potent. He
brought with him to Russia not only a love for enlightenment, but also what then was a necessary concomitant
of that culture, a love for German learning; hence his
exclusive imitation of German originals. At first the
privileges of Western education were not only enjoyed
by a small number of learned men, but there was no
attempt made at introducing them to the masses at
large, for that would have been a hazardous occupation
for those who entered in an unequal combat with the
superstitious people. It was only after J. B. Levinsohn
had pointed out in his Hebrew works the desirability
of educating them, and after he had undertaken to do
so single-handed, that the other writers, late in the
thirties and in the forties, began to approach the masses
in the least offensive manner, by means of the folksong.
Dr. Ettinger's activity, however, fell in the period
preceding the militant energy of the Haskala. If he
wished at all to write in Judeo-German, he could
appear only as the interpreter of German culture to a
public imbued with a love for it. What in the beginning was only a pastime of his leisure hours, soon
became a passion to try his ingenuity, and he proceeded
in writing original poems, and continued that practice
even at a time when the main purpose of Judeo-German
literature was to educate the people.

Judeo-German poetry has developed in Russia in precisely the opposite direction from the one generally taken by that branch of literature among other nations. Whereas the usual course would have been to pass from the simple utterings of the folksong to more and more elaborate forms, the process among the Jews in Russia has been inverted. The first poetical expressions were those of Dr. Ettinger, who may be regarded as a dialectic continuator of Schiller and Lessing. After that followed the school of popular poets of the Gordons, Goldfaden, Linetzki, Ehrenkranz, Berel Broder. In the seventies a few traces of that school are still to be found, but the majority of songs produced then smack of the badchen's art, while Goldfaden himself has deteriorated into a writer of theatre couplets. The explanation of this is found in the fact that in the sixties the efforts of the folk-singers were crowned with success. The Rabbinical schools had graduated several classes of men trained in the Reform, the Gymnasia and Universities had been thrown wide open to the Jewish youths, and in the next decade a large number of them had availed themselves of the highest advantages offered in these institutions of learning. The cloud of a stubborn ignorance had been successfully dispelled, the light shone brightly over the whole land. The bard's task was done; he had no need to spur the people on to progress, for that duty was now devolved on the large host of younger men who had tasted the privileges of a Russian education. But these had been identifying themselves with Russian thought, with Russian ideals. For them German culture had little of significance, except as it appeared in universal literature, or had affected Russian ideas. Still less were they interested in Jewish letters, whether in Hebrew, or in Judeo-German. On the contrary, they were trying hard to forget their humble beginnings. Neither for these nor by these could the Judeo-German language be employed for any literary purposes. The masses had become accustomed to look with favor on the new education, and one by one the better elements were disappearing from the narrow world of the Ghetto. There was still left a large proportion of those who could not avail themselves of the benefits offered them. They knew no other language than the homely dialect of their surroundings, and they were still thirsting for entertainment such as the folk-singers have offered to them. The older men, the champions of the Haskala, were dead, or too old to write; the younger men had other interests at heart, and thus it was left to a mediocre class of writers to supply them with poetry. This part naturally fell to the badchens. Another quarter of a century, and Judeo-German literature would have run its course; even the badchen would have been silenced. But it suddenly rose from its ashes with renewed vigor after the riots against the Jews in 1881.

VII. POETRY SINCE THE EIGHTIES IN RUSSIA

THE latest blood-bath was instituted against the Jews of Russia in 1881.   In the same year there was started in St. Petersburg a weekly periodical, *Jüdisches Volks-blatt*, by the editor of the *Kol-mewasser* which had gone out of existence ten years before.   The purpose of the new publication was to focus all the available forces that had been dispersed in the decade preceding through the agencies that made for assimilation, and to prepare the way for a renewed activity among the people.   These no longer needed to be urged on to progress, but had to be comforted in the misfortunes that had befallen them, and in the dangers that awaited them.   In the first number of the new periodical there appeared the poem of J. L. Gordon on 'The Law written on Parchment,' while the second brought one by the same author, outlining his plan to sing words of encouragement to his suffering, hard-working brothers and sisters.   However, very soon after all singing ceased. The year 1882 had been one of too much suffering, when even consolation is out of place.   Two years later S. Rabinowitsch, who was destined by his unresting energy and good example to cause a revival of Judeo-German literature, justly exclaimed in the same weekly [1] in a poem 'To Our Poet': "Arise, thou Poet ! Where have you been all this time ? Send us from afar your words of wisdom ! For what other pleasure

[1] Vol. IV. p. 175.

have your brothers if not your sweet and consoling songs ? "

While no other singers were forthcoming, Rabinowitsch composed himself a series of songs, although he was preparing himself to be a novelist. His heart was with the poetry of the Russian Nekrasov, and his native Judeo-German gave him Michel Gordon for a model. He imitated both, taking the structure from the Russian, and the manner of the folksong from Gordon. When his talent was just reaching its fullest development, he abandoned this branch of literature to devote his undivided attention to prose. Only twice afterwards he returned to the use of rhythm, once in a poem, entitled 'Progress, Civilization,' an imitation of Nekrasov's 'Who lives in Russia Happily,' and at another time in a legend in blank verse. The first has never been finished, the other appeared in a collective volume of poetry published in 1887 by M. Spektor, his friend and rival in the resuscitation of Judeo-German letters.

That volume, named 'Der Familienfreund,' was intended as an attempt to bring together all those who wrote poetry; but we find in it only names that had been known to us from the previous period: M. Gordon, Zunser, Goldfaden, Linetzki.[1] To these must be added the name of Rabinowitsch just mentioned, and of Samostschin, who had furnished a few poems to the *Kol-mewasser* nearly twenty years before. In the *Volksblatt* there were published in the meanwhile a few songs by various authors, most prominently by Moses Chaschkes. He also printed in 1889 a volume of his poems at Cracow, under the name of 'Songs

---

[1] This is also true of the poets who contributed to ' *Der jüdischer Wecker*,' a similar volume published in the same year at Odessa.

from the Heart,' in which are contained a number of reflections on the riots in Russia. There are some good thoughts in them, although the technique is not always faultless. He, too, belongs to the older type of folk-singers.

The Jews had at that time furnished three names to Russian poetry: those of Nadson, Vilenkin (Minski), and Frug. Of these the first had a Christian mother and died at the early age of twenty-four, in 1886. The second had begun his poetical career in the seventies, after having received a thorough Russian education. There was only Frug left, who had not entirely broken with his Jewish traditions, for he had gone directly from the Jewish farmer colony where he had been born to St. Petersburg to engage in literary work. His first Russian poem was published in 1879. In 1885 he began to compose also in Judeo-German, continuing to do so to the present time.[1] Like many other Jewish writers he had become convinced that his duties were above all with his race, as long as it was oppressed and persecuted, and his energy was thus unfortunately split in two by writing in two languages. For the same reason such poets as Perez, Winchevsky, Rosenfeld, have taken to Judeo-German, which is understood by few and which in a few decades is doomed to extinction, except in countries of persecution. They adorn their humble literature, but they would have been an honor to other literatures as well, and from these they have been alienated.

[1] His poems were printed in : *Jüd. Volksblatt*, Vol. V. p. 515 ; Vol. VII. No. 36 ; Vol. VIII. No. 10 ; Beilage No. 3 passim ; Vol. IX. No. 3 passim ; *Hausfreund*, Vol. I. p. 44 ; Vol. III. pp. 172–175 (*On the death of M. Gordon*); *Jüd. Volksbib.* Vol. I. pp. 260–263 ; Vol. II. pp. 1–6, 120–125, 139–141, 167–168, 195–204 ; *Jüd. Volkskalender*, Vol. III. pp. 117–124.

When Frug began to write in his native dialect, he had already acquired a reputation in a literary language. He had passed the severe school of the poet's technique, had been trained in the traditions of his vocation. One could not expect that in descending to speak to his coreligionists in their own tongue, he would return to the more primitive methods of the popular bard. He simply changed the language, but nothing of his art. By this transference he only gains in reputation, although he loses in popularity, for the accusation frequently brought against him, that he confines himself to too narrow a sphere, falls to the ground when he intends that that narrow sphere alone should be his audience. Half a century had gone by since Dr. Ettinger had introduced the form and subject-matter of German poetry, and since those days no such harmony had been heard to issue from the mouth of a Jewish poet. There were no literary traditions to fall back upon, except the folksong of the preceding generation; there scarcely existed a poetical diction for Judeo-German, and a variety of dialects were striving for supremacy. What he and the people owed to Michel Gordon, he expressed in two poems entitled 'To Michel Gordon' and 'On Michel Gordon's Grave'; both collectively he named 'One of the Best.' In an allegorical series, 'Songs of the Jewish Jargon,' he sings of the history of the language which is identical with that of his downtrodden race. The prologue is a model of beautiful style. The Slavic dactyllic diminutives, grafted on German stems, the gentle cadence of words, the simplicity of the diction, remind one rather of mellifluous Italian than of a disorderly mixture which, in the poem, he compares to the bits of bread in a beggar's wallet, or which, according to

another part in the same allegory, excludes the de-
ceased Jew from heaven, as the angel at the gate cannot understand him.

There are a few poems in his collection in which he
bewails the lot of a Jewish poet who has only tears for
his subject, but the most deal with incidents in the life
of his oppressed coreligionists, now painting pictures of
their misery, their poverty, their lack of orderliness,
now giving them words of consolation.   He never
passes the narrow frame of his people's surroundings,
no matter what he sings.   Even when he chooses
nature of which to sing, it appears to him transformed under a heavy cloud of his own sufferings
superinduced by the persecution of his brethren.   The
best of his poems are those entitled ' Night Songs,' in
which he depicts a few night scenes.   Here is the way
he describes the Melamed, the teacher of children in
those miserable quarters called a school : " Behold the
palace, oh, how beautiful, how magnificent : ivory and
velvet, silk, leather, bronze, cedar wood . . . here lives
a Jewish teacher. . . .   Of velvet is his skullcap — it
glistens and shines from afar; the fescue is made of
ivory; his girdle is of silk; the candelabrum is of
bronze; the knout is of leather; the stool, the stool
is cut out of cedar wood ! "   One can easily see that
the rest of the picture is in keeping with the glory
just described.   There is gloom everywhere in his
songs.   And how could it be otherwise?   It was
proper for Ettinger to smile and to jest, for he was
active at the dawn of better days ; it was natural for
the poets of the thirties and fifties to battle against
superstitions and to sound the cry of progress; for the
poets of the eighties there was nothing left but tears.

It has been Frug's ambition to be a continuator of

the bards who sang for the masses, to be a folk-poet,
and the people look upon him as such, although he
hardly appeals to them in the manner of the older
bards.   He is entirely too literary to be understood
without previous training, and his allegory is not so
easily unravelled.   His greatest faults are, perhaps, an
absence of dramatic qualities and a certain coldness of
colors.   Nevertheless, he is one of the best poets in
Judeo-German literature, who may also claim recognition by a wider class of readers.

The year 1888 is momentous in the history of Judeo-
German literature: it gave birth to two annuals, *Die
jüdische Volksbibliothēk* and *Der Hausfreund*, around
which were gathered all the best forces that could be
found among the Jewish writers.   The first, under the
leadership of S. Rabinowitsch, started out with the purpose of clearing away all rubbish from the field of Jewish letters and to prepare it for a new, a better harvest ;
the second set out to serve the people with the best
existing literary productions.   The latter was doomed
to a certain mediocrity on account of the bounds which
it had placed around itself; the first, in exercising a
severe criticism on the productions presented for publication, and in purifying the public taste, attracted
from the start the best talent obtainable and encouraged young promising men to try themselves in Jargon
letters.   In the *Volksbibliothēk* appeared the firstling
from the pen of Leon Perez, the poet and novelist, who
must be counted among the greatest writers not only
of Judeo-German literature, but of literature in general
at the end of the nineteenth century.   If he had
written nothing else but 'The Sewing of the Wedding
Gown,' his name would live as long as there could
be found people to interpret the language in which

he sings. But he has produced several large volumes of admirable works in prose and in verse.

Leon Perez, or Izchok Leibusch Perez, as he proudly prefers to be called, was born in 1855 in Zamoszcz, the city which has been the birthplace of so many famous men in Hebrew and Judeo-German letters, the home of Zederbaum and Ettinger. He obtained his education in a curious way. In his town there had lived a surgeon's assistant who, on becoming rich, had collected a library on all kinds of subjects, numbering nearly three thousand volumes. There came reverses to him, and his books were stored away pell mell in the loft. Perez somehow got hold of the key to that room, and without choice took to reading, until the whole library was swallowed up by his omnivorous appetite. He read everything he could get hold of, and he learned German through a work on physics which he had discovered in the loft. Then he passed on from science to science, all by himself. Then he studied Heine by heart, then Shelley, and then he became a mystic. This history of his education is also the history of his genius. There is reflected in it the subtleness of the Talmud, the wisdom of the ancients, the sparkle of Heine, the transcendency of Shelley, the mysticism of Hauptmann. He has treated masterfully the Talmudical legend, has composed in the style of the Romancero, and has carried allegory to the highest degree of perfection.

Perez is even less of a popular poet than Frug. He has entirely parted company with the people. Although he started with the avowed purpose of aiding his race to a better recognition of itself, yet his talents are of too high an order, where language, feelings, and thoughts soar far above the understanding of the masses. He can hardly be properly appreciated even by

those who enjoy the advantages of a fair school education, not to speak of those who are merely lettered.
It is only an unfortunate accident, the persecutions of
the Jews, that has thrown him into so unpromising a
field as that of Judeo-German letters, where to be great
is to be unknown to the world at large and to be subjected to the jealous attacks of less gifted writers.   He
could easily gain a reputation in any other language,
should he choose to try for it, but, like many of his
predecessors, he is pursued by the merciless allurements
of the Jewish Muse.   Her enchantment is the more
powerful on her devotees since she appears to them
only in the garb of their own weaving.   They spend
so much work in creating the outer form and fashion-
ing a poetic diction that they get fascinated by their
creative labor, and stick to their undertaking, even
though they have but few hearers for their utterances.

   'Monisch' is the name of the ballad with which Perez
made his debut ten years ago.[1]   It is the old story of
Satan's recovery of power over the saint by tempting
him with an earthly love.   But the setting of the story
is all new and original.   The fourth chapter, beginning
with

> Andersch wollt' mein Lied geklungen
> 'ch soll far Goim goisch singen,
> Nischt far Jüden, nischt Žargon

   (My song would sound quite differently, were I to sing to Gentiles in their language, not to Jews in Jargon)

is the best of all.   He describes there the difficulty of
singing of love in a dialect that has no words for 'love'
and 'sweetheart'; nevertheless he acquits himself well

---

[1] *Jüd. Volksbib.* Vol. I. pp. 148-158; better than this is his own
edition of the ballad in a separate pamphlet (*q.v.*).

of his task to tell of Monisch's infatuation, for which, of course, a saint and a Jew can only become Satan's prey. Perez has written a number of stories in verse. Some of them are mosaics of gems, in which the unity of the whole is frequently marred by a mystic cloud which it is hard to penetrate. Such, for example, is his ' He and She,'[1] a story of the Spanish inquisition, and ' Reb Jossel,'[2] the temptation of a teacher of children by his hostess, the wife of a shoemaker. The latter poem is very hard to grasp at one reading, but the details, such as the description of the teacher, his pale and ailing pupil with his endless school superstitions, the jolly shoemaker, are drawn very well. Much more comprehensible are his ' The Driver '[3] and ' Jossel Bers and Jossel Schmaies.'[4] The first is a sad picture of a Jewish town in Poland, in which the inhabitants have lost, one after the other, their means of subsistence after the railroad had connected them with Warsaw. The drivers, the merchants, the artisans who throve at their honest professions before, have become impoverished and are driven to despised occupations, only to keep body and soul together. It is a very sad picture indeed. In the other, the author tells of two boys who had been fellow-students out of the same prayer-book, but who soon separated at the parting of the roads. The one, a faithful believer in all the teacher told him, becomes a Rabbi ; the other asks for facts and reasons to fortify the statements of his mentor, and subjects himself to many privations in order to acquire worldly wisdom in the gymnasium and the university. The

---

[1] *Jüd. Bibliothēk*, Vol. II. pp. 170–180.
[2] *Ibid.*, Vol. III. pp. 123–155.
[3] *Ibid.*, Vol. I. pp. 246–257.
[4] *Ibid.*, Vol. I. pp. 276–285.

final picture is placed in Roumania (or Russia, had the censor permitted it), where the student is driven through the streets by a mob, while the Rabbi, unconscious of the outer world, is somewhere thinking hard over the solution of a question of ritual.

The shorter poems are either translations from the Russian poet Nadson, or imitations of Heine. They are well done, though some suffer somewhat by their veiled allegory, at least at a superficial reading. The best of these are those that deal with social questions, or describe the laborer's sufferings. Preëminent among them is 'The Sewing of the Wedding Gown.'[1] If Thomas Hood's 'Song of the Shirt' is to be compared to a fine instrument, then this poem is a whole orchestra, from the sounds of which the walls of Jericho would fall. Instead of a criticism, a short review of the story will be given here. The scene is at a dressmaker's; the cast: the modiste, two dressmakers, and sewing-girls. The modiste tells of the care with which the wedding gown has to be sewed. The choir of sewing-girls sing the song of the prison. The first dressmaker speaks of the beauty of the gown, and compares the bride to an angel from heaven, whereupon the choir sings of the misery at home, of asking the 'angel' to advance a rouble on the work, of the 'angel's' cruel refusal, of the pawning of her silks for a loaf of bread, and of the girl's arrest by the 'angel.' "And the angel has taken care of me during the great frosts, and for three months has provided me with board and lodging." The second dressmaker compares the rustle of the silk to the noise made by her tired bones, speaks of the diamond buttons that will be sewed on the gown "as

[1] *Jontew-blättlech, Zweite Serie, Ōneg Schabes,* pp. 27–31, *Chamischo Osser,* pp. 22–31.

large as tears of the poor," and bids the wheel of the
machine to drown the noise of her breaking bones.
The choir sings the song of the grave, where no sewing
is done, where all go down in a shroud forever. The
second dressmaker continues the song, whereupon a
girl, named 'Fond-of-Life,' protests, telling of her
good health, of her desire to pass her youth in pleasure. The choir chides her with the Ragpicker's song,
in which 'Fond-of-Life's' future is portrayed, and the
conclusion to the song is given by the first dressmaker.
The first dressmaker contrasts the luxury of the bride's
bed with her straw bed on the floor, the bride's splendor of light in her parlor with the two candles at her
head when she is dead. The modiste, oppressed by
the sad songs that portray their own unhappiness, bids
them sing of other people's happiness. To this the
choir responds by singing the happiness of the bride,
but the modiste sees in this only the girls' jealousy,
whereupon the choir tells of the obedient daughter who
is advised by her mother to scorn sweetness, getting
the promise of a gilded nut if she behaves properly.
When the nut is brought and cracked it is found to be
wormy and bitter. Of course, that is a picture of a
match made by the parents for their daughter. The
modiste answers that happiness does not always dwell
in high places; and the first dressmaker tells the story
of labor, which is quite unique: There lived two
brothers happily together. A stranger, who is no
other than the Biblical serpent, visits them; he is clad
in diamonds and costly stones, and dazzles the older
brother with his splendor. He, too, would like to be
rich. He follows the stranger out into the woods, and
seats himself at his side to inquire of the manner of
acquiring such wealth. "What a fool you are to allow

your opportunities to slip by," says the serpent. "You do not know that the sweat of your brother is nothing but diamonds, the tears are brilliants, his blood pearls." The elder brother returns home, beats his younger brother to elicit blood and sweat and tears. His wealth grows, but not his happiness, for he suffers as much from fear of his hoarded riches as his brother sighs under tears. They finally fall to blows, — but here the poet purposely breaks his story, for he will not undertake to tell the end of their hostility. The choir sings the ten o'clock song, when all must go to rest : "You are rested, and at times you dream of—a loaf of bread! The clock strikes ten, the work is done, — good night, madame!" The modiste answers : "Be back early in the morning!"

This is the bare skeleton of the poem, of whose painful beauties nothing but a perusal in the original can give an adequate idea. There is the making of a great poet in one who can sing like that; but Perez has chosen, like Rabinowitsch, to devote his best energies to prose, and to this part of his activity we shall return later. Of the minor poems of this period there might be mentioned those by David Frischmann, Rosa Goldstein, M. W. Satulowski, M. M. Penkowski, W. Kaiser, Paltiel Samostschin. Frischmann has produced but a few poems, but they are all of excellent quality. His best is a ballad, 'Ophir,'[1] but he has also written some clever satires in verse. Samostschin,[2] who had begun composing in the sixties, has translated several poems,

[1] His legend *Ophir*, printed in *Jüd. Volksbib.*, Vol. I. pp. 211–224.
[2] His poems appeared in *Jüd. Volksblatt*, Vol. I. Nos. 10, 11 ; Vol. II. Nos. 9, 46 ; Vol. III. pp. 402 ; Vol. IV. p. 94 ; Vol. V. pp. 565, 664 ; Vol. VI. pp. 190, 195 ; Vol. VII. pp. 277, 759 ; *Hausfreund*, Vol. III. pp. 304–306 ; Spektor's *Familienkalender*, Vol. V. p. 71 ; *Lamteren*, col. 26.

especially from the Hebrew of J. L. Gordon, and has written some clever feuilletons in rhymes. Minchas Perel has published a small collection of poems on the Fall of Jerusalem, of which the first, ' The Night of the Destruction of Jerusalem,' is a very spirited and dramatic story of the event. Another good book of poems is ' The Harp,' by G. O. Hornstein. Although some of them are in the style of the coupletists, others betray original talent that might be well developed. The best of these is the ballad, ' The Cat and the Mouse,' an allegory of Jewish persecutions, in which the Jew is represented as a mouse living on the fat of the oil candelabrum in the Temple at Jerusalem, and the Romans and other nations are represented as cats who drive the mouse out of her abiding place.

The riots of the early part of the eighties affected the whole mental attitude of the Jews of Russia by rousing them to a greater consciousness of themselves and by rallying them around distinctly Jewish standards. For hundreds of thousands life had become impossible at home, and they emigrated to various countries, but mostly to America, where, under the influence of entirely new conditions, Judeo-German literature, and with it poetry, developed in new channels.

VIII. POETRY SINCE THE EIGHTIES IN AMERICA

JUDEO-GERMAN poetry has developed in two directions in America, — downwards and upwards. Many
of the poets left Russia in the beginning of the eighties,
together with the involuntary emigration of the Russian
Jews, to escape the political oppression at home; but
once in America they came in contact with conditions
not less undesirable than those they had just left; for,
instead of the religious persecution to which they had
been subjected there, they now began to experience
the industrial oppression of the sweat-shops into which
they were driven in order to earn a livelihood. At
the same time, the greater political liberty which they
enjoy makes it possible for them to give free utterance
to their feelings and thoughts, without veiling them
in the garb of a far-fetched allegory. However, they
have not all suffered who have come here. Many
have found on the hospitable shores of the United
States opportunities to earn what to their humble
demands appears as a comfortable income. With the
increased well-being, there has come a stronger desire
to be entertained. The wedding day, Purim, and the
Feast of the Rejoicing of the Law no longer suffice
as days of amusements, and Goldfaden's theatre, which
had been proscribed in Russia, has found an asylum in
New York. Soon one theatre was not large enough
to hold the crowd that asked for admission; and three

companies, playing every evening, were doing a good business. But qualitatively the theatres rapidly deteriorated to the level of dime shows. The theatre, as established by Goldfaden, has never been of an elevated character even in Europe, except as it treated the Biblical and the historical drama. Still, it reflected in a certain respect the inner life of the Ghetto. In the New World, the Jewish life of the Russian Ghetto is rapidly losing all interest, and that part of New York which in common parlance is known as the Ghetto, deserves its name only in so far as it is inhabited by former denizens of other Ghettos. There is taking place a dulling of Jewish sensibilities which will ultimately result in the absorption of the Russian Jews by the American people. This lowered Jewish consciousness finds its expression in poetry in the development of the theatre couplet in imitation of the American song of the day. As in Russia, the plays are written by a host of incompetent men, not so much for the purpose of carrying out a plot as in order to weave into them songs of which Jews have always been fond. Nearly all the plays are melodramas, in which the contents go for nothing or are too absurd to count for anything. But the couplets have survived, and are fast becoming street ballads or folksongs, according to the quality of the same. Goldfaden's songs, in which there is always a ring of the true folksong, are giving place to the worthless jingles of Marks, Hurwitz, Awramowitsch, Mogulesco, and the like, and the old national poems are being superseded by weak imitations of 'Daisy Bell,' 'Do, do, my Huckleberry, Do,' 'The Bowery Girl,' and other American ballads. Now and then a couplet of a national character may be heard in the theatres, and more rarely a really good poem occurs in these dramatic performances, but otherwise the old folksong is rapidly decaying.

I. Reingold, of Chicago, is a fruitful balladist who at times strikes a good note in his songs; but in these he generally painfully resembles certain passages in Rosenfeld's poetry, from whom he evidently gets his wording if not his inspiration. Side by side with this deteriorated literature there goes on a more encouraging folk-singing. Zunser, who now owns a printing-office in New York, continues his career as a popular bard as before, and has written some of his best poems in the New World. It is interesting to note how America affects his Muse, for he sings now of the 'Pedlar' and the 'Plough.' The latter, a praise of the farmer's life, to which he would encourage his co-religionists, has had the honor of being translated into Russian. Among his later poetry there is also one on 'Columbus and Washington,' in which, of course, both are lauded. The Stars and Stripes have been the subject of many a song by Judeo-German poets, which is significant, since not a single ode has been produced praising Russia or the Czar.

Goldfaden, too, has written some of his songs in America, and Selikowitsch has furnished two or three translations and adaptations that may be classed as folksongs. Still more encouraging is the class of poetry which has had its rise entirely in America or in England, for among these poets it has received the highest development yet attained.

The volume entitled 'Jewish Tunes,' by A. M. Sharkansky, contains a number of real gems in poetry. Sharkansky has a good ear for rhythm and word jingling, and in this he always succeeds. But he is not equally fortunate in his ideas, for he either over-

loads a picture so as to bury the meaning of the poem
in it, or else he does not finish his thought, leaving an
impression that something ought to follow. Now and
then, however, he produces a fine song. Among his
best are 'Jewish Melodies,' in which he says that they
must always be sad, and 'Songs of Zion,' of similar
contents. 'Jossele Journeys to America,' which is a
parody on Schiller's 'Hektor and Andromache,' and
'The Cemetery,' a translation of Uhland's 'Das Grab,'
give evidence of a great mastery of his dialect. It is
hardly possible to suspect the second poem of being a
translation. Sharkansky has for some reason ceased to
sing, which is to be regretted, for with a little more
care in the development of his ideas he might have
come to occupy an honorable place among the best
Judeo-German poets.

New York is the place of refuge not only of the
laboring men among the Russian Jews, but also of
their cultured and professional people. These had
at home belonged to liberal organizations, which in
monarchical countries are of necessity extreme, either
Socialistic or Anarchistic. Such advanced opinions
they shared in Russia with their Gentile companions,
with whom they identified themselves by their education. Their relations to the Jewish community were
rather loose, for the tendency of the somewhat greater
privileges which the Jews enjoyed in the sixties and
the seventies had been to obliterate old lines of demarkation between Jew and Gentile. They had almost
forgotten that there were any ties that united them
with their race, when they were roused from their
peaceful occupations, to which they had been devoting
themselves, to the realization of their racial difference.
They then heard for the first time that they were

pariahs alike with the humblest of their brethren. The same feeling which prompted the Russian poet Frug to take up his despised Judeo-German, drove many a man into the Judeo-German literary field, who not only had never before written in that language, but who had hardly ever spoken it. In England and America such men could only hope to be understood by a Jewish public, and those who felt themselves called to write poetry wrote it in Judeo-German. But with them the language could only be the accidental vehicle of their thought, without confining them to the narrow circle of their nation's life. Their interests, like those of young Russia in general, are with humanity at large, not with the Jew in his Ghetto, and their songs would not have lost a particle of their significance had they been written in any other tongue. They suffer with the Jew, not because he is a Jew, but because, like many other oppressed people, he has a grievance, and they propose remedies for these according to their political and social convictions.

David Edelstadt was the poet of the Anarchistic party, as Morris Winchevsky represents Socialistic tendencies. The influence of both on their respective adherents has been great, but the latter has been a power for good among a wider circle of readers, within and without his party. Both show by the language which they use that it was mere accident that threw them into the ranks of Judeo-German writers, for while usually the diction of the older poets abounds in words of Hebrew origin, theirs is almost entirely free from them, so that one can read their productions with no other knowledge than that of the literary German language.

Edelstadt mastered neither his poetical subjects nor

the dialect. The latter is a composition of the literary German with dialectic forms, and his rhythms are halting, his ideas one-sided. There is not a poem among the fifty that he has written that is not didactic. Many of these are in praise of Anarchists and heroes of freedom who have fallen in the unequal combat with the present conditions of society. There are poems in memory of Sophia Perovskaya, Louise Michel, John Brown, and even Albert Parsons and Louis Ling. He sings of the eleventh of November, the Fall of the Bastile, of strikes, misery, and suffering. Most of these are a call to war with society. They are neither of the extreme character that one generally ascribes to the Anarchists, nor do they sound any sincere notes. They seem to be written not because Edelstadt is a poet, but because he belongs to the Anarchistic party. In all his collection there is one only in which he directs himself especially to the Jews, and one of its stanzas is significant, as it lies at the foundation of much of Rosenfeld's poetry: it tells that they have escaped the cruel Muscovite only to be jailed in the dusky sweat-shops where they slowly bleed at the sewing-machine.

Morris Winchevsky is a poet of a much higher type. He is a man of high culture, is conversant with the literatures of Russia, France, Germany, and England, is pervaded by what is best in universal literature, follows carefully all the rules of prosody and poetic composition, and above all is master of his dialect. His Socialistic bias is pronounced, but it does not interfere with the pictures that he portrays. They are true to life, though somewhat cold in coloring. His mastery of Judeo-German, nearly all of German origin, is displayed in his fine translation of Thomas Hood's 'Song of the Shirt' and some of Victor Hugo's poems. His other

songs show the same care in execution and are as
perfect in form as can be produced in his dialect.
Winchevsky began his poetical career in England,
where he was also active as a Socialistic agitator. The
small collection of his poetical works (unfortunately
unfinished) contains almost entirely songs which were
written there.   His American poems appeared in the
Emeth, which he published in Boston in 1895 and
in other periodicals.   Although he has tried himself
in all kinds of verses, he prefers dactyllic measures,
which in 'A Broom and a Sweeping' he uses most
elaborately.   The poems all treat on social questions
and describe the misery of the lower strata of society.
He speaks of the life of the orphan whose home is
in the street, of the eviction of the wretched widow,
of the imprisonment of the small boy for stealing a
few apples, of the blind fiddler, of night-scenes on
the Strand, of London at night.   A large number of
songs are devoted more strictly to Socialistic propaganda, while a series of forty-eight stanzas under the
collective title 'How the Rich Live' is a gloomy kaleido-
scope through which pass in succession the usurer, the
commercial traveller, the journalist, the preacher, the
cardplayer, the lawyer, the hypocrite, the old general,
the speculator, the lady of the world, the gambler at
races, the man enriched by arson, the dissatisfied rich
man, the doctor, the Rabbi.   Winchevsky has also
written some excellent fables, of which 'The Rag and
the Papershred' and 'The Noble Tom-Cat' are probably
the best.   In all those the language alone is Jewish,
everything else is of a universal nature, and the freeing
of society from the yoke of oppression is the burden of
his songs.

The most original poet among the Russian Jews of

America is Morris Rosenfeld. He was born in 1862 in
a small town in the Government of Suwalk in Russian
Poland. His ancestors for several generations back
had been fishermen, and he himself passed many days
of his childhood on the beautiful lake near his native
home. He had listened eagerly to the weird folk-
tales that his grandfather used to tell, and as a boy
had himself had the reputation of a good story-teller.
At home he received no other education than that which
is generally allotted to Jewish boys of humble families :
he studied Hebrew and the Talmud. But his father
was more ambitious for his son, and when he moved to
the city of Warsaw he provided him with teachers for
the study of German and Polish. However, Rosenfeld
did not acquire more than the mere rudiments of these
languages, for very soon his struggle for existence began. He went to England to avoid military service,
and there learned the tailor's trade. Thence he proceeded to Holland, where he tried himself in diamond
grinding. He very soon after came to America, where
for many weary years he has eked out an existence in
the sweat-shops of New York. He learned in them to
sing of misery and oppression. His first attempts were
very weak ; he felt himself called to be a poet, but he
had no training of any kind, least of all in poetic diction. For models in his own language he had only the
folk-singers of Russia, for Frug began his activity at the
same time as he, and Perez published his ' Monisch '
some years after Rosenfeld had discovered his own
gifts. A regular tonic structure had not been attempted before in Judeo-German, and a self-styled
critic of Judeo-German literature in New York tried
to convince him that his dialect was not fit for the
ordinary versification. One of his first poems, pub-

lished in the *Jüdisches Volksblatt* in St. Petersburg, was
curiously enough a greeting to the poet Frug, who had
just published his first songs in Judeo-German; however warm in sentiment, it is entirely devoid of that
imagery and word-painting which was soon to become
the chief characteristic of Rosenfeld's poetry.

Rosenfeld has read the best German and English
authors, and although he knows these languages only
superficially, he has instinctively guessed the inner
meaning contained in their works, and he has transfused the art of his predecessors into his own spirit
without imitating them directly. One cannot help, in
reading his verses, discovering his obligations to Heine,
Schiller, Moore, and Shelley; but it is equally apparent
that he owes nothing to them as regards the subject-
matter of his poems. He is original not only in Jewish
letters but in universal literature as well.

Himself in contact with the lower strata of society
and yet in spirit allied to the highest; at once the subject of religious and race persecutions and of industrial
oppression; tossed about among the opposition parties
or Anarchists, Socialists, Populists, without allying himself with any; by education and associations a Jew, and
yet not subscribing strictly to the tenets of the Mosaic
Law, — he voices the ominous foreboding of the tidal
wave which threatens to submerge our civilization, he
utters the cry of anguish and despair that rises in different quarters and condemns the present order of
things. Rosenfeld does not scoff, or scorn, or hate.
He is one with the oppressor and the oppressed; if he
sings more of the latter, it is only because he sees more
of that side of life. He is a sensitive plate that repro-
duces the pictures that arise before his mental vision,
and the gloom of his poems is rather that which he sees

than that which he feels; for he has also written songs
of spring and happiness in the few intervals when the
sky has looked down unclouded on the Ghetto in which
he has lived so long.

We shall confine ourselves to the small volume of his
poetry, 'The Songs from the Ghetto,' even though it
contains but one-tenth of all the verses that he has
written. Who can read his ' Songs of Labor' without
shedding tears ? We enter with the poet, who is the
tailor himself, the murky sweat-shop where the monotonous click of the sewing-machine, which kills thought
and feeling, mysteriously whispers in your ear: —

" Ich arbeit', un' arbeit', un' arbeit' ohn' Cheschben.
  Es schafft sich, un' schafft sich, un' schafft sich ohn' Zāhl,"

and we see the workman changed into just such an
unfeeling machine. During the short midday hour
he has but time to weep and dream of the end of his
slavery; when the whistle blows, the boss with his angry
look returns, the machine once more ticks, and the tailor
again loses his semblance of a human being. What
wonder, then, that tears should be the subject of so many
of his songs? Even when the laborer returns home he
does not find relief from his sorrows; his own child does
not see him from one end of the week to the other, for
it is asleep when he goes out to work or returns from
it (' My Boy'). Not only the workman, but even the
mendicant, who has no home and finds his only consolation in his children, has reason to curse the present
system when he sees the judge take them away from
him to send them to an orphan asylum, — a species of
misdirected philanthropy ('The Beggar Family'). Sad
are the simple words: 'Ich gēh' vardienen!' uttered
by a girl before the break of day, hurrying to the fac-

tory, and late at night, following a forced life of vice
('Whither'). Even death does not come to the unfortunate in the calm way of Goethe's 'Über allen Gipfeln
ist Ruh''; not the birds are silenced, but the worms are
waiting for their companion ('Despair'). Nay, after
death the laborer arises from his grave to accuse the
rich neighbor of having stolen the flowers from his bar-
ren mound ('In the Garden of the Dead').

Not less sad are his National Songs. In 'Sephirah'
he tells us that the Jew's year is but a succession
of periods for weeping. Most of his songs of that
class deal with the tragical conflict between religious
duties and actualities. Such is 'The First Bath of
Ablution,' which is one of the prettiest Jewish ballads.
The 'Measuring of the Graves,' which relates the
superstition of the Jews who study by candles with
the wicks of which graves have been measured, is
especially interesting, on account of the excellent use
of the language of the Tchines made in it. The
unanswered question of the boy in the 'Moon Prayer'
is one of many that the poet likes to propound. Perhaps the best poem under the same heading is 'On the
Bosom of the Ocean,' which is remarkable not only as a
sad portrayal of the misfortunes of the Jew who is
driven out of Russia and is sent back from America
because he has not the requisite amount of money
which would entitle him to stay here, but also on
account of the wonderful description of a storm at
sea. The same sad strain passes through the poems
classed as miscellaneous. Now it is the nightingale
that chooses the cemetery in which to sing his sweetest
songs ('The Cemetery Nightingale'). Or the flowers
in autumn do not call forth regrets, for they have not
been smiling on the poor laborer in his suffering ('To

the Flowers in Autumn '). Or again, the poet compares himself with the bird who sings in the wilderness
where 'the dead remain dead, and the silent remain
silent' ('In the Wilderness').

The gloom that lies over so many of Rosenfeld's
poems is the result of his own sad experiences in the
sweat-shop and during his struggle for existence ; but
this gloom is only the accident of his themes. Behind
it lies the inexhaustible field of the poet's genius which
adorns and beautifies every subject on which he chooses
to write. The most remarkable characteristic of his
genius is to weld into one the dramatic action and the
lyrical qualities of his verse, as has probably never been
attempted before. Whether he writes of the sweat-
shop, or of the storm on the ocean, or of the Jewish
soldier who rises nightly from his grave, we in every
instance get a drama and yet a lyric, not as separate
developments, but inextricably combined into one
whole. Thus, for example, 'In the Sweat-shop' is a
lyrical poem, if Hood's 'Song of the Shirt' is one, but
in so far as the poet, or operative, is turned into a
machine and is subjected to the exterior forces which
determine his moods and his destiny, we have the
evolution of a tragedy before us. Similarly, the exact
parallel of the storm on the ocean with the storm in
the hearts of the two Jews in the steerage is no less
of a dramatic nature than an utterance of subjective
feelings.

Rosenfeld does not confine himself to pointing out
the harmony which subsists between man and the elements that control his moods and actions; he carries
this parallelism into the minutest details of the more
technical structure of his poems : the amphibrachic
measure in the 'Sweat-shop' is that of the ticking

machine, which in the two lines given above reaches
the highest effect that can be produced by mere words.
In the 'Nightingale to the Laborer,' the intricate versification with its sonnet rhymes, the repetition of the
first line in each stanza with its returning repetition in
the tenth line, the slight variations of the same burden
in each succeeding stanza which saves it from monotony,
are all artifices that the poet has learned from the bird
along his native lake in Poland.   These two examples
will suffice to indicate the astonishing versatility of the
poet in that direction; add to this the wealth of
epithets, and yet extreme simplicity of diction which
never strives for effect, the musicalness of his rhythm,
the chasteness of expression even where the cynical
situations seem to make it difficult to withstand impre-
cations and curses, and we can conceive to what marvellous perfection this untutored poet of the Ghetto
has carried his dialect in which Russian, Polish, Hebrew,
and English words are jostling each other and contending their places with those from the German language.

It was left for a Russian Jew at the end of the
nineteenth century to see and paint hell in colors
not attempted by any one since the days of Dante;
Dante spoke of the hell in the after-life, while Rosenfeld sings of the hell on earth, the hell that he has not
only visited, but that he has lived through.   Another
twenty-five years, and the language in which he has
uttered his despair will be understood in America but
by few, used for literary purposes probably by none.
But Rosenfeld's poetry will survive as a witness of
that lowermost hell which political persecutions, religious and racial hatred, industrial oppression have
created for the Jew at the end of this our enlightened
nineteenth century.

IX. PROSE WRITERS FROM 1817–1863

THE beginning of this century found the Jews of the Russian Empire living in a state bordering on Asiatic barbarism. Ages of persecution had reduced the masses to the lowest condition of existence, had eliminated nearly all signs of civilized life in them, and had succeeded in making them the outcasts they really were. Incredibly dirty in their houses and uncleanly about their persons, ignorant and superstitious even beyond the most superstitious of their Gentile neighbors, dishonest and treacherous not only to others, but even more to their own kind, they presented a sad spectacle of a downtrodden race. The legislators made the effects of the maltreatment of previous lawgivers the pretext for greater oppression until the Jews bade fair to lose the last semblance of human beings. One need only go at this late hour to some small town, away from railroads and highways, where Jews live together compactly, in order to get an idea of what the whole of Russia was a century ago, for in those distant places people are still living as their grandfathers did. Only here and there an individual succeeded in tearing himself away from the realm of darkness to become acquainted with a better existence by means of the Mendelssohnian Haskala. In spite of the very unfavorable conditions of life, or rather on account of them, the Jews, although averse to all instruction, passed the greater part of their lives, that were not given to the earning of a livelihood, in sharpening their wits over Talmudical subtleties. When they came in contact with the learning in Germany, their minds had been trained in the unprofitable but severe school of abstruse casuistry, and they threw themselves with avidity on the new sciences, surpassing even their teachers in the philosophic grasp of the same. Such a man had been Salomon Maimon, the Kantian scholar; such men were later those followers of the Haskala who were active in the regeneration of a Hebrew literature, with whom we have also become acquainted in former chapters through their efforts of enlightening the masses; foremost of them, however, was J. B. Levinsohn, who wrote but little in Judeo-German. He was to the Jews of Russia what Mendelssohn had been half a century before to the Jews of Germany.

The light of the Haskala entered Russia in two ways: through Galicia and through Poland. Galicia was the natural gateway for German enlightenment, as its Jews were instructed by means of works written in Hebrew, which alone, outside of the native dialect, could be understood in the interior of Russia. But this influence was only an indirect one, for soon the German language began to be substituted and understood by the people of Galicia, whereas that has never become the case in the southwest of Russia, that is, in the contiguous territory. The case was different in Russian Poland and Lithuania, for there were many commercial relations between these countries and Germany, and there existed German colonies in that part of the Empire. Consequently the ground was here better prepared for the foreign culture. The seats of the Haskala of these more northern regions were such towns as Zamoszcz in the Government of Lublin, and Warsaw. Roughly speaking, the geographically favored portion of the Jewish Pale was inhabited by the Misnagdim, or strict ritualists, while the south-west was the seat of that fanatical and superstitious sect of the Khassidim against whom nearly all of the satirical literature of the last seventy-five years has been directed.

As early as 1824 there was published a periodical in Warsaw in which the German language, or a corrupt form of it, written with Hebrew characters, was employed to serve as an intermediary of German cul-ture. In the same year B. Lesselroth used this form of German in writing a Polish Grammar[1] for the use of his co-religionists. As has been pointed out before, this mixture of Judeo-German was to serve only as an inter-mediary for the introduction of the literary German which at that time appeared as the only possible alter-native for the homely dialects of the Russian Jews. This mixed language has unfortunately remained the literary norm of the northwest up to the present time, if one may at all speak of norm in arbitrary compounds. In the southwest the dialects were, in the first place, much more distant from the German than the varieties of Lithuania, and the greater distance from German in-fluence made the existence of that corrupt German less possible. At about the same time two books were pub-lished in Judeo-German, one in the south by Mendel Lefin, the other in the north by Chaikel Hurwitz, which became the standards of all future publications in the two divisions of the Jewish Pale. The first, by adhering to the spoken form of the dialect, has led to a normal development of both the language and the liter-

---

[1] B. Lesselroth, *Polnische volkommene Grammatik in jüdisch-deutscher Sprache, für solche, die diese Wissenschaft ohne Hilfe eines Lehrers erlernen wollen*, Warsaw, 1824, 16mo, 76 pp.

ature. The second, being unnatural from the start,
has produced the ugliest excrescences, culminating in
the ugliest productions of Schaikewitsch and his tribe
and still in progress of manufacture.

Hurwitz[1] was only following the natural tendencies of
the Haskala when he chose what he called a pure Judeo-
German for his literary style. In the introduction to
his translation of Campe's ' Discovery of America '
from his own Hebrew version of the same he says :
" This translation of the ' Discovery of America ' I have
made from my Hebrew version. It is written in a pure
Judeo-German without the mixture of Hebrew, Polish,
and Turkish words which one generally finds in the
spoken language." It must however, be noted that
he uses German forms very sparingly, and that but for
his avoiding Slavic and Hebrew words, his language is
really pure. It is only later, beginning with the writings of Dick, that the real deterioration takes place.

This book was published in 1824 at Wilna. Its effect
on the people was very great. Previous to that year
there were no other books to be had except such as
treated on ethical questions, or story-books, which had
been borrowed from older sources two or three centuries
before. Books of instruction there were none. This
was the first ray that penetrated the Ghettos from without. The people had no knowledge of America and

---

[1] This is the name given by Gottlober in his *Sichrōnes*, in *Jüd. Volksbib.*, Vol. I. p. 255, for the author of the ' Columbus,' but it appears
that it was Günsburg who wrote it in Hebrew ; and as in the Judeo-
German translation the translator speaks of having translated this work
from his Hebrew form, it is likely that Günsburg ought to be substituted for Hurwitz. There are four copies of that work in the Harvard
Library. Two of them are late remodellings ; the other two have no
title-pages and seem to have had none, so that I cannot ascertain the
dates of their printing.

Columbus, and now they were furnished not only with a
good story of adventure, but in the introduction to the
book they found a short treatise on geography, — the
first worldly science with which they now became acquainted. It is interesting to note here by way of parallel that a few years later the regeneration of Bulgaria
from its centuries of darkness began with a small work
on geography, a translation from an American school-
book, published at Smyrna. It is true that to the
disciples of the Haskala works on the sciences were
accessible in Hebrew translations, but these were confined to a very small circle of readers, and their influence on the masses was insignificant. If the followers
of the Haskala had not accepted blindly Mendelssohn's
verdict against the Judeo-German language, which was
true only of the language spoken by the Jews of Germany, but had furnished a literature of enlightenment
in the vernacular of the people instead of the language
of the select few, their efforts would have been crowned
with far greater success. By subscribing uncondition-
ally to the teachings of their leader, they retarded the
course of events by at least half a century and widened
the chasm between the learned and the people, which it
had been their desire to bridge. English missionaries
proceed much more wisely in their efforts to evangelize
a people. They always choose the everyday language
in which to speak to them, not the tongue of literature,
which is less accessible to them. Mainly by their
efforts the Modern Armenian and Bulgarian have been
raised to a literary dignity, and with it there has always
followed a regeneration of letters and a national consciousness that has in some cases led to political independence. The missionaries have not always reaped a
religious harvest, but their work has borne fruit in

many other ways. In the beginning of this century they also directed their attention to the Christianization of the Jews of Poland. The few works that they published in the pursuit of their aim, especially the New Testament, are written in an excellent vernacular, far superior to the one employed by Hurwitz and Lesselroth. It is a pity the Jewish writers of the succeeding generations, particularly in the northwest of Russia, did not learn wisdom from the English missionaries.

'The Discovery of America' has had edition after edition, and has been read, at first surreptitiously, then more openly, by all who could read, young and old, men and women. But Hurwitz was not forgiven by the fanatics for descending to write on worldly matters, and after his death it became the universal belief that the earth would not hold him for his misdeed and that he was walking around as a ghost, in vain seeking a resting-place.

In the south the first impulse for writing in Judeo-German was given by the translations of the Proverbs, the Psalms, and Ecclesiastes by Minchas Mendel Lefin. Of these only the Psalms were published in 1817; Ecclesiastes was printed in 1873, while the Proverbs and a novel said to be written by him have never been issued. To write in Jargon was to the men of the Haskala a crime against reason, and Lefin was violently attacked by Tobias Feder and others. He found, however, a sympathizer in Jacob Samuel Bick, who warmly defended him against Feder, and by degrees some of the best followers of the Haskala followed his good example. Ettinger and Gottlober are known to have received their first lessons in Judeo-German composition through the writings of Lefin, while by inference one may regard him also as the prototype of Aksenfeld and

Zweifel. It was not so easy to brave the world with the despised Jargon, and up to the sixties not one of the works of these writers appeared in print. They passed in manuscript form from hand to hand, until the favorable time had come for their publication ; and then they were generally not printed for those who wrote them, but for those who possessed a manuscript, so that on the first editions of their works their names do not appear at all.

Lefin's translations mark an era in Judeo-German literature. He broke with the traditional language used in story-books and ethical works of previous centuries, for that was merely a continuation of the language of the first prints, in which local differences were obliterated in order to make the works accessible to the German Jews of the East and the West. It was not a spoken language, and it had no literary norm. In the meanwhile the vernacular of the Slavic Jews had so far departed from the book language as to make the latter almost unintelligible to the masses. Lefin chose to remedy that by abandoning entirely the tradition, and by writing exactly as the people spoke. He has solved his problem in a remarkable way ; for although he certainly knew well the German language, there is not a trace of it in his writings. He is not at a loss for a single word ; if it does not exist in his dialect, he forms it in the spirit of the dialect, and does not borrow it from German. As linguistic material for the study of the Judeo-German in the beginning of this century the writings of Lefin, Aksenfeld, Ettinger, Levinsohn, and Gottlober are invaluable. But that is not the only value of Lefin's writings. By acknowledging the people's right to be instructed by means of an intelligible language, he at the same time opened up avenues

for the formation of a popular literature, based on an
intimate acquaintance with the mental life of the people.   In fact, he himself gave the example for that new
departure by writing a novel 'The First Khassid.'   In
the northwest the masses were not so much opposed to
the new culture as in the south, hence the writers could
at once proceed to bring out books of popular instruction
clad in the form of stories.   But the Khassidim of the
south would have rejected anything that in any way
reminded them of a civilization different from their
own.   In order to accomplish results among them, they
had to be more cautious and to approach their readers
in such a way that they were conscious only of the
entertainment and not of the instruction which was
couched in the story.   This demanded not only the use
of a pure vernacular, but also a detailed knowledge of
the mental habits of the people.   As their conditions
of life in no way resembled those of any other people in
Europe, their literature had to be quite unique ; and
the works of the earlier writers are so peculiar in regard to language, diction, and style as to baffle the
translator, who must remodel whole pages before he can
render the original intelligibly.   Of such a character
are the dramas of Aksenfeld, Ettinger, and J. B. Levinsohn.

Ettinger, the first modern Judeo-German poet, has
also written a drama under the name of 'Serkele, or
the False Anniversary.'   His bias for German culture
shows itself in the general structure of his play, which
is like that of Lessing's dramas.   The plot is laid in
Lemberg, and represents the struggle of German civilization with the mean and dishonest ways of the older
generation.   Serkele has but one virtue, — that of an
egotistical love for her only daughter, the half-edu-

cated, silly Freude Altele.   In order to get possession
of some jewels deposited with her by her brother for
his daughter Hinde, she invents the story of his death.
She is anxious to marry her daughter to Gavriel Händler,
who is represented to her as a rich speculator, but who
is in reality a common thief.   He steals the casket containing the jewels.   When the theft is discovered she
throws the guilt on Marcus Redlich, a student of medicine, her daughter's private teacher, and Hinde's lover.
Hinde, too, is accused of complicity, and both are taken
in chains through the town.   They pass a hostlery where
a stranger has just arrived, to whom Händler is trying
to sell the jewels.   The stranger is Hinde's father.
He recognizes his property, and seizes the thief just as
his daughter and her lover are taken by.   A general
recognition follows, and all is righted.   He finally for-
gives his sister, gives a dowry to Freude Altele, who
marries the innkeeper, while his daughter is united to
Marcus Redlich.

As in all the early productions of Judeo-German
literature, there are in that drama two distinct classes
of characters: the ideal persons, the uncle, Marcus
Redlich and Hinde, and the real men and women who
are taken out of actual life.   On the side of the first
is all virtue, while among the others are to be found
the ugliest forms of vice.   A worse shrew than Serkele
has hardly ever been depicted.   Her speeches are composed of a series of curses, in which the Jargon is peculiarly inventive, interrupted by a stereotyped complaint
of her ever failing health.   She hates her niece with the
hatred that the tyrant has for the object of his oppression, and she is quick to accuse her of improper conduct,
although herself of very lax morals.   Nobody in the
house escapes the fury of her tongue, and her honest

but weak husband has to yield to the inevitable. The other characters are all well drawn, and the play is an excellent portrayal of domestic life of seventy-five years ago. It was written early in the twenties, but was printed only in 1861, since when it has had several editions.

In 1828 J. B. Levinsohn wrote his Hebrew work, 'Teudo Beisroel,' by which the Haskala took a firm footing in Russia. About the same time there circulated manuscript copies of a Judeo-German essay by the same author, in which a sad picture of Jewish communal affairs was painted in vigorous and idiomatic words. This essay, called 'The World Turned Topsy-Turvy,'[1] is given in the form of a conversation by three persons, of whom one is a stranger from a better country where the affairs of the Jews are administered honestly. The other two in turn lay before him an array of facts which it is painful to regard as having existed in reality. It is interesting to note that the stranger, who is Levinsohn himself, advocates the formation of agricultural colonies for the Jews, by which he hoped to better their wretched condition and to gain for them respect among those who accused them of being averse to work.

The most original and most prolific Judeo-German writer of this early period was Israel Aksenfeld.[2] He was born in the last quarter of the eighteenth century, and had passed the early days of his life in the neigh-

[1] J. B. Levinsohn, *Die hefker Welt*, in *Jüd. Volksbib.*, Vol. I. pp. 133–147. His biography is given in the same place, by B. Natansohn, on pp. 122–132. Both together are to be found in Natansohn's *Die papierne Brück'* (*q.v.*).

[2] For review of his works see O. Lerner, *Kritičeskij razbor pojavivšichsja nedavno na evrejsko-německom žargoně sočinenij I. Aksenfelda*, etc., Odessa, 1868, 8vo, 15 pp.

borhood of the Rabbi of Braslow, a noted Khassid, being himself a follower of that sect. Later in life, in the fifties, he is remembered as a notary public in Odessa. He was a man of great culture. Those who knew him then speak in the highest terms of the kindly old man that he was. They also like to dwell on the remarkable qualities of his cultured wife, from whom he is supposed to have received much inspiration.[1] That is all that is known of his life. Gottlober mentions also in his 'Recollections' that he had written twenty-six books, and that according to Aksenfeld's own statements they had been written in the twenties or thereabout. Of these only five were printed in the sixties; the rest are said to be stored away in a loft in Odessa, where they are held as security for a debt incurred by the trustee of his estate. Although this fact is known to some of the Jews of that city, no one has taken any steps to redeem the valuable manuscripts. This is to be greatly regretted, as his books throw light on a period of history for which there is no other documentary evidence except that given by the writings of men who lived at that time.

Of the five books printed, one is a novel, the other four are dramas. The first, under the name of 'The Fillet of Pearls,' shows up the hypocrisy and rascality of the Khassidic miracle-workers, as only one who has himself been initiated in their doings could relate them. The hero of the novel is Mechel Mazeewe. He is discovered eating on a minor fast day, and the Rabbi uses this as an

---

[1] She was very fond of Jean Paul Richter, and it is not at all impossible that the peculiar humor contained in her husband's books is due to a transference of that author's style to the more primitive conditions of the Judeo-German novel. His was a gifted family : one of his sons became an artist, the other a famous professor of medicine at Paris.

excuse for extorting all the money the poor fellow had earned by teaching little children and young women. His engagement to one of his pupils, the daughter of the beadle, is broken off for the same reason. Disgusted with his town, he goes away from it in order to earn a living elsewhere. Good fortune takes him to Breslau, where he, for the first time, discovers that there are also clean, honest, peaceful Jews. He is regenerated, and returns to his native town, where in the meantime the miracle-working Rabbi has succeeded in rooting out the last vestige of heresy. At the house of the Rabbi, Mechel has an occasion to prove the falseness of his pretensions to the assembled people. Mechel is reunited with his bride.

This bare skeleton of the plot is developed with great care, and is adorned with a variety of incidents, each forming a story within the story. The biting satire, the sharp humor, the rapid development of situations, are only excelled by his dramatic sense, which makes him pass rapidly from descriptions, without elaborating them to the form of dialogue. His mastery of the dialect is remarkable; for although one can here and there detect his intimate acquaintance with German literature, there is not a single case where he has been led under obligations to the German language in thought or a word: German is as foreign to him as French or Latin. Of his dramas it will be sufficient to discuss one to show their general structure. The most dramatic of these is the one entitled 'The First Recruit' and tells of the terrible time in 1827 when the Ukase drafting Jewish young men into the army had for the first time been promulgated. To the ignorant masses it seemed as though the world would come to an end. To avoid the great misfortune of having their sons

taken away from them, they married them off before
they had reached their teens; finding that that did
not prevent the 'catchers' from seizing them, maimed,
halt, sickly men were preferred as husbands to their
daughters; in short, all was done to avert the unspeak-
able calamity of serving the Czar.   As in the novel,
there are plots within the plot, and didactic passages
are woven into the play without in the least disturbing
its unity.

The tragedy consists of eight scenes.   The first
opens with a noisy meeting at the house of Solomon
Rascal, a Parnes-Chōdesch (representative of the Jewish
community), on a Saturday afternoon.   The cause of
the disturbance is the order to furnish one recruit from
their town, which had just been brought in from the
capital of the district by two soldiers.   The assembled
kahal are wondering whether it is incumbent upon
them to sign the receipt of the order, while the infuriated mob without is clamoring that the Ukase will be
ineffective as long as not signed by the representatives
of the Congregation.   The kahal is divided on the
subject, and the women take a part in the discussion,
making matters lively.   Upon the advice of one of the
men, the meeting is adjourned to the house of Aaron
Wiseman, the honored merchant of their town of Nowhere, where they expect to get a satisfactory solution
in their perplexity.   The second scene is the ideal scene
of the play.   Here is depicted the happy and orderly
home life of the cultured merchant, — the reverse
of the picture just portrayed.   Jisrolik the Ukrainian
arrives and announces the decision of the kahal to refer
the matter to him.   Aaron Wiseman explains how the
Emperor had not intended to bring new misfortunes
upon the Jews by the mandate, but how by imposing

on them the honorable duty of defending their country, he was investing them with a new privilege upon which greater liberties would follow. This he farther elucidates in the next scene before the assembled representatives of the Congregation. The fourth scene is laid in the inn, where we are introduced to Nachman the Big, the practical joker and terror of the town. In the following scene, Aaron Wiseman advises the kahal to use a ruse by which Nachman will voluntarily offer himself as a soldier, thus freeing the town from the unpleasant duty of making a more worthy family unhappy. Wiseman explains that Nachman has been a source of trouble to all, and that military service would be the only thing that would keep him from a possible life of crime. The ruse is accomplished in the following manner : it is known that Nachman has been casting his eyes on Früme, the good and beautiful daughter of Risches the Red, the tax-gatherer. It is proposed to send a schadchen to Nachman, pretending that Früme's parents seek an alliance with him, and that Früme loves him, and that she wants to get a proof of his affection in his offering himself up as a soldier. The apparent incongruity of the request is amply accounted for in the play by the fact that he who has lost his heart also loses his reason. In the next two scenes the plot is carried out, and Nachman becomes a soldier. The last scene contains the tragic denouement. Chanzi, the go-between, comes to the house of Früme and tells her of the fraud perpetrated on Nachman. But, alas, Früme actually loves Nachman, and she silently suffers at the recital of the story. The climax is reached when her father arrives and tells of Nachman's self-sacrifice, how he has given himself up for the love he bears her, how they put him in chains and took him away. Früme bears her secret to the last, but her heart breaks, and she dies. The sorrow of her parents is great. During the lamentation Nachman's blind mother arrives, led by a little girl. She has learned of Chanzi's treachery, and breaks out in loud curses against those who took part in the plot. As she steps forward, she touches the dead body of her whom Nachman had thought to be his bride. She addresses her as though she were alive and consoles her that she need not be ashamed of Nachman, who had been an inoffensive, though somewhat wild, boy. While speaking this, she faints over her body.

The characters are all admirably delineated, and how true to nature the whole play is one can see from a matter-of-fact story, by Dick,[1] of the effects of the Ukase on the city of Wilna. Except for the tragic plot, the drama may serve as a historical document of the event, and is a valuable material for the study of the Jewish mind in the beginning of Nicholas's reign. This must also be said of the other plays of Aksenfeld, which all deal with conditions of contemporary Jewish society.

Similar to Aksenfeld's subject in 'The Fillet of Pearls' is the comedy 'The Marriage Veil' by Gottlober, which he wrote in 1838. Jossele, a young man with modern ideas, is to be married to a one-eyed monster, while his sweetheart, Freudele, is to be mated on the same day with a disfigured fool. By Jossele's machinations, in which he takes advantage of the superstitions of the people, he is united under the marriage veil to Freudele, while the two monstrosities are married to each other. This is found out too late to be mended. This plot is only an excuse to show

[1] A. M. Dick, *Der erster Nabor*, etc., Wilna, 1871.

up the hypocrisy and rascality of the miracle-working
Rabbi in even a more grotesque way than in 'The
Fillet of Pearls.' A much finer work is his story
'The Transmigration,' which, however, is said to be
based on a similar story in the Hebrew, by Erter. In
this a dead soul, previous to finding its final resting-
place, relates of its many transmigrations ere reaching
its last stage. The succession of mundane existences
is strictly in keeping with the previous moral life of
the soul. It starts out with being a Khassidic singer,
who, like all the followers of the Rabbi, is represented
as an ignorant dupe. After his death he naturally
is turned into a horse, the emblem of good-natured
stupidity according to the popular Jewish idea. Then
he is in turn a Precentor, a fish, a tax-gatherer, a dog,
a critic, an ass, a doctor, a leech, a usurer, a pig, a con-
tractor. By far the most interesting and dramatic
incident is that of the doctor, who is trying to pass for
a pious Jew, but who is caught eating lobsters, which
are forbidden by the Mosaic Law, and who dies from
strangulation in his attempt to swallow a lobster to
hide his crime. The story is told in a fluent manner,
is very witty, and puts in strong relief the various characters which are satirized.

Like the poetry of the same period, the prose literature of the writers previous to the sixties is of a militant
nature. It had for its aim the dispersion of ignorance
and superstition, and the introduction of the Haskala
and Western civilization among the Jews of Russia.
The main attack of all these early works was directed
against the fanaticism of the Khassidic sect, against
the hypocrisy of its miracle-working Rabbis in whose
interest it lay to oppose the light at all cost. But the
authors not only attacked the evil, they also showed

the way for a reform : this they did by contrasting the low, sordid instincts of the older generation with the quiet, honest lives of the new. Of course, the new generation is all German. The ideal characters of Ettinger's drama, Aksenfeld's hero in 'The Fillet of Pearls,' Gottlober's Jossele, have all received their training in Germany. At the same time, in accordance with the Mendelssohnian School, these ideal persons are not opposed to the tenets of Judaism ; on the contrary, they are represented as the advocates of a pure religion in place of the base substitute of Khassidism. Outside of the didactic purpose, which, however, does not obtrude on the artistic development of the story, the Judeo-German literature of that period owes its impulse to the three German authors, Lessing, Schiller, Jean Paul Richter. As regards its language, the example set by Lefin prevails, and all the productions are written in an idiomatic, pure dialect of the author's nearest surroundings. There is but one exception to that, and that is 'The Discovery of America,' which, being mainly intended for a Lithuanian public, is written in a language which makes approaches to the literary German, whereby it opened wide the way to misuses of various kinds.

X. PROSE WRITERS FROM 1863–1881:
ABRAMOWITSCH

ZEDERBAUM,[1] the friend and fellow-townsman of
Ettinger, began in 1863 to publish a Judeo-German
weekly under the name of *Kol-mewasser*, as a supplement to his Hebrew weekly, the *Hameliz*. This was the
first organ of the kind for Russia, for the one edited in
Warsaw forty years before was not written in the dialect
of the people. Let us look for the cause of such an innovation.

The advocates of the Haskala regarded it as one of
their sacred duties to spread culture wherever and
whenever they could do so. This they did through
the medium of the Hebrew and the Judeo-German.
The first was a literary language, the other was not
regarded as worthy of being such. If, therefore, there
was some cause to feel an author's pride in attaching
one's name to productions in the first tongue, there was
no inducement to subscribe it to works in the second.
It was, to a certain extent, a sacrifice that the authors
made in condescending to compose in Judeo-German,
and the only reward they could expect was the good
their books would do in disseminating the truth among
their people. The songs of M. Gordon and Gottlober,
and the works of Ettinger and Aksenfeld, were passed
anonymously throughout the whole land. The books
were not even printed, but were manifolded in manuscript form by those who had the Haskala at heart. A

---

[1] Short biography in *Sseefer Sikorōn*, p. 97.

few years before the issue of the *Kol-mewasser*, the efforts of these men began to bear ample fruit. It was no longer dangerous to be called a ' German,' and many Jewish children were being sent to the gymnasia, to which the Government had in the meanwhile admitted them.   The Rabbinical schools at Wilna and Zhitomir, too, were graduating sets of men who had been receiving religious instruction according to the improved methods of the Haskala.   It was then that some of the works written decades before, for the first time saw daylight, but more as a matter of curiosity of what had been done long ago, than with any purpose.   It would even then have been somewhat risky to sign one's name to them for fear of ridicule, and no native firm would readily undertake their publication.   Thus the first two works of Aksenfeld were issued from a press at Leipsic in 1862, while Ettinger's ' Serkele ' had appeared the year before at Johannisburg.   Only the following year Linetzki's ' Poems ' were published at Kiev, and, by degrees, the authors took courage to abandon their anonyms and pseudonyms for their own names.   The time was ripe for a periodical to collect the scattered forces, for there was still work to be done among those who had not mastered the sacred language, and they were in the majority.   At that juncture, Zederbaum began to issue his supplement to the *Hameliz*.

This new weekly was not only the crowning of the work of the past generation of writers, it became also the seminary of a new set of authors.   It fostered the talents of those who, for want of a medium of publication, might have devoted their strength entirely to Hebrew, or would have attempted to assimilate to themselves the language of the country.   In the second year of the existence of the periodical, there appeared in it

'The Little Man,' the first work of Abramowitsch, who was soon to lead Judeo-German literature to heights never attempted before by it, and with whom a new and more fruitful era begins.

Solomon Jacob Abramowitsch [1] was born in 1835, in the town of Kopyl, in the Government of Minsk. He received his Jewish instruction in a *Cheeder*, and later in a *Jeschiwe*, a kind of Jewish academy. He consequently, up to his seventeenth year, had had no other instruction except in religious lore. His knowledge of Hebrew was so thorough that, at the age of seventeen, he was able to compose verses in that language. He lost his father early, and his mother married a second time. When he was eighteen years old, there arrived in his native town a certain Awremel the Lame, who had been leading a vagabond's life over the southern part of Russia. He told so many wonderful stories about Volhynia, where, according to his words, there flowed milk and honey, that many of the inhabitants of Kopyl were thinking of emigrating to the south. Awremel also persuaded Abramowitsch's aunt to go with him in search of her absent husband. That she did, taking her nephew along with her. It soon turned out, however, that Awremel was exploiting them as objects of charity, by collecting alms over the breadth and length of the country. For several months he kept zigzagging in his wagon from town to town, wherever he expected to find charitable Jews, until at last they arrived a certain distance beyond Kremenets. Here they passed a carriage from which proceeded a voice call-

---

[1] For fuller information on the life and works of Abramowitsch see his autobiography in *Sseefer Sikorōn*, pp. 117–126; see also the references in the *Sistematičeskij ukazatel'*, p. 286, Nos. 4663–4669, of which No. 4665 is the most important.

ing Abramowitsch by his given name. They stopped,
and Abramowitsch was astonished to discover his friend
of his childhood, who had, in the meantime, become a
chorister in Kremenets. The latter invited his youth-
ful friend to go back to town with him, promising to
take care of him. This the young wanderer was only
too glad to do, for he wished to be rid of Awremel, who
had been tantalizing him with his almsbegging. The
Precentor, who was in the carriage with the chorister,
paid off the driver, and Abramowitsch started with
them back to town, where a new period began in his
life.

His thorough acquaintance with the Talmud and the
Hebrew language soon gained him many friends, and he
was able to make a living by teaching the children of
the wealthier inhabitants. One of his friends advised
him to make the acquaintance of the poet Gottlober,
who, at that time, was teaching in one of the local
Jewish schools. The old man who was giving him that
counsel added : " Go to see him some evening when no
one will notice you, and make his acquaintance. He is
an apostate who shaves his beard, and he does not enjoy
the confidence of our community. Nor do we permit
young men to cultivate an acquaintance with him ; but
you are a learned man, and you will know how to meet
the statements of that heretic. He is a fine Hebrew
scholar, and it might do you good to meet him. Remember the words of Rabbi Meier : ' Eat the wholesome fruit, and cast away the rind.' I'll tell the beadle
to show you the way to the apostate."

On the evening of the following day, Abramowitsch
betook himself, with a copy of a Hebrew drama he had
composed, to the house of Gottlober. The latter smiled
at the childish attempt of the young Talmudist, but he

did not fail to recognize the talent that needed only the fostering care of a teacher to reach its full development, and he himself offered his services to him, and invited him to be a frequent caller at his house. Here, under the guidance of Gottlober's elder daughter, he received his first instruction in European languages, and in the rudiments of arithmetic. He swallowed with avidity everything he could get, and soon he was able to write a Hebrew essay on education which was printed in the *Hamagid*, and which attracted much attention at the time. His fate soon led him to Berdichev, "the Jewish Moscow," where he married for a second time, and settled down for many years. In 1859 his first serious work, still in Hebrew, was published. In 1863 began his Judeo-German career, in which he still continues, and which has made him famous among all who read in that language.

The tradition of the Haskala came down to Abramowitsch in an uninterrupted succession, from Mendel Lefin through Ettinger and Gottlober. He, too, started out with the set purpose of spreading enlightenment among his people, and in his first two works we find a sharp demarkation between the two kinds of character, the ideal and the real. But he was too much of an artist by nature to persevere in his didactic attitude, and before long he abandoned entirely that field, to devote his undivided energy to the production of purely artistic works. Even his earlier books, in which he combats some public nuisance, differ materially from those of his predecessors in that they reflect not only conditions of society as they actually existed at his time, but in that his characters are true studies from nature. No one of his contemporaries reading, for example, his 'The Little Man,' could be in doubt of who was meant by this or that name. The portrait was so closely, and yet so artistically, copied from some well-known denizen of Berdichev that there could be no doubt as to the identity. There are even more essential points in his stories and dramas in which he widely departs from his predecessors. While these saw in a religious reform and in German culture a solution out of the degraded state into which their co-religionists had fallen, he preached that a reform from within must precede all regeneration from without. While they directed their attacks against the Khassidim as the enemies of light, and their Rabbis as their spiritual guides, he cautiously avoided all discussions of religion and culture, and sought in local communal reforms a basis for future improvements. To him the physical well-being of the masses was a more important question than their spiritual enlightenment, and according to his ideas a moral progress was only possible after the economical condition had been considerably bettered. His precursors had looked upon the Haskala as the most precious treasure, to be preferred to all else in life. Abramowitsch loves his people more than wisdom and culture, and the more oppressed and suffering those he loves, the more earnest and the more fervent are his words in their behalf. He is the advocate of the poor against the rich, the downtrodden against the oppressor, the meek and long-suffering against the haughty usurper of the people's rights. He is, consequently, worshipped by the masses, and has been hated and persecuted by those whose meanness, rascality, and hypocrisy he has painted in such glaring colors. He had even once to flee for his life, so enraged had the representatives of the kahal become at their lifelike pictures in one of his dramas. His love for the people is an all-pervading passion, for man is his

Godhead. There is a divine element in the lowest of human beings, and he thinks it worth while to discover it and to bring it to light, that it may outshine all the vices that have beclouded it. He turns beggar with the beggar he describes, becomes insane with him who ponders over the ills of this earth, and suffers the criminal's punishment. He at all times identifies himself with those of whom he speaks.

In the more external form of composition there is again a vast progress from the writings of Lefin to the style and diction of Abramowitsch. Lefin was the first to show what vigor there was in the use of the everyday vernacular. Ettinger, Aksenfeld, and Gottlober have well adapted that simple, unadorned speech to the requirements of literary productions; but it was only Abramowitsch who demonstrated what wealth of wordbuilding, what possibilities of expression, lay dormant in the undeveloped dialects of Judeo-German. He was peculiarly fitted to enrich the language by new formations, for having passed the first eighteen years of his life in Lithuania and passing the greater part of his later years in the Southwest, he was enabled to draw equally from the source of his native Lithuanian dialect and the spoken variety of his new home. He has welded the two so well that his works can be read with equal ease in the North and in the South, whereas the language of Aksenfeld offers a number of difficulties to the Lithuanians and even the Polish Jews whose dialect the Southern variety resembles. In diction he differs from his masters in that he substitutes a regular prose structure for the semi-dramatic utterances of the older narration, without affecting the natural speeches of the characters wherever these are introduced. In these cases he becomes so idiomatic as to baffle the best translator, who must be frequently satisfied with mere circumlocutions. He also abandons the anonym of the former generation for a pseudonym, Mendele the Book-pedler, which is, however, but a thin disguise for his real name, for his writings are of such an individuality that there can be no doubt about their authorship. Beginning with Abramowitsch style is regarded as an important requisite of a Judeo-German work.

— Now we shall turn to the discussion of his several books. The subject of his first, 'The Little Man,' is an autobiography of a man, who, by low flattery, vile ser-vility, and all dishonest ways, rises to high places of emolument which he uses entirely in order to enrich himself at the expense of the people. Such men had been the bane of Jewish communities in the middle of our century. In Berdichev it was, at the time of the publication of the book, Jacob Josef Alperin, who by similar means had come to be the right hand of the Governor General, Bibikov; but far more vile than he was Hersch Meier Held, who stood in the same relation to Alperin that the latter occupied to the Governor General. That flunky of a flunky is personified as the hero of the story, Isaac Abraham Takif. In this work we still have the ideal persons of the older writers. We are introduced there to a poor, honest, and cultured family, in whom one cannot fail to recognize his master and friend, Gottlober, and his daughter.

If this work made him a host of friends among those who were the victims of Alperin and Held, the next drama he wrote endangered his stay in Berdichev, for the persons attacked in it, the representatives of the kahal, would not shrink from any crime to rid them-selves of a man who, like Abramowitsch, had come to be a power and a stumbling-block to their incredible rascalities. The greatest curse of the Jewish community in Russia had ever been the meat and candle tax, which all had to pay, nominally to support communal institutions, but the greater part of which went into the pockets of the representatives of the kahal to whom the tax was farmed out. No meat and no candle could be purchased without that arbitrary imposition by the members of the kahal, who in their fiendish craving for money increased the original cost of meat several fold, and who spared no means, however criminal, to silence any opposition to their doings. It is these men that Abramowitsch had the courage to hold up to the scorn of the people in his 'The Meat-Tax, or the Gang of City Benefactors.'[1] He had to flee for his life, but the drama did its work. It even attracted the attention of the Government, which tried to remedy the evil. It became the possession of the people, and many of its salient sentences have become everyday proverbs. The revolt against that Gang of City Benefactors of Berdichev was so great that Moses Josef Chodrower, whom all recognized as the prototype of the arch-rascal Spodek in the play, and who had been a prominent and wealthy merchant, was soon driven into bankruptcy by the infuriated population that refused to support him. That was the first time that a literary production written in Judeo-German had become a factor in social affairs. A Russian troupe that was then playing at Berdichev wanted to give a Russian version of the drama, but was restrained from doing so by the machinations of the kahal. The book had done its work thoroughly.

In the same year there appeared his story from the life of the Jewish mendicants, 'Fischke the Lame.'[2]

---

[1] Translated into Russian by Petrikovski.

[2] Reviews of this work are in *Jüd. Volksblatt*, Vol. VIII. (Beilage),

This psychological study of the impulses of the lowest dregs of society is probably unique in all literature. It is a love story from the world of the lame and the halt that constitute the profession of mendicants in the Jewish part of every Russian town in the West. But it is not merely the love of Fischke the Lame for a beggar girl and the jealousy of his blind wife, who tyrannizes over him in spite of her affliction, that we are made acquainted with in that remarkable book. We are introduced there to a class of people with entirely different motives, different aims in life, from those we are accustomed to see about us. They hide from daylight and have a morality of their own; but yet they are possessed of the passions that we find in beings endowed with all the senses and enjoying the advantages of well-organized society. One must have lived among them, been one of them, so to reproduce their language, their thoughts, as Abramowitsch has done in this novel; and one must have broad sympathies with all humankind to be able to find the divine spark ablaze even in the lowest men.

His next work, ' The Dobbin,' [1] is the most perfect of his productions. It unites into one a psychological study of a demented man, with a delicate allegory, in which the history of his people in Russia is delineated, thus serving as a transition from the pure novel in his former production to the composite allegory in his poetical work ' Judel ' which was published a few years later. It combines a biting satire with a tragic story; it is a prophecy and a history in one. If the ' Meat Tax ' had made him the favorite of the masses who

pp. 1385-1396, by J. Levi; and *Voschod*, 1880, Nos. 1, 2, 4, by M. G. Morgulis.
    [1] Translated into Polish by Klemens Junosza.

suffered from the oppression of the members of the kahal, ' The Dobbin ' was calculated to endear him with all who professed the Jewish faith ; for while the first pointed out an internal evil which could be remedied, the second painted in vivid colors their sufferings in the present and the misfortunes which awaited them in the future, which were entirely of an external nature over which they had no control. It showed them more graphically than anything that had been said heretofore how helpless they were to meet the charges which were continually cast against them by the Gentiles and the Government. Abramowitsch foresaw that the turning-point in the inner life of his race was near at hand, that the call to progress of the early writers had availed them little in righting them with the world without, that his own productions acquainting them with their weak points from within were now out of place, and that soon they would need only words of consolation such as are uttered when a great calamity overtakes a people.

In 1873 hardly any one dreamed of the possibility of the riots against the Jews that were to be inaugurated eight years later, for it was just then that the highest privileges had been granted to them, and the assimilation had been going on to such an extent that Judeo-German literature would have been a thing of the past, had not the writers of the previous decade continued now and then to issue a volume of their works. But Abramowitsch saw that the reforms of Alexander II. were not conceived in the same liberal spirit as had been proposed by Nicholas I., and that sooner or later they would be followed by retrenchments such as would throw the Jews back into conditions far worse than those they had been in half a century before ; for they would find no avenues for their many new energies which they had developed in the meanwhile. It is this coming event that the author has depicted in his fantastic story, 'The Dobbin.' Jisrolik has made up his mind to acquire Gentile culture, and he is preparing himself for an examination in the Gymnasium. He falls in with a Dobbin that is pursued by everybody, and this so affects him, together with the worry over his examination, that he becomes demented, and he imagines that the Dobbin is talking to him. After that the animal is introduced as a transmigrated soul that tells its biography. The Dobbin is the personification of the Jewish race. The book was very popular, and although there was a demand for new editions, the Russian Government would not permit them, as even this veiled allegory appeared to it as too open an accusation of its acts. Only sixteen years later the censor relaxed and allowed a second edition to appear.

In 1879 there was published by Abramowitsch a volume entitled 'The Wanderings of Benjamin the Third,'[1] which is an excellent pendant to Cervantes's famous work and which has therefore been called by its Polish translator 'The Jewish Don Quixote.' The subject of his caricature was a real fellow, named Tscharny, who had been employed by some French society to undertake a scientific journey into the Caucasus, but who was entirely unfit for the work, as he had a very superficial knowledge of geography. For his more immediate purpose Abramowitsch copied a crazy fellow who was all the time citing passages from a fantastic Hebrew geography he had been poring over. Out of this Abramowitsch evolved the story of the Quixotic fellow who starts out to discover the mystic river Sambation and the tribe of the Red Jews, but who never gets any

---

[1] Translated into Polish by Klemens Junosza.

further than the town of Berdichev and its dirty river Gnilopyat.

Of the other works[1] of Abramowitsch the most important is his drama 'The Enlistment,' which deals with the same subject as Aksenfeld's 'The First Recruit,' but referring it to more modern times. After a long silence the author has again resumed his pen, and one may look forward for some new classics in Judeo-German. He has also written a number of popular scientific articles, which have been widely circulated by means of calendars which he has edited. His popularity as a writer is best illustrated by the fact that for a series of years his income from his books and calendars has amounted to three thousand roubles a year. Considering the poverty of the reading public, for whom cheap editions have to be issued, and the general custom of borrowing books rather than buying them, this will appear as a very great sum indeed. Many of the younger authors lovingly refer to him as the 'Grandfather,' although no one has attempted to imitate him either in manner or style. He forms by himself a school, and would have been the last to write in the dialect but for the occurrences of the eighties that have been the cause of a new set of writers who have no reason to follow the authors of the period of the Haskala, but who dip their pens in the blood that has been shed in the riots, or who from the same cause speak to their brethren, though not of them.

[1] His shorter stories have appeared in *Hausfreund*, Vol. I. pp. 128–134; Vol. III. pp. 1–9; Vol. IV. pp. 3–25; *Jüd. Volksbib.*, Vol. II. pp. 7–93; *Jüd. Volkskalender*, Vol. III. pp. 53–64.

XI. PROSE WRITERS FROM 1863-1881 : LINETZKI, DICK

In 1867 the *Kol-mewasser* began publishing a serial story by Linetzki[1] under the name of 'The Polish Boy.' Its popularity at once became so great that to satisfy the impatient public the editor was induced to print the whole in book form as a supplement long before it had been finished in the periodical. The interest in the book lay not so much in the fact that it was written with boundless humor as in its being practically an autobiography in which the readers found so much to bring back recollections of their own sad youth. They found there a graphic description of the whole course of a Khassid's life as no one before Linetzki had painted it, — as only one could paint it who had himself been one of the sect, standing in an even nearer relation to their Rabbis than had been the case with Aksenfeld. While the latter had been a follower of one, Linetzki had narrowly escaped being a Rabbi himself, had suffered all kinds of persecution for attempting to abandon the narrow sphere of a Khassid's activity, and knew from bitter experience all the facts related in his work. The story of his own life, unadorned by any fiction, was dramatic enough to be worth telling, but he has enriched it with so many details of everyday incidents as to change the simple biography into a valuable cyclopedia of the life and thoughts of his contemporaries, in

---

[1] Short notice of his works in *Sseefer Sikorōn*, pp. 59, 60; cf. also notices mentioned in *Sistematičeskij ukazatel*, p. 286, Nos. 4670–4672.

which one may get information on the folklore, games, education, superstitions, and habits of his people in the middle of our century.

Linetzki was born in 1839 in Vinitsa, in the Government of Podolsk. At the age of six he was far enough advanced in Hebrew to begin the study of the Talmud. At ten he had passed through all the Jewish schools, and there was nothing left for his teachers to teach him. He was an *Ilui*, an accomplished scholar, but his father, who was a Khassidic Rabbi, was not satisfied with his mere scholastic acquirements; he wanted him to be initiated in all the mysteries of the Cabbala which would make of him a fanatical Khassid. He was put for that purpose in the hands of a few of his blind followers, who did not spare any means to kill the last ray of reason in him, even if they had to resort to violent punishments, with which they were very liberal. Instead of curbing his spirit, they only succeeded in nurturing an undying hatred toward themselves and everything connected with their doctrine. But finding it impossible to tear himself away from their tyranny, he finally feigned submission and openly professed adherence to his sect, while he secretly visited the few intelligent people that the town could muster up and borrowed from them works that told of the Haskala or that gave some useful instruction. These books he would take with him to uninhabited houses, or to the empty synagogues, and pore over them until their contents had been appropriated by the precocious boy. His father began to suspect that something was wrong with his son, so at the age of fourteen he married him to a girl who, he hoped, would take him back on the road of Khassidism. But finding that, contrary to his expectations, she agreed in everything with her child-husband,

the father managed to divorce her from him.   Linetzki's
patience had come to an end ; he threw off the thin mask
he had been wearing, and began to make open attacks
on the fanatics.   He was again forced into marriage, but
with the same result as before.   The Khassidim now
wanted to get rid of him at all cost, and in a dark night
he was seized by them and thrown into the river.   He
was saved as if by a miracle.   After that he was carefully guarded by the police, and his enemies did not
dare to lay hands on him again.   At the age of eighteen
he escaped to Odessa, where he eked out his existence
by teaching Hebrew to children, all the time perfecting
himself in worldly sciences.   He was again pursued by
the Khassidim of the city, who got away with a box full
of his manuscripts, and he decided to leave Russia, to
take a course at the Rabbinical Seminary in Breslau.
What was his surprise when, upon arriving at the
Austrian frontier, he was put in chains by the Rabbi of
the border town, who threatened to present a forged
despatch from Odessa in which Linetzki was named as
a dangerous criminal.   He again pretended to repent,
and was taken back to his father, from whom the forged
despatch had emanated.   The latter compelled his son
to do penance at the house of the Rabbi of Sadugora.
After that he was divorced from his second wife, as it
was hoped that it would conciliate him to free him from
the ties which had been hateful to him.   Linetzki, however, took the first occasion to escape again.   This time
he went to Zhitomir, where at the age of twenty-three
he entered the third class of the Rabbinical school, as
his insufficient knowledge of Russian made it impossible
for him to attend a higher class.   His schoolmates were
about twelve years old, and ridiculed the man who was
sitting on the same bench with them.   He left the in-

stitution and went to Kiev, where in 1863 his Judeo-German literary career began by his volume of poetry discussed in a previous chapter.   His next work was 'The Polish Boy,' which has gained him a reputation as a classic writer.

Were it not for the many didactic passages which the author has interwoven in the second part of his story, it might easily be counted among the most perfect productions of Jewish literature. These unfortunately mar the unity of the whole.   Except for these, the book is characterized by a truly Rabelaisian humor.   Its greatest merit is that it follows so closely actual experiences as to become a photographic reproduction of scenes.   There is hardly any plot in it, and it is doubtful if Linetzki would have succeeded so well had he attempted a piece of fiction, for in his many later works he is signally defective in this direction.   The mere photographic quality of the story, the straightforward tone that pervades it, the grotesque, unbounded humor which one meets at every turn, have made it acceptable to the Khassidim themselves, who grin at their caricatures but must confess that it is absolutely true.   The copy of the book in my possession was sold to me by a pious itinerant Rabbi, who had treasured it as a precious work.

Linetzki was misled by his early success to regard his unchecked humor as his special domain, and into cultivating it to the exclusion of the finer qualities of style and sound reason. The farther he proceeds,[1] the less readable his works become, the coarser his wit. Later, in the eighties, he abandons entirely original

---

[1] Shorter stories have appeared in *Familienfreund*, Vol. I. pp. 84–86; *Hausfreund*, Vol. I. pp. 121–128; *Jüd. Volksbib.* Vol. I. pp. 62–92; Vol. II. pp. 98–119; *Volksfreund*, pp. 14–16.

work to devote himself to the translation of German books. We have from his pen versions of Lessing's 'Nathan the Wise' and Graetz's 'History of the Jews.' The first is rather a free paraphrase than an artistic translation, while the second is not as carefully done as one might have expected. But once has he returned to the style of his 'The Polish Boy,' in his 'The Maggot in the Horseradish,'[1] but that is but a reflection of his great work. Linetzki's reputation is based only on his first novel, which will ever remain a classic.

A number of men with less talent than those heretofore mentioned have attempted imitations of this or that popular book. Among these writers the attacks against the Khassidim still continue at a time when they have lost their power to sting, when the best authors have abandoned that field for more useful works. However, some of the minor productions are quite creditable performances. Such, for example, is the well-told story in verse by M. Epstein, entitled 'Lemech, the Miracle-worker,' published in 1880. It tells of Lemech the tailor who leaves his wife, and turns miracle-worker, which he finds more profitable than his tailoring. He settles in a distant town and persuades one of the wealthy men to give him his daughter in marriage. The miracle-worker must not be refused, and the daughter's previous engagement with Rosenblatt, her lover, is broken off. Just as the rings are to be exchanged which would unite Lemech with Rosenblatt's former bride, Rosenblatt steps up with Lemech's wife, who has been travelling about to find her unfaithful husband, whom she knows only as a tailor. The story is developed naturally, and the reflections interwoven in it are well worth reading. An earlier one-act drama

[1] *Jüd. Volksbib.*, Vol. I. pp. 62 ff.

by the same author, 'The Drubbing of the Apostate at Foolstown,' relates also in verse of the punishment inflicted by the Rabbi on the Jew who had been found reading one of Mendelssohn's books. Another, 'The Conversation of the Khassidim,' by Maschil Brettmann, gives in the form of a dialogue the best exposition of the tenets of that sect, and shows how the various stories of miracle-workings originate. The introduction contains a short historical sketch of this strange aberration of miracle-working, written in an excellent prose.

While these writers had in view the eradication of some error and the dissemination of culture by their works, the ancient story-telling for the mere love of amusing still continues to attract the masses. The better class of authors were too serious to condescend to compete with the badchen in their efforts to entertain. The lighter story was consequently left to an inferior set of men who frequently had no other excuse for writing their stories than the hope of earning a few roubles by them. Of such a character are 'Doctor Kugelmann,' 'Wigderl the Son of Wigderl.' There is, however, a wide difference in these from similar story-books of the previous generation. The older chap-books were based mainly on the romantic material of the West, generally reflecting nothing of the Jewish life in them. The newer stories of the Southwest of Russia have this in common with the works of the classical writers, that they reproduce scenes of contemporaneous Jewish life. At times these tales are well told and well worth reading. Such is the amusing *quid pro quo* in 'A Jew, then not a Jew, then a Good Jew [*i.e.* a Khassid], and Again a Jew,' by S. Hochbaum. Still more interesting is the charming comedy 'The Savings

of the Women' by Ludwig Levinsohn.[1]   Its plot is as
follows: Jekel, a Khassid, returns late at night to his
house, where he is awaited by his wife Selde. To
silence her torrent of invectives he invents a story that
the decree of Rabbi Gershon, by which monogamy had
been introduced among the Jews of Europe in the
eleventh century, was about to be dissolved in order
that by marrying several wives the Jews of the town
might get new dowries with which to pay the arrears
in their taxes. His wife spreads this news throughout
the community, to the great terror of the women. They
resolve to avert the calamity by offering up their savings stored away in stockings and bundles. These are
brought to the assembled brotherhood of the Khassidim,
who, of course, use the money for a jollification. There
are many amusing incidents in the play. The servant
of Selde is dreaming of the time when she shall be
married to Jekel and when she will lord it over her
former mistress; the scene in the women's galleries
when the news of the impending misfortune is reported
is very humorous, and the attempt of the Rabbi's wife
to learn the truth of the fact from her husband who had
not been initiated in the story by Jekel is quite dramatic. It is one of the best, if not the best, comedy
written in Judeo-German.

A number of witty stories in a semi-dramatic form
have been produced by Ulrich Kalmus; the most of
these are disfigured by coarse jokes, but a few of them
it would well pay to rearrange for scenic representation. One of his best is a version of the Talmudical
legend of the devil and the bad wife; it is almost pre-

---

[1] His name does not appear on any of the editions of his comedy.
Early in the seventies he had turned his work over to Wollmann for
publication ; the latter surreptitiously published it over his own initials.

cisely the same that Robert Browning has versified in his ' Doctor ——.' A good story, resembling Linetzki's 'The Polish Boy,' but with much less bitterness and humor, is given in ' Jekele Kundas,' by one who signs himself by the pseudonym Abasch. Translations from foreign tongues are not uncommon in this period. Some Russian stories are rendered into Judeo-German; also a few German dramas, such as Lessing's 'The Jews'; from the English we have Walter Scott's 'Ivanhoe' and Longfellow's 'Judas Maccabæus'; and from the French we get for that time Massé's 'The Story of a Piece of Bread,' and from the Hebrew one of Luzzato's dramas. To other useful works of a scientific character we shall return later.

There is a marked difference in the development of Judeo-German literature in the Khassidic Southwest and the Misnagdic North. While the first gave promise of a natural growth and a better future, the second showed early the seeds of decay. The nearness to Germany explains the deterioration of the literary Judeo-German of Lithuania, but the cause for the weaker activity in the literature itself is to be sought in the whole mental attitude of the Misnagdim, who as strict ritualists did not allow the promptings of the heart to interfere with their blind adherence to the Law. The very origin of Khassidism was due to a protest against that cold formalism which excluded everything imaginative. Unfortunately this protest opened the way to the Cabbala and admitted the wildest excesses of mysticism in the affairs of everyday life, and this soon gave rise to that form of the new sect with which we meet so frequently in the descriptions of the early authors of the Southwest. These, however, in tearing themselves away from their early associations abandoned only their degraded religious faith, not the love for the fanciful which, if properly directed by a controlling reason, would lead to an artistic career. The Misnagdim, on the contrary, in breaking with their traditions were predisposed to become rationalists with whom utilitarian motives prevailed over the finer sentiments. Their advocates of the Reform, who took to writing in the vernacular of the people, set about from the very start to create a useful, rather than an artistic, literature, to give positive instruction rather than to amuse. The outward form of language and style was immaterial to them; the information the story carried was their only excuse for writing it. Foremost of that class of writers was Aisik Meier Dick,[1] who in the introduction to one of his stories[2] speaks as follows of his purpose in publishing them:

"Our women have no ear and no feeling for pure ethical instruction. They want to hear only of miracles and wonderful deeds whether invented or true; they find delight in the story of Joseph de la Reyna, or of Elijah's appearance in the form of an old man to be the tenth in the Minyan on the eve of the Atonement day; they are even satisfied with the story of Bevys of Hamptoun and the Greyhound, with the Horse Drendsel and the Sword Familie, and with the beautiful Princess Deresna, or merely with a story of a Bride and Bridegroom.

"This sad fact, dear readers, I took deep to heart, and I resolved to make use of this very weakness for interesting stories for their own good by composing

[1] Short mention in *Sseefer Sikorōn*, p. 26; necrology in *Hausfreund*, Vol. III. p. 312.

[2] *Der Schiwim-māhlzeit*, p. 10.

books of an entertaining nature, which would at the same time carry moral lessons. Thanks to God I have succeeded in my undertaking, for my stories are being read diligently, and they are productive of good. Several hundred stories of all kinds have been so far issued by me, each having a different purpose. Even every witty tale and mere witticism teaches something useful. I am sure a great number of my readers do not suspect my good intentions, and read my stories, just as they read Bovo, for pastime only, and will accuse me, the writer of the same, as being a mere babbler who distracts the attention from serious studies, and as writing them for the money that there is in them. I know all that full well, and yet I keep on doing my duty, for even greater men than I have been treated in no better way by our nation; our prophets have been cursed by us, and beaten, and pulled by the hair, and spit upon, and some have even been killed. I am proud to be able to say that I am not making my living from my writings, and I should have been repaid tenfold better if I had passed my time in some more profitable work. But I do it only out of love for my nation, of whom the most do not know how far they are removed from mankind at large, and what a miserable position we occupy in these enlightened days among the civilized nations. . . . We must, whether we wish or not, enter into much closer relations with the outside world than our parents did. We must, therefore, be better acquainted with the world, that we may be tolerated by our fellow-men (the Gentiles), who surpass us in civilization. . . . Consequently, I regard it as a great favor to speak to you by means of my books, and as a still greater favor that the famous firm of Romm is willing to print them, for the publication of prayers is more

profitable than that of story-books that are only read
in circulating libraries or merely borrowed from a
friend."

This passage fully characterizes Dick's activity, which
lasted from the fifties until his death, in 1893. He was
not a man of deep learning, and did not produce any
masterpieces, such as the other writers of the time were
printing in the South. But he atoned for this by his
great earnestness and good common sense, which led
him to choose the best subjects for his stories, such as
would be of the most immediate good for his humble
readers. He translated or imitated the leading popular
books of his time, not limiting himself to such as were
taken out of Jewish life, but independently of their
religious tenor. Among his translations we find the
works of Bernstein, Campe, Beecher-Stowe; there are
imitations of Danish, French, Polish, and Russian
books; and many subjects, not easily traceable now,
have been suggested to him by other literatures. He
has also written many stories taken from the life of
the Lithuanian Jews. He ascribes great importance to
biographies, devoting several introductions to impress
the necessity of reading these. But he treats just as
frequently geographical and historical themes; among
the latter he has even dared to give an impartial discussion of the Reformation.

At first Dick's books were small 16mos of rarely more
than forty-eight pages, and up to the year 1871 the
abbreviation AMD, for his name, occurs but twice.
After that all his works bear the initials, or even the
name in full. The small size of the books is due to
his desire to make them accessible to the poorest of his
race; this necessitated a retrenchmert of nearly all the
works which he translated. Only in the eighties, when

reading had become universal and more expensive works could be published, did he issue octavos of considerable thickness, some of them being four-volumed books. Dick had no talent as a writer, and his style is but a weak reflection of the originals which he translated. The language he uses is a frightful mixture of Judeo-German with German, the latter frequently predominating over the first, so that he is often obliged to give in parentheses the explanation of unusual words. And so it happened that, although his purpose had been a good one, and his influence had at first been salutary on a very large circle of readers, he has set a bad example to a large host of scribblers who have taken all imaginable liberties with the language and the subjects they treated of, and have produced a flood of bastard literature under which the many better productions are entirely drowned. He has destroyed all feeling for a proper diction, and has cultivated only a passion for reading, so that it was necessary for his followers to write 'ein höchst interessanter Roman' on the title-page, and parade the book with crumbs of German words unintelligible to the public, in order to find a ready sale.

One of the first to write in the style of Dick was M. R. Schaikewitsch,[1] who began his prolific career in 1876, since which time he has brought out more than one hundred books, the most of which are of bulky proportions. At first he was satisfied to tell stories from the life of his immediate surroundings, but soon he

---

[1] Cf. S. Rabinowitsch, *Schomer's Mischpet*, and Seiffert's *Däs Tellerl vun 'm Himmel* (*Ein Entwer auf M. Schaikewitsch's Taines*), in *Die neue Welt*, No. 5, pp. 11–21. To his detractors Schaikewitsch answered in his pamphlet *Jehi Ōr*. Other reviews in *Jüd. Volksblatt*, Vol. VIII. (Beilage), pp. 335–361, 455–467, 707–714, 738–743, 763–773.

aspired to higher things, and began to drag in by the hair scenes and situations of which he did not have the slightest conception. As long as he wrote of what he had himself seen he produced books that, without doing any particular good, were to a certain extent harmless. He certainly has a better talent for telling a story than Dick ; his language is also nearer the spoken vernacular, and in the beginning he avoided Germanisms. He might, therefore, have developed into one of the best Jargonists, had he chosen to study, and had he worked less rapidly. In an adaptation of Gogol's 'The Inspector,' he has shown what he might have been had he had any earnest purpose in life. But he lacks entirely Dick's straightforwardness, and writes only to make money. The common people devoured his stories with the same zeal that formerly they showed towards the productions of Dick, and unwittingly they have imbibed a poison which the later authors of a nobler nature, who have the interests of the people at heart, are trying to eradicate. These try to point out directly by accusation, and indirectly by writing better novels, how dangerous and immoral Schaikewitsch is in his books. They go too far in their anxiety to bias the mind of the masses against him when they speak of his proneness to immoral scenes, for in that he is not worse than many of the better class of authors. The deleterious effect is produced not by these, but by his introducing a world to them that does not exist in reality, that gives them a most perverted idea of life, without teaching them any facts worth knowing. In his many historical novels, for example, he uses good sources for the fundamental facts on which he bases his tale, but the men and women are such as could never have existed at the period described and that do not exist now:

they are monstrosities of his imagination as they appear
to him in his very narrow sphere of experiences. His
treatment of these historical themes is not unlike the
one given to the stories of Alexander and other ancient
works during the Middle Ages. The resemblance is
still further increased by his extravagant, romantic
conception of love, on which he dwells with special
pleasure, to the great joy of his feminine public.

A much better attempt at transferring the method
of Dick to dramatic productions had been made as
early as 1867 and the following year by J. B. Falkowitsch. His two dramas 'Chaimel the Rich' and
'Rochele the Singer' were at one time very popular
in the South. The second is an adaptation of some
foreign work; the first is probably original. They are
written in a good vernacular, but are devoid of interest,
as the didactic element outweighs the plot, and the latter is very loosely developed. Schaikewitsch has had
many imitators, all of whom try to rival him in quantity.
Among these are to be counted Blaustein, Beckermann,
Seiffert, Budson, Buchbinder; the latter, a writer without talent, has at least given some useful translations,
and has also written some articles on the popular belief
of the Jews. Outside of Dick, the Northwest has produced two important writers, one in the beginning, the
other at the end, of the period. The first is Zweifel,
whom we already know from his poetical works; the
other is Schatzkes, the author of 'The Jewish Ante-
Passover.' Zweifel has produced several small works
of aphorisms which have been very popular and have
been frequently reprinted. Their fine moral tone, the
purity of the language used in them, the simple style
in which they are composed, place them among the best
books of Judeo-German literature. He has also written

a story, 'The Happy Reader of the Haphtora,' which is a discussion on piety and honesty clad in the form of a tale. The other, M. A. Schatzkes, has written but one book, which is not properly called a story, but an invaluable cyclopedia of Jewish customs, particularly such as directly or indirectly refer to the Passover, strung together in chronological order as a consecutive action. With the exception of Linetzki's 'The Polish Boy,' there has been written no one work that treats so comprehensively of the beliefs and habits of the Jews in Russia. Schatzkes is an indifferent story-teller, and his work is full of repetitions, but, nevertheless, 'The Jewish Ante-Passover' must be counted among the classics of the period under discussion. It is a sad picture that is portrayed in it; in a straightforward manner, without exaggeration, he tells of conditions that one would hardly believe possible as existing at the end of the nineteenth century.

Neither of these men has told stories in the manner of the Southern writers, for neither of them cared as much for the form as for the contents in which they told them. They differ from Dick in that they at least did not use a corrupt language in their works. All the other writers have no excuse for writing at all. This inferior literature had its rise in the seventies, when the better forces had been alienated from the people and had received instruction in Russian schools. The men who had been writing for the Haskala, finding their efforts crowned with success, had ceased to write; many of the older men had passed away. The newer generation had no reason to proceed in the path of the older men. There were only the lower classes left, who had had no advantages in the foreign education, and who were craving for reading matter of whatsoever kind.　It was to these alone that the newer writers spoke, and they were not animated by any high motives in addressing them.　They were left to themselves to do as they pleased, for the seventies are characterized by an absence of all criticism.　No one cared what they did or how they did it.　All felt and hoped that the last hour for the Jargon had come, and it was immaterial to them what was produced in Judeo-German literature before its final decay.　But Abramowitsch's prophecy in ‘The Dobbin’ was fulfilled, — the assimilation that had been going on peacefully had not produced the desired result, and one morning those who had had time to forget the language their mothers had been talking to them awoke to the bitter consciousness that they were despised Jews, on the same level with the most lowly of their race.　Among these arose a new school of writers who introduced the methods of the literary languages into their native dialect.　The next period, the present, is signalized by a spirit of sound criticism.

XII. PROSE WRITERS SINCE 1881: SPEKTOR

In the short period of two years Judeo-German literature lost four of its most prominent writers: in 1891 there passed away the veteran poet, Michel Gordon; the next year J. L. Gordon followed him; and soon after death gathered in Dick and Zederbaum. Without having himself produced any works of a permanent value, without having in any way accelerated or retarded the course of its literature, Zederbaum is peculiarly identified with its development and has on two important occasions in the history of the Jews of Russia served as a crystallizing body for the literary forces in the vernacular. He was born in 1816, and in his youth enjoyed the intimate friendship of Ettinger and Aksenfeld. He had fostered the budding talents of Abramowitsch and Linetzki at a time when the efforts of the first disciples of the Haskala were about to be crowned by a success they had hardly dreamed would be realized so soon. And he lived to see all his hopes crushed in the occurrences of 1881, when his race was threatened to be cast back into darkness more dense than at his birth. During a lifetime thus rich in momentous experiences, he has in his person reflected the succession of events as far as they affected his race. In 1861 he founded a Hebrew periodical, the *Hameliz*, as a mouthpiece of the more advanced ideas of culture for that restricted class of the learned and educated who still clung to the sacred language as the only medium for the advancement of worldly knowledge. But he felt that the time had

come when the masses who, on the one side, could not
be reached by that ancient tongue, and who, on the
other, had not yet had an opportunity of a Russian
instruction, must be approached directly in their own
mother-tongue. So, two years later, he started the
Judeo-German supplement to his Hebrew weekly, the
Kol-mewasser, which was for ten years the rallying
ground of all who could wield a Judeo-German pen.
Then the Government interfered in the publication,
and for another decade there was no periodical published in Russia in that language. Nor was that to
be regretted, for its usefulness had become very small.
The Russian schools were crowded with Jewish young
men and women, and there was not a science or an art
to which the Jews had not given a large contingent,
and this vanguard of the new culture, even if it had
not broken with the traditions of the past, could be
reached only by means of the Russian language. To
fall in line with these changed conditions, Zederbaum
founded two Russian periodicals for the discussion of
Jewish affairs.

After a great deal of trouble, he succeeded in October
of 1881 in getting the Government's permission to issue
a Judeo-German weekly, the *Jüdisches Volksblatt*. He
felt that his duty was once more with the masses, that
they needed the advice of better-informed men in the
impending danger, and at the advanced age of sixty-five
he once more took upon his shoulders a publication in
which he had no supporters. In the first two years the
weekly was bare of literary productions. Except for
an occasional poem by J. L. Gordon, and here and there
a feuilleton, the rest was occupied by political news, for
which Zederbaum had to supply the leaders. Abramowitsch and Linetzki had ceased writing, and no new

generation had had time to develop literary talents.
The tone of the new novel, to do any positive good, had
to be different from those current before. Dick had
been writing for the people with little regard to the
people's familiarity with the scenes described, while
Abramowitsch wrote of the people but not necessarily
to the level of an humble audience. Now the author
had to write both of and for the people, he had to be in
touch with them not as a critic or moralizer, but as a
sympathetic friend. In 1883, two such men made their
debut in the *Jüdisches Volksblatt:* Mordechai Spektor,
the calm observer of the life in the lower strata of society,
and Solomon Rabinowitsch, the impulsive painter of
scenes from the middle classes. Of these, the first
came nearest to what Zederbaum regarded as requisite
for a writer in those troublous times, and he called
Spektor to St. Petersburg to take charge of the literary
part of his weekly.

In the short time of his connection with the *Volksblatt*, and later as editor of several periodicals of his
own, Spektor[1] has developed a great activity. He has
written a large number of short sketches and more
extended novels,[2] and his talent is still in the ascendant.

[1] Cf. *Sseefer Sikorōn*, p. 80. Reviews of his works in *Voschod*,
Vol. VII. No. 12, pp. 18–21 ; Vol. IX. No. 7, pp. 30–37.

[2] In addition to his separate works the following periodicals contain
Spektor's stories: *Jüd. Volksblatt*, Vol. III. and following (very
many) ; *Hausfreund*, Vol. I. pp. 109–121, Supplement; Vol. II. pp.
1–5, 116–143 ; Vol. III. pp. 9–28, 38–101, 149–172, 277–294 ; Vol. IV.
pp. 81–95, 107–131 ; Vol. V. pp. 123–136 ; *Familienfreund*, Vol. II.
pp. 66–91 ; Spektor's *Familienkalender*, Vol. II. pp. 51–54 ; Vol. III.
pp. 81–85 ; Vol. IV. pp. 63–93 ; Vol. V. pp. 45–51, 52–58 ; *Widerkol*,
pp. 10 ff.; *Jontewblättlech*, I. Series, No. 3, 4, 9 ; *Kleiner Wecker*, pp.
43–48 ; *Literatur un' Leben*, pp. 67–89. Reviews by him, under the
pseudonym *Emes*, in *Hausfreund*, Vol. I. pp. 143–160 ; Vol. II. pp.
170–176 ; Vol. III. pp. 251–260.

All of his productions are characterized by the same melancholy dignity and even tenor. He is never in a hurry with his narration, and his characters are sketched with a firm hand and clearly outlined against the background of the story. He loves his subjects with a calm, dispassionate love, and he loves the meanest of his creations no less than his heroes. He likes to dwell with them and to inspect them from every coign of vantage. He fondly tells of their good qualities and suffers with them for their natural defects. And yet, though he loves them, he does not place a halo around them, he does not idealize them. The situations are developed in his stories naturally, independently of what he would like them to be.

Although he now and then describes the life of the middle classes, he more often treats incidents from the life of the artisans in the small towns, who have not been affected by the modern culture. Himself having had few advantages in life, he has been able to keep in closer touch with the men and women about whom and for whom he writes. He understands them thoroughly, and they like to listen to him. He does not sermonize to them, he does not attack them or their enemies; he merely speaks to them as their friend. The Khassid and the Anti-Khassid, the laborer and the man of culture, Jew and Non-Jew, can read him with equal pleasure. The student of manners finds in his faithful pictures as rich a store of information as in Schatzkes' or Linetzki's works, and he has the conviction that nothing is distorted or thrown out of its proper proportion, as the others sometimes have to do in order to strengthen their arguments. Spektor is a young man, having been born in 1859, and was a witness of the occurrences in the seventies and the eighties from which he draws the subjects for his stories. His style is simple, without any attempts at adornment, and his language, based on his native dialect of Uman in the Government of Kiev, is chaste and pure.

One of the most puzzling problems to the Judeo-German writers of modern times has been the treatment of love in the Jewish novel. They all agree that they have to follow Western models in that class of literature, and they are all equally sure that that passion does not exist among their people in any of the phases with which one meets elsewhere. The young woman's education in a Jewish home is such as to exclude a blind self-abandonment, with the consequent tragic results. Her desire to form family ties is greater than the natural promptings of her heart ; her infatuation of the moment is easily smothered by a cool calculation of her future welfare, by the consideration of her duties towards her future husband and children. Unless the author uses the greatest caution in this matter, he is liable to fall into exaggerations and sentimentalities which would soon land him among the writers of the type of Schaikewitsch. But Spektor, not departing even in this from his usual candor, intermingles the most romantic passages with the cold facts of stern reality. His unrequited lovers do not commit suicide, or pine their lives away; they get over their infatuations in a manner prescribed by their religious convictions, get married to others, and rear happy families. Here is an example :

In ' The Fashionable Shoemaker ' we are introduced to the sphere of a well-to-do shoemaker with no pretensions to any kind of culture. Having gotten on successfully in life, he is anxious to marry his daughter Breindele to Schlöme, the dandyish son of Sender

Liebersohn, the rich man of the town. The latter
looks favorably on the alliance in spite of the general
disinclination of business men to enter into family
ties with artisans, as he is desirous of feathering his
son's nest before an impending bankruptcy sweeps
away his fortune. Lipsche, Breindele's mother, in
vain tries to dissuade her husband from the step,
while Hirschel, the chief apprentice in the shop, is
earnestly pleading with Breindele to marry him, for he
loves her dearly. But she is too much attracted by the
wealth of Schlōme and her future social position to
listen to her father's simple-hearted, honest workman.
The marriage is consummated, and soon a complete
change takes place in the affairs of all concerned.
Liebersohn loses his possessions. Hirschel, bearing in
his heart his unrequited love, leaves his master and
establishes a shop of his own. He works with great
energy to forget his sorrow, and becomes a dangerous
competitor of Susje, the shoemaker, whose hard-earned
savings are slowly disappearing under the double obligation to support his family and that of his daughter
Breindele. In vain some of the 'modern' girls of the
town dress themselves in their best gowns and don
fine silk stockings when Hirschel comes to take a
measure of their feet for new pairs of shoes for them.
Their machinations have no effect on Hirschel, who
lives quietly for himself. But one day he notices
Leotschke, Breindele's younger sister, in the street,
and he is struck by her resemblance to his former
love. When he left his master she was but a child,
and now she is a pretty maiden. He cultivates her
acquaintance, falls in love with her and is loved by
her. There are no love scenes in the story. Hirschel
goes to Leotschke's mother and gets her willing con-

sent to the union. After the marriage he helps support Breindele and her family, for her husband, Schlöme, who has learned no trade, finds it hard to make a living.

One of his best sketches is the one entitled 'Two Companions.' It is a gem among the many good things he has written, — perfect in form and rounded off as few of his sketches are. It tells of two girls, Rösele and Perele, who have grown up together as dear friends. When they reach the age of sixteen Rösele notices that the young students of the gymnasium pay more attention to her beautiful companion than to her. She becomes jealous, suspects the seamstress of purposely favoring her friend with more carefully worked dresses, which enhance her natural beauty, accuses Rösele of drawing away her gentlemen friends by unfair means, and finally when she finds herself more and more abandoned by her acquaintances, she completely breaks off her relations with the friend of her childhood. They lead a separate existence. At the age of thirty-five Perele is bowed down with sorrows : she has buried a husband and two children, has again married, and her days are taken up in the care of her family and unpleasant discussions with her jealous husband. Rösele has married a sickly man with whom she has nothing in common. He married her only for her money. Their child is as frail as its father, and Rösele's days are passed in sordid cares and worry.

"So passed another twenty-five years. After a long severe winter there came at last the young, fresh spring in all his glory, with his many attendants of all kinds who warble, whistle, chatter, and clatter, in the trees, in the air, on the earth, and in the grass. The streets are dry, the air is warm. . . . . In an avenue of trees, on

the sunlit side of it, two old women are walking together. They are dressed in old-fashioned, long bur-
nouses, and hold umbrellas in their hands against which
they lean. Their faces are wrinkled, their heads drooping to one side, and they stop every few steps they
take, and speak with their toothless mouths :

" ' My dear Perele, this has been a long winter ! '

" ' Yes, a frightful winter ! Thanks to the Lord it is
over. To-day it is good — the sun shines so warmly !
But I have put on my burnous for all that ! You,
Rōsele, have done likewise ! No, it is not yet warm
enough for us.'

" They seated themselves on the nearest bench and
continued their conversation :

" ' I am getting tired ; I think we had better go home.'

" ' Yes, I am getting hungry, for I have eaten to-day
only a broth. I cannot eat anything except it be a
soft, fresh roll with milk or something like it.'

" ' I, too . . . '

" And thus old age has again made peace among the
two companions of long ago. They love each other
again just as before when they were children, and they
did not know that one was pretty and the other homely,
. . . for now they are again alike ! Perele and Rōsele
have both alike bent forms and wrinkled faces ; both
have no teeth in their mouths, and their heads droop
alike. Only Perele has come to it from living too
much, and Rōsele from not living at all. The two
gowns, which the same tailor has made for them for
the Passover from the same piece of cloth and according to the same fashion, have pleased them equally well,
and they need not complain of the workmanship."

Of the many other shorter sketches we might mention the touching scenes in his ' Purim and Passover,

in which ' How Grandfather's Child put on her First Shoes ' is the most pathetic. Not less pathetic is the one named ' The Uncle,' in which are contrasted the open-hearted reception of the wealthy uncle in the house of his poor nephew and the niggardly treatment of the nephew by his relative in the large city. Through all of Spektor's works passes the same melancholy strain, coupled with a strict objectivity of conception. This objectivity does not leave him even in cases where one would certainly expect him to express an opinion of his own. He has given us, for example, a most important series of sketches under the name of ' Three Persons,' in which the tendencies among the Russian Jews in the last quarter of a century are described with remarkable clearness; and he proceeds to point out their various modifications under the influence of the riots. Here, it seems, one would look for an individual conviction, for he must surely side with one of the parties discussed by him so thoroughly; and yet he does not once betray his personal preference. This series is indispensable to any one who wants to study the current of opinion among the Russian Jews, previous to the development of the Zionistic movement which now is uppermost in their minds. We are introduced successively to the Palestinian, the Assimilator, and the Neither-here-nor-there. A careful psychological study is made of all, with apparently negative results as to their respective merits. They are all three insincere with their fellow-sufferers and belong to their organizations only for personal advantage. The sad impression made by the reading of these interesting chapters is anticipated by the motto placed at the head of them : Laughing is not always in ridicule; laughing is sometimes a bitter weeping.

Among his best longer stories is 'Reb Treitel,' which gives a good insight into the life of a small town away from all railroads and off the highway of travel. One of the most necessary institutions in every Jewish town is the *Mikwe*, the bathhouse, not so much for sanitary purposes as for the ritual ablutions of the women. This mikwe is the centre of our story. Around it are grouped the various incidents which emanate from it like the arteries from the heart. The bathhouse is consumed by fire, and the town is all agog with excitement. There is no immediate outlook that a new one will be built, and in the interim Reb Treitel, the wagon-driver, who has been despairing of making both ends meet, is doing a splendid business by taking the women to the neighboring town for their ritual ablutions. He manages to keep all competition away and to lay a heavy tribute on the feminine population. Spektor has also begun a historical novel dealing on the life of the founder of the sects of the Khassidim. He does not represent him there as an impostor, but as a truly pious man, which he was, no doubt, in reality. So far he has published only chapters on his youth, but these promise a sympathetic treatment of which Spektor is eminently capable as an unbiassed author.

In 1887 Spektor severed his connection with the *Volksblatt* and settled in Warsaw. The time now being ripe for a purely literary periodical, he started the first of the kind in Judeo-German literature. He was, however, delayed for various reasons, and another collective volume appeared in the South before he was able to issue his own. He named it *Der Hausfreund* and intended it as an annual, but the Government having interfered on various occasions, there have appeared only five numbers so far. The annual reflects all of Spektor's peculiarities. Like his own writings, all of the articles and stories contained in it are adapted for the popular ear, and are written in a simple, comprehensible style. The scientific discussions are of a rudimentary character, and the criticisms of books and the Jewish theatre, which from now on becomes an important factor in Judeo-German literature, are intended more as guides to the reader than as correctives to the authors. Though somewhat primitive in its form, this periodical was calculated to advance the cause of letters among the masses of the people. Among his contributors we find in the first two numbers such names as Goldfaden, Zunser, Samostschin, Buchbinder, M. Gordon, Frug, Linetzki, Abramowitsch. Among the other writers there are some who had before written for the *Volksblatt* but whose productions are insignificant. A few of them, however, begin to develop a greater activity, and deserve special mention. Among these are the novelists ' Isabella,' Dienesohn, the collector of legends Meisach, and the critic Frischmann.

'Isabella' is the pseudonym of Spektor's wife. She has written but a few sketches,[1] but some of them show remarkable talent. She unites her husband's objectivity with a fine discrimination of humor which is her own. She likes to dwell on comparisons between the older and the newer generation, and to point out the evil effects of a superficial modern culture. In 'The Orphan' she introduces us to the house of Schmuel Dāwid, who tries to keep himself occupied by teaching children penmanship. He is too simple-minded and goodhearted to battle with the world. The supporter of the house is his wife, Treine, who makes a living by usury.

[1] In *Hausfreund*, Vol. I. p. 67 ; Vol. II. pp. 108–116 ; *Jüd. Bibliothēk*, Vol. I. pp. 41–74.

They shower their attentions on their only descendant, the peevish granddaughter Jentke. She is sent to the gymnasium and later is loved by a young scholar, a lank, consumptive-looking fellow, with whom she joins one of those narrower circles so common among the students of Russia, where they propose remedies for the betterment of the world and dream of the millennium near at hand. Their one desire is to identify themselves with the Russians at large. Then come the awful years 1881 and 1882. All of a sudden new ideals begin to animate the younger generation. Jentke's lover no longer calls himself Fyodor Sebastyanovitch, but his visiting card bears the homely Jewish name Peessach ben Schabsi, of which the former was only a Russified form. He becomes an ardent defender of his race. Later he marries Jentke, and a new career begins for them. They forget all their ideals of the period before the riots, to which they so readily subscribed; they do not persevere in their intention to devote their energies to their people. They live only for themselves. They begin to hoard money, and Jentke is much more hardhearted than her grandmother, for having abandoned the religious convictions of the older woman, she has not received any new moral basis for her actions. The grandmother dies, and the lonely, half-starved grandfather in vain tries to find a resting-place in their house. They send him away in a most cruel manner.

Her other sketches are of a similar character. In all of these, she points out the dangers from a superficial modern education, and the insincerity of the self-styled reformers who are ever ready to suggest a remedy for the ills that befall her people. Her characters are drawn from that new class of half-learned men and women who, receiving their training in the gymna-

sium, were just on the point of disappearing from the
fold of the Jewish Church, when they were violently
cast back into it by the persecutions from without.
Of an entirely different tendency are the writings of
Jacob Dienesohn, although akin to 'Isabella' in the
sympathy he shows for the older generation.   Dienesohn had begun his career in 1875, when he published
a novel 'The Dark Young Man,' after which he grew
silent.   In 1885 he took up his literary work, since
when he has produced two large novels and several
shorter sketches. His first work was very popular. He
depicted in it the machinations of an orthodox young
man of the older type, who felt it his duty to lay stum-
bling-blocks in the way of one who strove to acquire
worldly knowledge.   Dienesohn occupies a peculiar
place in Judeo-German literature.   He is the only one
who has attempted the lachrymose, the sentimental
novel. He began writing at a time when Dick had prepared the ground for the romantic story, and Schaikewitsch had started on his sentimental drivel.   But while
these entirely failed to produce something wholesome,
Dienesohn gained with his first book an unusual success. He drew his scenes from familiar circles, and his
men and women are all Jews, with a sphere of action
not unlike the one his readers moved in.   Readers consequently were more easily attracted to him, and carried away a greater fund of instruction.   His feminine
audiences have wept tears over his work, and the author
has received letters from orthodox young men, who
assured him that although the description of the Dark
Young Man fitted them, they would not descend to
the vile methods of the hero of the book in pursuing
differently minded men.

  During his renewed activity, which began in the

Volksblatt ten years after his first novel had been printed, he dwelt on that period in the history of the Russian Jews when they were just commencing to take to the new culture, when it still meant a struggle and a sacrifice to tear oneself away from the ties which united one with the older generation. In the 'Stone in the Way' he describes the many hardships which his hero had to overcome ere he succeeded in acquiring an education. In 'Herschele' (still unfinished) the same subject is treated in the case of a young mendicant Talmudical scholar, who is beset, not only by the usual difficulties, but who is, in addition, trying to suppress his earthly love for the daughter of the woman who furnishes him with a dinner on every Wednesday. Dienesohn treats with loving gentleness all the characters he writes about.[1] Like Spektor, he attacks no one directly, and, like him, sarcasm has no place in his works. His most touching and, at the same time, the most perfect of his shorter stories is the one entitled 'The Atonement Day.'[2] He introduces us there to a scene in the synagogue where an old woman is praying fervently. Her devotion is interrupted by her thoughts of her daughter at home whom she had enjoined to fast on that awful day, although she had just given birth to a son. For a long time her religious convictions outweigh her maternal feelings, but, at last, her natural sentiment is victorious, and she hurries home to insist on her daughter's eating something. In this way the new-born babe is saved. Thirty years

---

[1] Other articles by him: *Jüd. Volksblatt*, Vol. V. pp. 329 ff.; Vol. VIII. (Beilage), pp. 33–43; *Hausfreund*, Vol. I. pp. 1–21; Vol. II. pp. 75–99; *Jüd. Volksbib.*, Vol. I. pp. 244–248; *Jüd. Bibliothēk*, Supplements.

[2] *Hausfreund*, Vol. II. pp. 75–99.

pass.   The old woman has died, and her daughter
Chane is brought before us on the same Atonement
day.   She has grown old, while her son has, in the
meantime, finished at the university, and is a practising
physician.   She, too, is praying fervently, and thinking
with awe of the day when young and old, the pious and
the sinner alike, come to the synagogue and invoke the
mercy of the Lord with contrition of spirit.   Her eyes
search in vain for her son among the crowd congregated
below.   The hours pass, and he does not appear.   Faint
with hunger from the long fasting and grieving at her
son's apostasy, she falls sick and soon dies.   In her last
agony she makes her son promise her that he will, at
least once a year, on the Atonement day, visit the
synagogue.   After that, one can see every year, on the
awful day, the physician in deep devotion in the house
of the Lord.

The circle which has Spektor for its centre is characterized by the use of Western literary forms for its productions, which yet are all of a distinctly Jewish type.
The object of the authors is to create a sound literature
for the masses.   Incidentally, the literature is also to
give positive instruction ; but primarily, it is to draw
away attention from the worthless books of the previous decade, and to create a decided taste for good works.
These authors also intend to give the people a feeling
for their racial solidarity, to acquaint them with the
thought of the best of their race in an accessible form.
This period has completely broken its connection with
the older Haskala, for the writers no longer dream of
substituting German culture for the ignorance of the
masses.   Nor do they preach of assimilation and Russian education, for that has signally failed to be of any
use to the Jews in their struggle for recognition.   In the

nineties, the dream of Zionism was to haunt these writers, and many others who were to write then. But, in
the meanwhile, they have no other definite purpose than
to create a national consciousness, to instil in them the
idea of human dignity, to develop individual character.
While, on the one hand, they do not give them any new
cultural ideals for those of the past generations, they
have, on the other, no suggestions to make in regard to
the religious faith of the orthodox, or the absence of
religious convictions of the younger men and women.
They do not attack the old Law, they do not side with
any modern philosophy. Khassid and Misnaged, the
unenlightened and enlightened, are the same in the
scale of their judgment. It is not time, they think,
to discuss about any such matters, but to gather in all
the unfortunate ones into one brotherhood. The upper
classes who have had many advantages in life, can shift
for themselves in forming their convictions, but it is
the lower strata that need guidance, and it is the duty
of those who are better informed to devote their energies to the deliverance of their wretched brothers and
sisters. Such is the doctrine of these writers. These
sentiments are not alone the result of the riots of 1881.
They are a reflex of the Russian *Narodniks*, who, at
about the same time, were preaching the necessity of
going among the people, of identifying oneself with the
masses, of devoting all one's energies in the cause of the
peasant, the artisan, the factory hand.

The Jargon is not represented in a contemptuous
way, nor are apologies made for its use. On the contrary, the authors try to show the wealth of its expressions and to collect data for its history. Lerner writes
a good essay on the folksong in a popular style; Dienesohn gives a review of the older writings and their

authors; Spektor and Bernstein publish a large number
of Judeo-German proverbs; Buchbinder collects popular
superstitions; and Meisach writes a small book of Jewish folktales.   The latter has also told in Judeo-German
some of the legends from the Talmud and other sources.
He has written some stories in the style of Dick, but
like those they are disfigured by a disregard of style.
The activity of these men still continues, independently
of the new movements advocated by other writers and
unimpeded by the new faith of Zionism.

XIII. PROSE WRITERS SINCE 1881:
RABINOWITSCH, PEREZ

SOLOMON RABINOWITSCH began writing for the
Volksblatt[1] at about the same time as Spektor, and
shortly after the appearance of the *Hausfreund* he issued
an annual, *Die Jüdische Volksbibliothēk*, which was of
even a more pretentious character than its contemporary. Both authors were animated by the same ideas
when they started on their literary careers and when
they commenced publishing their periodicals. But a
glance at the writings of the two is sufficient to convince us that there is a wide difference in the methods
pursued by them, and in the results achieved. Rabinowitsch is impulsive, enthusiastic, quick-witted, sarcastic,
and these qualities of his character are discernible in all
his productions. He has attempted many things, poetry,
playwriting, novels, criticism, and he is successful in all.
He has been a merchant and an author, has vaulted
over from a pure realism to the illusive dream of Zionism, and bids fair to follow new ideals should such
present themselves to him. He is in every sense an
artistic nature.

While connected with the *Volksblatt* he wrote a
number of sketches and short stories. The first one

---

[1] His stories, dramas, and poems have appeared in *Jüd. Volksblatt*
Vol. III. p. 387, hence continuously up to the ninth volume of that
periodical; *Familienfreund*, Vol. I. pp. 73-84; *Hausfreund*, Vol. I
pp. 45-63; Vol. III. pp. 321-326; Vol. IV. pp. 63-81; Vol. V. pp. 97-
123; *Jüd. Volksbib.*, Vol. I. pp. 1-47, 241-243, 351-378; Vol. II
pp. 205-220, 304-310; *Wecker*, pp. 88-91.

to attract the attention of the critic in the *Voschod* was his 'Child's Play,'[1] after which his new books never failed of bringing out favorable comments in that Russian periodical. He depicts scenes from his own childhood, or from that middle class into which his fortune, an inheritance of his wife, brought him. His impulsiveness keeps him from elaborating his sketches into long novels, such as Spektor and Dienesohn have produced. There is rarely a complicated plot in them, but the separate situations are painted with great clearness and in bold relief. One may forget the story, but one will never forget his characters. They have all of them their sharply defined individuality, their language, their circle of thought. We get acquainted with them through their actions rather than through the author's description, and we like them not for the parts they play in the story, but for their strong personalities, equally pronounced in their virtues as in their weaknesses. The men and women he describes we have met somewhere, and we shall again recognize should we meet them in actual life. The Russian critic, who is naturally in touch with his own literature, unconsciously thinks of this and that well-known character in the writings of Gogol and Ostrovski, when he speaks of Rabinowitsch's creations, and at times he actually gives them their Russian names. But Rabinowitsch does not imitate Gogol and Ostrovski, at least not purposely. He is himself possessed of a humor which is not dissimilar to that of the Russian authors, and the society which

---

[1] *Voschod*, Vol. VII. No. 6. Reviews of his other works are in *Voschod*, Vol. VII. Nos. 7, 8; Vol. VIII. No. 10, and in later numbers; of *Sender Blank*, by J. J. Lerner (unfavorable), in *Jüd. Volksbib.*, Vol. VIII. (Beilage), No. 29, pp. 804–876, under the title *Lebendige Meessim*. Short mention of his works in *Sseefer Sikorōn*, p. 105.

he describes is not unlike the one Gogol knew half a
century ago, and Ostrovski found even at a later time
among the merchant class of Moscow. He is a close
observer, and knows how to separate the wheat from
the chaff, to present to the reader only the essential
characteristics, and not to burden the story with subjective discussions.

Although Rabinowitsch may have started in the
literary field with no other idea than the current one
of elevating the lower classes, there is certainly nothing
in his works to show that that has long remained his
main object. He writes to entertain, and not to instruct.
Moreover, he draws his subjects from a class of society
with which the masses are not particularly well acquainted. With him the last spark of the didactic
ideals of the Haskala has entirely vanished. He is
above all else a litterateur who is addressing an audience
with a decided taste for good literature. He is, therefore, more calculated to win the ears of the better
classes than of the lowly of his race, to exercise a cor-
rective influence on the manners of the middle class
than to educate or console the masses.

Of his longer works, 'Stempenju' is the most artistically conceived and most carefully executed. In his
previous productions such as 'Child's Play,' and 'Sender Blank,' he had humorously depicted scenes from
the life of the merchant class. In the first of these,
he introduces us into the life and love of a rich man's
spoiled, half-educated son. In the second, which he
names a novel without love, we get an excellent picture
of a tyrant and miser, the terror of his family, the
merchant Sender Blank. He is on his death-bed, and
his congregated children are, each in his own way,
dreaming of the moment when they shall be free to do

as they like, when they shall no longer be kept in poverty. But Sender Blank gets well again, and his
family departs, each one to his home with shattered
hopes. In 'Stempenju' we have a more carefully laid
plot, and his first attempt at a novel in which a romantic love plays a part. Stempenju is a violinist, the
leader of a band that plays at weddings. He has great
talent for music and has developed his powers entirely
by self-instruction. He is a real artist, and like many
others of his profession takes life easy, and is of amor-
ous propensities. He has frequently made love to
Jewish women, but the latter generally pay no attention to his assurances. But once he falls in with a girl
who takes his words in earnest, and in a prosaic way,
without any idea of love on her part, compels him
to marry her. She takes him in her hands and would
have him lead a settled, prosaic life also. But he
finds relief from his sordid existence every time he
journeys away with his band to play at some wedding.
Once he notices upon such an occasion a young married woman who awakes in him the first inkling of a
real, romantic love. Rochel — that is her name — is
both beautiful in form and kind and lovable in character. After many overtures he almost succeeds in
gaining her love. It is the easier to succumb to Stempenju's importunities since she has a silly, worthless
man for a husband. She finally comes out victoriously
from her inner struggle, for her religious conviction of
the holiness of the marriage ties are stronger in her
than her natural inclination. Stempenju returns home,
and tries to find his consolation and relief from his
scolding wife by having more frequent recourse to his
violin. He plays even more sweetly and more sadly
than before.

His other large novel, 'Jossele Ssolowee,' is also a characterization of the life of an artist, this time a singer. Of his shorter sketches it is hard to select one as the best, as they are all well written. We shall take at random the one entitled 'The Colonization of Palestine.' Selig, the tailor, has read something about the colonization scheme in Palestine. He joins a society for the promotion of that idea, and finally abandons his work to go to the neighboring town, where he has heard there is a society that has a fund from which to pay the travelling expenses of prospective settlers in the Holy Land. After a great deal of trouble, he finds the president of the society, who is vexed at having applicants but no members ready as settlers to support the scheme, for fund there is none. The tailor offers a small coin as his contribution, the first that has been given, and returns home a wiser man and more satisfied with his lot. The story is told humorously, and is meant as a sarcasm at the readiness of the Jews to form new schemes and support them with eloquence of speech, but not in a substantial manner.

Rabinowitsch has also attempted a kind of poetic prose in his 'Nosegay,' but in this he has not been very successful. He is at best where he can make use of wit and sarcasm, and that he has been able to apply better in his stories and comedies. Of the latter his 'Jaknehos' is a good picture taken from the life of the men who do business on 'Change. Here again the plot is the minor part of the play, but the separate scenes are drawn in bold strokes.

When Rabinowitsch came into his fortune, he conceived the idea of devoting his energy and his money to the creation of a periodical such as had never before existed in Judeo-German literature. Only two volumes

appeared, when bad speculations on 'Change made him
a poor man. These two annuals show that had he been
more fortunate, he soon would have brought Judeo-
German letters to a height where they would have taken
place by the side of the best in Europe. His enthusi-
asm, his critical acumen, his talents, fitted him emi- .
nently for that undertaking. Spektor's aim in issuing
the *Hausfreund* was the more modest one of furnish-
ing the people with wholesome reading. How difficult
his task has been can be seen from the fact that the
articles for his periodical are not paid for. They are
voluntary contributions by those who have the welfare
of the masses at heart. However good the forces may
be, it is not possible in these degenerate days to expect
a natural development of a literature when the writers
can hope to earn neither glory nor money by their
labors. No Judeo-German litterateur has ever been
able to make more than a scanty living, and that only
sporadically, out of his books. But here came Rabinowitsch, who paid liberally for all the articles furnished him. That was an innovation from which only
good could result. But the editor not only paid his
contributors; he demanded well-written articles, and
he accepted only the best of those. In his annual we
find departments, — Belles Lettres, Criticism, Science,
Bibliography, each being strictly defined in its proper
sphere. In the division of belles lettres we find all
the best authors of the time. Here also appeared for
the first time articles from the pen of Frischmann,
M. J. Rabinowitsch, and Perez, who belong among the
most talented of Judeo-German writers. Among the
scientific articles there are several of a historical character, such as 'On the History of the Jews in Podolia,'
by Litinski, 'The Massacres of Gonto in Uman and the

Ukraine,' by Dr. Skomarowski. There are several discussions on popular medicine, mainly from the pen of the indefatigable worker in that direction for more than a quarter of a century, Dr. Tscherny, and there is one on 'The History of Judeo-German Literature' by A. Schulmann. The latter is the result of years of investigation and is remarkably rich in bibliographical data. It would do honor to any scientific periodical. The part given to bibliography is of great importance to the student of Judeo-German literature, as that bibliography is in such a bad condition that it is not possible for certain periods, especially the older, to give absolutely correct data. But the most interesting department in the periodical is that of criticism, which is a new factor in Judeo-German. Heretofore a few scattered remarks on books might be found in the *Volksblatt*, but a systematic treatment of that branch of literature was unknown to the older writers, and would have been of no use to the readers. But here, in the *Volksbibliothēk*, we not only find this new departure, but there are not less than eighty pages devoted to it in the first volume.

Rabinowitsch had published but a short time before a volume entitled 'Schomer's Mischpet,' *i.e.* 'The Judgment of Schaikewitsch,' which marks a new era. In this book the author passes in review the writings of Schaikewitsch and his like who have been supplying the people with a worthless literature. It is written in an entertaining style, in the form of a judicial proceeding, and has produced to a certain extent the effect that it was intended to produce: the sale of those books fell off rapidly, and thus the field was again free for a new and better class of works. It cannot be said that Rabinowitsch has always been just

to the men under judgment, but on the whole his opinion
is sound, and his verdicts will stand.   In his zeal he has
sometimes been led to make sweeping statements, by
which he has left some loopholes to the opponents who
have taken him to task.   However, criticism from now
on becomes an established institution, and no author can
escape a thorough inspection.   The first to follow the
example of Rabinowitsch was Frischmann, who brought
out the same year a few sound reviews in the *Hausfreund*.   In the *Volksbibliothēk* that duty is attended to
by Rabnizki[1] and the editor.   They not only criticise
unworthy productions, but also direct the attention to
good books, and encourage young writers if they seem to
deserve encouragement.   Rabinowitsch's talent in this
direction is shown at its best in his biting sarcasm in
reviewing Perez's poetry[2] (although he is not entirely
just to him), and still better in his witty criticism of
the various dictions used in Judeo-German.   Perez,
who is a genius of no mean proportions and who has
started out in new directions in literature, has somehow aroused the displeasure of the critics, who will not
put up with his symbolism.   Frischmann has taken him
to task for his alleged obscurity and other imagined
faults in a series of masterly caricatures.[3]   Frischmann
also does not spare others who incur his wrath, and
though one need not subscribe to his judgments, one
cannot help learning useful things by his anatomies.
By these we see, among other things, what progress
Judeo-German is making ; for individuality of style

---

[1] Other articles by Rabnizki in *Wecker*, pp. 62–74, 115–122; *Heilige
Land*, pp. 13–25.

[2] In his *Kol-mewasser*, col. 31–34.

[3] *Lokschen* and *A Flōh vun Tischebow;* see Bibliography, under
Frischmann.

must be pronounced to deserve imitation and parody. Frischmann has also written some pretty tales of a fantastic nature, such as fairy tales, and a few from actual life.[1] His stories are all well worth reading, particularly on account of the excellent style he cultivates. M. J. Rabinowitsch's stories are mainly translations of his own Russian compositions.[2] They are all pictures from the Ghetto in Russia and Roumania, not unlike those by Bernstein and Kompert. They lack the spontaneity of the Judeo-German writers, but are carefully executed as to form.

By far the most original author of this latest period is Perez,[3] whose poetical works have been discussed before. With him Judeo-German letters enter into competition with what there is best in the world's literature, where he will some day occupy an honorable place. Among his voluminous works there is not one that is mediocre, not one that would lose anything of its comprehensibleness by being translated into another language. Although they at times deal with situations taken from Jewish life, it is their universal human import that interests him, not their specifically racial

---

[1] Frischmann's stories, reviews, and poems may be found in *Jüd. Volksblatt*, Vol. VIII. (Beilage), pp. 92, 93 ; Vol. IX. Nos. 23, 30, 32, 51, 52 ; *Familienfreund*, Vol. II. pp. 47–49 ; *Hausfreund*, Vol. II. pp. 22–25, 66–73, 151–170 ; Vol. III. pp. 175, 176 ; Vol. IV. pp. 167–176 ; Vol. V. pp. 7–21, 159–161 ; *Jüd. Volksbib.*, Vol. I. pp. 211–224 ; *Handelskalender*, pp. 100–104.

[2] His stories appeared in *Jüd. Volksbib.*, Vol. I. pp. 183–210 ; Vol. II. pp. 225–246 ; *Jüd. Volkskalender*, Vol. III. pp. 70–81.

[3] In addition to the very large number of stories, etc., in his own publications, Perez has contributed to *Jüd. Volksbib.*, Vol. I. pp. 148–158 ; Vol. II. pp. 126–129, 136–138, 142–147, 167, 168, 195–204; *Hausfreund*, Vol. III. pp. 111–113, 179–181 ; *Handelskalender*, pp. 79–83, 105–113 ; *Kleiner Wecker*, pp. 25–29 ; *Jüd. Volkskalender*, Vol. III. pp. 105–111.

characteristics.   It is mere inertia and the desire to serve his people that keep him in the ranks of Judeo-German writers.   He does not belong there by any criterions that we have applied to his confreres, who themselves complain that his symbolism is inaccessible to the masses for whom he pretends to write.   While this accusation is certainly just in the case of some of his works, it cannot be brought up in many other cases, where, in spite of the allegory, mysticism, or symbolism underlying his tale, there is a sufficient real residue of intelligible story for the humblest of his readers.   He, too, aims at the education of his people, but in a vastly different sense from his predecessors.   It is not the material information of mere facts that he strives for, nor even the broader culture of the schools that he would substitute for the Jewish lore and religious training, nor is he satisfied, with Spektor, to rouse the dormant national consciousness.   His sympathies are with humanity at large, and the Jews are but one of the units that are to be redeemed from the social slavery under which the wretched of the world groan.   It is those who have become timid under oppression of whatsoever form, who have lost the power of thinking, who have developed only the power of suffering, who are saints without knowing it, that Perez loves best.   To them he would restore the human rights so long withheld from them, not by political and social enfranchisement, but by a consciousness of their human dignity which must precede all reform.   To those to whom belongs the Kingdom of Heaven must also be given the Kingdom on Earth.   While, nevertheless, the material things are withheld from them, there is no reason why the spiritual things should not be turned over to them.   Perez, for one, offers gladly all he has, his genius, in the service of the lowly. Literature, according to him, is not to be a flimsy pastime of the otiose, but a consolation to those who have no other consolation, a safe and pleasurable retreat for those who are buffeted about on the stormy sea of life. For these reasons he writes in Judeo-German and not in any other language with which he is conversant, and for these same reasons he prefers to dwell with the downtrodden and the submerged.

To these people he devotes his best energies, and he uses the same care in filing and finishing his works that he would use if he were writing for a public trained in the best thoughts of the world and used to the highest type of literature. His first prose work, though not the first to be printed, was a small volume entitled 'Well-known Pictures,' containing three stories: 'The Messenger,' 'What Is a Soul?' and 'The Crazy Beggar-Student.' In the first he tells of the last errand of an aged messenger who through cold and rain and snow is making his way on foot to a distant village where he has to deliver an important document. He trudges along in hunger and pain, but not a word of complaint escapes his lips. Through his head pass old recollections of the time when his wife was still alive, when his children were all gathered about him. They have left him, but he is sure they are getting on well in their new homes, for, he consoles himself, bad news travels fast. His strength gives out, and he seats himself on a heap of snow to take a rest. He begins to dream of the not distant inn where the wife of the innkeeper will prepare a warm broth for him. He already sees himself seated at the table when strange persons enter the room. He soon recognizes them as his sons, and they embrace him and kiss him impetuously. In vain he begs them to desist from their choking embraces, for he is old and feeble. He begs them to be careful with him, for he has been intrusted with a sum of money that must be brought to its place of destination. . . . The old messenger was found dead, his hand upon his coat pocket in which he carried the intrusted document.

The second sketch is of a more cheerful character. It tells of the many troubles and doubts that a certain boy has ere he discovers what a soul really is. When very young his father dies, and they tell him that his soul has flown to heaven. Ever after he imagines the soul to be a bird. But he is ridiculed for that belief by his teacher's monitor. The teacher himself is accustomed to maltreat the boys and whip them mercilessly. He explains to them that the punishment of the body is good for the soul. What, then, is the soul? the young boy asks himself again. Then the teacher tells the children many fairy tales about the prenatal life of the soul, when the angel of life instructs it daily in the wisdom of the Bible and the Talmud. And that belief is soon taken from him by his instructor of penmanship, who has a turn to liberal ideas. So the boy keeps on wavering from belief to doubt and back again until the age of seventeen or eighteen, when he is studying the Talmud with a new teacher. Once, in his absence, it occurs to him to get the opinion of Gütele, his beautiful daughter, who is known by the name of the wise Gütele, on the question which has been puzzling him so long, and for which he has suffered so often in his life. With trembling he asks her:

"'They say, Gütele, that you are wise. Tell me, then, I beg you, what is a soul?'

"She smiled and answered:

"'Truly, I do not know.'

"Only all at once she grew sad, and tears filled her eyes.

"'I just happened to think,' she said, 'when my mother of blessed memory was alive, my father used to say that she was his soul . . . they loved each other so much! . . .'

"I do not know how it came to me, only I suddenly took hold of her hand, and trembling, said:

"'Gütele, would you like to be my soul?'

"She answered me, softly:

"'Yes.'"

From these two soulful, tender stories, we pass to one not less pathetic and an even more profound psychological study. The beggar-student, harmlessly insane, has grown faint from two days' fasting and long poring over the Talmud, and is discussing with himself whether he is one, or two, or more, and whether he is really himself. He has finally the same doubts of Wolf the Merchant, who is just reading in the Talmud. He imagines that three Wolfs are sitting there: one who is trying to cheat God with his piety; one who cheats his fellow-men in his shop; and one who beats his wife who furnishes the beggar-student with an occasional meal. He takes a violent dislike to the third Wolf, and would like to kill him, but he does not wish to injure the other two Wolfs. The monologue of this beggar-student, told in about twenty octavo pages, is one of the most remarkable to be found in any literature: it must be read in the original to be fully appreciated.

With such a book Perez made his entrance into the field of letters. To say that his future works show a riper talent would be to place too low an estimate on his first book, which, in spite of the many excellent

things he has written, still remains among the very
best. In 1891, when Spektor's annual was temporarily
suspended, and Rabinowitsch's periodical had ceased
appearing, Perez issued a new periodical, *Die jüdische
Bibliothēk*, which he intended to be a semi-annual, but of
which only three volumes have so far been issued. In
the introduction to the first volume Perez makes a plea
for the education of the people, in which are the following significant words: "Help us educate the poor,
wretched people; leave them not a prey to fanatics,
who will suck out the last trace of blood and the last
trace of marrow from their lean bones. Leave them
not in the hands of the visionaries, who will entice
them into wildernesses! Let not boys and school-chil-
dren lead them by the nose, — have pity on the people!
Let them not fall! The people have in themselves a
certain amount of vital power, a fund of energy. The
people are the carriers of a civilization that the world
does not undervalue, of ideas that would be of great
use to it. The people are an ever living flower. . . . In
daytime, when the sun shines, when the spirit of man
is developing, it revives and unfolds its leaves; but no
sooner does dark night approach than it closes up
again, shrivels up, and goes back into itself. . . . It is
then that it has the appearance of a common weed . . .
and when the sun once more rises, some time passes
before the sun seeks out the flower and the flower discovers that the sun shines. . . . At night it becomes
dusty and soiled, so that the beams of light cannot
penetrate it easily! Help the people to recognize the
sun early in the morning! . . . But the main thing,
means must be devised for the people to earn a living. . . ."

In conformity with this platform, Perez calls his new

periodical a literary, social, and economical periodical. Not only did the difficult task of editing this novel magazine devolve on Perez : he had also to supply the greater part of the literature himself, for there existed no writers in Judeo-German who could follow him readily in his new departure. He had to write the greater part of the scientific department, all of the reviews, all the editorials. In addition, he furnished most of the poetry and the novels. The few other writers who published their articles in this magazine owed their development to the editor's fostering care : they had nearly all been encouraged for the first time by him. Of his scientific articles particular mention must be made of his long essay ' On Trades,' which is a popularization of political economy, brought down to the level of the humblest reader. The admirable, entertaining style, the aptness of the illustrations, and the absence of doctrinarianism make it one of the most remarkable productions in popular science. Still more literary and perfect in form are his ' Pictures of a Provincial Journey.' It seems that Perez had been sent into the province for the sake of collecting statistical data on the condition of the Jews resident there. This essay is apparently a diary of his experiences on that trip. We do not remember of having read in any literature any journal approaching this one in literary value. What makes it particularly interesting is that it is written so that it will interest those very humble people about whom he is writing. The picture of misery which he unrolls before us, however saddening and distressing, is made so attractive by the manner of its telling that one cannot lay aside the book until one has read the whole seventy quarto pages.

Perez has written more than fifty sketches, all of

them of the same sterling value as the three described
above. Every new one is an additional gem in the
crown he is making for himself. They are all characterized by the same tender pathos, the same excellence
of style, the same delicacy of feeling. He generally
prefers the tragic moments in life as fit objects for his
sympathetic pen, but he has also treated in a masterly
manner the gentle sentiment of love. But it is an
entirely different kind from the romantic love, that he
deems worthy of attention. It is the marital affection
of the humblest families, which is developed under difficulties, strengthened by adversity, checkered by misfortune; it is the saintliest of all loves that he tells about
as no one before him has ever told. In the same manner
he likes to dwell on all the virtues which are brought
out by suffering, which are evolved through misery and
oppression, which are more gentle, more unselfish, more
divine, the lower we descend in the scale of humanity.
Nor need one suppose that in order to show his characters from that most advantageous side, the author has
to resort to disguises of idealization. They are no
better and no worse than one meets every day and all
around us; but they are such as only he knows who is
not deterred by the shabbiness of their dress and the
squalor of their homes from making their intimate
acquaintance. They do not carry their virtues for
show, they do not give monetary contributions for
charities, they do not join societies for the promotion
of philanthropic institutions, they do not preach on
duties to God and on the future life, they are not even
given to the expression of moral indignation at the
sight of sin. But they are none the less possessed of
the finer sentiments which come to the surface only in
the narrower circle of their families, in their relations

to their fellow-sufferers.   Not even the eloquent advocate of the people generally cares to enter that un-
familiar sphere as Perez has done.   His affection for
the meanest of his race is not merely platonic.   He not
only knows whereof he speaks : he feels it; and thus we
get the saddest, the tenderest, the sweetest stories from
the life of the lowliest of the Jews that have ever been
written.

In 1894 Perez published a collective volume, 'Literature and Life,' which contains, like his periodical,
mostly productions of his own.   As they were composed at some later time than those spoken of above,
and as they contain some matter in which he appears
in a new rôle, we shall discuss the volume at some
length.   In the introduction are given his general aims,
which are not different from those expressed in his
former publication.   The final words of it are : "We
want the Jew to feel like a man, to take part in all
that is human, to live and strive humanly, and if he
is offended, to feel offended like a man !"   The first
sketch is entitled 'In the Basement.'   It is the story
of the incipient marital love of a young couple who
are so poor that they live in a dark basement, in a room
that serves as a dwelling for several families whose
separate 'rooms' are divided off from each other only
by thin, low partitions.   The second is 'Bontsie Silent,'
which is given in our Chrestomathy.   It belongs to the
same category of sketches as his 'The Messenger.'   It
presents, probably better than any other, the author's
conception of the character of the virtues of the long-
suffering masses.   Who can read it without being
moved to the depth of his heart?   There is no exaggeration in it, no melodrama, nothing but the bitter
reality.   It expresses, in a more direct way than any-

thing else he has written, his faith that the Kingdom of Heaven belongs to the lowly.

The sketch named 'The Fur-Cap' is one of the very few that he has written as an attack on the Khassidic Rabbi. There is here, however, a vast difference in the manner of Perez and of Linetzki. While the latter goes at it in a direct way, with club in hand, and bluntly lets it fall on the head of the fanatic, Perez has above all in mind the literary form in which he clothes his attack, and we get from him an artistic story which must please even if the thrusts be not relished. The Rabbi never appears in public without his enormous fur-cap, which is really the insignia of his office. In this story we find the furrier engaged in a monologue, in which he tells of his delight in making the Rabbi's cap. He feels that it is he who gives all importance to that dignitary, for it is the cap that makes the Rabbi. He relates of the transformation of a common mortal into an awe-inspiring interpreter of God's will on earth. No important occurrence in life, no birth, marriage, or death, can take place without the approval of him who wears that fur-cap. It is the cap, not the man, and his wisdom, that sanctions and legalizes his various acts. Were it not for the cap, it would not be possible to tell right from wrong. This fine bit of sarcasm is not a mere attack at the sect of the Khassidim; it is also meant as an accusation of our whole social system, with its conventional lies. Perez does not show by his writings to what particular party he belongs, but he is certainly not with the conservatives. He is with those who advocate progress in its most advanced form. He is opposed to everything that means the enslavement of any class of people. In Russia, where one may not express freely views which are not in accord with the sentiments of the governing class, authors have to resort frequently to the form of allegory, fable, or distant allusion, instead of the more direct way of writers in constitutional countries. For these reasons pure literature is generally something more to the Russians than mere artistic productions. The novel takes frequently the place of a political pamphlet, of an essay on social questions. The stories of the Judeo-German authors share naturally the same fate with those of the Russians, and, consequently, cannot be free of 'tendencies' whenever the writers have in mind the treatment of subjects which would be dealt with severely by the censor. Much of the alleged obscurity of Perez's writings is just due to the desire of avoiding the censor's blue pencil, and the more dangerous a more direct approach becomes, the more delicate must be the allegory. The best of that class of literature is contained in this volume in a series entitled 'Little Stories for Big Men.'

The first of these is called 'The Stagnant Pool.' We are introduced here to the world of worms who live in the pool, who regard the green scum as their heaven, and pieces of eggshells that have fallen into it as the stars and the moon upon it. A number of cows stepping into the pool tear their heaven and kill all who are not hidden away in the slime. Only one worm survives to tell the story of the catastrophe, and he suggests to his fellows that that was not the heaven that was destroyed, that there is another heaven which exists eternally. For this the narrator was thought to be insane and was sent to an insane asylum. The second sketch, 'The Sermon of the Lamps,' in which the hanging lamp instructs a small table lamp to send its flame heavenwards and not to flicker in anar-

chistic fashion, is a fine allegory in which the social
order of things is criticised. There are altogether ten
such excellent allegories, or fables, in the collection, all
of the same value. The last of Perez's articles in the
book is a popular discussion of what constitutes property; it is written in the same style as his scientific
works spoken of before.

From 1894 to 1896 Perez has been issuing small
pamphlets of about thirty octavo pages at irregular ·
intervals. They are called 'Holiday Leaves,' and bear
each a special name appropriate for each particular
occasion. A certain part of these pamphlets has stories
and discussions to suit the occasions for which they are
written, but on the whole their contents do not differ
from those of his periodicals. Here again Perez has
furnished· most· of the matter. The other writers are
David Pinski, J. Goido, Solomon Grossglück, M. J.
Freid, who also contributed to his earlier magazines.
It is evident that they follow their master in the
general manner of composition, though at a respectable
distance. Of these, Freid[1] has written some good
sketches of animal life. His 'Mursa' is the story of a
bitch who has given birth to some puppies : — her love
for her offspring, her madness when she finds her young
ones drowned and gone, and her death by strangulation.
'Red Caroline, a Novel of Animal Life,' is a similar
story from the life of a cow. They are well told and
display talent in the author. Of the others, Pinski[2]
deserves to be mentioned specially, both on account of

[1] In *Hausfreund*, Vol. V. pp. 136–145 ; Spektor's *Familienkalender*,
Vol. V. pp. 45–51 ; *Widerkol*, pp. 5–18 ; *Jüd. Bibliothēk*, Vol. III. pp.
89–94 ; *Literatur un' Leben*, pp. 89–95 ; *Jontew-blättlech*, No. 16.

[2] In *Hausfreund*, Vol. III. pp. 231-241, 265–277 ; *Jüd. Bibliothēk*,
Vol. III. pp. 84–89 ; *Literatur un' Leben*, pp. 23–47, 163. *Jontew-
blättlech*, Nos. 1, 3, 20, 22, 24, 29 ; 2d Series, Nos. 1, 2, 5.

the quantity and the quality of his work. Most of his sketches do not rise above the mediocre, but there are several that are as good as those of Spektor. The best of his are those that are entitled 'The Oppressed,' the first of which appeared in 'Literature and Life.' In this he tells of the tyranny exercised by a shopkeeper on his clerk, and of the timidity of his wretched subordinate, who merely ekes out an existence by working for him from daybreak until late at night from one end of the year to the other. The brutal master, the cowardly, downtrodden clerk, his courageous daughter who urges her father to leave the store in spite of the shopkeeper's protest, the scene at home, where his wife has just given birth to a child, where there is no money for a fire or for medicine, — all this is drawn dramatically and naturally. Goido[1] began to issue a series of stories in Wilna, in the manner of Perez's 'Holiday Leaves,' and they attracted Perez's attention, who encouraged him in his literary career. Regarding his career in America, we shall find him more especially mentioned in the next chapter.

After the financial failure of the different magazines started since 1887, only Spektor's *Hausfreund* has been able to survive with some degree of regularity. The last of this series appeared in 1896, after which Judeo-German letters seem to have been checked entirely. There still appear publications by societies, but they are all of a Zionistic nature. It is hard to foretell what the future of this literature will be. But having worked out such a variety of styles in the last fifteen years, it can hardly fail of presenting the same interesting features with which

[1] In addition to his own publications see *Hausfreund*, Vol. III. pp. 294–304; *Jüd. Bibliothek*, Vol. I. pp. 90–98; *Jontew-blättlech*, Nos. 7, 8, 18.

we have just become acquainted, unless, indeed, the intelligent classes abandon this field for other European
languages and turn it over to the class of writers who
have in view the filling of their pockets and not the
good of the people. Then it will revert to the chaos into
which it was led by Schaikewitsch and the like. In any
case it will reflect the conditions from without; it will
flourish in proportion as the Jews are oppressed by the
government and public opinion; it will disappear when
full rights shall have been accorded them. The latter
are not to be hoped for in any appreciably near time,
hence Judeo-German letters will continue to be an
anomaly in Russia, in Galicia, and in Roumania for
some time to come.

Although this literature has assumed such great proportions and has produced a score or more of good writers, it has still remained an unknown quantity to a large
number of the better classes who have not yet broken
entirely with their mother-tongue. They continue
looking with disdain at the popular language and thus
make it hard for those who devote themselves to the
service of the people to produce the desired effect; for,
failing to get the support of those whose opinion might
weigh with the masses, the latter are somewhat indifferent themselves. Another unfortunate factor in the
development of this literature is the petty jealousies
of many of the writers, which have again and again kept
them from uniting for concerted action. If in spite of
all this it has been able to hold its own and to evolve
to such perfection, it is due to the untiring, self-sacrificing, noble efforts of Zederbaum, Spektor, Rabinowitsch,
and Perez. All honor to these men!

XIV. PROSE WRITERS SINCE 1881: IN AMERICA

MANY years before the great immigration of the Jews had begun, there was a sufficiently large community of Russian Jews resident in New York to support a newspaper. In the seventies there existed there a weekly, *The Jewish Gazette*, and there was at least one book store, that of the firm of Kantrowitz, that furnished the colony with Judeo-German reading matter. The centre of that Jewish quarter was then as now on Canal Street, where there was also the Jewish printing office of M. Topolowsky, from which, in 1877, was issued a small volume of Judeo-German poetry by Jacob Zwi Sobel, probably the first of the kind in America. His few songs are all in the style of Goldfaden. One, entitled 'The Polish Scholar in America,' is especially interesting, not from a literary standpoint, but from the light it throws on the condition of the Jews before the eighties. Whether they wished so or not, they were rapidly being amalgamated, on the one side by the German Jews, on the other by the American people at large. Many tried to hide their nationality, and even their religion, since the Russian Jews did not stand in good repute then. The vernacular was only used as the last resort by those who had not succeeded in acquiring a ready use of the English language, and its approach to the literary German was even greater than that attempted by Dick at about the same time in Russia. However, English words had begun to creep in freely and to modify the Germanized dialect. It is evident that the seeds of the American Judeo-German, as it may now be found in the majority of works printed in New York, had been sown even then. The proneness to use a large number of German words is derived from the time when the smaller community had been laboring to pass into American Judaism by means of the German Jewish congregations.

Suddenly, in 1881, began the great forced emigration of the Jews from Russia, and in the same year the main stream of the unfortunate wanderers commenced to flood the city of New York, and from there to spread over the breadth and the length of the United States. At present there are, probably, not less than three hundred thousand Russian Jews to be found in New York alone. The aspect of the Jewish colony was at once changed. It was thrown back into conditions resembling those in congested Russian cities. There came misery, poverty, and squalor. The struggle for existence was even harder than it had been at home. They had exchanged the tyranny of the autocracy for the liberty of the republic, but they did not at the same time better their material well-being. It was then that the sweat-shop with all its horrors had its beginning, or at least found its most objectionable development. And they were not all laborers who were forced to tread the sewing-machine, or roll cigars and fill cigarettes. Many of them had seen better days at home, some had even been students at gymnasia and at universities. Without any previous training in their particular occupations, forced to do ten and twelve hours' work of the hardest labor, they had no time to think of any but the most sordid, more immediate physical needs. Some indeed succeeded in establishing themselves perma- .

nently, but the majority groaned under a heavy yoke.
Only by degrees did more and more of them issue from
the sweat-shops, to take up other occupations ; but few
of them ever forgot the horrors of their first years in
America.   The whole course of the Judeo-German
literature is a reflex, on the one side, of their sufferings,
on the other, of the greater liberty, the slowly increasing well-being.

With the large immigration came also some of the
literary men : Zunser, Schaikewitsch, Seiffert, Goldfaden.   They at once set about to produce books with
the same vim that they had developed at home.   But
the field was not so profitable, and they had to turn to
other work.   Schaikewitsch and Zunser have become
printers instead of writers of books, and Goldfaden
gave up his attempt in despair and returned finally
to Europe.   However, in the short time that they
have been active in America, they have succeeded in
doing immeasurable harm not only to Judeo-German
literature, but to the people for whom they wrote as
well.   They have corrupted the language in accord
with the forms which they found in vogue among the
Jews who had been here before them, and they started
out to minister to the sensational tastes of the masses
who received their nourishment from the lower English
press of New York.   The amount of many-volumed so-
called novels that they have produced is simply appall-
ing.   These are mainly adaptations of the most sensational novels in whatsoever language they could lay their
hands on.   Goldfaden also started *The New York Illustrated Gazette*, the first of the kind in Judeo-German,
but it lived only a short time.   In spite of the mass of
printed matter in the vernacular, literature did not pay
in America, and Goldfaden left the country in disgust.

But the eighties were not by any means devoid of interest and far-reaching importance to Jewish letters. During that time Judeo-German journalism received its fullest development. In Russia a daily press could not exist at all, and the few weeklies that had been issued from time to time had to move in such closely circumscribed limits that journalism ever remained there in its infancy. But on the other side of the Atlantic, the first thing the Jews learned to value and to make free use of was the newspaper. A large number of these were started in the first ten years of the great immigration, but most of them have been of short duration. In the struggle for existence the oldest newspaper, that had had its beginning in•1874, came out victorious. It bought out and consolidated twenty Jewish dailies and weeklies and now appears in the form of *The Jewish Gazette*, as the representative of the more conservative faction of the Russian Jews of America. But the most active in that field of literature were those who at the end of the eighties clustered around the newspapers that were published in the interest of the Jewish laborers. Of these *Die Arbeiterzeitung* was the most prominent.

A number of causes united in making the socialistic propaganda strongest among the Russian Jews. They had come from a country where all the elements of opposition naturally gathered around the political parties that stood in secret conflict with the Government and also the social order of things. In America, they came at once in contact with the sweat-shop and similar industrial oppressions, which only sharpened their dislike of the social structure. Intellectually they stood higher than those of their brethren who persevered with the conservatives, for they had at least come to think about their condition and the affairs of the world, while the others clung to old superstitions and did nothing to drag themselves out from the slough of ignorance into which they had fallen in Russia. At the same time the many intelligent men who had been driven to the United States nearly all had belonged to the opposition parties at home, and it was from them alone that the masses could be saved from the clutches of the sensational novelists. This struggle between Schaikewitsch and his tribe on the one side and the intelligent writers on the other began towards the end of the last decade, and the older men are being as surely driven to the wall here as they have been in Russia by Rabinowitsch and the newer school of writers. These younger men have, with but one exception, been driven to Judeo-German letters as their last resort. Some of them had never before published anything in any language, and none of them had ever practised writing in their vernacular. They all belonged to that class of Jewish young men who had received their instruction in Russian schools, or who had in any way identified themselves completely with their Gentile comrades. They had all reached their school age in the seventies, when everybody was as eager to become Russianized as two decades before their parents had been to oppose the new culture. Either as belonging to the Jewish race, or because of their sympathies with the Nihilists, they had to flee from the country. These form to a great extent the basis for the Russian intelligence in the United States.

They brought with them the idea of the Narodniks, which was that their energies ought to be devoted to the uplifting of the masses. They could not hope to become in any way influential among the native population in the American cities. They, consequently, directed their attention to their own race. One of the first to arrive in America with the great immigration, was Abraham Cahan. He was born in the year 1860 in Podberezhe, in the government of Wilna. His early years had been passed in a Jewish school perfecting himself in Jewish lore. At the age of fourteen he entered the Hebrew Teachers' Institute at Wilna, from which he graduated in 1881. He was appointed a teacher in a government school in a small town in the province of Witebsk, but he had soon to flee, having been discovered by the police as a participant in the nihilistic movement. The next year he arrived in New York penniless. He had a hard struggle for three or four years. Since that time he has been active as the founder of several excellent Judeo-German periodicals, as a writer in the dialect himself, as a contributor to the English press, and, finally, as a writer of English books. Of the latter, 'Yekl' was published a short time ago by Appleton & Co., and 'The Imported Bridegroom and Other Stories,' by Houghton, Mifflin & Co. He has also contributed to the *Cosmopolitan*, *Short Stories*, and the *Atlantic Monthly*.

His Judeo-German activity began with the foundation of the *Arbeiterzeitung*, devoted to the interest of socialism and enlightenment among the Jewish masses. To this gazette he contributed largely. Most of his articles are popularizations of sciences, but he has also written several books of stories, mostly from the life of the New York Ghetto. Like his English stories, they are composed in a good literary style, and present vivid pictures of Jewish life as it is modified under American conditions. It may be safely asserted that his English sketches are conceived by him first in the Judeo-German, after which they are adapted for an American

public. While showing great merit, it cannot be said
of his novels that they equal those of the writers in
Russia. In fact, there has not arisen in America any
author who has shown the same degree of originality
as those of the mother-country, even though they frequently surpass them in regularity of structure, and in
the fund of information they possess. Among the large
number of writers in New York who have contributed
to the literature, it can hardly be said that any individual style has been developed. They resemble each
other very much, both in the manner of their compositions, and the subjects they treat. Nor could it be
otherwise. They nearly all are busy popularizing science in one way or other, or they write novels from the
life of the Jewish community, which, in the less than
two decades of its existence, has not developed, as
yet, many new characteristics. They imitate Russian
models for their stories and novels, mainly Chekhov.
They are all of them realists, and some have carried
their realism to the utmost extent.

One of the most fruitful popularizers of science has
been Abner Tannenbaum. His works have all the
merit of being based on real facts, though these are
presented in the attractive form of novels, whether
original or translated. He is now exerting an influence also on the Jews of Russia, where his works are
much valued. He was born in 1847, and, up to the
year 1889, was a wholesale druggist. In that year he
arrived in America, and, for the first time, began writing in the vernacular. At first, he translated novels
from German and French, especially the works of Jules
Verne. Later, he wrote some novels after the fashion
of the German pedagogue, J. H. Campe, in his works
'Robinson the Younger' and 'The Discovery of Amer-

ica.' Since 1893, he has been a permanent contributor to *The Jewish Gazette*, where he has been writing and popularizing encyclopedic items.

The early history of J. Rombro, who is writing under the pseudonym of Philip Krantz, does not differ much from that of Abraham Cahan, with whom he has been active in the publication of the same periodicals. He had to flee from Russia about the same time. He went to London and Paris, from which place he contributed to various Russian magazines. In London he met Winchevsky, who, at that time, had been editing a Judeo-German newspaper, *The Polish Jew*. He was asked by him to write a description of the riots against the Jews. " It was a hard job for me," so writes the author, " and it took me a long time to do it. I never thought of writing in the Jewish Jargon, but fate ordered otherwise, and, contrary to all my aspirations, I am now nothing more than a poor Jargon journalist." The author's evil plight has, however, been the people's gain, for to his untiring activity is due no small amount of the enlightenment that they have received in the last ten years. In 1885 he was invited by a group of Hebrew workingmen, rather anarchistic than social-democratic, to edit a socialistic monthly, *The Workers' Friend*. Against his will, for he was a social-democrat, he accepted the offer. This monthly became the next year a weekly. Later, he translated Lassale's ' Workingmen's Program' into Judeo-German. About that time, in 1890, he was invited by the Jewish socialists of New York to come to the United States and edit a strictly social-democratic paper. He gladly accepted this invitation, and March 6, 1890, the first number of the *Arbeiterzeitung* was issued; since 1894 it has been appearing under the name of the *Abend-Blatt* as a daily, and it is now the official Jewish organ of the socialist labor party. He was also the first editor of the *Zukunft*, started by the Jewish socialist sections of the United States in 1892. Now he is contributing to the monthlies *Neuer Geist* and *Neue Zeit*. His articles are all characterized by great earnestness, and by a good flowing style. He is far from being a blind partisan, and he knows how to treat impartially questions of a general import.

The nineties have passed in the United States in the often-repeated attempt to establish permanent Judeo-German magazines. There have been a large number of them in existence, and one after the other has met with financial failure. Now, however, there are several that promise to last a longer time. Never before has the periodical press in Judeo-German been brought to such a perfection as regards its outward form and the variety of subjects that it has incorporated in its pages. The first of the kind was the *Zukunft* just mentioned. It lasted until the year 1897, when it gave way to the *Neue Zeit*, which is practically a continuation of the first. It differs little from similar popular science magazines in other languages. We find in it such articles as, What is Socialism? Philosophy and Revolution; A Dog's Brain, by John Lubbock; Shakespeare, his Life and his Works; Pasteur and his Discoveries; and similar scientific articles. To these must be added many literary articles, stories, poems, reviews, and the like. Among the several good contributors of the latter class of literature we shall dwell at a greater length on B. Gorin and Leon Kobrin.

B. Gorin is the pseudonym of J. Goido, of whose activity in Russia we have spoken before. After the failure of his undertaking in Wilna, mainly through the interference of the censor, who delayed his publication in every possible way, he went to Berlin to attend lectures at the University. He soon went to America, where shortly after, in 1895, he became the editor of a Philadelphia Judeo-German newspaper. From there he went to New York, where he published the 'Jewish American Popular Library,' a collection of short stories in the manner of his Wilna edition; but its life was cut short after the seventh number. He has since been the editor of the *Neuer Geist*. The most of his sketches were published in the *Arbeiterzeitung* and in the *Abend-Blatt*, when it was still edited by A. Cahan. At first he confined himself exclusively to short sketches in the style of the Russian writer, Shchedrin, but soon he followed the example of all of those who have written in America, and has translated foreign authors, has written reviews, and popularized science. In Russia he had begun the translation of 'David Copperfield.' In America he has translated Chekhov, and has in one way or other introduced the Russian Jews to the works of Daudet, Maupassant, Sienkiewicz, Korolenko, Dostoyevski, Bourget, Garshin, Potapenko, and many German and English novelists.

One of the most original writers of the realistic school in the manner of the Russian Chekhov is Leon Kobrin. He has lately started the publication of a 'Realistic Library,' of which the first number so far issued contains several sketches that have been written by him in the last two years. One of the best in that volume is the first, 'Jankel Boile,' a story from the life of Jewish fishermen. One is rather inclined to doubt that his Jewish characters really exist as he has depicted them ; it almost seems as if they were a transference of Russian men to Jewish surroundings, for they

seem to do things that are not met with as peculiarities
of the Jews in the many novels by Judeo-German writers.   But it may be that he speaks from intimate
acquaintance with a class of people that is not generally
accessible to the average writer.   Barring this, the
story is very vividly told.   It is a sketch of a Jewish
boy who has grown up with the village boys, and who
has but the faintest idea of his Jewish faith.   He falls
in love with one of the peasant girls of his acquaintance,
whom he courts, and for whom he is about to give up
the faith of his fathers.   In the last moment, when out
in the night on a fishing tour on the stormy lake, he is
caught with remorse at his impending apostasy, and he
commits suicide by jumping in the lake.   This is but a
bare outline of a most excellently developed story, in
which realism has been carried to a *ne plus ultra*.   His
portrayal of the lower classes with their indomitable
passions reminds one very much of the remarkable
sketches of the Russian Gorki.

At this juncture mention must be made of the many
short sketches by Gurewitsch, who writes under the
pseudonym of Z. Libin.   They belong among the best
Ghetto stories that have been written in New York,
and they display undoubted talent.   Cahan, Goido,
Kobrin, and Libin are all young men yet, and from
them alone a regeneration of the Jewish novel may be
expected.

In 1893 Krantz and Sharkansky started a monthly
magazine, *The City Guide*, but only two numbers of
it appeared.   Two years later Winchevsky began issuing in Boston *The Emeth*, a weekly family paper for
literature and culture.   It is a pity it was stopped
before the year was out, for of all the magazines that
have seen daylight in America, it was by far the most

ably edited. Among his contributors of belles lettres
we find the names of the authors just mentioned, and
also several others. Nearly everything else is from the
pen of the editor. While in many of the leaders his
socialistic bias is pronounced, yet most of his articles
deal with subjects of a general interest. Of his poetry
we have spoken before. His prose style is even better.
It is smooth, idiomatic, and carefully balanced. He is
one of the few authors who bestow great care on a good
Judeo-German style, and file and finish it. Most interesting are his epigrams and philosophical reflections,
and his satirical sketches, which he generally ascribes
to the 'Insane Philosopher.' Winchevsky has been
very productive. Outside of his many original stories
and sketches, his poetry, and sociological articles, he
has translated a number of works, among others the
Russian Korolenko and Victor Hugo's 'Les Misérables.'
His translations are the very best in the Judeo-German language. Few have equalled him in the art of
translation. The distinguishing characteristics of all
his productions are dignity and refinement. Although
he frequently depicts Jewish life, the Jew is but an
accident of his themes, for he has ever in mind the
social questions at large, as they affect the whole world.

The year before Schaikewitsch began the publication
of the *Hebrew Puck* in imitation of the English
Puck. Being of a humorous nature, that magazine
does not show the glaring defects of his other works
to any great extent. In the same year Alexander
Harkavy started *The American People's Calendar*,
which in addition to the matter that more strictly
belongs to an almanac contains also several useful articles of a literary value. Harkavy has developed an
untiring activity in the publication of books by which

his countrymen should be introduced to the English language and to a right understanding of American citizenship. He has written all kinds of text-books, has translated the Constitution and the Declaration of Independence, and published *The Hebrew American*, an English weekly with footnotes in Judeo-German. He has also written a large number of popular articles on linguistic subjects. Many of these contain valuable matter, but it is often difficult to disentangle the facts from his personal speculations, which are not always based on scientific truths. He lacks training, and his style is otherwise colorless. But for all that, his deserts in the education of the Russian Jews of New York must not be undervalued. Of his translations we might also mention the 'Don Quixote,' of which so far only the first part has appeared in Judeo-German. Among the writers of historical essays, the most promising is the Roumanian, D. M. Hermalin, whose 'Mohammed' and 'Jesus the Nazarene' are not only fair and unbiassed statements of the foreign religious teachings, but also belong among the very few books in Judeo-German that are supplied with a critical apparatus.

The best magazine now in existence is the *Neuer Geist*, of which the first seven numbers were edited by Harkavy, but which now appears under the editorship of Gorin. It is a periodical of science, literature, and art, and has no special political bias. We find here the same contributors as in former monthlies. To those mentioned before may be added the names of Budianov, Feigenbaum, and Solotkov, who have written many good articles on sociological and philosophical matters, and Katz, who is an astute critic. Here has also appeared the best translation in verse of one of Shakespeare's dramas, 'The Merchant of Venice,' from the pen of the poet Bovchover. Another, smaller magazine, *Die Zeit*,[1] is published by the Hebrew poet M. M. Dolizki. Another well-conducted monthly is the *Neue Zeit*, issued by the Jewish-speaking sections of the Socialist Labor Party of the United States. There is no material difference in the composition of the contributors' staff. A few more names might be added to the list of men who have been active in spreading information among the Russian Jews, such as Feigenbaum, Wiernik, Bukanski. Seiffert has written some interesting accounts of the Jewish stage in America, but his language is of the order of Dick or even worse; Rosenfeld and Sharkansky have at various times produced some sketches and even dramas, but they are more strictly poets, as which alone they will survive.

The time is not far away when there will not be a Judeo-German press in America. The younger generation never looks inside of a Jewish paper now, and the next following generation will no longer speak the dialect, unless something unforeseen happens by which the existence of that anomaly shall be made possible. Already *The Jewish Gazette*, taking time by the forelock, has begun issuing an English supplement to its Judeo-German weekly. It wants to secure its lease of life by passing over by successive steps to a periodical published entirely in English, without a violent loss of its subscribers. Several of the intelligent writers in the vernacular are at the same time contributing to the English press, while some have entirely abandoned their Judeo-German. In the meanwhile that literature is developing a feverish activity. From its ashes will rise new forces in the English literature of America

[1] Since writing this, both the *Neuer Geist* and *Die Zeit* have ceased appearing.

that will add no small mite to its pages. In the short time of the existence of the Judeo-German in America, it has passed through three distinct stages : the first was the era of the sensational novel ; then followed the socialistic propaganda, coupled with the evolution of the press, but particularly the magazine. Now, without abandoning entirely the social and political ideals, the writers are combining to popularize science and to produce a pure literature. The latter is more or less under the sway of the Russian writers Chekhov, Korolenko, and Garshin. What Russia has done for the Jews in the seventies is reaped by the masses in the nineties in America.

XV. THE JEWISH THEATRE

In the beginning of the eighteenth century two plays written in Judeo-German appeared in print, 'The Sale of Joseph' and the 'Ahasuerus-play.'[1] They were intended for scenic representation on the feast of Purim, which even before that time had been given to mimic performances. These mysteries, together with another written at about the same time, 'David and Goliath,' have held uninterrupted sway up to our own time wherever the Jargon has been spoken. Schudt has left us in his 'Jüdische Merkwürdigkeiten'[2] a detailed account of the popularity of one of these plays from the start, of the manner of its performance at the house of the Rabbi of Mannheim, of the formation of the first travelling company for the execution of the drama at other towns, and many other interesting facts connected with it. These mysteries differ little from the coarse comedies and burlesques current at the time among the Gentiles, from whom, no doubt, many of the details were borrowed. Soon many imitations of the original 'Ahasuerus-play'[3] and 'The Sale of Joseph' came to rival

---

[1] For the bibliography of the older plays see Steinschneider, in the *Serapeum* (1848, '49, '64, '66, '69): *Ahasuerus*, Nos. 11 a, 387; *Purim-play*, No. 417; *Acta Esther* (Ahas.), No. 17 (cf. *Litteraturblatt des Orients*, 1843, p. 59, and *Jüd. Litteratur*, in Ersch und Gruber, § XX. Anmerkung 36); *Action von König David und Goliath dem Philister*, No. 18; *Mechiras Josef*, No. 146. On the ancient theatre, see Abrahams, *Jewish Life*, pp. 260-272.

[2] pp. 36 ff.

[3] Part of the *Ahasuerus-play*, as given at present on the day of Purim, may be found in Abramowitsch's *Prizyw*, pp. 62-65.

the older plays in popularity. Of the first a form is known to me in which the Leckerläufer is substituted for the original Pickleherring, the grotesque harlequin, while of the second I possess at least two widely different versions, not to speak of Zunser's large drama of the same subject. Altogether, this matter has not, as far as I know, been properly investigated, so that little can be said with certainty about the relations that they bear to each other. 'The Sale of Joseph,' or 'The Greatness of Joseph,' as it is frequently called, was translated at the end of the last or the beginning of this century into Judeo-German by Elieser Pawier from the original Hebrew under the title ' Milchomo be-Scholom.' It is a much more serious production than the older work, and this, rather than the one printed in 1710, has lain at the foundation of future adaptations. At least one, the versified drama under the name of 'Geschichte vun Mechiras Jössef u-Gdulas Jössef,' published in 1876 in Jusefov, distinctly claims to be a translation from the same Hebrew source. How many such plays have been actually performed it is not possible to determine now without a more careful inquiry among older men in various parts of Russia. There have just come to light a number of mysteries once popular in the Government of Kowno, while some have been printed within our own days. Such, for example, is 'The Book of the Wisdom of Solomon,' which is based on the Biblical story of Solomon's life, but which contains also Talmudical commentaries on certain facts connected with his reign. The latest, and by far the best, drama on the 'Sale of Joseph' comes from the pen of Zunser, who not only has given it a literary finish, but has perused all the sources that throw any light on several difficult points connected with the play, and has furnished in some perplexing problems solutions of his own, so as to make the whole uniform and historically correct. In his introduction he mentions a few important facts about the popularity of the subject, and the manner of its performance, or recitation. He says: "No other story from our Holy Scripture has made such an impression or has become so known to the masses of the Jews as the 'Sale of Joseph.' . . . As far back as we can remember it has been played among us by beggar-students, or by the old-fashioned badchens at weddings."

It is not uncommon to see a performance of this play given at the present time in some small town. The actors are generally the beggar-students who have to play both the male and female parts, as no women are allowed to perform together with the men. Some large unoccupied room is furnished with benches on which the sexes are generally seated separately. The stage is of the most primitive character, without decorations of any kind; and the actors like to parade in fantastic clothes which have nothing in common with the historical truth. Either the whole of the play, or at least certain passages are sung according to traditional tunes. In the 'Sale of Joseph' it is always the monologue of Joseph before his mother's grave upon which the greatest care is bestowed, as it is the most pathetic part of the drama. It is probably the prototype of M. Gordon's ballad of 'The Stepmother' and similar popular versions, for in them, as in Gordon's version, Joseph's mother sends up her consoling words to her son from her grave. An excellent description of such a performance is given in Dienesohn's 'Herschele,'[1] where the hero of the novel plays the part of Joseph.

[1] Cf. Dienesohn, *Herschele*, pp. 47 ff.

These mysteries are not the only form of histrionic art. On the Purim, many masqueraders may be seen passing from house to house, followed by a curious crowd of children, anxious to catch a glimpse of the strange mummery of men and impossible animals. In some places the children and even grown persons manage to enter the house either by sheer force, or under the proverbial pretext that they are the "bear's brother." The actors begin in a chanting way: "Good evening, my good people, do you know what Purim means?" after which they proceed with the explanation and the performance of some grotesque scene. Each group has its own Purim play, which is generally some unrecognizable fragment of the 'Ahasuerus-play,' but frequently also some original production which is jealously guarded from being imitated by rival boy performers. There is no merit in them, but an investigation even of this form of the Purim play might bring out some interesting points or bits of antiquity. The length of the burlesque is graded according to the expectation of the final monetary reward, to which they allude with the stereotyped phrase: "The play is out, give us a coin, and throw us out of doors!" [1]

The possibility is not excluded that in addition to this semi-religious form of the drama, there may also have been given performances of profane plays at an early date in Russia. It is not known whether any of the dramas written by Aksenfeld, Gottlober, or Ettinger have been played by amateur actors, but we have at least one well-attested case of a performance of that kind in 1855, — twenty years before the establish-

---

[1] Cf. Abramowitsch, *Prizyw*, p. 64: "Heunt is' Purim un' morgen is' aus, Gi't mir a Groschen un' stupt mich araus!"

ment of the Judeo-German theatre by Goldfaden. In that year the students of the Zhitomir Rabbinical school celebrated the coronation of Emperor Alexander II. by a play in which the life of the Jewish soldier and the kahal were depicted. This drama is said to have been written by one Kamrasch, but never to have been printed. It is also asserted that it served as the first impulse to Goldfaden to create a Jewish theatre, which, however, he realized only much later.

There existed a dramatic literature long before Goldfaden. We have had occasion to mention the works of Ettinger, Aksenfeld, Gottlober, Abramowitsch, Falkowitsch, Levinsohn, Epstein. After the popular poetry a semi-dramatic style was better calculated to impress the people with the new culture than simple prose, which at that time had not been well worked out. Nearly all of the prose style of the early days is more or less affected by the drama, and even Abramowitsch has not entirely got away from it. Nearly all of his stories are introduced by the stereotyped words: "Says Mendele Möcher Sforim," and there are other similar dramatic effects scattered through them. This, which is an imitation of Hebrew originals, has also been the usual way of introduction with other Judeo-German writers of the early days. The drama of Ettinger is entirely constructed after the manner of a German play, has five acts, and the laws of dramaturgy are carefully carried out. It really looks as though he had intended it for the stage. In Aksenfeld the adaptation to the stage is less apparent, while the others do not seem to have had the performance of their plays in mind at all. What is surprising is that Aksenfeld and Gottlober should have introduced in their dramas a number of couplets and songs which have no meaning unless they were meant

to be sung by the actors.   Possibly they followed the
precedent of familiar German plays even in this particular, without any other purpose before them ; or it may
be that they foresaw the possibility of their future representation and thought it best to imitate the Purim plays,
which had always some songs intermingled with the
spoken dialogue of the actors.

In 1872 Goldfaden published two of his comedies.[1]
The first, 'The Two Neighbors,' is a splendid farce,
in which two women are discussing the prospective
marriage of their two babies playing on the floor.
The children get to fighting, and one of them is hurt.
This changes the tone of their mothers, and they heap
curses on each other in the vilest manner.   The other,
'Aunt Sosie,' is the best he has ever written.   We do
not find in it the rant of his later dramas, and the
subject is taken strictly from Jewish life.   Aunt Sosie
is a woman of the type of Serkele.   She is anxious to
get her sister married, and maltreats her husband's
niece.   Her husband is under her thumb.   By the aid
of his friend Ispanski he manages to cheat his wife and
to get his niece married to his wife's brother.   Sosie is
about to marry her sister to a Lithuanian Jew, a cloak-
maker, who is already married to another woman.   His
lawful wife comes in time to prevent the bigamy of her
husband.   It is easy to see that the whole is a close
imitation of Ettinger's comedy.

During the Turco-Russian War, in 1876 and 1877,
the city of Bukarest in Roumania presented a lively
spectacle.   It was the seat of the Russian staff, and all
the news from the field of war was carried there, and
all the contracts for the commissariat were let there.
The city swarmed with Jews from Russia and Galicia,

[1] In *Die Jüdene, q.v.*

who had come there to find, in one way or another, some means to earn a fortune. Bukarest became a Mecca of all those who did not succeed at home. And, indeed, as long as the war lasted most of them managed to fill their pockets. With the easily gotten gains there came also a desire to be amused, and coffee-houses were crowded by Jews who came to them to listen to the songs of some local ballad singer. It was also not uncommon for such singers to give performances of their art in private houses to assembled guests. Goldfaden had also come there in the hope of bettering his condition. It occurred to him that he might widen the activity of the balladists by uniting several of them into a company for the sake of theatrical performances. This he did at once. Bearing in mind the fact that Jews had not been used to the regular drama, but that they were fond of music, he wrote hurriedly half a dozen light burlesques, mostly imitations of French originals, in which the songs written and set to music by him were the most important thing. There is no other merit whatsoever in the plays, as their Jewish setting is merely such in name, and as otherwise the plot is too trivial.[1] But the songs have survived in the form of popular ballads. It is interesting to note that this first Roumanian troupe consisted exclusively of men, who had also to take the women's parts.

After the conclusion of the war, in 1878, Goldfaden returned to Odessa, where he established a regular Jewish theatre.[2] Women were added to the personnel,

---

[1] Cf. Abramsky, *Bomas Jischok*, which gives an account of that period.

[2] See *Die Jüdische Bühne*. (*The Jewish Stage.*) *Herausgegeben zum 20 jährigen Jubiläum vun dem jüdischen Theater.* Publisher, J. Katzenellenbogen, New York, 1897; about 800 pages, irregularly marked. In this volume the most important contribution, though

and a number of writers began to write plays specially adapted for the stage. Katzenellenbogen, Lerner, Schaikewitsch, Lilienblum, and the founder of the theatre were busy increasing the repertoire. Of these, Katzenellenbogen was the most original and most literary. It does not appear that his dramas have been printed, but the songs taken out of several of them and issued by him in a volume of his poetry attest a high merit in them. Lerner was satisfied with reproducing some of the best German plays in a Jewish garb. Of these he later published, ' Uncle Moses Mendelssohn,' a one-act drama; a translation of Gutzkow's 'Uriel Acosta'; a rearrangement of Scribe's 'The Jewess'; and a historical drama, 'Chanuka,' of which the original is not mentioned by him. The dramas of the other two are quite weak, but they do not yet indicate that degree of platitude which they have reached later in America. The success of the theatre was complete. The original company divided in two, and one part began to play independently under the leadership of Lerner, while the other started on a tour through the Jewish cities of Russia, visiting Kharkov, Minsk, and even Moscow and St. Petersburg. In many towns

far from exhaustive, is by M. Seiffert, *Die Geschichte vun jüdischen Theater, In drei Zeit-perioden*, 47 pp. For the condition of the theatre at its beginning, in Roumania, see Abramsky, *Bomas Jischok*. For its later development cf. J. Lifschitz, *Dās jüdische Theater un' die jüdische Schauspieler, Rezensie über dās jüdische Theater in Warschau*, in *Jüd. Volksblatt*, Vol. VIII. (Beilage), pp. 773–784 (No. 20); Meisach, *Dās jüdische Theater*, in *Hausfreund*, Vol. I. pp. 160–165; *Unser Theater*, in *Jüd. Volkskalender*, Vol. III. pp. 81–86; Rombro, *Der jüdischer Theater in America*, in *Städt-anzeiger*, No. I. pp. 5–9; No. II. pp. 8–13; J. Jaffa, *Der jüdischer Theater wie er is'*, in *Jüd.-Amer. Volkskalender*, 1895–96, pp. 60–63. See also the bibliography in *Sistematičeskij ukazatel'*, p. 211 (Nos. 3137–3149), and pp. 286, 287 (Nos. 4675 and 4676).

they were received with open hands, in others the intelligent classes saw in the formation of a specifically Jewish theatre a menace to the higher intelligence which was trying to emancipate itself from the Judeo-German language and all its traditions. They went so far as to get the police's prohibition against the performances of Goldfaden's troupe.

This procedure was only just in so far as it affected the character of the plays, for there was nothing in them to recommend them as means of elevating or educating the masses. They had had their origin at a time when amusement was the only watchword, and they had had no time to evolve new phases. Seeing that in order to succeed he would have to furnish something more substantial than his farces, Goldfaden produced in succession three historical dramas : 'Doctor Almosado,' 'Sulamith,' and 'Bar-Kochba,' to which at a later time were added 'Rabbi Joselmann, or the Persecution in Alsace,' 'King Ahasuerus, or Queen Esther,' and 'The Sacrifice of Isaac,' and a fantastic opera, 'The Tenth Commandment.' None of these are, properly speaking, dramas, but operas or melodramas. They have at least the merit of being placed on a historical or Biblical basis and of following good German models. Their popularity has been very great, and the many songs which they contain, especially those from 'Sulamith' and 'Bar-Kochba,' rank among the author's best and most widely known. The latter two operas were translated into Polish, and given in a theatre in Warsaw. Just as the Jewish theatre was entering on its new course of the historical drama, the Government, by a rescript of September, 1883, closed them in Russia, and this was followed later by another prohibition of Jewish performances at Warsaw, where the first law had been obviated by giving them in the so-called German theatre.

About that time two young men, Tomaschewski and Golubok, of New York, started a theatre in New York. The troupe consisted of actors who had just arrived from London, where they found it too difficult to establish themselves. The first performance was given in the Fourth Street Turner Hall. As formerly in Russia, the Reformed Jews of the city used their utmost efforts to prevent the playing of a Jewish comedy, but in vain. It was given in spite of all remonstrances and threats. After that the theatre was permanently established in the Bowery Garden, under the name of the Oriental Theatre, which soon passed under the directorship of J. Lateiner. In 1886 another theatre, The Roumania Opera House, was opened in the old National Theatre, at 104–106 Bowery. It would not be profitable to enter into the further vicissitudes of the companies, their jealousies and ridiculous pretensions at equalling the best American troupes. Unfortunately, the authors upon whom they had to depend for their repertoires were Lateiner, Hurwitz, and other worthy followers of Schaikewitsch, who by rapid steps brought the Jewish stage down to the lowest degrees of insipidity. Not satisfied with producing dramas from a sphere they knew something about, they began to imitate, or rather corrupt, existing foreign plays, to give foolish versions of 'Mary Stuart,' 'Don Carlos,' 'Trilby,' and similar popular dramas. There were, indeed, some men who might have saved the stage from its frightful degeneration, but the theatre managers would not listen to them, preferring to pander to the low taste of the masses by giving them worthless productions that bore some distant resemblance to the performances in the lower grades of American theatres.

Only during a short period of time, early in the nineties, it looked as though things were going to be improved, for the managers accepted a number of adaptations and original plays by J. Gordin. Gordin belonged to that class of educated men who, though they had been carried across the ocean with one of the waves that bore the Jewish masses from Russia to the shores of the United States, had never stood in any relation whatsoever to their fellow-emigrants. He had been a Russian journalist, and in America he was confronted with the alternative of devoting himself to Judeo-German literature or starving. He naturally chose the first. Although he had had a good literary training, he had never before written a word in the vernacular of his people. At first he tried himself in the composition of short sketches from the life of the Russian Jews, and finding that his articles found a ready acceptance with the Judeo-German press, he attempted dramatic compositions. He has translated, adapted, or composed in all more than thirty plays, of which, however, only one has been printed. As his large variety of dramas give a good idea of the condition of the stage during its best period, they will be shortly mentioned here. Among the translations we find Ibsen's 'Nora'; among the adaptations we have Victor Hugo's 'Ruy Blas,' 'Hernani'; Lessing's 'Nathan the Wise'; Schiller's 'Kabale und Liebe,' under the name of 'Rösele'; 'The Parnes-chōdesch,' from Gogol's 'The Inspector'; 'Elischewa' and 'Dworele,' imitations of two of Ostrovski's comedies; Grillparzer's 'Medea'; and 'Meir Esofowitsch,' on a subject taken from Mrs. Orzeszko's novel of the same name. Several of his plays display more original creative power. Of these

it will suffice to mention : 'The Wild Man,' treating of
the degeneration among the Jews ; 'The Jewish Priest,'
illustrating the struggle between the progressive Jews
and the old orthodox factions; 'The Russian Jew in
America,' dealing with the condition of the Russian
Jews in New York; 'The Pogrom,' in which the late
riots against the Jews in Russia are depicted.

Gordin and a few other men, such as Rosenfeld,
Korbin, Winchevsky, might have introduced new blood
and life into the Jewish drama, but the managers and
the silly actors who in their pride permit their names
to go down on the billboards as second Salvinis and
Booths have willed otherwise. But then they are
following in this the common course pursued by all
dying literatures, and they are not, after all, to be
blamed more than the public that permits such things,
and the public in its turn is merely succumbing rapidly
to the influence of American institutions, which before
long will overwhelm peaceably, but none the less surely,
the Jewish theatre and the Judeo-German language.
Before the inevitable shall happen, they have attempted
to cling to their old traditions; but it is only a very faint
glimpse of their old life they are getting now, and in
the very weak performances that one may still see on
the Jewish stage there is already a great deal more of
the reflex of their new home than the glow of their old.
It is very doubtful whether the Jewish theatre can
subsist in America another ten years.

Of late the theatre has been revived in Galicia and
Roumania; if I am not mistaken, there exists also a
Jewish theatre in Warsaw. The plays performed there
are mainly the productions of Goldfaden, Lerner, and
a few other writers of the older period. Occasionally
a play is given there that has previously been played

in New York. If the theatre is to survive in Europe, it will naturally develop quite independently from the American stage. It must remain more national if it is at all to be Jewish. And such we really find it to be. In addition to the several dramas mentioned throughout the book there might be added David Sahik's 'A Rose between Thorns' and Sanwill Frumkis's 'A Faithful Love,' which are among the best comedies produced in Judeo-German.

Excepting the peculiar development of the theatre in America, the Judeo-German drama has remained more or less a popular form of poetry. In the form of Goldfaden's farces we may see an evolution of the farcical Purim plays, while his historical dramas stand in very much the same relation to our time that the mysteries occupied two centuries ago. Similarly the theatre, even at its best, has remained of a primitive nature.

XVI. OTHER ASPECTS OF LITERATURE

In spite of the brilliant evolution of Judeo-German literature in the last fifty years, the older ethical works of the preceding period continue in power and are reprinted from time to time, mostly in the printing offices at Warsaw and Lublin. Among these we find a large number of biographies of famous Rabbis, testamentary instructions of wise men, essays on charity, faith, and other virtues, and an endless mass of commentaries on the Bible and other religious books. Most of these are translations from the Hebrew. Of late there have also begun to appear treatises on moral subjects written specially in the vernacular. We have had occasion to mention the works of Zweifel. There have also been written sermons of a more pretentious character in Judeo-German, and even the missionaries have used the dialect for the purpose of making propaganda among them: the first to attempt this were the English missionaries, the last have been emissaries from the Greek Church. Of course these have had no influence of any kind on the minds of the people. One of the most fruitful branches of the liturgical literature has been the Tchines, or Prayers. They are intended for women, and there is a vast variety of them for every occasion in life. Some of the older ones are quite poetical, being translations or imitations of good models. But many of the newer ones have been manufactured without rhyme or reason by young scholars in the Rabbinical seminaries of

Wilna and Zhitomir. These were frequently in sore straits for a living, and knowing the proneness of women to purchase new, tearful prayers, have composed them to their tastes. They have hardly any merit, except as they form a sad chapter in the sad lives of Russian Jewish women. The old story-books and the prayers have been almost the only consolation they have had in their lives fraught with woe.

In one of Abramowitsch's novels a woman, purchasing a prayer from an itinerant bookseller, gives the following reason for being so addicted to them: " For us poor women, the Tchines are the only remedy for hearts full of sores and wounds ; they furnish us with the only means of weeping to our hearts' content, and of finding relief for our saddened spirits in a warm stream of tears. . . . It is truly aggravating and painful to see men who do not understand and who do not wish to understand our hearts make light of women's Tchines and begrudge us the only consolation we have. Let them take a seat in the women's synagogue on a Saturday or some holiday, and let them watch the many poor, unfortunate women who have come away from their homes under difficulties : — one suffering an evil fate from her husband, another a forlorn widow ; one heavy with child, another downhearted and exhausted from watching long nights at the bed of her sick, suckling babe ; one with swollen, blistered hands from standing at the stove, and another with her face careworn, and pale from heavy slave's work, from walking eternally under a yoke ; — let them watch all these sad, downtrodden women standing around the Reader, let them hear them wail and lament with eyes uplifted to their merciful, all-kind Father in heaven, bathing in tears and ready to tear their hearts out of their bosoms. If the men could see such a scene with their own eyes, they would, I am sure, never open their mouths again to ridicule the prayers of women."

Outside of these prayers and ethical treatises the most popular books since the middle of our century have been two elementary works, — one on arithmetic, teaching the rudiments of the art, the other a letterwriter. It is probably no exaggeration to say that a hundred editions of the latter book have appeared in print. It was composed by Lewin Abraham Liondor, and was intended as a guide for Judeo-German spelling and letter-writing by children and women. This has been almost the only text-book written in and for the vernacular. Liondor knew how to make it entertaining by having a series of connected stories in the form of letters and an occasional song interspersed in them. The book begins with an interesting dialogue in the form of letters between the letterwriter and the author, and ends with a number of letters from and to a schadchen, the go-between in marriage affairs. From the dialogue one can see what great popularity this humble work has had in its time. There have been issued in the last ten years a number of similar letterwriters, more in accord with the demands of the time, but the naïveté of Liondor's book has all disappeared in them, and they present no interest to the reader.

It has never occurred to Judeo-German writers to treat their language grammatically. They all started out with the idea that it was not a language, but merely a corrupted dialect which could not be brought under any grammatical rules. In this opinion they have persevered up to the present. Where they felt it, nevertheless, their duty to establish some kind of system, they have dealt only with orthography, and thus of late a few pamphlets on that subject, but of no scientific value, have been produced by them. Much greater has been the attempt of Judeo-German authors to furnish their people with text-books for the study of foreign tongues. As early as 1824 a Polish grammar appeared in Warsaw. Wherever the conditions have been favorable for it, the Jews have tried to learn the languages of their Gentile fellow-citizens. If they have so long persevered in the use of their dialect in Russia and Poland, the fault is with the Government and not with them, as we shall soon see. In the seventies Jewish youths were admitted liberally to the gymnasia and universities, and they eagerly availed themselves of the privilege and threw themselves with ardor upon the study of the Russian language. The most encouraging time for them was from the year 1874 to 1875, when all seemed to presage better days for them. The schools were crowded with ambitious children, and there were many left at home who had to get their Russian education privately or through self-instruction. To help these, a number of excellent text-books were written. Such were the books of Skurchowitsch, Lifschitz, Zazkin, Chadak, Feigensohn. All these appeared within the short period of two years. Later a number of other similar productions followed. Lifschitz also published at the same time a Russian-Judeo-German and Judeo-German-Russian dictionary, which is one of the most valuable stores of Judeo-German that we possess. Everything was preparing the way for the extermination of the native dialect in favor of the literary language of the country, when the short-sightedness of the Government drove them once more back into their separate existence.

Previous to the seventies there could be found only grammars for the study of German, French, and even English, but no works to make the study of Russian easy. Since the year 1881, when the forced emigration began, new interests have taken hold of the minds of the Jews. They have been scattered to the four winds, have formed colonies in Germany and France, but more especially in England, South Africa, and the United States. Most of those who have gone to their new homes, and who still intend going there, hardly know any other language than Judeo-German. But they must learn the tongues of their adopted countries, and we find a large number of text-books of all descriptions prepared for them. They have been driven also to Spanish America, and we find Spanish word-books and grammars written for them. Sadder still, they have begun to dream of returning to their former home in Palestine, and Arabic word-books have become their latest necessity. It must not be forgotten that this class of publications has no claim to scientific recognition; though they are sometimes written by educated men, they are meant to serve only for the immediate needs of the wandering Jew. They consequently reflect, like the belles lettres, the conditions under which the Jews are laboring.

At the dawn of the new era, in the first half of this century, few thought of the study of foreign languages. The masses were too ignorant in more essential things to be ready for that kind of instruction. It was more important that they be made acquainted with the most obvious facts around them. We saw how one of the most popular books of those days was 'The Discovery of America,' which also gave some facts in regard to physical geography. In the sixties, when books of instruction for the first time were being printed, history and geography were the first to receive the attention of those who wished to further popular instruction. Almost one of the very first to be issued then was Resser's 'Universal History,' and this was followed not long after by a primer on geography. Only after the riots, a more direct attempt was begun at the education of the people from the standpoint of their vernacular, and since then geographies and histories of the best foreign authors have been adapted to their humble needs. We find then, among others, a translation of Graetz's 'Popular History of the Jews.'

When we reach the nineties, we get a whole literature of popular science. We have Bernstein's 'Natural Science,' Brehm's 'Essays on Animals,' and a large number of other similar adaptations for this period. The most systematic distribution of such books was carried on by A. Kotik and Bressler, who published a series of text-books on the useful sciences. Among these are several on anthropology, on political economy, and even on Darwinism. But none of these can compare in literary value with the excellent essays of Perez, or even with some of the articles in the various periodicals. Within the last few years the popular stories of Tannenbaum in New York have become very popular in Russia, where nearly all of his works are being reprinted as soon as they have appeared in America. One of the most persistent kinds of this class of literature has been the one that gives instruction in popular medicine. We find such information teaching what to do in case of cholera in the first half of the century, and later for nearly forty years many such useful essays have been written by Dr. Tscherny. This exhausts the scanty collection of a scientific nature that has been produced for the masses.

Conditions have not been favorable in Russia for the development of a periodical literature such as the leaders of the people have always had in mind, and such as the writers now would like to see inaugurated. The Government has put so many obstacles in the way of their publications that they have nearly all been of an ephemeral nature, and have had successively to give place to new and just as short-lived periodicals. The earliest use of Judeo-German, at least of German written with Hebrew letters, we find in a gazette published in Prague in the beginning of the century; the next was a similar paper that was published in Warsaw in 1824. After that there ensued a long silence until the year 1848, when a constitution and the freedom of the press were announced in Austria. The happy news was brought to the Jews of Galicia by a Judeo-German proclamation issued by Jizchok Jehuda Ben Awraham in Lemberg. In a simple language the author tells his co-religionists of the change that has come over them, of the formation of a National Guard, of the Freedom of the Press, and of the Constitution. It proceeds to give the late occurrences in Lemberg, and expresses the hope of a close union with the Gentile population. "And to-day when the Gentiles cast away their hatred against us, we Jews who have always had good hearts shall certainly be one body and one soul with the Christians." A month later A. M. Mohr started a political gazette under the name of *Zeitung*, in which a corrupt German, rather than Judeo-German, was employed. This paper has subsisted, with some interruptions and various changes of form, up to the present time. The following year there was issued a rival paper, *Die jüdische Post*, which added a commercial column to the political news.

In Russia no periodical appeared until Zederbaum issued his supplement, *Kol-mewasser*, to the *Hameliz* in 1863. This weekly was not only a gazette of political news, but also a literary magazine which, as we have seen, has fostered the Judeo-German literature and has made it possible for Abramowitsch and Linetzki to develop themselves. In 1871 its life was cut short. In 1867 a short-lived attempt was made in Warsaw to issue a weekly, *Die Warschauer-jüdische Zeitung*, which followed closely the precedent set by the *Kol-mewasser*. Many of the contributors to the older magazine have written articles for the same. For some reason, emanating mainly from the censor, no periodical in Judeo-German was published in Russia during the seventies. The Jews were, however, not entirely without reading matter of that class, for at different times magazines and gazettes were issued for them abroad. The first of the kind was the *Jisrulik*, which appeared in Lemberg in 1875 under the joint editorship of Linetzki and Goldfaden. This differed from its predecessors in so far as it made the literary part the most important division in its columns. Most of the matter was furnished by the editors themselves, or rather by Linetzki alone, for Goldfaden's name does not figure upon it after the first few numbers. In less than half a year, the *Jisrulik* was discontinued. From 1877 up to 1881 Brüll issued in Mainz a weekly, *Hajisroeli*, devoted to the interests of the Russian Jews. Upon its pages one may now and then find the names of some of the older writers, but on the whole it seems to have been only in distant contact with its countrymen at home. Another weekly of the same character was started in 1880 under the name of *Kol-leom* in Königsberg. Only the next year Zederbaum succeeded in obtaining the Government's permission for his *Volksblatt*, which appeared uninterruptedly until 1889, some time after its chief contributors, Spektor and Rabinowitsch had discontinued their connection with it and had started annuals of their own. Since then, several new ones, all of them of very short duration, have seen daylight. At the moment of writing this, permission has been granted by the Russian government to a Zionistic society, in Warsaw, to publish a magazine under the name of *Bas-kol*.

There has been a steady progress in the periodical press, such as could be expected under the tantalizing restrictions attendant on a Judeo-German press in Russia. The *Volksblatt* is both quantitatively and qualitatively an improvement over the *Kol-mewasser*, which in its turn is far superior to the gazettes preceding it. The *Hausfreund* and the *Volksbibliothēk*, *Dās heilige Land*, and *Die jüdische Bibliothēk* are all more systematic, more in accord with the modern form of periodicals, than the *Volksblatt*.

There has been and still is another potent factor in the dissemination of useful knowledge and even of good literature, that is furnished by the almanacs, of which a large number have been issued at various times. The best of these were started in the seventies, just at the time when the periodical press was discontinued. One of the earliest of the kind was *The Useful Calendar*, the first of which was issued in Wilna in 1875 by Abramowitsch. In addition to the usual information given in publications of this sort, there are in it tabular data on geography, history, statistics, and similar sciences, all gotten together from the best and most reliable sources. It is a close reproduction of similar almanacs in the Russian language. Soon after a similar series was begun by Linetzki, who added a column of anecdotes to those of a more serious nature. In the nineties, when there was again a lull in the publication of the annuals and magazines, the almanac was revived, but in a still more improved form than before. In fact, it now differs little from the annuals, for the calendar is the minor part in it, while the literary division is worked out with great care. The first of this new kind was edited by J. Bernas under the name of *The Jewish Commercial Calendar* for the years 1891–1896. Among the contributors to the literary department we find the familiar names of Perez, Dienesohn, Goldfaden, Frischmann. Since 1893 Spektor has been issuing an annual almanac, *The Warsaw Jewish Family Calendar*, which is constructed after the manner of Bernas's publication. Another similar series is that issued by Eppelberg of Warsaw. The most perfect of the almanacs is the one which was started in 1894 by G. Bader in Lemberg under the name of the *Jewish Popular Calendar*, of which not less than two-thirds is occupied by literature. As contributing editors are mentioned Abramowitsch, Frug, Perez, J. M. Rabinowitsch, and a few others who have not appeared before in Judeo-German literature. These almanacs are calculated to do a great deal of good among the masses, as they are circulated in much larger editions than any other books, and as they generally escape destruction at least for the period of one year, whereas the people have not learned to preserve printed works longer than during the time they are perusing them. The rapidity with which books disappear from the market and from the possession

of private individuals is something astounding.   Of
books printed in the sixties one need hardly hope to be
able to find more than one in ten asked for, while even
those that have been printed comparatively late, in
the eighties, have frequently become a rarity.   This
is partly due to their being sold in uncut, unstitched
sheets which easily fall to pieces.   But much more
often it is the result of indifference to the printed word
which, to a certain extent, is also shared by the corresponding classes of their Gentile countrymen.   The
works that have been published in the last twenty
years stand a better chance of being preserved, as they
are well stitched and not seldom even bound.   They
are also printed on much better paper than the majority
of books of the older time.

What few Judeo-German books were issued in Russia
before the sixties were printed mostly in the printing
offices of Wilna and Warsaw.   Up to the forties, the
books that proceeded from the first place bear the
names of the printers Manes and Simel, after which
begins the activity of the firm Romm, which is still in
existence ; but Romm is not the only firm there now
as it has been for nearly fifty years.   In Warsaw we
find in the beginning of our century the office of Levinsohn ; in the forties many works were also printed at
Orgelbrand's.   In the sixties and the seventies, most
of the better works were published in the South.   The
firms of Nitsche, and Beilinsohn in Odessa and of Scha-
dow, and Bakst in Zhitomir printed nearly all the Judeo-
German books of the Southern group of writers.   The
books of the Odessa firms are particularly well printed,
and put together in an attractive form.   In the last
twenty years Berdichev, Kiev, Wilna, Warsaw, have
been the leading cities to print such books, while

Lublin in Poland, and Lemberg in Galicia, have brought out a mass of religious and legendary literature. The Lemberg chapbooks can hardly be equalled for the miserable way in which they are gotten up and printed.

Anciently Jewish bookstores could be found only in the largest cities. In the towns and villages the books were disseminated by the itinerant bookseller who carried with him a variety of things which did not have anything in common with the book trade, such as candlesticks, show-threads, prayer shawls, and other things necessary in the observance of the Mosaic Law. Even now this wandering bookseller has not gone out of existence. All the stories of Abramowitch are told in the person of Mendele Mōcher Sforim, *i.e.* Mendel the Bookseller, of whose part played in the distribution of literature and as a newsmonger many interesting details will be found in his works. It is interesting to note that a few years ago several Russians who had undertaken to spread good books among the people resorted to the same means that for a hundred years, if not longer, had been in vogue among the Jews. The books were hawked about in a wagon from village to village, and to attract the peasants, many other useful things were sold by these itinerant bookstores.

Since the dispersion of the Russian Jews in Europe and America, there has arisen in the diaspora a large number of periodical publications which serve as the medium for the dissemination of all kinds of knowledge. In England there were issued in the eighties the weeklies *The Future* and *The Polish Jew*, and in the nineties a monthly *The Free World*. Some good essays on sociological questions, mostly of a socialistic nature, were issued by the 'Socialistic Library' and

'The People's Library' in London. In Paris there has appeared since 1896 a weekly, *The Hatikwoh*, under the editorship of Bernas, the former compiler of a calendar. In that city Zuckermann is publishing also a 'Library of Novels,' in which one may find translations of many of the popular French works. Roumania has had a gazette, the *Hajōez*, ever since the seventies, which has published a number of novels in book form. The most of these are translations; the few original ones that have appeared in that collection are of little value. A few other papers may be found in Jassy and other places. In 1896 H. L. Gottlieb started a monthly in M.-Sziget in Hungary, but it lived only two months. Most of the articles in prose and poetry are by the editor himself, whose style resembles that of Linetzki and Goldfaden. There have also been published a dozen books, mostly farces or parodies, in Judeo-German, but with German letters. Nearly all of these appeared in Austria and Hungary. They add nothing to the store of the Judeo-German literature.

CHRESTOMATHY

As the main intention of the present Chrestomathy is to give a conception of the literary value of Judeo-German literature, and not of its linguistic development, the texts have all been normalized to the Lithuanian variety of speech. The translations make no pretence to literary form: they are as literal as is consistent with the spirit of the English language; only in the case of Abramowitsch's writings it was necessary frequently to depart considerably from the text, in order to give an adequate idea of the original meaning which, in the Judeo-German, on account of the allusions, is not always clear to the reader. The choice of the extracts has been such as to illustrate the various styles, and only incidentally to reproduce the story; hence their fragmentariness. Should the present work rouse any interest in the humble literature of the Russian Jews, the author will undertake a more complete Chrestomathy which will do justice to the linguistic requirements as well.

I. SSEEFER KOHELES

(Chap. I. 1–11)

1. Dās senen die Wörter Koheles, Dāwids Suhn, Melech in Jeruscholaim.

2. Hawel Hawolim, flegt Koheles zu sāgen, Hawel Hawolim, All'sding is Howel.

3. Wās kummt dem Menschen draus mit all' sein Horewanie, wās er derhorewet sich nor unter der Sunn'.

4. Ein Dor gēht varbei un' ein anderer Dor kummt wieder auf, nor die Erd' bleibt asō ēbig stēhn.

5. Gēht wieder auf die Sunn', vargēht wieder die Sunn', all's wieder in ihr Ruh' arein, sie scheint, sie schnappt nor ahin.

6. Er gēht kein Dorem un' drēht sich aus kein Zoffen, arum un' arum drēht sich aus der Wind, un' asō kummt āber a Māl araus der ēigener Wind.

7. Alle Teichen gēhn in Jam arein un' der Jam gēht noch all's nischt über; wuhin die Teichen gēhn, varstēh', dorten araus gēhn see take wieder zurück.

8. Alle Sachen mutschen sich, nor es känn kēin Mensch gār nischt all's ausreden, kēin Äug känn sich drān nit satt ānkucken, kēin Ōher känn sich nit genug vull ānhören.

9. Wās a Māl is gewesen, dās Eigene wet take wieder a Māl sein, un' wās es flegt sich zu thun, dās wet sich wieder alle Māl thun : es is' gār all's kēin Neues nischt unter der Sunn'.

10. Oftmāls wet sich a Sach mit geben, wās me sāgt : " Owa, o dās is' schōn jā spogel neu, es is lō hojo ! " Es is' schōn a Māl asō äuch gewe'n, far Zeiten, as mir senen noch efscher auf der Welt nischt gewe'n.

I. ECCLESIASTES

(Chap. I. 1-11)

1. The words of the Preacher, the son of David, king in Jerusalem.

2. Vanity of vanities, saith the Preacher, vanity of vanities ; all is vanity.

3. What profit has a man of all his labour which he taketh under the sun ?

4. One generation passeth away, and another generation cometh : but the earth abideth forever.

5. The sun also ariseth, and the sun goeth down, and hasteth to his place where he arose.

6. The wind goeth toward the south, and turneth about unto the north; it whirleth about continually, and the wind returneth again according to his circuits.

7. All the rivers run into the sea ; yet the sea is not full ; unto the place from whence the rivers come, thither they return again.

8. All things are full of labour ; man cannot utter it ; the eye is not satisfied with seeing, nor the ear filled with hearing.

9. The thing that hath been, it is that which shall be ; and that which is done is that which shall be done ; and there is no new thing under the sun.

10. Is there any thing whereof it may be said, See, this is new ? it hath been already of old time, which was before us.

11. Es gedenkt sich schōn azund nischt in dem, wās
a Māl früher is gewe'n, āber in die spätere Sachen, wās
wöllen sich erst thun, wet män noch später äuch in see
vargessen.

M. M. LEFIN.

II. DIE MALPE

('Mescholim,' etc., p. 106)

" Weis' mir chotsch ēine zwischen die Chajes,
" Ich soll nischt nāchmachen ihre Hawajes ! "
Asō thut sich a Malpele berühmen
Var a Fuchs, wās is' zu ihr gekümmen.
Dās Füchsel entwert teekef zurück :
" Sāg' nor du, parschiwe Marschelik !
" Wemen wet āber dās einfallen a ganz Jāhr,
" Er soll wöllen dir nāchmachen auf a Hāar ? "

*　*　*　*　*

Dās Moschel mäg, chleben, ohn' a Nimschel bleiben,
Itlicher wēisst es allēin, wemen zuzuschreiben.

S. ETTINGER.

III. DAIGES NĀCH DEM TŌDT

('Mescholim,' etc., p. 225)

Der karger Chaim liegt begrāben oto dā !
Kēin Āremen flegt er zu geben a Dreier ;
Er hāt noch Daiges bis der itztiger Scho,
Wās sein Mazeewe hāt gekost' ihm teuer.

S. ETTINGER.

IV. DER ELENDER SUCHT DIE RUHE

('Makel Noam,' Vol. I. pp. 71-75)

Sāg' mir, ich bett' dich, du Wind,
Du schwebst dich auf der ganzer Welt,
Wēisst nischt, wu der Elender sich gefindt
Zu ruhen ein Gezelt,

11. There is no remembrance of former things; neither shall there be any remembrance of things that are to come with those that shall come after.

KING JAMES BIBLE.

II. THE MONKEY

"Show me but one among all the animals whose grimaces I cannot imitate!" Thus a little monkey boasted to a fox that came to visit him. The fox bluntly replied to him: "Tell me, you nasty marshelik! To whom would it ever occur in a year to want to imitate you a whit?"

*　　*　　*　　*　　*

The parable, I am sure, may remain without a moral, for each one knows himself to whom to ascribe it.

III. WORRY AFTER DEATH

Stingy Chaim lies buried in this place! He never gave a penny to a poor man; he is worried even at the present hour because his tombstone has cost him so much.

IV. THE FORLORN MAN LOOKING FOR REST

Tell me, I pray you, O Wind, you who hover over the whole world, do you not know where the forlorn man may find a tent in which to rest, — where injustice has ceased, where there is never a complaint, where no

Wu Reziches hāt aufgehört,
Me hāt kēinmal nischt geklāgt,
Wu kēin Äug' hāt nischt getrährt,
Der Gerechter werd nischt geplāgt?
Der Wind schweigt un' bleibt still stēhn,
Süfzt un' entwert: "Nēin, nēin!"

Sāg' mir, du tiefes, du grōsses Meer,
Du stromst asō weit
Bei deine Inslen hin un' her,
Wēisst nischt ergez in a Seit',
Wu der Frummer gefindt a Trōst,
Zu ruhen a sicher Ort?
Wēisst nischt, wie die Stādt hēisst?
Sāg' dās gute Wort!
Der Jam stromt un' brummt: "Nēin!
"Ich hāb' sō ein Ort nischt gesehn."

Du schoene Lewone mit dein Pracht,
Du kuckst doch überall
Wenn es is' still bei der Nacht,
Verdeckt mit der schwarzer Schal.
Du gehst doch aus die ganze Welt
Tomid durch die Nacht', —
Wēisst nischt ergez ein Gezelt,
Wu dem Guten is' nischt schlecht?
Me seht sie in a Wolken bald vergēhn,
Süfzt un' entwert: "Nēin, nēin!"

Sāg' že du mir, mein Seele, fort,
Liebe un' Hoffnung derneben,
Wu die Sunn' gēht auf jeden Ort,
Wu gefindt mān a ruhig Leben,
Wu kēin Schlechts is' nischt derbei,
Me lebt nor in Frēuden,

eye has ever been in tears, and the just man is not vexed? — The Wind remains mute and arrests its course, sighs and answers : "No, no!"

Tell me, you deep, you large Sea, you flow so far around your islands here and there, — know you not somewhere in some corner, where the godly man may find his consolation and a safe place of rest? Know you not the name of that city? Tell the good word! — The Ocean flows onward and murmurs : "No! I have not seen such a place."

You beautiful Moon, in your glory! You look everywhere when all is still at night and covered with a black shroud. You pass over the whole world ever through the nights, — know you not somewhere a tent, where the good have no sorrow? — You may see the Moon disappear behind a cloud, and sigh and answer : "No, no!"

Tell me, then, my Soul, and Love and Hope also, — wherever the Sun passes is there not to be found a quiet life, where no evil goes with it, where one may live but in joy, where one may be free of sins and sorrows, of troubles and of sufferings? — They all give the one answer : "They live quietly up there in heaven!"

Vun Sünd' un' Sorgen is' män frei,
Vun Zores un' vun Lēiden?
See geben Alle ēin Antwort:
"Ruhig lebt män in Himmel dort!"

B. W. EHRENKRANZ-ZBARŻER.

V. DIWREE CHOCHMO
('Sseefer Musser Haskel,' pp. 22, 23)

Der Mensch darf sein gut, un' klug, un' frumm. Gut allēin känn a Scharlatan äuch sein; klug allēin känn an Apikōres äuch sein; un' frumm allēin känn a Narr äuch sein.

Die grösste Reichkeit is' as män is' gesund; däs grösste Vergenügen is' as män hāt a ruhig Harz; däs grösste Glück is' as män is' frumm, wie män darf zu sein.

A grōsser Mensch is' wie a Feuer: sein mit ihm vun weiten, leucht' er un' waremt; vun nähnten, brennt er.

Der Narr bei an Unglück beschuldigt dem Anderen; der Frummer beschuldigt sich allēin; der Kluger Kēinem nit.

Vun zu viel Ahawo känn män äuch viel leiden, wie vun zu viel Ssino: Jōssef hat zwēi Māl gelitten, bēide Māl vun zu viel Ahawo, ēin Māl vun Vāter's, däs andere Māl vun Potifar's Weib.

Nit alle Māl känn män gläuben Trähren: Jōssef's Brüder hāben äuch gewēint, beschas see hāben gebracht Jainkefn däs varblutigte Hemdel.

E. Z. ZWEIFEL.

VI. DIE STIEFMUTTER
('Jüdische Lieder,' pp. 40–43)

Auf'n Bess-hakwores, unter a Mazeewe,
Hört sich bitter a Kol vun a Nekeewe;

V. WORDS OF WISDOM

Man must be good, and wise, and pious. Even a charlatan can be good alone; an apostate can be wise alone; a fool can be pious alone.

The greatest riches is to be well; the greatest pleasure is to have a peaceful heart; the greatest happiness is to be pious as one ought to be.

A great man is like fire : approach it from a distance, and it shines and warms you; come close to it, and it burns you.

The fool, in misfortune, accuses another of it; the pious man accuses himself; the wise man no one.

One may suffer from too much love even as from too much hatred : Joseph had suffered twice, both times from too much love, once from his father's love, a second time from that of Potiphar's wife.

You cannot always believe tears : even Joseph's brothers wept as they brought to Jacob the bloodstained shirt.

VI. THE STEPMOTHER

In the cemetery, under a tombstone the bitter words of a woman are heard; it is a mother that cries : "Oh,

Dās schreit a Mutter : "Oi wēh mir, oi wünd !
Wās thut a Stiefmutter mein teueren Kind ?

" Mein ganzes Leben, wās ich hāb' verbracht,
Is' dās nor gewe'n a finstere Nacht ;
Mein Kind is' mir gewe'n mein Licht, mein Schein, —
Itzt leidet es nebech grōss Zores un' Pein.

" Mit Blut vun Harzen hāb' ich ihm erzōgen,
'Ch hāb' ihm gewaschen mit Trähren vun meine
    Äugen ;—
Itzt zappt män sein Blut, män brecht seine Bēiner ;
Er schreit, er wēint, — es helft ihm nit Kēiner.

" Es stēhen Menschen vun arum un' arum ;
Wās schweigt ihr Alle ? Zu seid ihr stumm ?
Wenn euer Harz is' vun Eisen un' Stēin,
Vun Kind's hēisse Trähren darf es zugēhn.

" Ot seht ! Die Stiefmutter schlāgt ihm in Kopp,
Sie drapet sein Ponim, — Blut rinnt arāb ;
Sie schlägt ihm, warft ihm auf die Erd' anieder ;
Sie beisst ihm, reisst ihm, brecht seine Glieder.

" Er schreit : — O Mutter, O Mutter, helf' mir!
Wenn kännst nit helfen, to nemm mich zu dir ! —
Stēht auf, alle Tōte, stēht auf geschwind !
Stēht auf, alle Tōte, ratewet mein Kind !

" Alle Tōte liegen ruhig in sejer Ruh' ;
Zu Gott's Kisse-kowed flieh' ich bald zu.
Vun Gott's Kisse-kowed well ich nit ābtreten,
Bis Er wet derhören mein Schreien, mein Beten."

* * * * *

" Ribōne-schel-ōlem, wu senen Deine Rachmones ?
Der Vāter bist Du vun Jessōmim un' Almones,
Wie kännst Du sehen, wie die Marschas
Giesst aus auf mein Jossem ihr giftigen Kas ?

woe to me ! What does the stepmother do to my beloved child ?

" My whole life that I have passed was nothing but a dark night ; my child had been my light, my lustre, — and now he suffers both sorrow and pain.

" With the blood of my heart I have reared him, I have washed him with the tears of my eyes ; — now they tap his blood, they break his bones ; he weeps, he cries, — but no one helps him.

" People stand all round about ; why are you silent ? Are you dumb ? Even if your heart is of iron and stone, it ought to melt from the child's hot tears.

" Now look ! The stepmother strikes him upon his head, she scratches his face, — blood trickles down ; she beats him, throws him down on the ground ; she bites him, tears him, breaks his limbs.

" He cries : — O mother, O mother, help me ! If you cannot help me take me to you ! — Arise, all you dead, arise quickly ! Arise, all you dead, and save my child !

" All the dead lie quietly in their rest ; to God's own throne I shall soon fly. From God's own throne I shall not depart, ere He will hear my cries, my entreaty."

*　　*　　*　　*　　*

" Lord of the World, where are Your mercies ? You are the father of orphans and widows, — how can You look at the evil woman pouring forth her venomous anger upon my orphan ?

"Meine junge Jāhren hāst Du mir ābgeschnitten,
Bist Du mechujew mein Jossem zu hüten;
Vun dein Welt hāb' ich nit geha't Vergenügen,
To lās mich chotsch ruhig in Keewer einliegen!

"Wie känn ich in Keewer einliegen beruht,
Wenn 's rinnt mir arein mein Jossem's Blut?
Wie känn ich zum Grub zurück sich umkehren,
Wenn mein Grub is' vull mit mein Jossem's Trähren?"

       *   *   *   *   *

"Nu, schweig schōn, mein Kind, sei ruhig mein Ne-
schome!
Ich hāb' schōn gehört vun Gott a Nechome:
Gott sāgt, 's wet sein zu deine Zores an End',
Er wet ausloesen dich vun der Stiefmutter's Händ'.

"Die Reschas, die Stiefmutter wet Gott besträfen,
Un' du, mein Kind, schweig! Zu Gott sollst nor hoffen!
Far alle deine Zores, far alle deine Lēid,
Wet Gott dir bezāhlen mit Nechomes un' Frēud'.

"Nu, schweig schōn, mein Kind, wisch' āb deine Träh-
ren!
Du sollst mich nit mehr vun mein Ruh' stören!
Gott wet erfüllen sein hēiliges Wort;
Nu känn ich schōn liegen ruhig in mein Ort."

M. Gordon.

VII. DIE MUME SOSJE
('Die Jüdene,' pp. 65–67)
VIERTE SCENE

(*Chanzi-Ginendel kummt arein; Sosje un' Silberseid
hēben sich auf vun die Pläze.*)

SOSJE.   Awade, awade! Seht ihr? O dās is' mein
Schwesterl!

SILBERSEID.   (*Nemmt bei ihr die Hand un' nēigt sich
hoeflich.*)   Es freut mich Ihre Kanntschaft.

"You have cut off my young years, You ought at least to watch over my child; I have not enjoyed much pleasure in Your world, — at least let me lie in peace in my grave!

"How can I lie in peace in my grave, when my orphan's blood flows into it? How can I return to my grave, when my grave is full of the tears of my orphaned child?"

    *   *   *   *   *

"Now, be silent, my child, be quiet, my own soul! I have had good news from the Lord! God says there will be an end to your troubles, He will save you from your stepmother's hands.

"God will punish the evil woman, and you, my child, be quiet and hope in God! For all your sorrows, for all your suffering, God will pay you with pleasures and joys.

"Now, be silent, my child, wipe off your tears! You must not disturb me in my rest! God will fulfil His holy word; and now I may lie quietly in my place!"

VII. AUNT SOSIE

FOURTH SCENE

(Chanzi-Ginendel enters; Sosie and Silberseid rise from their seats.)·

SOSIE. Certainly, certainly! Do you see? Here is my sister!

SILBERSEID. (*Takes her hand and greets her politely.*) I am glad to make your acquaintance.

Sosje. No, meine liebe Kinderlech! Sitzt euch dā a Bissele! Plaudert euch a Bissel! Un' ich mus gēhn — ihr sent junge Leut', un' mir senen schōn, chleben, ältere. Uns is' schōn der Kopp verschlägen mit andere Sachen. Män darf balebosten in Stub'. Sitzt euch dā! Ich kumm' bald. (*Sie lāst sicht aweggēhn un' leben der Thür' thut sie a Ruf.*) Chanzi-Ginendenju, mein Leben! Auf ēin Minut! (*Chanzi-Ginendel gēht zu zu-n ihr.*)

Sosje. (*Ihr in Ōher.*) Vergess' nor nit, wu du bist in der Welt! Wēiss nor mit ihm wie asō zu rēden, — der Iker, wās wēniger rēden! (*Sie gēht araus un' kuckt sich unter durch der Thür'.*)

FÜNFTE SCENE

(*Silberseid un' Chanzi-Ginendel nehmen Stuhlen un' setzen sich Ēins leben's Andere.*)

Silberseid. (*Auf der Seit.*) Ich wēiss? Soll mich asō wissen Boes', wie ich wēiss, vun wās-er a Sprache mit ihr ānzuhēben rēden! Ta, lā-mir prüwen! (*Zu Chanzi-Ginendeln, hōch.*) Et comment vous portez-vous, mademoiselle?

Chanzi-Ginendel. (*Thut a Schmēichel.*) Hm! Hm! Ihr frägt, zi bin ich noch a Mamzell! Jā! Gläubt mir, me hāt mir schōn übergeredt Schiduchim ohn' an Eck. Die Schadchonim schlägen āb die Thüren bei mein Schwester. Einer hāt mich gewollt nehmen, asō wie ich stēh' un' gēh'. Er hāt mich gewollt beklēiden vun Kopp bis Fuss, wāren er allēin is' sēhr reich, un' bei mir will er nit ēin Pitak; abi die Schwester soll nor araussāgen 'Jā.' ·Nor ich hāb' sich betracht, wās hāb' ich sich dā zu eilen, zi ich bin dā schōn asa-n-alte Māid? Erst heuntigen Summer is' mir gewor'en fufzehn Jāhr. (*Sie tracht.*) Sieben un' neun un' neun is fufzehn.

Sosie. Well, my dear children! Sit here a little while! Talk to each other! I must go away! You are young people, but we have grown to be old. Our head is filled with worries of all kind. I must look after the household. Sit down! I shall be back after a while. (*She starts away, but calls back from the door.*) Darling Chanzi-Ginendel, my dear! Just for a minute! (*Chanzi-Ginendel goes to her.*)

Sosie. (*In a whisper.*) Do not lose your head and do not forget where you are in the world. Be sure you say the right thing to him, — above all, don't talk too much. (*She goes out, but peeps in through the door.*)

Fifth Scene

(*Silberseid and Chanzi-Ginendel take their chairs and seat themselves near each other.*)

SILBERSEID. (*Aside.*) I declare! May I know of something evil if ever I know in what language to begin to speak to her! Well, let us try. (*To Chanzi-Ginendel, loud.*) Et comment vous portez-vous, mademoiselle?

Chanzi-Ginendel. (*Smiling.*) Hm! Hm! You want to know if I am still a Miss! Yes, believe me, they have been making matches for me without end. The go-betweens have been tearing down the doors of my sister's house. There was one who wanted to take me just as I am. He wanted to dress me up from head to foot, for he is himself very rich, and he does not ask for a nickel of mine; he is only waiting for my sister to give her consent. But I have thought over the matter; I thought there was no hurry yet, that I was not yet an old maid. I am fifteen years this summer. (*She thinks.*) Seven and nine and nine is fifteen.

SILBERSEID. (*Die ganze Zeit verwundert, bei der Seit.*)
No, no! A gut Min Franzoesisch! Lā-mir prüwen
weiter! (*Hōch.*) Haben Sie nicht ein Bändchen Saphir?

CHANZI-GINENDEL. Wās täug' euch a safirn Bän-
dele? Awade auf a Halstüchel! Wēiss ich, heunt is'
der Kolir schōn araus vun der Mode. Heunt trāgt
män Havana oder Bismarck. Ich hāb' erst nit lang
a Jungermann geschenkt asōns! Willt ihr? Känn ich
euch schenken.

A. GOLDFADEN.

VIII. SEMER LE-SSIMCHAS TŌRE
('Ssichas Chulin,' pp. 30–34)

1

Lechajim, Brüder, lechajim, lechajim !
Heunt senen mir die Tōre messajim,
Heunt hēben mir sie ān noch a Māl wieder ; —
Drum lechajim ulescholem, liebe Brüder !
Seid froehlich un' dankt dem Gott dem lieben
Far die hēilige Tōre, auf Parmet geschrieben !

2

Die hēilige Tōre, geschrieben auf Parmet,
Is' doch unser Trōst in unser Armut !
All's auf der Welt hāben mir verloren :
Der Bees-hamikdesch is' chorew gewor'en,
Chorew dās Land, wu mir senen gesessen,
Afile unser Loschen hāben mir vergessen ;
Nit dā unser Meluche, nit dā unser Kehune,
Nor uns is' geblieben unser Emune.
Gott in Harzen, die Tōre in der Hand,
Senen mir gegangen vun Land zu Land,
Viel Zores gelitten, doch leben geblieben,
Durch die hēilige Tōre, auf Parmet geschrieben.

SILBERSEID. (*Wondering all the time, aside.*) Well, well! That's a fine kind of French! Let us try again! (*Loud.*) Haben Sie nicht ein Bändchen Saphir?

CHANZI-GINENDEL. What do you want with a sapphire ribbon? Oh, I suppose for a tie! I declare, that color has now gone out of fashion. Now they wear Havana or Bismarck. I just lately gave a young man such a ribbon. If you want, I will give you one.

VIII. SONG OF THE REJOICING OF THE LAW

1

Your health, brethren, your health! Your health! To-day we finish the Law, to-day we begin to read it anew; hence, may you prosper in peace, dear brethren! Be merry and thank the kind Lord for the holy Law written upon parchment!

2

The holy Law written upon parchment has been our consolation in our poverty! All in the world we have lost: the Temple has been laid in ruins, in ruins the land which we have inhabited; even our tongue we have forgotten, — we have lost our kingdom and our priesthood, only our faith is left to us. God in our hearts, the Law in our hands, we went from land to land, suffered many tribulations, yet have lived through it all by means of the Law written upon parchment.

3

Kummt, liebe Brüder, kummt aher gicher!
Kummt, lā' mir öffenen die historische Bücher!
Wās derzaehlt die Geschichte? Wās schreiben die
    Chronikes?
Nor Raübergeschichten, Maisses vun Rasbojnikes!
Unser Geschichte, asō gröss wie die Erd',
Is' nit mit a Feder, nor mit a Schwert,
Nit mit Tint' geschrieben, nor mit Blut un' Trähren,
Nit in Leipzig gedruckt, nor in Goles dem schweren,
Nit in Goldschnitt gebunden, nor in Kētten un' Eisen.
Lās mir chotsch Einer kummen un' weisen,
Wu hāt men uns nit verfolgt un' vertrieben
Far die hēilige Tōre, auf Parmet geschrieben?

4

Noch gār in Ānhēb, var ganz langer Zeit,
As mir senen gewesen noch Stücklech Leut,
Wie Balebatim in der Hēim nor gesessen
Un' in fremde Haüser kēin Täg' nit gegessen,
Densmāl noch, ach! soll dās nit treffen Kēinem
Wās mir hāben ausgelitten vun unsere Schcheenim!
Wer red't schōn dernāch, wēh unsere Jāhren!
As die Schcheenim seinen Balebatim gewor'en. . . . .
Un' mir hāben gemust nit geren, beōnes,
Areinziehen wōhnen bei see in Schcheenes.
Wie hāben mir gelebt, wie senen mir gelegen?
Ach, ihr wollt't schōn besser gār nit frägen!
Wie Köpplech Kraut, wie a Haufen Rüben,
Mit der hēiliger Tōre, auf Parmet geschrieben.

5

Zwēitausend Jāhr, a Klēinigkeit zu sägen!
Zwēitausend Jāhr gemattert, geschlägen!

3

Come, dear brethren, come quickly! Come, let us open the historical books! What does history tell? What do the chronicles write? Nothing but tales of robbers, stories of highwaymen! Our history, as large as earth, has been written, not with a pen, but with a sword; not with ink, but with blood and tears; has been printed, not in Leipsic, but in heavy exile; is bound, not in gold carving, but in chains and iron. Let a man come and show me where they have not persecuted us and expelled us for the holy Law written upon parchment!

4

In the very beginning, a long time ago, when we still were of some importance, when we were sitting at home and did not lodge in strangers' homes — alas, may that not befall any one, what we have suffered from our neighbors! Not to mention later — woe unto our years! — when our neighbors became our masters. . . . And we were compelled against our will to take lodgings in their homes. How did we live, how did we rest? Oh, you had better not ask at all! Like cabbage heads, like turnip heaps, with our holy Law written upon parchment.

5

Two thousand years, no small matter that! Two thousand years of torture and vexation! Seventy-

Sieben un' siebezig finstere Dōres
Gestoppt mit Zores, gefüllt mit Gseeres !
As ich wollt' nehmen derzaehlen jede Gseere,
Wollt' heunt nit gewe'n Ssimchas-Tōre ;
Nor dās darf ich gār nit, es is' sēhr gut
Bei Jedem eingeschrieben in sein March, in sein Blut.
Mir hāben All's ausgehalten, All's aweggegeben,
Unser Geld, unser Kowed, unser Gesund, un' Leben,
Wie a Māl Chane ihre Kinder, die sieben, —
Far die hēilige Tōre, auf Parmet geschrieben.

6

Un' itzt?   Is' schōn besser?   Lāst män uns zufrieden?
Hāt män schōn a Māl derkennt, as mir Jüden
Senen äuch Menschen asō wie die Andern?
Wellen mir nit mehr in der Welt arumwandern?
Wet män sich auf uns mehr nit beklāgen?
Dās wēiss ich nit, dās känn ich euch nit sāgen.
Eins wēiss ich, es lebt noch der alter Gott ōben,
Die alte Tōre unten un' der alter Gläuben ;
Drum sorgt nit un' hofft auf Gott dem lieben
Un' auf die hēilige Tōre, auf Parmet geschrieben !

7

Lechajim, Brüder, lechajim, lechajim !
Heunt senen mir die Tōre messajim,
Heunt hēben mir sie ān noch a Māl wieder : —
Drum lechajim, lescholem, liebe Brüder !
Sorgt nit un' hofft auf Gott dem lieben
Un' auf die hēilige Tōre, auf Parmet geschrieben !

J. L. Gordon.

IX.   DIE KLATSCHE
('Die Klatsche,' Odessa, 1889, pp. 17-20)

Auf dem Feld, seh' ich, füttern sich panske Zapes,
Ēslen, ganze Tabunes Ferd, wās hāben a Jiches-brief,

seven gloomy generations surfeited with sorrows, filled with misfortunes! Were I to begin to tell all the persecutions, we should not have the Rejoicing of the Law to-day; but I need not do that, it is too well written in each man's marrow, in his blood. We have suffered all, given away all, our money, our honor, our health, our lives, as Hannah once her seven children, — for the holy Law written upon parchment.

6

And now? Is it better? Do they leave us in peace? Have they come to recognize that we Jews are also men like all others? Shall we no longer wander about in the world? Will they no longer complain of us? That I do not know, that I cannot tell you. Thus much I know, there still lives the old God above, the old Law below, and the old faith; therefore do not worry, and hope in the kind Lord and in the holy Law written upon parchment!

7

Your health, brethren, your health! To-day we finish the Law, to-day we begin to read it anew; hence, may you prosper in peace, dear brethren! Do not worry, and hope in the kind Lord and in the Law written upon parchment!

IX. THE DOBBIN

In the field I see feeding noble goats, asses, whole herds of horses who have genealogies that prove their

as see stammen araus vun ēdle Eltern. Einems Seede
is' an englischer Oger, wās hāt varzeitens, durchfäh-
rendig durch dem Land Kenoan, Chassene geha't mit
an arabischer Schkape. Dem Anderens Babe wachst
vun a berühmter Mischpoche, wās hāt in Leben genug
Pulwer geschmeckt, un' Jenems Älter-bābe hāt genos-
sen a gute Erziehung, a Edukazje, ergez in a berühmten Sawod, is' gewesen a Melumedes un' hāt in ihr
Zeit gegeben Konzert in Tanzen un' Springen in-ēinem
mit noch assach gebildete, gelernte Ferd. Denn ihr
musst wissen, as bei Ferd spielt Jiches a grōsse Rolje,
bei see kuckt män stark auf ēdel Blut, un' die wās
fun a guten Sawod hēissen ēdel oder wōhlgeborene.
Die dāsige ēdele Ferd hāben sich gefüttert frank un'
frei, senen äuch gegangen in Schāden, kalje gemacht
die Twues, welche āreme Pauern hāben gesaet mit
Schwēiss nebech, un' män hāt sich nischt wissendig
gemacht, see nischt gesāgt kein umtarbisch Wort. Die
Ferd hāben gesprungen, gehirset, gedriget mit die
Füss'. Sejer Kōach, sejer Starkkeit, un' sejer Wildkeit is' gewe'n " schelo kederech hatewa " ! Plutzlim
hör' ich vun der weitens a schrecklich Geschrēi, a Rasch
vun Menschen un' a Billen vun Hünd'. Ich hāb' tchilas
gemēint, dās hāben die Pauern sich zunaufgenummen
un' läufen mit a Geschrēi, arauszutreiben die panske
Zapes, die Ferd vun sejere Twues ; nor āber nein.
Die Kōles hāben sich alls derweitert un' sich varträgen
gār in ein ander Seit'. Ich bin gewe'n zikawe un'
gegangen nāch dem Kol, gegangen bis ich bin gekummen zu a ganz grōssen Platz varwachsen mit Grās.
Dort hāt var meine Äugen sich vürgestellt a schreckliche Scene. Jünglech, Kundeessim, hāben vun alle
Seiten sich gejägt nāch a darer, a māgerer Klatsche,
geworfen Stēiner un' ängerēizt auf ihr a ganze Tschate

descent from aristocratic parents. The grandfather of
one had been an English steed who once, during a journey through the country of Canaan, had been married
to an Arabian mare. Again, the grandmother of another was descended from a famous family, and had
smelled much powder in her lifetime, while the great-
grandmother of still another had been well educated in
some famous stud, and had, in her time, given performances in dancing and jumping in company with many
other educated, well-trained horses. For you must
know that with horses breed is of great importance ;
much attention is paid to noble blood, and those who
come from a good stud are called noble or well born.
These noble horses were grazing at their will ; now and
then they did some damage by ruining the standing
grain which poor peasants had sown in the sweat of their
brows, and no one noticed that, or said a harsh word
to them. The horses jumped about, neighed, kicked.
Their strength, their power, and their wildness were out
of the common. Suddenly I heard from afar a terrible
noise, a hollowing of men and barking of dogs. At
first, I thought that the peasants had come together and
were starting on a run with a noise, in order to drive
out the noble goats and the horses from their corn ; but
no ! . . . The voice grew more distant, and could be
heard from an entirely different direction. I became
curious, and followed the noise until I came to a very
large place overgrown with grass. There a frightful
scene presented itself to my eyes. Street urchins were
pursuing from all sides a thin, lean dobbin ; they threw
stones at her, and urged on against her a whole pack of
dogs of all kinds. Some of these dogs were whining,
barking, gnashing their teeth ; others again were biting
her as best they could. I could not stand there looking

Hünd' vun allerlēi Minim. A Thēil Hünd' hāben gār
geheult, gebillt, gekrizt die Zaehn', a Thēil āber hāben
äuch take gebissen, wie nor see hāben gekännt. Ich
hāb' nischt gekännt stēhn un' zusehn asa Majsse-ra vun
der weitens. Einmāl is' doch glatt a Rachmones, dās
Menschlichkeit derlāst nischt zuzusehn asa Achsorjes,
un' zwēitens, awekgenummen schōn Rachmones, hāt
doch die Schkape auf mir take a grōss Recht geha't,
ich soll ihr helfen, machmas ich bin eingekäuft in der
Chewre " Zar-bal-hachaim," wās ihr is' nischt niche,
män soll peinigen, änthon Leid lebedige Beschäffenisch,
wārim see senen äuch Bossor-wedom, Flēisch un' Blut,
un' hāben äuch dās Recht zu leben auf Gotts Welt wie
mir. Ich will mich dā nischt areinlāsen in dem alten
un' sēhr tiefen Schmues mikōach dem Menschen un'
die Beheemes. Lās sich sein chotsche wie Jene sāgen,
as ich, Mensch, bin der Tachles, der Zimmes, der Antik
vun alle Beschäffenisch ; nor zu lieb mir, Tachschit, zu
lieb mein Bederfenisch un' mein Vergenügen leben see
alle auf der Welt ; lās sich sein chotsch, as ich, Tachschit, bin der Meelach, der Ōberharr über alle Beheemes,
wās musen mir dienen, wās musen gēhn in Joch un'
makriw sein far mir sejer Leben, — vun destwegen,
dacht sich mir, wie bald afile a Klatsche, asa proste
Podane, hāt auf mir eppes a Recht, mus ich al-pi
Din, wenn nischt al-pi Menschlichkeit, akegen ihr jōze
sein. . . .

"Kundeessim ! " sāg' ich, zugēhendig zu die weisse
Chewre, " Wās hā't ihr, ich bett' euch, zu der Schkape
nebech ? "

A Thēil vun die Kundeessim hāben mich gārnischt
gehört, andere hāben jä eppes wie gehört un' gelacht
mit Ases. A Thēil Hünd' hāben mich eppes varwundert āngekuckt, etliche hāben gebillt vun der weitens,

quietly at such misdeeds. In the first place it is a question of pity — humanity does not permit to look unmoved at such wrong-doing. Secondly, leaving pity out, the mare had a great right to my protection, for I am a member of the Society for the Prevention of Cruelty to Animals, which is opposed to vexing and torturing any living being, for they, too, are flesh and blood, and have the same right to live in God's world that we have. . . . I shall not enter here into the old and profound discussion in regard to man and beast. Let it be as they say that I, man, am the highest aim, the perfection of all creation, that only for me and for my wants and pleasures they all live upon this world. Let it be that I, man, am the king, the supreme lord of all the animals who must serve me, must walk under the yoke and sacrifice their lives for me, nevertheless, it seems to me that even to that dobbin, who is my lowest subject, I have certain duties, and I must, in accordance with the law if not with humanity, do what is right by her. . . .

" Urchins ! " I said, as I approached the crowd of wild boys, " what have you, I pray, against that mare ? "

Some of the urchins paid no attention at all to me ; others did hear me, but they laughed at me with brazen faces. Some of the dogs looked at me somewhat astonished ; others barked at me from afar, while others

noch etliche häben ausgeschtschiret die Äugen, gekuckt schrecklich boes, senen gewe'n berēit ānzufallen auf mir vun hinten un' zureissen mich auf Stücker.

"Kundeessim!" ruf' ich mich noch a Māl ān. "Wās jägt ihr un' peinigt Gotts Beschäffenisch, die Klatsche nebech?"

"A schoener Nebech!" häben see mit Gespött geëntwert. "Far wās füttert sie sich dā? Far wās füttert sich die schoene Klatsche dā?"

"Steutsch!" thu' ich a Sāg, "dā is' doch a Pasche, dā füttern sich doch alle Städt-beheemes vun ēbige Jāhren!"

"Die Stādt-beheemes," häben see geëntwert, "senen eppes andersch, see mögen un' sie tor nischt."

"Far wās nischt sie?" ruf' ich mich ān, "sie hāt denn nischt kēin Neschome wie alle Städt-beheemes?"

"Efscher take nischt!" häben see a Sāg gethan.

"Schkozim!" sāg' ich zu see, "āber sie hāt doch sicher a Balebos, wās zāhlt in der Städt Zinsch un' alle andere Ābgāben. Sie is' doch äuch a Städt-beheeme!"

"Ot dās take wēissen mir nischt!" entwern see mir mit a Gespött. "Ōb sie is' äuch a Städt-beheeme, dās is' erscht a Schaile!"

"Es māg sein, wie es will sich," häb' ich gesāgt, "āber die Klatsche is' doch derweil hungerig, sie will doch nebech essen!"

"Lās sie essen Werem, Kränk', Makes!" sāgen see zurück. "Wās hāt sie zu uns? Far wās soll a sölche auffressen un' zunehmen bei die Städt-beheemes?"

"Gaslonim!" häb' ich schōn mehr nischt gekönnt mich einhalten un' a Geschrēi gethān mit Kas. "Far

again opened their eyes wide open, scanned me in great anger, and were ready to fall upon me from behind, and to tear me to pieces.

"Urchins!" I cried out again. "Why do you pursue and torture one of God's creatures — the miserable dobbin?"

"Miserable indeed!" they cried out scoffingly. "Why does she graze here? Why does that fine-looking mare graze here?"

"How is that?" I exclaimed, "is this not a pasture, and have not all the animals of the town grazed here from time immemorial!"

"The animals of the town," they answered, "are an entirely different matter; they may, but she may not."

"Why not she?" I called out, "has she not a soul like all the animals of the town?"

"Maybe she has not!" they retorted.

"Urchins!" I said to them, "but she certainly has a master who pays all the taxes of the town and other duties. She is a town animal like all the others!"

"That's exactly what we do not know!" they answered in scorn. "Whether she is a town animal, that's the question!"

"Let it be as it may," I said, "but in the meanwhile the mare is hungry and wants to eat!"

"Let her eat worms, get sick and die!" they replied. "What does she want of us? Why should such a creature eat up that which belongs to the town animals?"

"Murderers!" I could no longer hold myself and cried out in anger. "Why do you not pay any attention

wās kuckt ihr nischt, wās dort gēhen arum panske Zapes, ganze Tabunes Ferd zwischen die Twues un' fressen auf ārem Blut, ārem Schwēiss nebech? Dā vargünnt ihr nischt a bidner Schkape a Haufen Grās un' es art euch klal nischt, as dort thuen Ferd ān a Jam Heskejes un' machen umglücklich viel Menschen. Dās nor allēin, wās see zutreten, wās see machen kalje glatt asō, wollt' genug gewe'n der Klatsche bis Kinds- kinds-kinds-kinder! Kundeessim, ihr hā't nischt kein Jōscher afile auf a Hāar, ihr sent Kēinem nischt getreu un' ihr hāt noch a Hose sich arauszustellen klomerscht far die Stādt-beheemes!"

"He, he!" hāben die Kundeessim sich āngerufen, "er is' gār in Kas, er frägt gār eppes Kasches! Kummt Chewre! Wās täug' uns die Taines? Lās er sich schreien! Wer hört ihm? Kummt, Chewre, kummt!"

Ein Kundas hāt a Feif gethān un' bald hāben die weisse Chewre mit sejere Hünd' sich gelāst nāch der Klatsche un' auf ihr wieder āngefallen. A lange Zeit hāt mān sie getrieben, gerissen un' gebissen, bis mān hāt sie zum Ssof vartrieben in a tiefer Grub un' dort hāt sie sich eingegrisnet in Blote.

S. J. Abramowitsch.

X. TUNEJADEWKE
('Binjāmin ha-Schlischi,' pp. 6-9)

Tunejadewke, dās klēine Städtel, is' a varworfen Winkel, ān der Seit' vun dem potschtowen Trakt, kimat ābgerissen vun der Welt asō, as wenn a Māl macht sich, Einer kummt ahin zufāhren, öffent mān die Fenster, die Thüren, un' mān kuckt varwundert ān dem frischen Parschōn; Schcheenim frägen Einer beim Andern, arauskuckendig vun die offene Fenster, assach mehr wie vier Kasches: Ha, wer soll es asōns sein?

to the noblemen's goats, the whole herds of horses who run around in the grain and eat up the blood and the sweat of the poor? Here you begrudge the poor dobbin a handful of hay, and do not at all care that there the horses are doing no end of damage and making many people unhappy. That alone which they trod under foot, which they simply destroy, would be enough for the mare and her future generations! You, urchins, have no sense of justice, not a hair's-breadth of it, you are not true to anybody, and yet you take it upon yourself to take the part of the town animals!"

"Ho, ho!" the urchins exclaimed, "he is getting angry, and he asks questions of us! Come, boys! What is the use of discussing? Let him cry! Pay no attention to him! Come, boys, come!"

An urchin blew his whistle, and the rude company started with their dogs to attack once more the dobbin. They drove her for a long time; she was bitten and torn until at last she was driven into a deep ditch where she sank down in the mud.

X. PARASITEVILLE

The small town of Parasiteville is a forgotten corner of the earth, to one side of the highway, almost torn away from the world. When by accident some one visits it, the windows and doors are opened and people look in astonishment at the stranger; neighbors ask of each other, as they look out of the open windows, more than the usual four questions: I wonder who he may be? How did he all of a sudden get here? What may

Vun wannen hāt er plutzlim vun der heller Haut aher
sich genummen? Wās känn asölcher bedarfen? Eppes
asō glatt känn es nit sein, glatt asō denn nemmt män
un' män kummt? Mistome liegt doch dā eppes, wās
män mus es dergēhn. . . . Derbei will Itlicher araus-
weisen sein Chochme, sein Genitschaft, un' Bauch-
swores fallen wie Mist. Alte Leut' derzaehlen Maisses
un' brengen Mescholim vun Orchim, wās senen in dem
un' dem Jāhr gekummen aher zufāhren, Balamzojes
sāgen mikōach dem Wörtlich, a Bissel eppes nischt
kein schoene; Mannsbill' halten sich bei die Bärdlich
un' schmēichlen; alte Weiber siedlen āb die Balamzojes
auf Katowes, mit a Boeser i mit a Lachen in ēinem;
junge Weiblich derlangen vun die arābgelāsene Äugen
a gebōgenem Kuck´vun unten arauf, halten die Händ'
auf'n Maul un' sticken sich lachendig in Kulak. Der
Schmues mikōach dem dāsigen Injen kaukelt sich vun
Stub' zu Stub' wie a Kaul vun Schnee un' werd kau-
klendig sich all's grösser, grösser, bis er kaukelt sich
arein in Bessmedresch ssame unter'n Ōwen, in dem Ort,
wās ahin varkauklen sich alle Schmuessen vun allerlēi
Injonim, hen Sōdes vun Stubsachen, hen Politike mikōach Stambul, mikōach dem Tōger u-mikōach Kiren,
hen Geldgeschäften mikōach Rothschild's Varmögen in
Vargleich mit die grösse Prizim un' die andere gewisse
Negidim, we-hen Potschten mikōach die Gseeres u-mikōach die rōthe Jüdlich uchdōme, un' wās dort rasbi-
rajet see kesseeder a besunder Komität vun schoene
betāgte Jüden, wās sitzen ständig a ganzen Tāg bis
spät in der Nacht, senen mafker Weib i Kinder un'
giben sich mit die alle Geschäften take emes getreu
āb, thuen sejer Sach' bischleemes, glatt asō le-Schem-
schomajim, nischt zu nehmen far sejer Müh', far sejer
Praze, afile a zubrochenem Heller.

such a one want here? There is something wrong, for
without good reason no one would come to this place!
There is some secret in it which I must find out. . . .
And each one wants to show his wisdom, his skill, and
all kinds of speculations come as fast as hail. All tell
stories and make allusions to strangers who had visited
them in such and such a year; jesters relate anecdotes
about it, and they are not always within the bounds
of propriety; men twirl their beards and smile; old
women jokingly scold the jesters, angered and laughing
at the same time; young married women stealthily look
upwards with their drooping eyes, hold their hands
before their mouths and choke with laughter. The
conversation in regard to that matter rolls on from
house to house like a snowball and rolling grows larger,
larger, until it rolls into the synagogue near the stove,
the very place where find their final abode gossips of
all kinds, whether domestic secrets, or politics in regard to Stamboul, in regard to the Mogul and Cyrus,
or money matters regarding the wealth of Rothschild
as compared with that of great lords and the other well-
known millionnaires, or reports of persecutions and the
tribe of the Red Jews, and so forth. And there these
matters are discussed one after the other by a special
committee of pious Jews advanced in years, who sit
there whole days until late into the night, who abandon
their wives and children and earnestly devote themselves to those affairs, doing their business in peace,
just for the glory of God, without receiving a broken
penny for their labor and their work.

Vun dem däsigen Komität gēhen oft die Injonim
aweg in Bād auf der ōberster Bank, un' in a polner
Ssobranje vun Städt-balebatim wer'en see dort utwerdet, "wehakol schorir wekajom," as dernāch sollen afile
kummen kol Malchej Misrach un' Majrew, sich stellen
mit dem Kopp arāb un' mit die Füss' arauf, wellen see
gār nischt pōeln.　Der Tōger is' schier ein Māl nischt
umglücklich gewor'en in asa Ssobranje auf der ōberster Bank, wenn etliche juste Balebatim sollen nischt
gewe'n halten mit ihm Blatt, wer wēisst, wu er wollt'
itzt āngesparrt.　Rothschild nebech hāt schier nit var-
lōren dort eppes a zehn, fufzehn Milljon; derfar hāt
ihm Gott geholfen in a Pāar Wochen arum: der Ōlem
is' gewe'n, wie män sāgt, begelufin; auf der ōberster
Bank is' grād' gewe'n a Bissel leblich; die Besemlich
hāben sich gehōben, — un' män hat ihm mit a Māl
zugelāst rēin Vardienst akegen a kan Milljon Kärblich!
Die Einwōhner allēin in Tunejadewke senen nebech
kimat alle, lō-aleechem, grōsse Ewjōnim, starke Dal-
fonim.　Nor dem Emes mus män sāgen, see senen
froehliche Ewjōnim, lustige Kabzonim, wilde Bal-bito-
chens.　As män soll, a Stēiger, plutzlim a Fräg geben
a Tunejadewker Jüden, vun wannen un' wie asō er is
sich mefarnes, bleibt er tchilas stēhn wie zumischt,
wēisst nebech nischt, wās zu entwern, nor später a
Bissel āber kummt er zu sich un' entwert bitmimes:
Ich, wie arum ich leb', ich?　Et, 's is' dā a Gott, sāg'
ich euch, ot-o, wās varlāst nischt alle seine Beschäffenisch, Er schickt zu un' wet mistome weiter zuschicken,
sāg' ich euch, ot-o! — Fort, wās thut ihr asōns?　Hā't
ihr chotsch eppes wās 's is' far a Meloche oder a Parnosse in der Hand? — Gelōbt is' ha-Schem-jisborach!
Ich hāb', borchaschem, asō wie ihr kuckt mich ān, ot-o,
a Matone vun sein lieben Nāmen, a Keele, a Kol-negine,

From this committee the affairs are frequently transferred to the upper bench in the bathhouse, and in a
plenary assembly of householders they are confirmed,
" resolved and decreed." If after that even all the kings
of the East and the West were to come and walk with
their heads downwards and their feet in the air, they
could not move . them to change their decrees. The
Mogul came once very near falling into misfortune in
such an assembly of the higher bench; if some of the
householders had not taken his part, who knows where
he would now be resting his head. Rothschild very
nearly lost there ten or fifteen millions; but God came
to his rescue a few weeks later : the people felt, as they
say, in high spirits; all was alive upon the highest
bench; the bathing brooms were dancing over their
backs, and they all at once gave him a clean gain of one
hundred and fifty million roubles.

Nearly all the inhabitants of Parasiteville are, may it
be no evil omen to you, nothing but poor people and
quite destitute. But the truth must be told, they are
merry beggars, joyful mendicants, possessed of unbounded hope. If one, for example, suddenly asks a
Parasiteville Jew where and how he manages to make
a living, he stops at first bewildered, and does not know
what to answer, but after a while he collects himself
and answers in good spirits : I, how I make a living, I ?
Well, there is a God, I tell you, you see, who does not
abandon His creatures ; He sends us a living and will
no doubt continue to send us, I tell you ! — After all,
what is your occupation? Have you some kind of
trade that you ply, or have you some kind of income? — Praised be the Lord ! I have, thanks to the
Lord, as you see me, a gift from Him, a good voice, and
I lead the prayers of the Mussafim on the great holidays

un' dawen' Mussofim Jomim-nōrojim in der Swiwe; ich
bin a Mohel un' a Maze-rädler, Einer in der Welt; ich
führ' a Māl aus a Schidech, führ' ich aus. Ich hāb' a
Stāat, wie ihr kuckt mich ān, ot-o, in der Schul';
heunt halt' ich äuch, zwischen uns soll es bleiben, a
Schēnkel, wās melkt sich zu bisslich; ich hāb' a Zieg',
wās melkt sich ohn' Anore sēhr gut, un' hāb' nischt
weit vun dannen a reichen Korew, ot-o, wās lāst sich
unter a schlechter Zeit äuch a Bissel melken. Heunt,
chuz die alle Sachen, sāg' ich euch ot-o, is' Gott a Tate
un' die Jisroejel senen Rachmonim-bnee-rachmonim, sāg'
ich euch ot-o, nischt zu varsündigen! . . .

Äuch mus män die Tunejadewker Einwōhner dem
Schwach nāchsāgen, as see senen zufrieden mit wās
Gott gi't un' klauben cholile in der Halbosche un' in
dem Essen stark nischt über. As die schabesdige
Kapote, a Stēiger, is' zuhackt, zufallen, zurissen, a Bissel varschlumpert un' eppes nischt asō rēin, macht äuch
nit aus, abi sie is' fort vun Atlas un' glanzt. Ai örter-
weis kuckt wie vun a Reschete araus dās hōhle Leib,
meele wās art es wemen? Wer wet sich dā asō stellen
zukucken? Lemai Pjates, mit wās is' dās ärger vun
ausgerissene Pjates? Pjates is' denn nischt kēin Leib,
kēin Menschenflēisch? . . .

A Stückel Brōt mit a Kolisch, abi 's is' nor dā, is'
sēhr a guter Mittāg. Wer schmuest a Bulke mit a
Rosselflēisch Freitāg, wer es hāt nor, — dās is' take
a Maichel-Mecholim, kēin Besseres dervun is' schōn,
dacht sich, auf der Welt nischt dā. Lās män see derzaehlen, a Stēiger, vun andere Minee Potrawes chuz
Fischjauch, Gebrāten's un' a Māhren- oder Posternak-
zimmes, kummt see dās aus eppes meschune wild un'
sāgen darauf āb varschiedene Wörtlich mit dem grössi-
ten Gelächter, gleich wie der, wās sāgt es, is' narrisch,

in the towns hereabout; I am a Mohel and a roller of matzoth, an expert in my work; I sometimes make a match and get people married. I have a pew in the synagogue, although you may not think it of me; besides I have a grog-shop, between us be it said, that brings me in a little income; I have a goat that gives a great deal of milk, and not far from here I have a rich relative who in bad times lets himself be milked a little too. Besides all these things, I tell you, God is a father and the Jews are the recipients of His mercy, I tell you, and may we not sin against Him! . . .

We must give the inhabitants of Parasiteville their due, — they are contented with anything God may give them, and they are not by any means dainty in their garments and their food. If, for example, the Sabbath coat is all crushed, threadbare, and torn, a little bedraggled and of questionable cleanliness, that does not trouble them much, provided it is of satin and has a sheen. You will say that in places the bare body looks out of it as from a sieve! What of that? Whose concern is it? Who will stop to look at it inquisitively? Is that at all worse than bare heels? Are heels no body, no human flesh? . . .

A piece of bread with a buckwheat cake, if only it can be procured, is a very good dinner indeed. And just think of a white roll with some braized meat on a Friday! Whoever can get that, regards it as the finest dainty, better than which, it seems, nothing can be found in the world. Let anybody tell of any other kinds of choice dishes than fish juice, roast meat, and carrot or parsnip scallop, he will be looked upon as a madman, and they will make all kinds of jests about him and burst out in loud laughter, as if he who had

meschuge un' will see äuch machen meschuge, einrēden
see a Kind in Bauch, a Kuh is' geflōgen über'n Dach
un' gelēgt an Ei. A Stückel Bockser in Chamischo-
ossor dās is' asa Peere, wās is' mechaje Nefosches;
kuckendig derauf dermāhnt män sich in Erzesrojel,
nischt ēin Māl varglotzt män derbei die Äugen mit a
Krächz: Ach, "wessōlicheenu kōmmius," sollst uns,
harzediger Vāter, führen kōmmius, take was kōmmius
hēisst, "learzeenu " — zu unser Land, wās Ziegen essen
dort Bocksern! . . . Al-pi Mikre hāt Einer a Māl in
dem Städtel gebracht a Tēitel, hā't ihr bedarft sehn,
wie asō män is' dās geläufen ānkucken auf Chidesch !
Män hāt aufgemischt a Chumesch un' gewiesen, as
"Tomer" der Tēitel stēht in Chumesch! Steutsch, der
Tēitel, ot der Tēitel wachst doch vun Erzesrojel ! . . .
Kuckendig auf'n Tēitel, hāt sich ausgedacht, Erzesrojel
is var die Äugen, ot gēht män über dem Jarden, ot is'
die Meoras-hamachpeelo, der Mutter Rochel's Keewer,
dās Kōssel-maarowi, ot bādt män sich in Chamee-te-
warjo, män kriecht arauf auf'n Har-haseessim, män esst
sich ān mit Bocksern, mit Tēitlen, un' män lēgt ān
fulle Keschenjes mit Erzesrojel-erd'. Ach, hāt män ge-
krächzt, un' in die Äugen hāben Itlichen sich gestellt
Trähren. "Jene Zeit," asō sāgt Binjāmin, "is' ganz
Tunejadewke, wie grōss sie is', gewe'n in Erzesrojel.
Män hāt geschmack geredt vun Moschiach'n, ot, ot,
is' schōn Gott's Freitāg noch halben Tāg. . . . Der
neuer Pristaw, wās is' nischt lang āngekummen, hāt
grād be-jod-romo denstmāl geführt dās Städtel. Bei a
Pāar Jüden hāt er arābgerissen die Jarmelkes, Einem
ābgeschnitten a Peje, Etliche nebech gechappt spät bei
der Nacht in a Gässel ohn' Pasporten, bei noch Einem
varnummen a Zieg', wās hāt aufgegessen a neuem

told that had actually become crazy and wanted to drive them crazy too by making them believe of a child in the stomach,[1] of a cow that has flown over the roof and has laid an egg. A piece of buck's-horn on the fifteenth day in the month of Shebat is regarded as a fruit that delights the heart. Looking at it they are reminded of Palestine, and they frequently raise their eyes in ecstasy and say with a sigh: " Oh, wessolicheenu kōmmius," lead us, O merciful Father, upwards, yes, upwards indeed, "learzeenu," into our land where goats feed on buck's-horn. . . . By chance some one brought a date to town. You ought to have seen how people rushed up to see the wonder! They opened the Pentateuch and pointed out that " Tomer," the date, was mentioned in the Bible! Just think of it! The date, that very date grows in Palestine! . . . Looking at the date it appeared to them that Palestine was before their very eyes, that, behold, they were crossing the Jordan; right there was the cave of Machpelah, Rachel's grave, the western wall; that now they were bathing in the Pool of Tiberias, they were climbing the Olive Mount, they were eating their fill of bucks'-horn and dates, and swelling their pockets with earth of Palestine. Ah, they sighed, and tears filled the eyes of all. " In those days," says Benjamin, "all of Parasiteville, as large as it is, was in Palestine. They talked with zest of Moses; and behold, it is already past noon on God's Friday. . . . The new police captain who had only lately arrived in town ruled it with a firm hand. He had torn off the skullcaps from the heads of a few Jews, he had lopped off an earlock, had bagged a few men late at night in a side street without passports, had confiscated another man's goat that had eaten up a

---

[1] This is a common saying for an impossible thing.

ströhenem Dach ; un' er is' dermit äuch gewe'n die
Ssibe dervun, wās der Komität unter'n Ōwen hāt sich
stark geduret mit'n Tōger, ad-mossaj wet der Schar-
schel-jischmoel asō schōlet sein?   Män hāt aufgemischt
dem gewoehntlichen Schmues mikōach die Ascheres-
haschwotim, wie glücklich see leben dort in jene weite
Mekōmes, in Gdule-ōscher un' Kowed ; män hāt avür-
genummen die rōthe Jüdlech, die Bneemōsche, mit
Gusmes Maisses vun sejere Gwures uchdōme ; Eldād
ha-Dāni, es varstēht sich, hāt äuch getanzt in dermit.
Jene Zeit, zum Mēisten, hāb' ich zu vardanken die Nessie meine, wās ich hāb' dernāch gemacht."

XI. A HARTER BISSEN
(*Hausfreund*, Vol. II. pp. 22-25)

Beim Breg vun dem Wasser, vun Jāffō bis Tarschisch,
Dort hört sich a Žummen un' Brummen —
Beim Breg vun dem Wasser, vun Jāffō bis Tarschisch,
Is' finster die Nacht āngekummen.

Un' tief aus dem Wasser dort hört sich dās Brummen,
A Kol vun a Wallfisch gār, dacht sich :
"Rabōssai!   Heunt hāt mich der Teuwel genummen,
Ich starb' heunt, ich spür' schōn, es macht sich !

"Ich eck' bald !   Mein Bauch, oi, mein Bauch mus mir
     platzen —
Heunt hāb' ich a Nowi verschlungen !
Dā helft mehr kēin Glätten, kēin Reiben, kēin Kratzen —
Bald is' schōn der Bauch mir zusprungen !

"A Nowi, dās is' gār a zu harter Bissen,
Es känn ihm gār Kēiner vertrāgen ;
Zu fett is' sein Frummkeit — es soll schōn nit wissen
Vun ihm kēin schum ehrlicher Māgen !

newly laid strawthatch. And it was he that was the
cause of the committee's preoccupation with the Mogul,
and their discussion of how much longer the Prince of
the Ishmaelites would be reigning. They returned to
the usual conversation of the Ten Tribes, how happy
they lived in those distant lands, enjoying wealth and
honor; they recalled the Red Jews, the Sons of Moses,
and told a mass of stories of their bravery, etc.; Eldad
the Danite was naturally also dished up. I owe it
mainly to those times that I later undertook my journey."

XI. A TOUGH MORSEL

On the shore of the waters, from Jaffa to Tarshish,
one may hear a grumbling and growling; — on the
shore of the waters, from Jaffa to Tarshish, the night
descended in darkness.

And deep out of the water one may hear a growling,
— it seems, the voice of a whale. "My lords! To-day
the devil has taken me, I am going to die to-day, I feel
it, I am sure!

"My end has come! My belly, O my belly will burst;
— I have swallowed this day a prophet! No massag-
ing, no rubbing, no scratching will help me; — ere long
my belly will certainly burst!

"A prophet is entirely too tough a morsel, and no
one can digest him; his piety is too fat, — may no
honest stomach ever know the like.

" A Nowi, derzu noch gār ēiner, a klēiner !
(Punkt zwölf auf a Tutz gār in Ganzen)
Gār hart is' sein Nefesch, gār hart seine Bēiner —
Er löchert mir 's Harz mit sein Tanzen !

" Un' Stēiner, un' Bēiner, un' kolerlēi Sachen,
See hāt schōn mein Māgen zurieben ;
Un' nor mit Newiim känn gār ich nit machen —
A Make, wās stēht nit geschrieben !

" A Nowi is' gār nit varhanden a wēicher —
Nit känn män ihm essen, nit nāgen :
Es wollt' sein a Mizwe, nit lāsen kēin Seecher
Vun Frumme, wās grablen beim Māgen !

" A Frummer is' gār nit varhanden kēin wēicher —
Mir kennen die dāsige Helden !
Es wollt' sein a Mizwe, nit lāsen a Seecher
Vun see — mit Respekt dās zu melden !

" Rabōssai ! Ich spür' jetzt, er grabelt in Bauch mir —
Gewalt ! 's is' die Tewa vun Frumme
Rak grablen in Jenems Gedārem — nu, äuch mir
A Nowi, — nor, ach, vun die Krumme !

" Rabōssai ! Mir dacht sich, er murmelt jetzt eppes
Un' krümmt sich, un' bēugt sich gār plutzim —
Du darschenst umsüst gār, du darschenst in Steppes
Un' wartst gār umsüst auf Tiruzim !

" Rabōssai ! Ich spür' jetzt sein Grablen, sein Zapplen,
Es dacht sich, er dawent a Bissel !
Un' halt' ich's noch länger jetzt aus, mus ich mapplen —
Gewald ! Gi't mir Brechwein a Schüssel !

"A prophet, and one of the smaller kind at that! — Just twelve of them to the dozen. Too tough is his body, too tough are his bones, he pierces my heart with his dancing!

"And stones, and bones, and all other kinds of things my stomach has digested; but I am powerless with prophets, — they are a plague not mentioned in the Scriptures.

"There does not exist a tender prophet, — you can never eat them or gnaw them. It would be meritorious not to leave a trace of pious men who rummage in your stomachs!

"There does not exist a pious man who is tender, — we know that class of heroes! It would be meritorious not to leave a trace of them — with all due respect permit me to say that!

"My lords! I feel he is now rummaging in my stomach, oh, help me! It has ever been the business of pious people to rummage in other people's entrails, — that's the kind of a prophet he is, only, alas, he is crooked!

"My lords! meseems, he is now mumbling something, and he is writhing and bending up all of a sudden, — you preach in vain, you preach in the wilderness, and you are waiting in vain for an answer!

"My lords! I now feel his crawling, his sprawling, it seems, he is praying now a bit! And if I am to endure it much longer, I shall have to abort. Help! Give me a dish full of emetic!

"Ich känn nit derhalten sein Dawnen, sein Singen, —
Dās Tanzen arum, wie die Rinder,
Die falsche, verwilderte Tnues, dās Springen. . . .
Gewald! Gi't mir Brechwein geschwinder!

"Gewald! Gi't mir Brechwein, gi't Zeitungsmaimorim,
Gi't Nechbi-ben-Wofsi's Artiklen;
Gi't gich Feuilletonen, gi't jüdische Sforim —
Un' thut mir dās All's zunaufwicklen,

"Un' macht mir a Mittel zum Brechen, zum Brechen!
Gi't Sforim vun spätere Dōres!
Gi't Schomer's Romanen, see senen, ich rechen'
Zum Brechen vorzügliche S-chōres —

"Gi't Sforim vun neunzehnten klugen Jāhrhundert,
Gi't kluge 'Kritiken' — vun wemen
Ihr willt sich allein nor; gi't gicher — mich wundert,
Wie brech' ich schōn nit bei die Nämen!" —

Beim Breg vun dem Wasser, vun Jāffō bis Tarschisch,
Dort hört sich a Žummen un' Brummen —
A Mittel zu Brechen, vun Jāffō bis Tarschisch,
Hāt dorten a Fisch eingenummen.

Un' still is' un' ruhig; es kraüselt die Nacht sich
Un' flecht ihre tunkele Locken;
In Himmel die Steren, — see flammen, es dacht sich,
Wie gelbliche, goldene Pocken.

Un' still is' un' ruhig, es flecht gār die Nacht sich
Un' kraüselt die finstere Locken;
Es wandelt gār still die Natur, un' es dacht sich,
Sie gēht wie auf seidene Socken.

"I cannot stand his praying, his chanting, — his dancing, like a calf, his false, barbaric doings, — his leaping. . . . Help! Give me quickly some emetic!

"Help! Give me some emetic, give me newspaper discussions, give me Nechbi-ben-Wofsi's articles. Give me feuilletons, give me Jewish books, — and put them all in a bundle,

"And make me a medicine to vomit, to vomit! Give me books of later generations! Give me the novels of Schaikewitsch, — I think they are excellent stuff for vomiting.

"Give me books of the wise nineteenth century; give me criticisms, whosesoever you wish yourself; only give them quickly, — I am surprised I am not vomiting at mentioning these names!"

On the shore of the waters, from Jaffa to Tarshish, one may hear a grumbling and growling; — an emetic, from Jaffa to Tarshish, a fish has swallowed there.

And all is still and quiet; night is curling and braiding her sable locks; the stars in the sky, — they flame, it seems, like yellow, golden pustules.

And all is still and quiet, and night is braiding and curling her dusky locks; nature wanders in silence, and it seems she walks on silken stockings.

Un' plutzling derhört sich a Kol in der Finster,
Gār fürchterlich hāt er geschriegen ;
Es hāt dort a Wallfisch, vun alle der dünster,
A groben Frummak ausgespiegen.

Un' nāch dem Ausspeien, un' g'rād zu Oleenu,
Dā thut er noch philosophiren ;
Er sāgt : " Zu Newiim, überhaupt zu die klēine,
Dā tor män sich gār nit zurühren ! "

D. Frischmann.

XII. STEMPENJU'S FIEDELE
(' Stempenju,' pp. 8–10)

Ach, ich fühl', as mein Feder is' schwach zu beschrei-
ben, wie Stempenju hāt besetzt a Kale ! Dās is' nit
gewe'n glatt gespielt, gerümpelt : dās is' gewe'n a Min
Aweede, a Gott's Dienst mit eppes sēhr a hōchen
Gefühl, mit eppes sēhr an ēdlen Geist. Stempenju hāt
sich gestellt akegen der Kale un' hāt ihr Drosche
gehalten auf'n Fiedel, — a schoene, a lange Drosche, a
rührende Drosche über dem frei un' glücklich Leben
vun der Kale bis aher, vun ihr Maedelstand, un' über
dem finsteren, bitteren Leben, wās erwartet sie später,
später : Aus Maedel ! übergedeckt dem Kopp, var-
stellt die schoene, lange Hāar auf ēbig . . . nit dā dās
Froehlichkeit ! Sei gesund, Jugend, ot werst du a
Jüdene ! . . . Eppes sēhr nischt froehlich, Gott soll
nischt strāfen far die Rēd' ! . . .

Ot asölche Wörter hören sich kimat araus vun Stempenju's Fiedele ; alle Weiber varstēhen gut dem Pschat
vun der dāsiger stummer Drosche, alle Weiber fühlen
es ; see fühlen dās, un' wēinen derauf mit bittere
Trähren.

—Wie lang bin ich asō gesessen, — klährt sich a

And suddenly a voice is heard in the darkness; terribly he did cry; a whale, the thinnest of them all, has there spit out a bigot.

And after his spitting up, just at the last prayer of Oleenu, he still continues to philosophize; he says: "With prophets, particularly the little ones, you must have nothing to do!"

XII. STEMPENJU'S VIOLIN

Oh, I feel that my pen is too weak to describe the manner of Stempenju's playing at the Enthronement of the Bride. That was not mere playing, mere fingering of the strings: that was a kind of religious service, devotion to the Lord, with a very elevated feeling, with such a noble spirit! Stempenju took his stand in front of the bride and began to address her with a sermon on his violin, a beautiful, a long sermon, a touching sermon, on the free and happy life she had led heretofore, on her girlish state, and the gloomy, bitter life that awaited her later, later. No longer a girl! the head covered, the beautiful long hair disguised forever . . . gone all merriment! Farewell, youth, you are now turned into a married Jewess! . . . 'Tis somehow very sad! May God not visit us with punishment for such words ! . . .

Almost these words are heard on Stempenju's violin. The women all understand well the purport of that silent sermon, all the women feel it; they feel it, and weep thereupon bitter tears.

"How long have I been sitting," meditates a young

jung Weibel, schlingendig die Trähren, — wie lang bin
ich asō gesessen mit zulāste, zuflochtene Zöpp' un' hāb'
nor gemēint, as Malochim spielen sich gār mit mir, as
ich bin Eine, a glückliche? Zum Ssof . . . ach, zum
Ssof . . .

— Bescher' ihr Gott, — thut beten an ältere Jüdene,
a Mutter vun derwachsene Töchter, — bescher' ihr
Gott, mein älterer Tochter, ihr Siweg in Gichen, nor
mit mehr Masel wie mir, nor mit a schönere Dolje, wie
ich hāb' bei mein Mann, Gott soll nit strāfen far die
Rēd'!

Ot in asölche Machschowes fallen arein die Weiber
un' Stempenju thut sich sein's: Er arbeit't mit alle
Keelim, un' dās Fiedele redt. Dās spielt Stempenju a
Wēinendig's, un' die Kapelje halt't ihm unter, es werd
still, aus-Ljarem, aus-Gepilder! Alle, alle willen hören
Stempenjun. Jüden wer'en vartracht, Weiber weren
anschwiegen; Jünglech, Maedlech kletteren arauf auf
Bänk' un' auf Tischen, — Jeder will hören Stempenjun!

— Sch — scha! Stiller! Ōlem, lās sein still!!!
Un Stempenju zugiesst sich auf'n Fiedele un' zugēht
sich wie a Wachs: Tjoch, tjoch, tjoch, — mehr hört män
nischt. A Hand flieht auf un' āb, — mehr seht män
nit, un' es hören sich allerlēi Kōles, un' es giessen sich
verschiedene Minee Gesangen, un' alls umetige, trauerige, as es nemmt ān beim Harzen, es zieht die Neschome,
es nemmt araus dās Chijes; Der Ōlem gēht aus mit
alle Kōches, der Ōlem starbt, starbt mit alle Eewrim,
dās Harz werd eppes asō vull, un' es stellen sich Trähren in die Äugen; Jüden süfzen, Jüden krächzen,
Jüden wēinen . . . un' Stempenju? Wer Stempenju?
Me sēht ihm gār nit, me sēht kein Fiedele, me hört nor
die süsse Kōles, die göttliche Gesangen, wās füllen ān

woman, swallowing her tears, "how long have I been sitting with flowing, unbraided hair, and thinking that angels are playing with me, that I am the happiest creature! And yet . . . ah, and yet . . ."

"God grant her," so begins her prayer an elderly woman, a mother of grown-up daughters, "God grant her, my oldest daughter, to be soon united in wedlock, but with more happiness than I have had, with a better lot than I have had with my husband, — may God not visit me with punishment for my words!"

Such are the thoughts that fall upon the women, and Stempenju keeps on playing his way: he directs the whole band, and his violin talks eloquently. Stempenju is now playing a sad tune, and his musicians support him. All is quiet, there is no noise, not a sound! All, all want to hear Stempenju. Men fall to musing, women are grown silent. Boys and girls have climbed on benches and tables, — all want to hear Stempenju!

"Hush! Keep still! People, let there be quiet!"

And Stempenju dissolves on his violin and melts like wax; pitapat is all you may hear. An arm flies up and down, — that's all you may see, and you hear all kinds of voices, and all kinds of tunes are poured forth, all melancholy, sad, so that it tears out your heart, draws out your soul, takes away your life. The people grow faint, the people grow weak in all their limbs; the heart is full to overflowing, and tears appear in the eyes. Men sigh, men groan, women weep . . . and Stempenju? But who pays attention to him? No one sees him, no one sees his violin; they only hear his sweet tones, the divine music which fills the whole room. . . . And Rochele the beautiful who had never

die ganze Stub' . . . Un' Rochele die schoene, wās hāt noch bis aher nischt gehört Stempenju's Spielen, Rochele, wās hāt gehört, as 's is' dā a Stempenju, nor sie hāt noch nischt gehört asa Min Spielen, stēht un' hört sich zu zu die kischefdige Gesangen, zu die seltene Kōles, un' verstēht nit, wās dās is'. Eppes zieht dās ihr dās Harz, eppes glätt't dās sie, — nor wās dās is' verstēht sie nit. Sie hōbt auf die Äugen ahin, vun wannen es giessen sich die süsse Kōles un' derseht a Pāar wunderschoene, schwarze Äugen, feuerdige Augen, wās kucken gleich auf ihr un' nehmen sie durch, wie Spiesen, wie scharfe Spiesen. Die wunderschoene, schwarze, feuerdige Äugen kucken auf ihr un' winken zu ihr un' reden mit ihr; Rochele will arāblāsen ihre Äugen arāb, — un' kānn nit.

— Ot dās is' Stempenju?

Asō klährt sich Rochele die schoene, wenn dās Besetzen hāt sich schōn geëndigt un' die Mechutonim hōben schōn ān zu trachten mikōach Führen zu der Chupe.

— Wu senen ergez die Licht? frägt Chossen's Zad.

— Die Licht wu senen? entfert Kale's Zad.

Un' asō werd wieder der ēigener Gepilder, wās früher; Alle läufen un' me wēisst nit wuhin. Me kwetscht sich, me stuppt sich, me tret't ān auf Masolim, me reisst Klēidlech, me schwitzt, me siedelt die Ssarwers mit die Schamossim, un' see siedlen zurück die Mechutonim, un' die Mechutonim amperen sich zwischen sich, — es is' borchaschem ganz lebedig!

S. Rabinowitsch.

before heard Stempenju's playing, Rochele who had heard before of Stempenju, but who had never before heard such playing, stands and listens to the enticing music, the rare sounds, and does not understand what that all means. Something has touched her heart, a soft feeling has passed over her, but she does not understand what that is. She lifts her eyes to the place from which the sweet sounds proceed, and notices a pair of very beautiful black eyes, fiery eyes that are looking straight at her, and that transfix her like spears, like sharp spears. The beautiful, black, fiery eyes look at her and beckon to her and speak to her; Rochele wants to lower her eyes, and she cannot.

"Oh, that is Stempenju!"

So meditates Rochele the beautiful, as the Enthronement is ended, and the parents of the contracting parties are getting ready to lead them under the Baldachin.

"Where are the candles?" comes the question from the bridegroom's side.

"The candles, where are they?" comes the reply from the bride's side.

And thus the same noise begins as before. All are running, not knowing whither. There is a jam, and they push each other, and step on people's toes, and tear dresses; they perspire, they scold the ushers and the beadles, and these again scold the parents of the marrying couple, and the parents wrangle among themselves, — praised be the Lord, all is lively!

XIII. DER TALMUD

(*Jüdische Volksbibliothēk*, Vol. II. pp. 195–197)

Alte Blätter vun'm Talmud,
Alte Sagen un' Legenden!
In mein trauerigen Leben
Oft thu' ich zu euch mich wenden.

Bei der Nacht, wenn in der Finster
Läuft der Schläf vun meine Äugen,
Un' ich sitz' allēin un' elend,
Zu der Brust dem Kopp gebōgen,

In die trauerige Stunden,
Wie a Steren in der blauer
Summernacht, hēbt ān zu scheinen
Der Sikoren in mein Trauer.

Ich dermāhn sich auf die Liebe,
Auf die süsse Kindheitsjähren,
Wenn ich bin noch frei gewesen
Vun mein Kummer, Lēid un' Zoren;

Ich dermāhn' sich auf die Zeiten,
Wenn ich fleg' dem ersten, süssen,
Besten Koss vun Leben, Freiheit,
Frēud' un' Lustigkeit geniessen.

Ich dermāhn' sich auf die alte,
Auf die süsse, liebe Jāhren,
Un' die Blätter vun'm Talmud
Stēhen auf in mein Sikoren.

Ach, die alte, alte Blätter!
Wie viel Licht un' wie viel Steren
Brennen, scheinen un' see können
Ēbig nit verloschen wer'en.

XIII. THE TALMUD

Old leaves of the Talmud, old stories and legends! In my saddened life I frequently turn to you.

At night, when in the darkness sleep evades my eyes, and I sit alone and deserted, my head bowed to my breast,

In those sad hours, like a star in the azure summer night, there begin to shine memories in my sadness.

I recall my love, my sweet years of childhood, when I was still free from sorrow, pain and anger ;

I recall those times when I quaffed the first, sweet, the best chalice of life, freedom, joy and merriness.

I recall the old, the sweet, delightful years, and the leaves of the Talmud arise in my memory.

Oh, the old, old leaves! As many lights and as many stars there burn and shine, they can never be extinguished.

Tausend Stromen, tausend Teichen
Hāben see gethun verfliessen,
Samd hāt sich auf see geschotten,
Sturems hāben see gerissen,

Un' die alte, alte Blätter
Leben noch . . . see senen take
Gell, verchōschecht, ābgerissen,
Dort a Loch un' dā a Make;

Dā a Stückel ābgesmalet,
Dort a Schure täug' auf Zores,
Un' in Ganzen hāt a Ponim
Vun an alten Bess-hakwores . . .

Meele wās?   Nu, is' dās take
A Bessalmen, wu begrāben
Liegt in Keewer All's, wās ēbig
Wöllen mir schon mehr nit hāben. . . .

Un' ich, alter, kranker Jossem,
Vull mit Lēid, mit Eemas-mowes,
Stēh', mein grauen Kopp gebōgen,
Stēh' un' wēin' auf Keewer-owes. . . .

                                        S. Frug.

XIV. DĀS JÜDISCHE KIND
(*Hausfreund,* p. 44)

Tief begrāben in der Finster,
Weit vun Luft un' Licht, —
Sehst du dort dem blinden Worem,
Wie er kriecht?

In der Erd' is' er gebōren,
Un' beschert
Is' ihm, ēbig, ēbig kriechen
In der Erd'. . . .

Thousands of streams, thousands of rivers have passed over them, sand has covered them, storms have torn them,

Yet the old, old leaves live on . . . though they be yellow, darkened, torn, — a hole here, a spot there ;

Here a bit charred, there a line obliterated, and the whole has the appearance of an old cemetery. . . .

What of that? Yes, indeed, that is a burial-ground where lies buried in the grave all that which we shall never have again. . . .

And I, old, sick orphan, full of sorrow, of the awe of death, stand with bent head, stand and weep at the grave of our fathers. . . .

XIV. THE JEWISH CHILD

Deeply buried in darkness, far from air and light, — do you see yonder the blind worm, as he creeps?

In the ground he was born, and it is decreed that forever, yes forever, he shall creep upon the earth. . . .

Wie a Worem in der Finster,
Schwach un' stumm un' blind,—
Lebst du āb die Kindheit's Jāhren,
Jüdisch Kind!

Auf dein Wiegel singt die Mame
Nit kēin Lied
Vun a ruhig stillen Leben,
Freiheit, Fried,

Vun die Gärtner, vun die Felder,
Wu dās frische Kind
Spielt un' frēut sich frei un' lustig,
Wie der Wind.

Nēin! A Quall vun tiefen Jāmmer
Rauscht un' klingt. . . .
Oi, wie bitter is' dās Liedel,
Wās sie singt!

Tiefe Süfzen, hēisse Trähren
Mit a starke Macht
Klingen, rauschen in dem Liedel
Tāg un' Nacht.

Tiefe Süfzen, hēisse Trähren,
Hunger, Kält
Schleppen sich mit dir zusammen
Auf der Welt.

Un' vun Wiegel bis zum Keewer,
Auf dem langen Weg,
Wachsen ganze Wälder Zores
Ohn' a Breg. . . .

S. FRUG.

Like a worm in the darkness, weak and mute and blind,—you live through the years of childhood, Jewish child !

At your cradle your mother sings not a song of a quiet, peaceful life, of freedom, peace,

Of the gardens, of the fields, where the blooming child plays and gladdens free and merry like the wind.

No, a spring of deep sorrow bubbles and resounds. . . . Oh, how bitter is the song that she sings !

Deep sobs, hot tears with a mighty power resound, bubble in the song day and night.

Deep sobs, hot tears, hunger, cold, drag along with you in the world.

And from your cradle to your grave, upon the long journey, there grow whole forests of sorrows without end. . . .

XV. DER ADELIGER KĀTER

(*Emeth*, Vol. I. p. 62)

A Fuchs, a chitrer Kerl un' a Lez
Hāt in an Unterhaltung mit a Kāter
Gemacht asō viel Chōsek vun die Kätz',
As Jener is' in Kas gewor'en.
" Du wēisst nit, Füchsel-chazuf " — hāt er
Zu ihm gesāgt mit Zorn, —
" As ich gehör' zum allerhöchsten Adel
" Vun Chajes, weil ich kumm' vun a Mischpoche
" Vun Helden ohne Furcht un' Tadel,
" Wās seinen kēinmāl nit gegangen in Gespann,
" Nit in a Fuhr', nit in a Ssoche,
" Zum Führen Hēu, zum Ackern a Feld,
" Zum Thon, wās passt nit far a Thieren-held ;
" Nor lebendig in Wöltāg, Jederer a Pan,
" Durch ehrenhafte Raub.
" Ich stamm' bekizer āb vun flinken Tiger,
" Wās känn verzucken jeden Rind ;
" Ich bin dem Lempert's Schwesterkind,
" Sogar vun seine Majestät, dem Loeb
" A Korew nit kēin weiter.
" Ōbgleich ich bin allēin vielleicht,
" Kēin Held nit, nit kēin grösser Krieger,
" Un' nit kēin mōrediger Streiter."
— "As du bist nit kēin Held, is' leicht
" Zu sehn " — hāt ihm geëntwert unser Fuchs —
" I vun dein schwache Lapke,
" I vun dein Blick, i vun dein Wuchs.
" Wer wēiss nit, as dem klensten Hüntel's Eck
" (Schōn gār nit rēdendig vun seine Zaehner)
" Verjāgt dich, wie die schwachste Žabke,
" In Thom arein var hōle Schreck ?

XV. THE NOBLE TOM-CAT

A Fox, a cunning fellow and a jester, conversing once with a Tom-cat, made light of all the cats, so that he made him angry. " You know not, arrant Fox," said he to him, growing angry, "that I belong to the noblest tribe of beasts, for I am descended from a family of heroes without fear and reproach, who never have walked under a yoke of wain, nor plough, to gather in the hay, to till the field, to do what is not meet for a beast-hero, — nay, living aye in plenty, each his own master, by honorable robbery. In short, I am descended from the swift Tiger, who knows how to slay the kine; I am cousin to the Leopard, and even of his Majesty, the Lion, a not distant relative, although I myself, perhaps, be not a hero, nor great warrior, nor awful champion.

" That you are not a hero is easily discerned," our Fox retorted, "both by your weak paw, and by your looks, and by your size. Who does not know that the tail of the smallest dog — not to speak of his teeth — will chase you away like the weakest frog into some hole, agog with fear? You, my friend, are bold only with bones, in a corner of the room, making war on a quiet, hungry mouse. I know of the high deeds of

" Du bist nor, Freund, a Chwat mit Bēiner
" In Winkele, in Haus,
" Bekämpfendig a stille, hungerige Maus.
" Ich wēiss nit vun die Maissim-tōwim,
" Vun deine adelige Krōwim,
" Nor du lebst nit vun ehrenhaften Raub allēin,
" Du, Bruder, schämst sich nit zu ganwenen,
" Zu bettlen un' zu chanfenen,
" Afile naschen is' far dir nit zu gemēin."
Dās sägendig hāt er sein ängepelzten Eck
Mit Spott a Hōb gethān un' is' aweg.

* * * * *

Die alte Welt
Is vull mit tausende asölche Kāters,
Jachsonim puste, adelige Pimpernätters,
Mit Wonzes lange, bliszendige Äugen,
Ohn' Macht, ohn' Sinn, ohn' Geld,
Nefosches, welche täugen
Zum Klettern mit Pläner in der Hōch,
Vun welche jeder endigt sich in Räuch;
Wās lecken Teller bei dem Reichen
Un' mjauken sich mit sejersgleichen
Aristokratisch fein zusammen,
Un' Alles, wās see wēissen,
Is' mehr nit, wie see hēissen,
Un' dann, vun welche Tigerkätz' see stammen.

M. Winchevsky.

XVI. JONKIPER
(*Hausfreund*, Vol. II. pp. 88–91)

... Es is' wieder Jonkiper, nor dreissig Jāhr senen
vun jener Zeit arüber.

Wieder is' die Schul vull mit Tales un' Kittel einge-
wickelte Jüden; der Pol is' mit Hēu ausgebett' itzt

your noble relatives,—but you do not live by honorable prey alone; you, my friend, are not ashamed to steal, to beg, and to flatter; you do not think it beneath you to nibble secretly at dainties." Saying that, he raised his furry tail in scorn and went away.

＊ ＊ ＊ ＊ ＊

The Old World is full of thousands of such Tomcats, empty-headed braggarts, noble dragons, with long mustaches and glittering eyes, without power, without sense, or money, souls that are good only to crawl on high with plans that all end in smoke; who lick the plates of the rich, and miaul together with their kind in aristocratic fashion, and all they know is only their own names, and then from what Tiger they are descended.

XVI. THE ATONEMENT DAY

. . . It is again the day of Atonement, but since that time thirty years have passed.

Again the synagogue is full of men wrapped in taliths and shrouds! The floor is strewn with hay now

wie demālt; in zwēi grösse Kastens vull mit Samd vun
bēide Seiten Bime brennen heunt die wächsene Ne-
schome-licht wie mit dreissig Jāhr zurück, chotsch nāch
andere, frische Neschomes, wās senen erst in die dreissig
Jāhr Neschomes gewor'en. Un' see brennen manche
still un' ruhig un' manche flackerndig un' schmelzendig,
un' Jünglech Kundeessim chappen die Stücklech āb-
geschmolzene Wachs äuch heunt wie a Māl.

Chotsch die Stimme vun dem Chasen is' itzt andersch,
āber die Wörter, wās er sagt, un' der Nigen, wās er
singt, senen dieselbe, gār dieselbe, nit geändert auf ēin
Hāar.

Dieselbe senen äuch die Trähren, wās giessen sich
heunt teichenweis dort hinter die varhangene Fen-
sterlech in der weiberscher Schul, chotsch vun andere
Äugen, vun andere gepeinigte Herzer fliessen see. . . .

Auf dem Ort, wu mit dreissig Jāhr früher is' die
unglückliche Mutter gestan'en un' bewēint ihr liebe
Tochter, wās is' asō jung vun der Welt aweg, stēht
heunt äuch a Mutter un' zugiesst ihr schwer Harz in
hēisse Trähren. Sie wēint un' klāgt über ihr schoene
Tochter, wās sie hāt sich a Māl gebentscht mit ihr,
a Maedel, schoen wie Gold, wās is' pluzling wie vun a
Kischef varführt gewor'en, un' wās mit ihr thut sich
itzt, is' schwer un' bitter selbst auszurēden; un' die
ständig getreue Mutter bet' itzt mit Trähren, hēiss wie
Feuer, nit Gesund, nit lange Jāhren far ihr Kind, āber
a Tōdt a gichen, wās wet gleicher sein far dem Kind
noch mehr wie far der Mutter.

Sie hāt noch ihr mütterliche Treuheit in ihr Harzen,
wie noch ēhder dās Unglück is' geschehn. . . . Nor take
derfar bett' sie bei Gott asō hēiss ot dem Tōdt auf ihr
Kind. Kēin bessere Sach seht sie nit in der Welt un'
kēin ander Sach kānn sie bei Gott dem lebedigen heunt

as then; in two large boxes filled with sand on both sides of the altar there are burning to-day the waxen soul-lights just as thirty years ago, though for other, fresh souls that have become souls only within the last thirty years. And they burn, some quietly and softly, and some flickering and melting, and urchins are now as then picking up the pieces of molten wax.

Although the voice of the Precentor is now different, yet the words which he says, and the tune which he sings, are the same, precisely the same, not a bit changed.

And the tears are the same that flow to-day in streams there behind the curtained windows in the woman's gallery, though from other eyes they flow, from other tortured hearts. . . .

On the same spot where thirty years ago the unfortunate mother had been standing and mourning her beloved daughter who had departed so young from this world, there is to-day also standing a mother and dissolving her heart in hot tears. She is bewailing and lamenting her beautiful daughter who had once been her blessing, a girl, as pure as gold, who had been misled as if by witchery, and of whom it would be hard and bitter to say what she is doing now; and the ever-true mother prays now with tears, as hot as fire, not for health, not for long years for her child, but for quick death, which would be better for the child even than for the mother.

She still harbors her mother's truth in her heart, even as before the calamity had happened. . . . For that very reason she prays to God so fervently to grant death to her child. She sees no better thing in the world, and she can ask for no better thing to-day of the living God.

nit betten. Un' es giessen sich ihre Trähren still un'
fallen über die Wörter vun ihre Tchines; sie halt dem
Kopp in Ssider eingegräben un' schämt sich ihre Äugen
arauszunehmen, tomer begegnen see sich mit Äugen,
wäs wöllen ihr Schand' dersehn, wäs is' wie a Fleck
auf ihr Ponim gewor'en. . . .

Un' punkt dort, wu die äreme Almone is' gestan'en
mit dreissig Jähr zurück un' hät minutenweis gekuckt,
ihre Jessomim in Schul zu sehn, öb see dawnen, öb see
nehmen a jüdisch Wort in Maul arein, un' hät gechlipet
wöinendig, as ihre Äugen häben nit gefun'en, wäs see
häben gesucht, stëht heunt a jüdische Tochter un' kuckt
durch däs Vorhangel, un' sie wëiss allëin nit, auf wemen
sie kuckt mehr, zi auf ihr Mann, wäs macht wilde Be-
wegungen mit bëide Händ' un' mit sein ganzen Körper,
oder auf dem jungen Menschen, wäs sitzt äuch in
Misrach-wand nit weit vun ihm un' dawent wie a Jüd'
un' sitzt ruhig wie a Mensch.

Welche Gedanken läufen ihr durch ihr Kopp itzund!
Wieviel Trähren hät sie vargossen vun jenem Täg än,
as der junger Mann is' gewor'en aus Chossen ihrer un'
der wilder Chossen is' ihr Mann, ihr Brötgeber gewor'en!
Wieviel Wunden trägt sie seitdem still un' tief varschlossen in ihr jüdischen Harzen un' peinigt sich vun
ihre ëigene Gedanken, wäs tracht sich ihr nit wöllendig,
nor sie hät këin Köach nit, nit zu trachten. Un' wie bett'
sie itzt Gott, er soll auslöschen däs sündige Feuer vun
ihr sündig Harz, auslöschen All's, wäs brennt un' kocht
in ihr, sie soll vargessen, wäs is' gewesen, nit wissen,
wie es darf zu sein, nor ëin Sach soll sie wissen, wie lieb
zu häben ihr Mann, welcher wet un' mus ihr Mann
bleiben bis ihr Tödt! Sie soll ihm lieben bei alle seine
Unmenschlichkeit, bei sein Wildkeit, un' selbst wenn

And her tears flow quietly and fall on the words of her Prayer; she holds her head buried on the Prayer-book and is ashamed to lift her eyes, lest they meet some eyes that may recognize her shame which has become as a spot upon her face. . . .

And precisely there where the poor widow had been standing thirty years before and had looked every minute to catch a glimpse of her orphans, to see whether they were praying, whether they were reciting the Hebrew words, and had burst out in sobs when her eyes did not find that which she had been looking for, there is standing to-day a young Jewess, and she peeps through the curtain, and she does not know herself at whom she is looking more, whether at her husband who is wildly gesticulating with both his arms and his whole body, or at the young man who is also seated at the Eastern wall not far from him and is praying as behooves a Jew and is sitting quietly as behooves a man.

What thoughts are now rushing through her head! How many tears she has shed since that day when the young man broke off his relations with her, and the uncouth man had become her husband, her breadgiver! How many wounds she has been carrying since then quietly and deeply buried in her Jewish heart, and has been tortured by her own thoughts which crowd upon her against her will, and which she has no strength to repel! And how she now implores God that He may extinguish the sinful fire from her sinful heart, that He may extinguish all that burns and boils within her, that she should forget all that had been, that she should not know how it ought to have been, that she should know but one thing, how to love her husband, who is and must remain her husband until her death! To love

er schlägt sie, soll sie nor allēin wissen, Ssonim sollen
nit derfrēut wer'en un' sie soll alle ihre Pein far Gut
können ānnehmen, wie Der, wās thēilt dem Gōrel ein
jeder Ischo, hāt a jüdischer Frau geboten. . . .

Un' es fliessen ihre Trähren auf dem ēigenem Ort,
wu es hāben asölche Trähren gegossen mit dreissig
Jāhr zurück vun a ganz ander Grund un' Quelle.   Un'
see fallen auf dieselbe Wörter vun Machser, wās jede
jüdische Frau varstēht see andersch als die andere.

Nor dort in Mairew-seit, nit weit vun Thür', wēinen
die āreme jüdische Frauen äuch heunt mit dem ēigenem
Nigen, mit dem ēigenem betrübten Harzen wie mit
dreissig Jāhr zurück.

Āremkeit, Hunger, Nōt un' Mangel hāben alle Māl
ēin Ponim, ēin Tam un' ēin Ort bei der Thür.   Asō
sauer un' bitter dās Gewēin, wās kummt vun Nieder-
geschlāgene, is' a Māl gewesen, wet äuch ēbig sein.
Alle Wünsche un' Gelüste vun Menschen wöllen sich
überbeiten un' beiten sich, nor der Wunsch vun dem
Hungerigen wet ēbig bleiben dās Stückele Brōt; die
Gelüste vun dem Nōtbedürftigen wet äuch ēbig hēissen : Vun der Nōt befreit zu wer'en un' nit mehr zu
wissen vun dem Tam, wās es hāt ! . . .

Un' dort bei der Thür stēhn itzt äuch nit wēniger
Finstere, Ausgetruckente un Schofele, nebech, hören
oder hören nit die Sāgerke un' wēinen, wie see zum
Harzen is', — es is' Jonkiper.

Nor in rechten mitten Misrach-wand, auf dem ēigenem Ort, wu die frumme Gütele hāt mit dreissig Jāhr
zurück gedawent, seht män itzt äuch a choschewe Frau,
korew zu fufzig Jāhr, sitzt still un' trauerig, wie a Der-
hargete, ihre Lippen varschlossen.   Die Äugen kucken
in offenem Korben-minche, nor see sehn die Wörter nit.

him with all his inhumanity, with all his uncouthness, and even when he beats her, she alone to know it, lest her enemies be not rejoiced, and that she may accept all her troubles in good spirits, just as He who gives each woman her lot, has bidden a Jewish woman to do. . . .

And her tears flow on the same spot where just such tears have flowed thirty years before for another reason and from another source. And they fall on the same words of the Prayer-book, which every Jewish woman interprets in her own way.

Only at the Western wall, not far from the door, the poor women are weeping to-day with the same intonation, with the same burdened heart as thirty years ago.

Poverty, hunger, misery, and want have always the same face, the same appearance, and the same place at the door. Just as oppressive and as bitter as the weeping that issues from the downtrodden has been before, it will eternally be. All desires and longings will change and are actually changing, but the want of the hungry will eternally remain a piece of bread; the longings of the needy will eternally be: To be freed from want and not to know the feeling thereof! . . .

And there at the door there now stand just such gloomy, emaciated, and dispirited women, who listen or do not listen to the Reader and weep out of the fulness of their hearts, — it is the Atonement day.

In the very centre of the Eastern wall, in the same spot where the pious Gütele had been praying thirty years before, one may even now discern a woman, nigh unto fifty years, sitting quietly and sadly, like one struck dead, with closely pressed lips. Her eyes look into the open Prayer-book, but they do not see the words.

Farwās wēint sie nit?

Is' ihr asō gut zu Muth, as selbst Jonkiper känn sie ihr Harz nit zuthun, zu dermāhnen, as kēin Gut's is' nit ēbig un' der lebediger Mensch wēiss nit, wās morgen känn sein?

Oder is' sie nit a jüdische Frau, a Frau vun a Mann un' Kinder, un' welche jüdische Frau hāt nit ergez ēine oder mehrere Ursachen, wegen wās Jonkiper zu betten un' a hēissen Trähr lāsen fallen?

Is' sie efscher asō hart un' asō schlecht, asō stolz un' vornehm bei sich, as ihr passt nit zu wēinen, Leut' sollen ihre Trähren nit sehn un' nit klähren, sie is gleich zu Allemen?

Nēin! Chanele, "die Gute, die Kluge" is' ihr Namen, — ihre jetzt truckene Äugen sāgen noch Eedes, as see hāben in sejer Zeit viel, viel gewēint; sie is' nit stolz un' schämt sich nit zu wēinen, bifrat Jonkiper, wās wēint sich memeele!

Farwās-že wēint sie nit?

Es kucken auf ihr viel Äugen un' wundern sich: Wās is' heunt mit ihr der Mähr mehr als alle Jāhr? Nor sie kuckt trucken, wie varstēinert, in ihr Ssider; nit sie wēint, nit sie dawent. A Pāar Māl hāt sie dās Vorhangel varbōgen, a Kuck gethun in männerscher Schul, sich bald zurück aweggesetzt un' jeder Māl alls traueriger un' beklemmter wie früher.

As der Chasen hāt āngehōben dawnen Mussaf, hāt sie noch a Māl a Kuck gethun durch dās Fensterl, die Äugen senen unruhig umgeloffen über der ganzer Schul, — sie hāt sich zurück aweggesetzt.

"Er is' noch alls nitdā!" hāt ihr Harz geredt innerlich, "Zu Mussaf afile hāt er nit gekönnt kummen?

Why does she not weep?

Is she so happy that even on the day of Atonement she cannot prevail over her heart to consider that no good is eternal, and mortal man does not know what to-morrow may be?

Or is she not a Jewish woman, a woman having husband and children? and where is there a Jewish woman that has not some one or more reasons for weeping on the Atonement day, and shedding hot tears?

Is she, perhaps, so hard of heart and so bad, so haughty and conceited, that she does not think it proper to weep, lest people should see her tears and deem her equal with the others?

No! Chanele,—they call her the good, the wise Chanele,—her very dry eyes are witness that she has wept much, very much in her time; she is not proud and is not ashamed to weep, especially on the Atonement day, when tears come of their own accord!

Why, then, does she not weep?

Many eyes are looking at her and wondering why she is so different from other years, why she looks stolidly, like one turned to stone, into the Prayer-book, why she is neither weeping nor praying. A few times she pushed aside the curtain, looked down into the men's division, seated herself again in her place and looked each time sadder and more oppressed than before.

When the Precentor began to read the Mussaf-prayer, she once more peeped through the window, her eyes ran restlessly over the whole synagogue, and she went back to her seat.

"He has not come yet!" her heart spoke to her inwardly. "Even to the Mussaf he could not come?

Och, un' dās is' mein Kind, mein Bchor! Vun ihm
hāb' ich dās asō viel Jessurim un' Schmerzen arüber-
getrāgen, bis ich hāb' ihm auf die Füss' gestellt!

"Jā, mein Kind, mein Wund'! Ein ander Mutter
wollt' ihm sein Gebēin varscholten, sie wollt' gesāgt:
Nit du bist mein Suhn, nit ich bin dein Mutter, — ich
känn es āber nit, — sei mir mōchel, Gott in Himmel,
wās ich ruf' ihm noch "mein Kind, mein Suhn!" . . .
O, ich känn bei Dir auf sich betten a Tōdt, āber nit
auf mein Kind! — Strāf' mich, Ribōne-schel-ōlem, mich,
sein sündige Mutter, efscher bin ich schuldig in dem,
wās er is' vun rechten Weg arāb un' hāt Dich, lebediger
Gott, vargessen un' hāt dein Tōre varlāsen un' thut
dein Gebot nit? Jā, ich bin schuldig, ich hāb' ihm zu
viel lieb geha't; wās er hāt gebeten, hāb' ich gethun;
ich hāb' sich mit sein frummen Vāter ständig arumge-
kriegt, as er flegt ihm bestrāfen wöllen. Ich hāb' ihm
ausgehodewet, wie er is', un' mich strāf' far ihm!" . . .

J. Dienesohn.

XVII. AUF'N BUSEN VUN JAM

('Songs from the Ghetto,'[1] pp. 70-76)

Der schrecklicher Wind, der gefährlicher Sturem,
Er rangelt sich dort mit a Schiff auf 'n Meer;
Er will sie zubrechen, un' sie mit Jessurim
Schneid't durch alle Tiefeniss, krächzendig schwer.

Es treschtschet der Mastbaum, der Segel, er zittert,
Der rauschender Wasser is' mōredig tief; —
Es kämpfen mit Zoren, es streiten varbittert
Auf Tōdt un' auf Leben der Wind mit der Schiff.

---

[1] Published by Copeland and Day; with permission of the publishers.

Oh, and that is my child, my first-born! For his sake I have borne so many privations and pains, that I might be able to place him on his feet!

"Yes, my child, my sore vexation! Another mother would have cursed his bones; she would have said: 'You are not my son, I am not your mother,' — But I cannot do that, — forgive me, O Lord, that I still call him 'my child, my son'! . . . Oh, I can ask for my death of You, but not for the death of my child! Punish me, Lord of the Universe, me, his sinful mother! Maybe I am to be blamed that he has departed from the road of righteousness, and has forgotten You, O living God, and has abandoned Your Law and does not do Your commandments! Yes, I am to be blamed for it, I have loved him too much; I always did what he wanted me to do; I have always quarrelled with his pious father when he wanted to punish him. I have raised him such as he is, and do punish me for him!" . . .

XVII. ON THE BOSOM OF THE OCEAN

The terrible wind, the dangerous storm, is wrestling with a ship on the ocean; it is trying to break her, but she in distress cuts through the deep, groaning heavily.

The mast cracks, the sail trembles, frightful is the depth of the roaring waters; the wind struggles desperately with the ship in a life and death combat.

Ot mus sie sich lēgen, ot mus sie sich stellen,
Ot treibt es zurück ihr, ot treibt es varaus, —
A Spielchel is' itzter die Schiff bei die Wellen,
See schlingen sie ein un' see speien sie aus.

Es laremt der Jam, un' es hēben sich Chwales;
Es huzet, es pildert mit Schreck un' mit Graul; —
Der Sturem, der Gaslen, will umbrengen Alles,
Der Thom öffent auf sein varschlossene Maul.

Es hören sich Süfzen, es hört sich ēin Beten,
's is' grōss die Ssakone, 's is' schrecklich die Nōt,
Un' Jederer bet't bei sein Gott, er soll retten,
Befreien die Menschen vun sicheren Tōdt.

Dās wēinen die Kinder, es klāgen die Weiber,
Män schreit un' män is' sich miswade azünd:
Es flatteren Sēelen, es zitteren Leiber
Var Schreck var dem boesen, varnichtenden Wind.

Doch unten, in Zwischendeck, sitzen zwēi Männer
Ganz ruhig, see rührt nit der mindester Wēh;
See suchen kēin Rettung, see klären kēin Pläner,
Wie Alls wollt' sein sicher un' still arum see.

Es laremt dās Wasser, die Wellen, see schäumen,
Es wojet, es mojet meschune der Wind;
Es ssappet der Késsel, es huzet der Kōmen;
Doch unten die Zwēi, seht, see schweigen azünd.

See kucken mit Kaltkeit dem Tōdt in die Äugen,
See rührt nit dem Sturem's gefährliche Macht;
Es scheint, as der Tōdt hāt allēin nor erzōgen
See Bēiden, in Schreck un' in finsterer Nacht.

Now she must lie down, now again she must rise, now she is driven back, now forward ; — the ship is a plaything of the waves that swallow her up and spit her out again.

The ocean roars, the billows rise, and lash, and thunder in awful terror, the murderous storm wants to destroy everything, — the abyss opens up its closed jaws.

There are heard sighs and prayers. Great is the danger and dreadful the calamity, — and everybody prays to his God that He may save and liberate the people from sure death.

Children weep, women wail ; the people cry and confess their sins ; souls flutter, bodies tremble in terror of the angry, destructive wind.

But below, in the steerage, two men sit quietly ; no pain assails them ; they seek no salvation, they make no plans, just as if all were safe and calm about them.

The water roars, the billows foam ; the wind whines and howls insanely ; the boiler gasps, the chimney buzzes, — but the men below, behold, they are silent now !

They look coolly into the eyes of Death ; the dangerous might of the storm touches them not ; it seems as though Death had reared the two in terror and dark night.

" Wer seid ihr, Unglückliche, — lässt es doch hören, —
Wās können varschweigen die gwaldigste Nōt,
Wās hāben kēin Süfzen, un' hāben kēin Trähren,
Afile bei'm schrecklichen Thōer vun Tōdt?

" Sāgt, hāben euch take nor Kworim geboren?
Ihr lāsst gār kēin Elteren, Weib oder Kind,
Zu wēinen auf euch, wenn ihr werd't dā varloren
In tiefen, in schrecklichen Ābgrund azünd?

" Wie?   Lāsst ihr nit Kēinem, wās ihm soll vardriessen,
Wās er soll wenn baenken, zu lāsen a Trähr,
Wenn euch wet der nasser Bessōlem vargiessen,
Wenn ihr wet dā kēin Māl zurückkehren mehr?

" Wie?   Hā't ihr kēin Vāterland gār, kēin Medine,
Kēin Hēim, wu zu kummen, kēin freundliche Stub',
Wās ihr hā't behalten in sich asa Ssine
Zum Leben un' wart't auf der finsterer Grub'?

" Ihr hā't gār nit Kēinem in Himmel dort ōben,
Zu wemen zu schreien, wenn ihr seid in Zar?
Ihr hā't gār kēin Volk nit, ihr hā't gār kēin Gläuben?
Varlorene, wās is' mit euch far a Gsar? "

Es gänezt der Ābgrund, es brausen die Inden,
Es krachen die Leiters vun Schiff, un' es trägt,
Es hulet der Sturem, es pfeifen die Winden,
Un' Einer hāt endlich mit Trähren gesāgt:

" Der schwarzer Bessōlem is' nit unser Mutter,
Nit is' unser Wiegel der Keewer gewe'n; —
Es hāt uns geboren a Malach a guter,
A teuere Mutter, mit Liebe varṣehn.

" Who are you, wretched ones, tell me, that you can suppress the most terrible sufferings, that you have no sighs and no tears even at the awful gates of Death?

" Say, have, indeed, graves brought you forth? Do you leave behind you no parents, no wife, no child who will lament you when you are lost here in the deep and dreadful abyss ?

" How ? Have you no one to be sorry for you, to long for you, or shed a tear, when the wet cemetery will cover you, when you will no more return to this earth ?

" How ? Have you no fatherland, no country, no home where to go to, no friendly house, that you bear such a contempt for life, and are waiting for the dark grave ?

" Have you no one in heaven above to whom to cry when you are in trouble ? Have you no nation, have you no faith ? Miserable ones, what is your fate ? "

The abyss yawns, the waves bellow, the shipladders crack, the storm rages madly, the winds whistle, — and finally one says in tears :

" The black cemetery is not our mother, the grave has not been our cradle ; a good angel has borne us, a dear mother, endowed with love.

" Es hät uns gepjestet a Mame, erzōgen
A zärtliche, wareme, freundliche Brust ;
Gekichelt un' ständig gekuckt in die Äugen
Hät uns äuch a Vāter, un' lieblich gekusst.

" Mir hāben a Haus, nor män hät sie zubrochen,
Un' unsere hēiligste Sachen varbrennt,
Die Liebste un' Beste varwandelt in Knochen,
Die Letzte varjägt mit gebundene Händ'.

" Män kenn' unser Land, o, sie lässt sich derkennen :
Durch Jāgen, durch Schlägen nit werendig müd',
Durch wilde Pogromen, durch Brechen, durch Brennen,
Durch Suchen dem Tōdt far dem elenden Jüd.

" Un' mir seinen Jüden, varwogelte Jüden,
Ohn' Freund un' ohn' Frēuden, ohn' Hoffnung auf
    Glück. —
Nit frägt mehr, o, frägt nit, o, seht, lässt zufrieden !
Amerika treibt uns nāch Russland zurück,

" Nāch Russland, vun wannen mir seinen antloffen,
Nāch Russland derfar, wās mir hāben kēin Geld;
Auf wās bleibt uns itzter zu warten, zu hoffen ?
Wās täug' uns dās Leben, die finstere Welt ?

" Ihr hā't wās zu wēinen, ihr hā't wās zu brummen,
Ihr hā't wās zu schrecken sich itzt far dem Tōdt,
Ihr hā't gewiss Alle a Hēim, wu zu kummen,
Un' fährt vun Amerika äuch nit aus Nōt.

" Doch mir seinen Elende, gleich zu die Stēiner:
Die Erd' is' zu schlecht, uns zu schenken an Ort —
Mir fāhren, doch leider, es wart't auf uns Kēiner,
Erklärt mir, ich bet' euch, wu reisen mir fort !

" A mother has fondled us, a tender, warm, friendly breast has nurtured us ; a father, too, has stroked us and looked into our eyes, and kissed us tenderly.

" We have a house, but it has been destroyed, and our holy things have been burned ; our dearest and best have been turned into bones, and those who survive have been driven away with fettered hands.

" You know our country ; it is easily recognized by its unceasing baiting and beating, by its cruel riots, its ruthless destruction, and dealing death to the wretched Jew.

" Yes, we are Jews, miserable Jews, without friends or joys, without hopes or happiness. Oh, ask us no more, ask no more, oh, leave us in peace ! America drives us back to Russia,

" To Russia, whence we have run away, to Russia, because we have no money. What is there left for us to expect, to hope for ? Of what good is life, and the gloomy world to us ?

" You have something to weep for ; you have reason to murmur and to be afraid of Death ! You have, no doubt, a home where to go to, and you have left America not from necessity.

" But we are forlorn and alone like a rock. Earth is too mean to give us a resting-place ; we are voyaging, but, unfortunately, no one waits for us. Explain to me, pray, whither we are bound !

"Soll sturmen der Wind, soll er brummen mit Zoren,
Soll sieden, soll kochen, soll rauschen der Grund!
Denn 's sei wie 's sei seinen mir Jüden varloren,
Der Jam nor varlöscht unser brennende Wund'. . . ."

M. ROSENFELD.

XVIII. BONZJE SCHWEIG'
(*Literatur un' Leben*, pp. 11-22)

Dā, auf der Welt, hāt Bonzje Schweig's Tōdt gār kēin Rōschem nischt gemacht! Frägt Emizen becheerem, wer Bonzje is' gewesen, wie asō er hāt gelebt, aúf wās er is' gestorben! Zu hāt in ihm dās Harz geplatzt, zu die Kōches senen ihm ausgegangen, oder der March-bēin hāt sich übergebrochen unter a schwerer Last . . . wer wēisst? Efscher is' er gār var Hunger gestorben!

A Ferd in Tramwaj soll fallen, wollt' män sich mehr interessirt, es wollten Zeitungen geschrieben, hunderter Menschen wollten vun alle Gassen geloffen un' die Neweele bekuckt, betracht't afile dem Ort, wu die Mapole is' gewe'n. . . .

Nor dās Ferd in Tramwaj wollt' äuch die S-chie nischt geha't, es soll sein tausend Milljon Ferd' wie Menschen!

Bonzje hāt still gelebt un' is' still gestorben; wie a Schātten is' er durch durch unser Welt.

Auf Bonzje's Bris hāt män kēin Wein nischt getrunken, es hāben kēin Kōsses geklungen. Zu Barmizwe hāt er kēin klingendige Drosche nischt gesāgt . . . gelebt hāt er wie a gro, klēin Kerndel Samd beim Breg vun'm Jam, zwischen Milljonen seins Gleichen; un' as der Wind hāt ihm aufgehōben un' auf der anderer Seit Jam arüber gejägt, hāt es Kēiner nischt bemerkt.

.Beim Leben hāt die nasse Blote kēin Schlad vun sein

"Let storm the wind, let it howl in anger : let the deep seethe, and boil, and roar ! However it be, we Jews are lost, the ocean alone can allay our burning wound. . . ."

XVIII. BONTSIE SILENT

Here, in this world, the death of Bontsie Silent produced no impression. You will ask in vain who Bontsie was, how he lived, and what caused his death. Did his heart burst, did his strength give out, or were his bones crushed under a heavy load . . . who knows? Maybe, after all, he died of starvation !

There would have been displayed more interest if it had been a street-car horse that had fallen dead. Newspapers would have reported about it, hundreds of people would have congregated from all the streets to look at the carcass and even to survey the spot where the accident had occurred !

But even the street-car horse would not be honored in such a distinguished way if there were as many millions of them in existence as there are men.

Bontsie had lived quietly, and he died quietly. He passed through the world like a shadow.

No wine was drunk on the day of Bontsie's circumcision ; no cups were clinked. At his confirmation he made no flowery speech . . . he lived like a small, yellow grain of sand on the seashore, among millions of its kind, and no one noticed how the wind lifted it up and carried it on the other side of the Ocean.

In his lifetime the wet mud kept no impression of his

Fuss nischt behalten; nách'n Tōdt hāt der Wind dās
klēine Brettel vun sein Keewer umgeworfen, un' dem
Kabren's Weib hāt es gefun'en weit vun Keewer un'
derbei a Töppel Kartoffles ābgekocht. . . . Es is' drei
Täg' nāch Bonzje's Tōdt, frägt dem Kabren becheerem,
wu er hāt ihm gelēgt!

Wollt' Bonzje chotsch a Mazeewe geha't, wollt' efscher
über hundert Jāhr sie an Alterthumsforscher gefun'en
un' Bonzje Schweig wollt' noch a Māl übergeklungen in
unser Luft.

A Schätten, sein Photographje is' nischt geblieben
bei Kēinem in Harz; es is' vun ihm kēin Seecher in
Kēinem's Mōach nischt geblieben!

"Kēin Kind, kēin Rind," — elend gelebt, elend gestorben!

Wenn nischt dās menschliche Geruder, wollt' efscher
Emizer a Māl gehört, wie Bonzje's Marchbein hāt unter
der Masse geknackt: wollt' die Welt mehr Zeit geha't,
wollt' Emizer efscher a Māl bemerkt, as Bonzje (äuch
a Mensch) hāt lebedigerhēit zwēi ausgeloschene Äugen
un' schrecklich eingefallene Backen; as afile wenn er
hāt gār schōn kēin Masse nit auf die Pleezes, is' ihm
äuch der Kopp zu der Erd' gebōgen, gleich er wollt'
lebedigerhēit sein Keewer gesucht! Wollten asō wēnig
Menschen wie Ferd in Tramwaj gewesen, wollt' efscher
a Māl Emizer gefrägt: Wu is' Bonzje ahin gekummen?

Wenn män hāt Bonzjen in Spital areingeführt, is'
sein Winkel in Suterine nischt lēdig geblieben, — es
hāben derauf zehn Seins-gleichen gewart't, un' zwischen
sich dem Winkel " In-pljum " lizitirt; wenn män hāt'n
vun Spitalbett in Tötenstübel arein geträgen, hāben
auf'n Bett zwanzig āreme Chaluim gewart't. . . .
Wenn er is' araus vun Tōtenstübel, hāt män zwanzig
Harugim vun unter ēin eingefallen Haus gebrengt, —

footsteps; after his death the wind threw down the small board over his grave, and the grave-digger's wife found it far away from the mound and made a fire with it over which she boiled a pot of potatoes. . . . It is but three days since Bontsie's death, but you will ask in vain of the grave-digger where he has laid him at rest!

If Bontsie had had a tombstone, an archæologist might have found it a hundred years later, and Bontsie's name would have resounded again in our atmosphere.

He was but a shadow: his picture does not live in anybody's heart; his memory does not exist in anybody's mind!

He left no child, no possessions! He had lived in misery, and he died in misery.

Had it not been for the noise of the crowd, some one might have heard the snapping of Bontsie's bones under a heavy burden; if the world had had more time, some one might have noticed that Bontsie's eyes were dim and his eyes frightfully sunken for one alive; that even when he carried no load on his shoulders, his head was bent to the ground as if he were looking for the grave! If there were as few people as there are horses in the street cars, some one might, perhaps, have asked: What has become of Bontsie?

When Bontsie was taken to the hospital, his corner in the basement was not left unoccupied; ten people of his sort had been waiting for it, and it was auctioned off to the highest bidder; when they carried him from the hospital bed to the morgue, twenty poor people were waiting for his bed. When he left the morgue, they brought in twenty people who had been killed by a falling wall. . . . Who knows how long he will rest

wer wēisst, wie lang er wet ruhig wōhnen in Keewer?
Wer wēisst, wieviel es warten schōn auf dem Stückel
Platz. . . .

Still gebōren, still gelebt, still gestorben un' noch
stiller begrāben.

Nor nischt asō is' gewesen auf jener Welt! Dorten
hāt Bonzje's Tōdt a grōssen Rōschem gemacht!

Der grōsser Schōfer vun Moschiach's Zeiten hāt geklungen in alle sieben Himmlen: Bonzje Schweig is'
nifter gewor'en! Die grösste Malochim mit die brēit'ste
Flügel senen geflōgen un' Einer dem Anderen übergegeben: Bonzje is' "nischbakesch" gewor'en "bischiwo
schel majlo"! In Ganeeden is' a Rasch, a Ssimche, a Geruder: "Bonzje Schweig! A Spass Bonzje Schweig!!!"

Junge Malochimlech mit brilljantene Aeugelech,
goldene drāht-arbeitene Flügelech un' silberene Pantöffelech senen Bonzjen ankegen geloffen mit Ssimche!
Der Gerasch vun die Flügel, dās Klappen vun die
Pantöffelech un' dās froehliche Lachen vun die junge,
frische, rosige Maülechlech hāt verfüllt alle Himmlen
un' is' zugekummen bis zum Kisse-ha-kowed, un' Gott
allēin hāt äuch schōn gewusst, as Bonzje Schweig
kummt!

Awrohom Owinu hāt sich in Thōer vun Himmel
gestellt, die rechte Hand ausgestellt zum brēiten
"Scholem-aleechem!" un' a süsser Schmēichel scheint
asō hell auf sein alten Ponim!

Wās rädelt asō in Himmel?

Dās hāben zwēi Malochim in Ganeeden arein far
Bonzje's wegen a gingoldene Vāterstuhl äuf Rädlech
geführt!

Wās hāt asō hell geblitzt?

Dās hāt män durchgeführt a goldene Krōn', mit die
theuerste Stēiner gesetzt! All's far Bonzjen!

quietly in his grave? Who knows how many are already waiting for his place?

Born quietly, lived quietly, died quietly, and still more quietly buried!

But matters went differently in the other world! There Bontsie's death produced a sensation!

The sound of Moses' ram's horn was heard in all the seven heavens: Bontsie Silent has died! The greatest angels, with the broadest wings, were flying about and announcing the news to each other: Bontsie has been summoned before the Judgment Seat! There is a noise, an excitement, a joy in Heaven: Bontsie Silent! Just think of it, — Bontsie Silent!!!

Young little angels with sparkling eyes, gold-worked wings, and silver slippers rushed out to receive Bontsie with joy! The buzzing of their wings, the clatter of their slippers, and the merry laughter of the young, fresh, and rosy little mouths filled the heavens and reached the Seat of Honor, and God himself knew that Bontsie Silent was coming!

Father Abraham placed himself at the gate of Heaven, and he stretched out his right hand for a friendly "Peace be with you!" and a sweet smile lit up his old face!

What are they rolling there in Heaven?

Two angels are rolling into Paradise an armchair of pure gold on wheels for Bontsie!

What caused that lightning?

They are carrying a golden crown, all set in the most precious stones! All for Bontsie!

— Noch var'n Psak vun Bess-din-schel-majle? frägen
die Zadikim verwundert un' nischt gār ohn' Kine.

— Oh! entwern die Malochim, dās wet sein a proste,
puste Forme!   Gegen Bonzje Schweig wet afile der
Katēgor kēin Wort in Maul nischt gefin'en!   Die Djele
wet dauern fünf Minut!
Ihr spielt sich mit Bonzje Schweig?

*   *   *   *   *

As die Malochimlech hāben Bonzjen gechappt in der
Luft un' ābgespielt ihm a Semer; as Awrohom Owinu
hāt ihm wie an alten Kamrat die Hand geschockelt;
as er hāt gehört, as sein Stuhl is' grēit in Ganeeden;
as auf sein Kopp wart't a Krōn', as in Bess-din-schel-
majle wet män über ihm kēin übrig Wort nischt reden,
— hāt Bonzje, gleich wie auf jener Welt, geschwiegen
var Schreck!   Es is' ihm dās Harz entgangen.   Er is'
sicher, as dās mus sein a Cholem, oder a proster Toes!
Er is' Bēide gewōhnt!   Nischt ēin Māl hāt sich ihm
auf jener Welt gecholemt, as er klaubt Geld auf der
Podloge, ganze Ōzres liegen . . . un' hāt sich auf-
gechappt noch a grösserer Kabzen wie nächten. . . .
Nischt ēin Māl hāt män in'm a Toes gehāt, es hāt ihm
Emiz zugeschmēichelt, a gut Wort gesāgt un' bald sich
übergedrēht un' ausgespiegen. . . .
— Mein Masel, tracht er, is' schōn asō!
Un' er hāt Mōre, die Äugen aufzuhēben, der Cholem
soll nischt verschwunden wer'en; er soll sich nischt
aufchappen ergez in a Hoehl' zwischen Schlangen un'
Egdissen!   Er hāt Mōre vun Maul a Klang arauszu-
lāsen, a Tnue mit an Eewer zu machen, — män soll
ihm nischt derkennen un' nischt awegschleudern auf
Kaf-hakal. . . .
Er zittert un' hört nit die Malochim's Komplimenten,

"What? Even before the sentence of the Supreme Court has been passed?" the saints ask not without envy.

"Oh!" answer the angels, "that will be a mere formality. The Prosecuting Attorney himself will find no words against Bontsie! The case will last but five minutes!"

Bontsie Silent — that's no trifling matter!

* * * * *

As the angels carried Bontsie through the air and played sweet tunes to him; as Father Abraham shook his hand like that of an old comrade; as he heard that his chair was ready for him in Paradise, that a crown was waiting for his head, that no trifling words would be spoken against him before the Supreme Court, — Bontsie was frightened into silence just as in the other world! His heart failed him. He was sure that this was but a dream, or a mere mistake!

He had been used to both. Many a time he had dreamed in the other world of picking up money from the floor where fortunes were lying. . . . More than once they had mistaken him for some one else; they had smiled at him, had said a good word, and then had turned aside, and spit out. . . .

"That's just my luck!" thought he.

And he is afraid to raise his eyes for fear that the dream would disappear, that he should not awaken somewhere in a cave full of serpents and lizards. He is afraid to utter a sound, to move a limb, lest he be recognized and hurled to perdition.

He trembles and does not hear the compliments of

seht nischt sejer Arumtanzen arum ihm, er entwert
nischt Awrohom Owinu auf'n herzlichen Scholem-
aleechem, un'—geführt zum Bess-din-schel-majle, sägt
er ihm kein "Gut Morgen" nischt. . . .

Bonzje is' ausser sich var Schreck!

Un' sein schreckliche Schreck is' noch grösser gewor'en as er hāt, nischt willendig, unter seine Füss'
dersehn die Podloge vun Bess-din-schel-majle. Ssame
Alabaster mit Brilljanten! "Auf asa Podloge stēhen
meine Füss'!" Er wert in Ganzen verstarrt. "Wer
wēisst, welchen Gwir, welchen Row, welchen Zadik
män mēint . . . er wet kummen, wet sein mein finsterer
Ssof!"

Var Schreck hāt er afile nit gehört, wie der Präses
hāt befeeresch ausgerufen: "Die Djele vun Bonzje
Schweig!" un', derlangendig dem Meeliz-jöscher die
Akten, gesāgt: "Les', nor bekizer!"

Mit Bonzjen drēht sich der ganzer Salon, es rauscht
ihm in die Ōheren, nor in'm Gerausch hört er alle Māl
scharfer un' scharfer dem Malech-meeliz's süss Kol wie
a Fiedel:

— Sein Nāmen, hört er, hāt ihm gepasst, wie zum
schlank Leib a Klēid vun an Artist a Schneider's Hand."

— Wās redt er? frägt sich Bonzje, un' er hört, wie
an umgeduldig Kol hackt ihm über un' sägt:

— Nor ohn' Mescholim!

— Er hāt kēin Māl, hēbt weiter ān der Meeliz-jöscher,
auf Kēinem nischt geklāgt, nischt auf Gott, nischt auf
Leut'; in sein Äug' hāt kēin Māl nischt aufgeflammt
kēin Funk' Ssine, er hāt es kēin Māl nischt aufgehōben
mit a Pretensje zum Himmel.

Bonzje verstēht weiter nischt a Wort, un' dās harte
Kol schlägt weiter über:

the angels, does not see their dancing around him, does not reply to Father Abraham's hearty "Peace be with you!" and being led before the Supreme Court he does not say "Good morning" to them.

Bontsie is beside himself with terror.

And his terrible fear is still increased when by accident he notices the floor of the Court Hall under his feet. Pure alabaster and brilliants! "On such a floor do my feet tread!" He grows stiff with fright. "Who knows what rich man, what Rabbi, what saint they mean! ... I shall fare ill when he will come!"

In his terror he did not even hear the Presiding Officer's call: "The case of Bontsie Silent!" and his saying to the Advocate, as he handed him the documents: "Read, but be short!"

The whole hall is turning around with Bontsie, there is a din in his ears, and through it he can distinguish more sharply and more sharply the voice of the Advocate as sweet as a violin:

"His name," he hears him saying, "has fit him like an artist-tailor's gown on a graceful body."

"What is he talking about?" Bontsie asks himself. And he hears an impatient voice interrupting him, and saying:

"Pray, without similes!"

"He has never, proceeds the Advocate, complained against any one, neither against God nor against man! There has never flamed up a spark of hatred in his eyes; he has never uplifted them with any pretensions to Heaven."

Bontsie again does not understand a word, and the harsh voice interrupts him:

— Ohn' Retorik!

— Iow hāt nischt ausgehalten, er is' umglücklicher
gewesen —

— Fakten, truckene Fakten! ruft noch umgeduldiger
der Präses.

— Zu acht Tāg' hāt men ihm male gewesen —

— Nor ohn' Realism!

— A Mōhel, a Fuscher hāt dās Blut nit verhalten —

— Weiter!

— Er hāt alls geschwiegen, führt weiter der Meeliz-
jōscher, afile wenn die Mutter is' ihm gestorben un' er
hāt zu dreizehn Jāhr a Stiefmame bekummen . . . a
Stiefmame — a Schlang, a Marschaas. . . .

— Mēint män doch efscher fort mich? tracht Bonzje.

— Ohn' Insinuazjes auf dritte Personen, boesert sich
der Präses.

— Sie flegt ihm žałewen dem Bissen . . . ēher-nächtig
verschimmelt Brōt . . . Hāar-flachs far Flēisch . . . un'
sie hāt Kawe mit Schmetten getrunken —

— Zu der Sach' — schreit der Präses.

— Sie hāt ihm far dās kēin Nägel nischt gekargt un'
sein blo-un'-blo Leib flegt arauskucken vun alle Löcher
vun seine verschimmelt-zurissene Klēider. . . . Winter,
in die grösste Fröst', hāt er ihr bārwess auf'n Hōf
Holz gehackt, un' die Händ' senen zu jung un' schwach
gewesen, die Klötzlech zu dick, die Hack zu stumpig
. . . nischt ēin Māl hāt er sich die Händ' vun die
Stawes ausgelenkt, nischt ēin Māl hāt er sich die Füss'
ābgefrōren, nor geschwiegen hāt er afile sich var'n
Väter —

— Var'n Schiker! lacht arein der Katēgor, un'
Bonzje werd kalt in alle Eewrim —

" Please, without rhetoric ! "

" Job did not endure, but he has been more unfortunate — "

" Facts ! Dry facts ! " the President calls out more impatiently.

" On the eighth day he was circumcised — "

" Pray, without realism ! "

" The surgeon was a quack, and he did not stanch the blood."

" Go on ! "

" He was always silent," the Advocate proceeds, " even when his mother died, and he got upon his thirteenth year a stepmother . . . a stepmother — a snake, a witch."

" Maybe he really means me ? " Bontsie thinks to himself.

" Leave out insinuations against third persons ! " says the President, angrily.

" She begrudged him every morsel. . . . Musty bread, three days old . . . tendons for meat . . . and she drank coffee with cream. . . ."

" Let's come to business ! " cries the President.

" And she did not spare him her finger nails, and his blue-and-black body peeped through all the holes of his musty clothes. . . . In winter, in the severest frosts, he chopped wood for her in his bare feet, and his hands were too young and too weak, the blocks too large, the axe too dull. . . . More than once he had sprained his wrists, more than once he had frozen his feet, but he was silent, and even to his father — "

" The drunkard ! " the Prosecuting Attorney laughs out loud, and a shiver passes over Bontsie's body.

— Nischt geklāgt, — endigt der Meeliz-jöscher dem Satz.

— Un' ständig elend, führt er weiter, kēin Chawer, kēin Talmud-tōre, kēin Cheeder, kēin Schkole . . . kēin ganz Beged . . . kēin freie Minut —

— Fakten! ruft weiter der Präses.

— Er hāt geschwiegen afile später, wenn der Vāter hāt'n schikerhēit a Māl āngechappt bei die Hāar un' in Mitten a schneewindiger Winternacht arausgeworfen vun Stub'! Er hāt sich still aufgehōben vun Schnee un' is'·entloffen, wu die Äugen hāben ihm getrāgen. . . .

Auf'n ganzen Weg hāt er geschwiegen . . . beim grössten Hunger hāt er nor mit die Äugen gebettelt.

Erscht in a schwindeldige, nasse Wjosne-nacht is' er in a grōsse Städt areingekummen; er is' arein wie a Troppen in a Jam un' doch hāt er die ēigene Nacht in Kose genächtigt. . . . Er hāt geschwiegen, nischt gefrägt far wās, far wenn? Er is' araus un' die schwerste Arbēit gesucht! Nor er hāt geschwiegen! Noch schwerer far der Arbeit is' gewesen sie zu gefin'en, — er hāt geschwiegen!

Bādendig sich in kalten Schwēiss, zusammengedrückt unter der schwerster Last, beim grössten Krampf vun'm lēdigen Māgen, hāt er geschwiegen!

Bespritzt vun fremder Blote, bespiegen vun fremde Maüler, gejägt vun Trotuaren mit der schwerster Last arāb in Gassen zwischen Droschkes, Kareten un' Tramwajs, kuckendig jede Minut dem Tōdt in die Äugen arein, — hāt er geschwiegen!

Er hāt kēin Māl nischt übergerechent, wieviel vun Masse es kummt aus auf a Groschen, wieviel Māl er is' gefallen bei jeden Gang far a Dreier, wieviel Māl er hāt schier nischt die Neschome ausgespiegen, māhnendig sein Verdienst, er hāt nischt gerechent, nischt sein, nischt Jenem's Masel, nor geschwiegen!

"He did not complain!" the Advocate concludes his sentence.

"And eternally alone, he proceeds, — no friend, no religious instruction, no school . . . not a whole garb . . . not a free minute!"

"Stick to facts!" calls out the President.

"He was silent even later, when his father, in a drunken fit, once grabbed him by his hair and kicked him out of the house into a stormy winter night. He quietly picked himself up and ran whither his eyes carried him.

"He was silent on his whole journey . . . in the greatest frost he begged only with his eyes.

"In a nasty, wet spring night he arrived in a large city; he fell in like a drop in the Ocean, and yet he passed that very night in the police jail. . . . He was silent, did not ask why. He came out of it, and looked for the hardest work! And he was all the time silent.

"Much harder than the work was the finding of the same, — and he was silent.

"Bathing in cold sweat, bent under the heaviest burdens, during the severest cramps of his empty stomach, — he was silent!

"Besmutted by strangers' mud, bespit by strangers' mouths, driven with his heavy load from the sidewalks into the streets among buggies, coaches, and street cars, looking every moment into the eyes of death, — he was silent!

"He never calculated how many pounds of load came to every penny, how many times he stumbled on every three kopeks' errand, how many times he almost exhaled his soul collecting his pay; he did not beseech or curse, — he only was silent!

Sein ēigen Verdienst hāt er nischt hōch gemāhnt.
Wie a Bettler hāt er sich bei der Thür gestellt, un' in
die Äugen hāt sich a hüntische Bakosche gemält!
"Kumm' später!" un' er is' wie a Schātten still verschwunden gewor'en, kedee später noch stiller aus-
zubettlen sein Verdienst!

Er hāt afile geschwiegen, wenn män flegt ihm ābreissen
vun sein Verdienst, oder ihm areinzuwarfen a falsche
Matbeje . . . er hāt alls geschwiegen. . . .

— Mēint män doch take mich! troest't sich Bonzje.

* * * * *

— Ein Māl, führt weiter der Meeliz-jōscher noch a
Trunk Wasser, is' in sein Leben a Schinui gewor'en
. . . es is' durchgeflōgen a Kotsch mit gummene Räder
mit zuploschete Ferd' . . . der Schmeisser is' schōn
lang vun weitens gelegen mit a zuspaltenem Kopp auf'n
Bruk . . . vun die derschrockene Ferd's Maüler spritzt
der Schaum, vun unter die Podkowes jägen sich Funken,
wie vun Lokomotiw, die Äugen blischtschen wie bren-
nendige Sturkatzen in a finsterer Nacht, — un' in Kotsch
sitzt nischt tōt, nischt lebedig, a Mensch.

Bonzje hāt die Ferd' verhalten!

Der Gerateweter is' gewesen a Jüd, a Balzdoke, un'
hāt Bonzjen die Tōwe nischt vergessen.

Er hāt ihm dem Gehargenten's Kelnje übergegeben; Bonzje is' a Schmeisser gewor'en! Noch mehr,
— er hāt ihm Chassene gemacht, noch mehr, — er hāt
ihm afile mit a Kind versorgt, — un' Bonzje hāt alls
geschwiegen!

— Mich mēint män, mich! befestigt sich Bonzje in
der Deje, un' hāt sich die Hose nischt, an Äug' zu
warfen auf'n Bess-din-schel-majle. . . .

Er hört sich weiter ein zum Malech-meeliz:

" He did not ask loud for his pay. Like a mendicant he stood at the door with a doglike prayer in his eyes. ' Come later ! ' and he disappeared quietly like a shadow, in order to ask later still more quietly for his dues !

" He was silent even when they knocked off something from his pay, or paid him in a counterfeit coin . . . he was silent. . . ."

" It seems they really mean me ! " Bontsie consoles himself.

* * * * *

" Once," proceeds the Advocate, after taking a drink of water, " there came a change in his life . . . a coach with rubber wheels and frightened horses rushed by . . . the driver lay way back on the pavement with his head split open . . . foam spurted from the mouths of the frightened horses, and sparks flew from under their feet, as from a locomotive ; their eyes sparkled like glowing coals in a dark night, — and in the coach there was sitting, more dead than alive, a man !

" Bontsie stopped the runaway.

" The person thus saved was a Jew, a charitable man, and he did not forget Bontsie's kindness.

" He transferred to him the seat of the killed man ; Bontsie became a driver ! More than that, — he got him married ; still more, he provided him with a child . . . and Bontsie kept silent all the time ! "

" They mean me, they mean me ! " Bontsie strengthens himself in his belief, and he has no courage to raise his eyes on the Supreme Judge.

He listens again to the Advocate.

—Er hāt geschwiegen afile, wenn sein Baltōwe hāt in Kurzen bankrottirt un' ihm sein S-chires äuch. . . .
Er hāt geschwiegen afile, wenn dās Weib is' ihm entloffen un' übergelāst ihm a Kind vun der Brust. . . .

Er hāt geschwiegen afile mit fufzehn Jāhr später, wenn dās Kind is' aufgewachsen un' genug stark gewesen, — Bonzjen arauszuwarfen vun Stub'. . . .

〤 —Mich mēint män, mich ! frēut sich Bonzje.

* * * * *

—Er hāt afile geschwiegen, hēbt ān wēicher un' traueriger der Malech-meeliz, wenn der ēigener Baltōwe hāt sich mit Alle ausgegleicht, nor ihm kēin Groschen S-chires nischt zurückgegeben, — un' afile demelt, wenn er is' Bonzjen (weiter fāhrendig auf a Kotsch mit gummene Räder un' Ferd' wie Loeben) übergefāhren. . . .

—Er hāt alls geschwiegen ! Er hāt afile der Polizēi nischt gesāgt, wer es hāt ihm zurecht gemacht. . . .

* * * * *

—Er hāt geschwiegen afile in Spital, wu män māg schön schreien !

Er hāt geschwiegen afile, wenn der Doktor hāt ohn' fufzehn Kop. nischt gewollt zu'n ihm zugēhn, un' der Wächter ohn' fünf Kop. — tauschen die Wäsch' !

Er hāt geschwiegen beim Gōssen, er hāt geschwiegen in der letzter Rege, beim Starben. . . .

Kēin Wort gegen Gott, kēin Wort gegen Leut' !
Dixi !

* * * * *

Bonzje hēbt ān weiter zu zittern auf'n ganzen Leib. Er wēisst, as nāch'n Meeliz-jöscher gēht der Katēgor. Wer wēisst, wās der wet sāgen? Er allēin hāt sein ganz Leben nischt gedenkt, noch auf jener Welt hāt er jede Minut die früherdige vergessen . . . der Meeliz-

"He was silent even when his benefactor became bankrupt and did not pay him his wages. . . . He was silent even when his wife ran away and left him with a nursing babe. . . .

"He was silent even fifteen years later when the child grew up, and was strong enough to throw Bontsie out of doors. . . ."

"They mean me, they mean me!" Bontsie says joyfully.

"He was silent," the Advocate begins again with a softer and sadder voice, "when his benefactor resumed business, but did not pay him a cent, and even then, when he ran over him, again riding in a carriage with rubber tires, and horses like lions.

"He was all that time silent! He did not even tell the police who had maimed him so.

* * * * *

"He was silent even in the hospital, where one may cry!

"He was silent even when the doctor would not come to him unless he was paid fifteen kopeks, and the janitor would not change his shirt without five kopeks!

"He was silent during the last moments of his life, he was silent in his death agony. . . .

"Not a word against God, not a word against man! Dixi!"

* * * * *

Bontsie begins again to tremble in his whole body. He knows that after the Advocate comes the Prosecuting Attorney. Who knows what he will say? He himself had never, during his whole life, preserved the memory of anything . . . in the other world, he forgot jōscher hāt ihm All's dermāhnt . . . wer wēisst, wās der Katēgor wet ihm dermāhnen!

— Rabōssai! hēbt ān a scharf-stichedig, brühendig Kol —
Nor er hackt āb —
— Rabōssai! hēbt er noch a Māl ān, nor wēicher un' hackt weiter āb.

Endlich hört sich, vun dem ēigenem Hals araus, a wēich Kol, wie a Putter:

— Rabōssai! Er hāt geschwiegen! Ich will äuch schweigen!

Es werd still, un' vun vorent hört sich a neue wēiche, zitterdige Stimme:

— Bonzje, mein Kind Bonzje! ruft es wie a Harfe. . . . Mein harzig Kind Bonzje! In Bonzjen zuwēint sich dās Harz . . . er wollt' schōn die Äugen geöffent, nor see senen verfinstert vun Trähren. . . . Es is' ihm asō süss-wēinendig kēin Māl nischt gewesen. . . . "Mein Kind," "Mein Bonzje," — seit die Mutter is' gestorben, hāt er asa Kol un' asōne Wörter nischt gehört —

— Mein Kind! führt weiter der Ow-bess-din, — du hāst alls gelitten un' geschwiegen! Es is' nischt dā kein ganz Eewer, kēin ganz Bēindel in dein Leib ohn' a Rane, ohn' a blutig Ort, es is' nischt dā kēin ēin behalten Ort in dein Neschome, wu es soll nischt bluten . . . un' du hāst alls geschwiegen. . . .

Dort hāt män sich nischt verstan'en derauf! Du allēin hāst gār efscher nischt gewusst, as du kännst schreien un' vun dein Geschrēi können Jereecho's Mauern zittern un' einfallen! Du allēin hāst vun dein verschläfenem Kōach nischt gewusst. . . .

Auf jener Welt hāt män dein Schweigen nischt be-

every moment the previous . . . the Advocate brought
back so many recollections . . . who knows what the
Prosecuting Attorney will remind him of?

"Judges!" he begins with a sharp, stinging voice —

But he stops short.

"Judges!" he begins once more, but more softly, and
he interrupts himself again.

At last there issues from the same throat a voice as
soft as butter:

"Judges! He has been silent! I shall be silent
too!"

All is still, and in front a new soft, trembling voice
is heard:

"Bontsie, my child Bontsie!" Bontsie's heart is dissolved in tears . . . he would have opened his eyes,
but they are covered with tears . . . he has never
wept such sweet tears before. . . . "My child," "My
Bontsie!" — ever since his mother had died, he had not
heard such a voice and such words.

"My child!" the Highest Judge proceeds, "you have
suffered all, and you were silent! There is not a member, not a bone in your body without wounds, without
a spot of blood. There is not a hidden place in your
soul where it does not bleed, and yet you were always
silent. . . .

"There they did not understand such things! It
may be you yourself did not know that you can cry
and that from your cries the walls of Jericho could
tremble and fall! You yourself did not know of your
hidden power. . . .

"They did not reward your silence in the other

löhnt, nor dort is' der Ōlem-hascheker, dā auf'n Ōlem-emes west du dein Lōb bekummen !

Dich wet dās Bess-din-schel-majle nischt mischpe-ten, dir wet es nischt paskenen, dir wet es kēin Cheelek nischt aus- un' nischt āb-thēilen ! Nemm dir, wās du willst ! Alles is' dein !

Bonzje hēbt dās erste Māl die Äugen auf ! Er werd wie verblend't vun der Licht vun alle Seiten ; Alles blankt, Alles blischtschet, vun Alles jägen Strahlen : vun die Wänd', vun die Keelim, vun die Malochim, vun die Dajonim ! Ssame Sunnen !

Er lāst die müde Äugen arāb.

— Take ? frägt er messupek un' verschämt.

— Sicher ! entfert fest der Ow-bess-din ! Sicher, sāg' ich dir, as Alles is' dein, Alles in Himmel gehör' zu dir ! Klaub' un' nemm, wās du willst, du nemmst nor bei dir allēin !

— Take ? frägt Bonzje noch a Māl, nor schōn mit a sicheren Kol.

— Take ! Take ! Take ! entfert män ihm auf sicher vun alle Seiten.

— Nu, ōb asō, schmēichelt Bonzje, will ich take alle Tāg' in der Früh' a hēisse Bulke mit frischer Putter !

Dajonim un' Malochim hāben arābgelāst die Köpp' verschämt. Der Katēgor hāt sich zulacht.

J. L. PEREZ.

world, but that was the World of Delusion; here, in the World of Truth, you will receive your reward!

" The Supreme Court shall not pass sentence against you! It will not weigh and dole out your part to you. Take what you wish, — all is yours ! "

Bontsie lifts his eyes for the first time ! He is dazed by the light on all sides: everything sparkles, everything flashes, beams issue everywhere: from the walls, from the vessels, from the angels, from the judges! Nothing but suns around him!

He wearily droops his eyes.

" Really ? " he asks doubtfully and abashed.

" Indeed! " answers the Highest Judge. " Indeed, I tell you — all is yours ! All in Heaven belongs to you ! Choose and take what you wish ! You take your own."

" Really? " asks Bontsie once more, but in a firmer voice.

" Really, really, really! " they answer him on all sides.

" Well, if so," Bontsie smiles, " I should like to have every morning a hot roll with fresh butter ! "

Judges and angels drooped their heads abashed. The Prosecuting Attorney laughed out loud.

I. APPENDIX

BIBLIOGRAPHY

(This Bibliography is a partial list of the works consulted in the preparation of the present book. Those marked with an asterisk are not in the Harvard Library; the others were formerly in my private possession, together with a large number (1800 titles in all) not given here. They now form in the Harvard Library the nucleus of a Judeo-German collection, the largest in America. For an additional list of newspapers, see Ch. D. Lippe, *Bibliographisches Lexicon der gesammten jüdischen Literatur der Gegenwart*, Vienna, 1881, pp. 666, 667.)

I. APPENDIX

BIBLIOGRAPHY

PERIODICALS AND ALMANACS

* **Monatschrift, Jüdisch-deutsche.** Prague and Brünn, 1802. 8vo.

* **Beobachter, Der, an der Weichsel.** Dostrzegacz nadwislański. Warsaw, 1824. 4to.

Zeitung. Redacteur: A. M. Mohr; Verleger: A. I. Madfis. Lemberg. (First number appeared in April, 1848.) 4to.

Post, Die jüdische. Däs is' a politische un' komerzische Zeitung. Verantwortlicher Redakteur, A. N. Blücher? Lemberg, 1849. (First number appeared Nov. 2, 1849.) 8vo.

* **Kol-mewasser.** In jüdisch-deutscher Sprache von A. Zederbaum un' A. I. Goldenblum. Odessa, 1863–1871. Fol.

* **Zeitung, Warschauer jüdische.** Erscheint jeden Freitäg. Warsaw, 1867. Fol.

Jisrulik. Zeitungsblatt far kol Jisroel. Erscheint Freitäg vun die Herausgeber J. J. Linetzki and A. Goldfaden. Lemberg, July 23, 1875–Feb. 2, 1876. Fol.

Kalender, Der nützlicher. Far die russische Jüden. Vun S. Abramowitsch. Wilna, 1876–. 8vo.

Volkskalender, Praktischer. Vun J. J. Linetzki. Lemberg, 1876–; Warsaw, 1883–. 8vo. 64 pp.

Volksblatt, Jüdisches. A politisch-literarische Zeitung. Erscheint in St. Petersburg ēin Māl in der Woch', Donnerstäg. St. Petersburg, Oct. 1/13, 1881–1889. Fol., except for 1888, which consists of the newspaper in large fol., and the Beilage, 4to. Editors, A. Zederbaum, –1887, Dr. L. O. Cantor, 1888–1889.

* **Pölischer Jüdel, Der. The Polish Yidel.** Editor, M. Winchevsky. London, 1884. 4to. Weekly. Only sixteen numbers appeared, after which it was named

* **Zukunft, Die. The Future.** First three numbers of 4 pp. each, later of 8 pp. each. London, 1884–August, 1885. 4to.

* **Arbeiterfreund, Der.** **The Worker's Friend.** Published by the International Workingmen's Educational Club. London, 1886–1891. Folio, of 8 pp. each. Started as monthly, then weekly of 4 pp., then 8, then again 4 pp.

Wecker, Der jüdischer. Redaktirt vun M. L. Lilienblum, herausgegeben vun J. H. Rabnizki un' Z. S. Frankfeld. Odessa, 1887. 8vo.

Familienfreund, Der. Herausgegeben vun M. Spektor. 2 vols. Warsaw, 1887–1888. 8vo.

Hausfreund, Der. A historisch-literarisches Buch. Herausgegeben vun M. Spektor. Warsaw, 1888–. 8vo. Vol. I. 1888, 2d ed., 1894; Vol. II. 1889; Vol. III., 2 eds., 1894; Vol. IV. 1895; Vol. V. 1896.

Kalender, Warschawer jüdischer, Eppelberg's. A historisch-literarisch-wissenschaftliches Buch, mit Annoncen. Warsaw, 1888. 8vo.

Volksbibliothēk, Die jüdische. A Buch für Literatur, Kritik un' Wissenschaft. Herausgegeben vun Scholem Aleechem (S. Rabinowitsch). 2 vols. Kiev, 1888–1889. 8vo.

Bibliothēk, Die klēine jüdische. A Sammlung vun Gedichte, Feuilletons, Erzaehlungen un' Jedies vun die jüdische Kolonies in Erzisroel. Herausgegeben vun der jüdischer Bibliothēk in Odessa, 1888. 4to.

Volksfreund. The Volksfreund. The only Jewish Weekly Journal of America. Editor, J. S. Glick. New York, 1889. 8vo.

Menschenfreund, Der. Belletristische Wochenschrift für Neues, Literatur, Kunst un' Unterhaltung, von N. M. Schaikewitsch. New York, 1889–1891. 4to.

Wecker, Der klēiner. A Sammlung vun verschiedene Artikel un' Gedichte. Herausgegeben vun Odessar gute Freund' vun'm jüdischen Loschen. 1890. 4to.

Bibliothēk, Die jüdische. A Žurnal für Literatur, Gesellschaft un' Oekonomie. Erscheint zwēi Māl jährlich. Redaktirt un' herausgegeben durch J. L. Perez. Warsaw, 1891–. (Only three numbers have so far been issued.) 8vo.

* **Freie Welt, Die.** **The Free World.** A monatlicher sozialistischer Žurnal, arausgegeben vun der Gruppe 'Freie Welt.' London, 1891–1892. 4to. Only ten numbers of 24 pp. each have appeared.

Handelskalender, Der jüdischer. Auf fünf Jähr, 1891–1896. A historisch-literarisch wissenschaftliches Buch mit Annoncen. Redaktor un' Herausgeber J. Bernas. Warsaw, 1891. 8vo.

Hëilige Land, Däs. Verschiedene Artiklen, Lieder un' Erzaehlungen wegen Jischuw Erez Jisroel. Herausgegeben vun Berthe Flekser un' Jisroel Narodizki. Zhitomir, 1891. 8vo.

Zukunft, Die. The Future. A wissenschaftlich-sozialistische Monatschrift. Arausgegeben vun die jüdisch-sprechende Sekzionen, S. A. P. vun Nord-Amerika. New York, 1892–1897. 4to.

Familienkalender, Warschawer jüdischer. A Buch vun Literatur un' Gesellschaft. Herausgegeben vun M. Spektor. Warsaw, 1893–. 8vo.

Städtanzeiger, Der. Wissenschaftlicher Žurnal für Literatur, Kunst, Wissenschaft un' Kommerz. Arausgegeben vun Philip Krantz un' A. M. Sharkansky. New York, 1893. 8vo.

Volksfreund, Der. A literarisch-wissenschaftliche Sammlung herausgegeben vun N. Rosenblum. Odessa, 1894. (One number only.) 8vo.

Literatur un' Leben. A Sammelbuch für Literatur un' Gesellschaft. Herausgegeben durch J. L. Perez. Warsaw, 1894. 8vo.

Jontew-blättlech. J. L. Perez's Ausgaben. Warsaw, 1894–1896. 8vo. Vun Peessach bis Peessach. Erste Serie. 10 Jontewblättlech (1894–1895). 32 columns each. 1) Lekowed Peessach. 2) Feilenbögen. 3) Grünes. 4) Tones. 5) Tröst. 6) Schöfer. 7) Hoschane. 8) Lichtel. 9) Schabes-öbs. 10) Hämen-tasch'.
Zwëite Serie, 1895–1896. 1) Kol Chamiro. 2) Der Ömer. 3) Bikurim. 4) Tamus. 5) Le-Schono-töwo. 6) Chamischo Osser. 7) Öneg Schabes. The first five of 64 columns each, the last two of 32 columns.

Widerkol, Däs. Spektor's Verlag. A Blättel auf wochendige Täg'. Warsaw, 1894. 8vo, 32 col.

Lamteren, Der. Spektor's Verlag. A Blättel auf wochendige Täg'. Warsaw, 1894. 8vo, 32 col.

Volkskalender, Der amerikanischer. The American People's Calendar. A Yearly Literary Review. By Alexander Harkavy. New York, 1894–. 8vo.

Neue Welt, Die. The New World. Ein wöchentlicher Žurnal vun S. J. Silberstein. Published weekly in Jewish-German language. New York, 1894. (Only two numbers were issued.) 8vo.

Puck, Der jüdischer. **The Hebrew 'Puck.'** Weekly, editor M. R. Schaikewitsch. New York, 1894–1896. Fol.

Freie Gesellschaft, Die. A monatlicher Žurnal für die fortgeschrittene Ideen, arausgegeben vun die 'Freie Gesellschaft Publ. Association.' Editors, M. Leontiev and M. Katz. New York, Vol. I. No. 1, October, 1895. 4to, 32 pp.

Emes, Der. The Emeth (Truth). A wöchentliches Familienblatt für Literatur un' Aufklärung. Editor, M. Winchevsky. Boston, 1895. Fol.

Volkskalender, Jüdischer. Redigirt vun Gerschom Bader. Lemberg, 1895. 8vo.

Wahrheit, Die. Monatschrift zur Unterhaltung und Belehrung, von Hirsch Loeb Gottlieb. M.-Sziget. 1896 (2 numbers only). 8vo.

Hatikwoh, Die Hoffnung. Journal Hebdomadaire pour les Israélites. Erscheint jeden Freitāg. Organ für Politik, Literatur, Wissenschaft und hauptsächlich jüdisch-nationale Interessen. Redaktor un' Herausgeber J. Bernas. Paris, 1897–. Fol.

Neuer Geist, Der. The New Spirit. Monatschrift für Wissenschaft, Literatur un' Kunst. Erscheint jeden Monat. Publisher, Sigmund Kantrowitz. New York, 1897–1898. 4to.

Neue Welt, Die. The New World. Erscheint monatlich. Arausgegeben vun A. M. Sharkansky. New York, 1897. 8vo.

Arbeiter, Der jüdischer. Organ für die Interessen der jüdischen Arbeiter in Russland, herausgegeben vun der "Gruppe jüdischer Sozial-demokraten in Russland," 1897. 4to.

Zeit, Die. The Time. Monatlicher Žurnal far Literatur, Unterhaltung un' jüdische Interessen. Redaktirt un' arausgegeben vun M. M. Dolitzky. New York, 1898. 4to.

Neue Zeit, Die. The New Time. Wissenschaftliche Monatschrift. Arausgegeben vun die jüdisch-sprechende Sekzion vun der sozialist. Arbeiterpartei vun Nord-Amerika. New York, 1898–. 4to.

SONG-BOOKS

Lieder-magasin. Magazine of Songs. Published by J. Katzenellenbogen. New York, 1898. Folio. Pt. I. 10 pp.; Pt. II. 10 pp.; Pt. III. 10 pp.; Pt. IV. 11 pp.

Neuer Singer, Der. In 3 Thēilen. 1. Thēil. Die neueste Theaterlieder vun die beste Verfasser. II. Thēil. Sēhr schoene Witzen mit Pictures zum Lachen. III. Thēil. Der Album. Verschiedene Bilder vun jüdische Verfasser. New York, s. a. 16mo, 29 and (30) pp. and adv.

Liederalbum, Der. A Sammlung vun alle jüdische Theaterlieder, Konzertlieder, Kupleten un' Volkslieder. Erster Buch. Alle Theaterlieder, mehr wie 200 Lieder vun alle jüdische Theaterstücke, gesammelt un' zusammengestellt in Ordnung vun Rosenbaum un' Werbelowski. The Song-Album. New York, s. a. 16mo, 240 pp.

Kupleten un' jüdische Theaterlieder. Alle Kupleten, komische un' humoristische, für der jüdischer Bühne verfasst vun Sigmund Mogulesco, un' alle Theaterlieder vun Kaprisne Tochter vun A. Goldfaden, Katoržnik, un' Der Jüdischer Prinz vun Schomer. New York, 1888. 10mo, 36 pp.

Jüdische Theaterlieder. 25. Auflage. In 4 Thēilen, etc. Die alle Lieder vun dem Buch seinen verfasst vun die beste Verfassers un' Dichters sō wie A. Goldfaden, A. Zunser, Ben Nez, A. Harkavy, Professor Selikowitsch, Edelstadt, D. Apothēker, M. Rosenfeld, u. s. w. New York, 1894. 16mo, 74 pp. and adv.

Jüdische Theater un' Volkslieder. Ausgewählte Lieder vun die beste jüdische Dichter. Erster Thēil. Dās Fiedele. New York, s. a. 16mo, 56 and (5)·pp. and adv.

AUTHORS

A. R. S. Reb Tanchum der Mekabel. Einige neue jüdische Volkslieder aus dem Panorama des russisch-polnischen jüdischen Lebens. Jassy, 1883. 16mo, 16 pp.

Abasch. Jekele Kundas. Sēhr a schoenè Maisse, wās hāt sich nit lang verloffen in a klēin Städtel in Pōlen. Geschrieben vun dem Korewer Bocher. Warsaw, 1879. 8vo, 95 pp.

Abramowitsch, Ch. E. Die Jüden. Ein Lustspiel in drei un' zwanzig Vorstellungen von dem weltberühmten Verfasser in der deutschescher Sprache, A. W. Lessing. Wilna, 1879. 16mo, 68 pp.

Abramowitsch, S. J. * Dās klēine Menschele, oder A Lebensbeschreibung vun Jizchok Awrohom Takif. Gedruckt be-Hischtadlus Mendele Mōcher Sforim. . . . Begun in Kol-mewasser, Vol. II. No. 45. (Odessa, 1864.)

The same. (Gār in ganzen auf dās Neu übergemacht.) Wilna, 1879. 8vo, 132 pp.

* Dās Wünschfingerl, wās mit dem känn itlicher Mensch dergrēichen allsding, wās sein Harz wünscht un' begehrt, un' durchdem nützlich sein sich un' der Welt. Warsaw, 1865. (?)

The same, greatly increased, but unfinished, in Die jüdische Volksbibliothēk, Vols. I. and II.

* Die Takse, oder Die Bande Städt-bal-tōwes. Zhitomir, 1869. 8vo.

The same. Wilna, 1872. 8vo, 88 pp.

* Fischke der Krummer, a Maisse vun jüdische āreme Leut'. Zhitomir, 1869.

The same. (In Alle Ksowim vun Mendele Mōcher Sforim, Vol. I.) Odessa, 1888. (Second edition, written entirely anew.) 8vo, 158 pp.

* Der Luftballon. (Written in conjunction with L. Bienstock.) Zhitomir, 1869.

Der Fisch, wās hāt eingeschlungen Jōne Hanowi. Vun die Mechabrim vun'm Luftballon A. B. (Herausgegeben vun der Redakzje vun'm Kol-mewasser.) (In conjunction with L. Bienstock.) Odessa, 1870. 16mo, 21 pp.

Die Klatsche, oder Zar-bale-chaim. A Maisse, wās hāt sich varwalgert zwischen die Ksowim vun Jisrolik dem Meschugenem. Wilna, 1873. 8vo, 119 pp.

The same. (In Alle Ksowim vun M. M. S., Vol. II.) Odessa, 1889. 8vo, 128 pp.

The same. (In Jewish Classics Issued Quarterly, Vol. I. No. I.) New York, 1898. 8vo, 121 pp.

The same. Polish translation : Szkapa ("Die Klatsche") Z oryginału napisanego w żargonie żydowskim przez S. Abramowicza, przełożył i objaśnieniami opatrzył Klemens Junosza. Warszawa. Nakładem księgarni A. Gruszeckiego, 1886. 16mo, 197 pp.

Der Ustaw über woinski Powinnost, wissotschaische utwerdet dem ersten Januar in Jāhr 1874. Übersetzt vun S. Abramowitsch un' L. Bienstock. Zhitomir, 1874. 8vo, 135 pp.

Jüdel. A Ssipur-ha-Maisse in Schirim. In two parts. Warsaw, 1875. 16mo, 105 + 117 pp.

The same. (In Jewish Classics Issued Quarterly, Vol. I. No. 2.) New York, 1898. 8vo, 123 pp.

Smires Jisroel. Schabesdige Smires, vardeutscht in Schirim un' gut derklärt, Bichdej itlicher Jüd' besunder Soll varstēhn sejer teuern Wert, Wie schoen see senen a Gott's Wunder. Zhitomir, 1875. 16mo, 82 pp.

Perek Schiro. Zhitomir, 1875. 8vo, 124 pp.

Kizur Maisses Binjāmin ha-Schlischi, dās hēisst Die Nessie, oder a Reisebeschreibung vun Binjāmin dem Dritten, wās er is auf seine Nessies vergangen het weit aż unter die Horee Chōschech un' hāt sich genug āngesehn un' āngehört Chiduschim schoene Sachen, wās see senen arausgegeben gewor'en in alle schiwim Leschones un' heunt äuch in unser Loschen. Sseefer rischōn. Wilna, 1878. 8vo, 96 pp.

* *The same.* Polish translation: Donkiszot żydowski, szkic z literatury żargonowej żydowskiéj. Przez K. Junoszy. Warszawa. 8vo, 156 pp.

Der Prizyw. A Drame in fünf Akten. St. Petersburg, 1884. 8vo, 87 pp.

Abramsky, G. Bomas Jischok, etc. s. l. e. a. 8vo, 30 pp.

Aksenfeld, I. Der erste jüdische Rekrut in Russland im Jahre 5587 (1827) am Tage der Publicirung des betreffenden Ukases. Ein komisch-tragischer Roman in jüdisch-deutschem Jargon. (Leipsic, 1862.) 8vo, 58 pp.

Dās Sterntüchel, oder Schabes Chanuke in Mesibis. (Leipsic, K. W. Vollrath, 1862?.) 8vo, 140 pp.

Mann un' Weib. Schwester un' Bruder. Ein emesse Maisse, bearbet in a Theaterstück, in zwēi Akten. Odessa, M. Beilinsohn, 1867. 8vo, 68 pp.

Sämmtliche Werke. *Dās vierte Büchel. Die genarrte Welt. Odessa, 1870. 16mo.

The same. Das fünfte Büchel. Kabzen-Ōscher-Spiel. A Drama in zwēi Akten. Odessa, 1870. 16mo, 72 pp.

Apotheker, D. Hanewel. Die Leier. Czernowitz, 1881. 8vo, 79 pp.

Beilinsohn, M. A. Gwures Jehudo Michabi oder Nes-Chanuko (Chanuke-spiel). A Drama in fünf Akten. Verfasst in Englisch vun dem berühmten amerikanischen Dichter (Poet)

Longfellow unter'n Nāmen "Judas Maccabaeus "; übergesetzt kimat in alle europäische Sprachen, un' auf Russisch in Evrejskaja Biblioteka (Vol. 5, 1875); jetzt in Jüdisch-deutsch. Odessa, 1882. 4to, 20 pp.

Golus Schpania. A historischer Roman aus der jüdischen Geschichte, etc. Übersetzt (from the German of Philippsohn) im Jüdischen. Odessa, 1894. 8vo, 158 and (2) pp.

Berenstein, S. Magasin vun jüdische Lieder far dem jüdischen Volk. Zhitomir, 1869. 16mo, 84 pp.

The same. Warsaw, 1880. 8vo, 73 pp.

Bernstein, S. Reb Jochze Dalgeje. A Komödie mit a Roman in 5 Akten. Erster Theil. Kishinev, 1884. 8vo, 32 pp.

Blaustein, E. Die finstere Welt. Ein Bild der vergangenen Zeiten. Ein Roman in vier Thēilen. Wilna, 1881. 8vo, 269 pp.

Die Weisse mit die Schwarze, oder Die Liebe vun a Wilden. Frei übersetzt aus dem Franzoesischen, verbreitet un' bearbeitet. (2 parts.) Wilna, 1894. 8vo, 80 and 78 pp.

Wichne Dwosche fährt zurück vun Amerika. Ein humoristische Erzaehlung. (2 parts.) Wilna, 1894. 8vo, 40 and 50 pp.

Wichne Dwosche fährt nāch Amerika. Eine humoristische Erzaehlung. Wilna, 1895. 16mo, 32 pp.

Brettmann, M. Der chsidischer Unterhalt. Ein emesse Maisse. Odessa, 1868. 8vo, 42 pp.

Brjanski, I. Die erste Aweere. Erinnerungen vun die kindersche Jāhren. St. Petersburg, 1887. 16mo, 23 pp.

Brodawski, Ch. Die Assife in der Städt Ezjōn Gower. Berdichev, 1889. 16mo, 100 pp.

Broder, Berel. Schiree Simro. Zhitomir, 1876. 16mo, 95 pp.

The same. Warsaw, 1882. 16mo, 96 pp.

Buchbinder, A. I. Der Blumengärten. Satirische scharfkritische erenste Maimorim; Anekdoten, Schailes u-Tschuwes, Mischlee Mussor, Schirim, kurze interessante Erzaehlungen un' wissenschaftliche Artiklen. Wilna, 1885. 8vo, 76 pp.

Der jüdischer Minister. A historischer Roman vun der letzter Zeit, ēhder man hat die Jüden arausgetrieben vun Spanien. Frei übersetzt. Odessa, 1890. 8vo, 48 pp.

Dās jüdische Aschires in Palestina. Material zu der Historie vun Jischuw Erez Isroel. Wilna, 1891. 8vo, 40 pp.

Die blutige Inquisizie. A historischer Roman, übersetzt. Wilna, 1895. 8vo, 104 pp.

Cahan, Ab. Wie asō Refoeel Naarizoch is' gewor'en a Sozialist. New York, 1896. 8vo, 80 pp.

Chaschkes, M. Lieder vom Herzen. Cracow, 1888. 16mo, 48 pp.

Dick, A. M. (Anonymous.) Der Göel. Wilna, 1866. 16mo, 88 pp.

(Anonymous.) Der Miljonär. Wilna, 1868. 16mo, 48 pp.

(Anonymous.) Die freundliche Brüder Elieser un' Naftali. Wilna, 1868. 16mo, 56 pp.

(Anonymous.) Der tödte Gast. Wilna, 1869. 16mo, 64 pp.

(Anonymous.) Der Litwak in Wolinien. Wilna, 1870. 16mo, 40 pp.

(Anonymous.) Die Bluthochzeit in Paris und ein Etwäs vun der Reformazion in Teutschland. Wilna, 1870. 16mo, 48 pp.

(A. M. D.) Fēigele der Magid. (Translation from A. Bernstein.) Wilna, 1868. 16mo, 44 pp.

(A. M. D.) Reb Schlōmele der Pair vun der Khile N., oder der Depo (Magasin) vun Bakalejen (Bsomim). (Translation from the Russian of Lewanda.) Wilna, 1870. 16mo, 144 pp.

(A. M. D.) Der erster Nabor, wäs war in dem Jāhr ThKPCh (1828). Wilna, 1871. 16mo, 36 pp.

(A. M. D.) Der ungebetene Gast. Wilna, 1871. 16mo, 47 pp.

(A. M. D.) Der Hauslehrer. Wilna, 1872. 16mo, 48 pp.

(A. M. D.) Der jüdischer Student Josef Kamenicki. (From the Polish.) Wilna, 1872. 16mo, 46 pp.

(A. M. D.) Witzen un' Spitzen, oder Anekdoten. Wilna, 1873. 16mo, 44 pp.

(A. M. D.) Eine Reise in Afrika. (Translation.) Wilna, 1873. 16mo, 48 pp.

(A. M. D.) Die ēdele Rache, oder Die Nekome. Wilna, 1875. 16mo, 44 pp.

(A. M. D.) Ssipuree Mussor, oder Moralische Erzaehlungen. Wilna, 1875. 16mo, 42 pp.

(A. M. D.) Alte jüdische Sagen oder Ssipurim. Wilna, 1876. 16mo, 43 pp.

(A. M. D.) Die alte Liebe rostet nicht. Wilna, 1876. 16mo, 79 pp.

(A. M. D.) Der Schiwim-mählzeit. Wilna, 1877. 16mo, 90 pp.

(A. M. D.) Die Grisetke, oder Die Naehterke un' Putzmacherin. Wilna, 1877. 16mo, 50 pp.

(A. M. D.) Der Fortepianist. Wilna, 1878. 16mo, 88 pp.

(A. M. D.) Der jüdische Poslanik un' Die Nacht var der Chupe. Wilna, 1880. 8vo, 64 and 36 pp.

(A. M. D.) Die Lebensgeschichte vun Note Ganew. Wilna, 1887. 8vo, 76 pp.

(A. M. D.) Dās grösse Gehēimniss. Eine sēhr interessante Erzaehlung. Wilna, 1887. 8vo, 63 pp.

(A. M. D.) Ewgenie oder die Gehēimnisse vun dem franzoesischen Hof. (From the French of F. Born.) Wilna, 1889. 8vo, 102 and 122 and 112 and 96 pp.

(A. M. D.) Der Sultan oder Die Gehēimnisse vun dem türkischen Hof. (From the French of F. Born.) Wilna, 1895. 8vo, Vol. I. 80 and 80 pp.; Vol. II. 80 and 84 pp.; Vol. III. 76 and 88 pp.; Vol. IV. 80 and 74 pp.

Dienesohn, J. *Himmel un' Erd', Dunner un' Blitz. Wilna.

Ha-Neehowim weha-Nimim, oder Der schwarzer junger Manzik. Roman. Wilna, 1875. 8vo, in four parts; 64 and 102, and?

The same. Vierte Auflage. Wilna, 1889. 8vo, 53 and 72 and 57 and 76 pp.

Zwēi Brief' zu a Mechaber. (Reprint from the Volksblatt.) St. Petersburg, 1885. 8vo, 42 pp.

Ewen Negef, oder A Stēin in Weg. Roman. (Two parts.) Warsaw, 1890. 8vo, 358 pp.

Herschele. A Roman vun klēinstädteldigen Leben. (Reprint from Jüdische Bibliothēk.) Warsaw, 1895. 4to, 179 pp.

Dlugatsch, M. Der Schlimmasel. A verschleppte, kritische, humoristische Kränk. Pankiwet nit Kēinem un' sägt Jeden aus dem Emes. Lemberg, 1883. 8vo, 30 pp.

Die Welt-messōre. Zusammengeklieben, zunaufgežebert, zunaufgeklapotschet vun alte, verschimmelte, verzwjetete Jüden. . . . Warsaw, 1895. 8vo, 68 pp.

Edelstadt, D. Volksgedichte. Popular poems. New York, 1895. 16mo, 124 pp.

Ehrenkranz-Zbarżer, B. W. Makel Noam. Volkslieder in polnisch jüdischer Mundart mit hebräischer Uebersetzung. Lemberg, Erstes Heft (second edition), 1969 (sic!), 8vo, 164 pp; (second part), 1868. 8vo, 200 pp.; Drittes Heft, 1873. 8vo, 125 + (3) pp.; Viertes Heft, 1878. 8vo, 127 pp.

Makal Chowlim. Przemyśl, 1869. 8vo, 39 pp.

Eiserkes, M. M. Der Privatlehrer. Bilder aus dem galizischen Leben. Drohobycz, 1897–1898. 8vo, 4 vols. 124 and 153 and 131 and 138 pp.

Eppelberg, H. Esterke. Drama in 5 Akten, nāch verschiedene Quellen bearbeitet. Warsaw, 1890. 8vo, 76 pp.

Epstein, M. Der geschmissener Apikōres, oder A Cholere in Duranowke. A Theater-spiel. Warsaw, 1879. 16mo, 37 pp.

Lemech der Balschem, oder Zwēi Chassanim unter ēin Chupe. A Maisse in Schirim geschrieben. Odessa, 1880. 16mo, 64 pp.

Ettinger, S. Serkele, oder Die falsche Jāhrzeit. Komödie in fünf Akten, geschehn in Lemberg. (New edition from the Johannisburg edition of 1861.) Warsaw, 1875. 8vo, 80 pp.

Mescholim, Liedelech, klēine Maisselech un' Katoweslech, ēigene un' nāchgemachte, vun Dr. Schlōme Ettinger. Herausgegeben durch W. Ettinger. St. Petersburg, 1889. 8vo, 254 pp.

The same. Zwēite Ausgabe. St. Petersburg, 1890.

F., A. Der Varblondziter, oder Dās Lebensbeschreibung vun Wigderil ben Wigderil. Warsaw, 1870. 8vo, 64 pp.

Falkowitsch, J. B. Reb Chaimel der Kozen. Ein Theater in 4 Akten. Bearbeitet nāch K. Geschrieben in St. Petersburg in 1864. Odessa, 1866. 8vo, 166 pp.

Rochele die Singerin. Ein Theater in 4 Akten, bearbeitet nāch S. und R. K. Zhitomir, 1868. 8vo, 125 pp.

Feder, S. S. Schiro Chadoscho. Ganz neue unterhaltliche Erzaehlungen. Vorstellungen mit grōssartige Volkslieder. Lemberg, 1891. 16mo, 78 and 78 pp.

Fischsohn, A. Der neuer Singer. Kiev, 1890. 16mo, 24 pp.

Frischmann, D. Jüdische Volksbibliothēk. I. Klēinigkeiten. (Tarnow, 1894.) 16mo, 32 pp.

Lokschen, a Blättel zur Unterhaltung. Verfasst durch A. Goldberg. Warsaw, 1894. 8vo, 26 col.

A Flōh vun Tische-bow, verfasst vun Awrohom Goldberg. A schwarz, springendig, lebedig, beissendig Blättel. Warsaw, 1894. 8vo, 30 col.

Frug, S. Lieder un' Gedanken. Odessa, 1896. 8vo, 160 pp.

Frumkis, S. Die treue Liebe. Ein Roman der neuer Zeit als Lustspiel (Komödie) in 4 Akten. Wilna, 1891. 8vo, 103 pp.

Gildenblatt, Ch. D. Bei'n Sāten in Hand, oder Der verkäufter Chossen. A Roman in zwēi Theil. Wilna, 1895. 8vo, 112 pp.

Awremele Bal-agole. Ein klēine Erzaehlung. Wilna, 1895. 16mo, 32 pp.

Aisikel Lez, oder Zurück auf'n gleichen Weg. Ein emesse Maisse, wās hāt sich getroffen in zwēi Städtlach "Naiwke" un' "Dumowiz." Wilna, 1895. 16mo, 32 pp.

Ein lebedige Mazeewe. A Bild vun a jüdische Tochter. Wilna, 1895. 16mo, 32 pp.

Goido, J. Der neuer Prozentnik. A Maisse. Wilna, 1893. 16mo, 62 pp. (Two parts.)

Vun Sawod in Bād. A Bild. (Vun A. Lebensohn.) Wilna, 1893. 16mo, 32 pp.

Der Ssowest is' verfallen. Nāch Schtschedrin. Wilna, 1894. 16mo, 32 pp.

Dāwid ben Dāwid (Copperfield). A Roman. Frei übersetzt vun Englisch. (4 parts, only half of the novel published.) Wilna, 1894. 8vo, 104 and 116 and 127 and 83 pp.

Die jüdisch-amerikanische Volksbibliothēk. Erscheint periodisch, ēin Māl in zwēi Wochen. Brooklyn, N.Y., 1897. 8vo, 16 pp. each.

No. 1. Die Geschmissene. A Bild vun A. Lebensohn. Erster Thēil.

No. 2. *The same.* Zwēiter Thēil.

No. 3. Die Agune. Vun B. Gorin. Erster Thēil.

No. 4. Schalach Mones. Vun B. Gorin.

No. 5. Die Agune. Zwēiter Thēil.

No. 6. Lekowed Peessach.

No. 7. Wemes Korben? Erster Thēil.

Goldfaden, A. Dās Jüdele. Jüdische Lieder auf prost jüdischer Sprach'. Herausgegeben vun J. Bernas un' N. A. Jakobi. Warsaw, 1892. 16mo, 108 pp.

Die Jüdene. Verschēidene Gedichte un' Theater in Prostjüdischen. Odessa, 1872. 8vo, 92 pp.

Schabssiel. Poema in zehn Kapitel. (Gedanken nāch dem Pogrom in Russland.) Cracow, 1896. 8vo, 44 pp.

Hozmach's Krämel vun verschiedene Antiken, 25 jüdische Volkslieder, wās senen gesungen gewor'en in Goldfaden's jüdischen Theater, zusammengeklieben vun Awrohom Jizchok Tanzmann. Warsaw, 1891. 16mo, 88 pp.

Schmendrig, oder Die komische Chassene. A Komödie in drei Akten. Warsaw, 1890. 8vo, 40 pp.

Die Kischefmacherin (Zauberin). Operette in 5 Akten un' in 8 Bilder. New York, 1893. 8vo, 66 pp.

Die kaprisne Kale-māid, oder Kabzensohn et Hungermann. Melodrama in 4 Akten un' in 5 Bilder. Warsaw, 1887. 8vo, 46 pp.

Der Fanatik, oder Die bēide Kuni-Lemel. Operette in 4 Akten un' in 8 Bilder. Warsaw, 1887. 8vo, 62 pp.

Die Bobe mit dem Enikel, oder Bonzje die Knōtlechlēgerin. Melodrama in 3 Akten mit Gesang. Warsaw, 1891. 8vo, 40 pp.

Doktor Almosado, oder Die Jüden in Palermo. Historische Operette in 5 Akten un' in 11 Bilder, bearbeitet vun einem deutschen Roman. Warsaw, 1887. 8vo, 62 pp.

Bar Kochba (Der Suhn vun dem Stern), oder Die letzte Tāg' vuu Jeruscholaim. Eine musikalische Melodrama in Reimen, in 4 Akten un' ein Prolog mit vierzehn Bilder. Warsaw, 1887. 8vo, 84 pp.

Schulamis, oder Bas Jeruscholaim. Eine musikalische Melodrama in Reimen un' in 4 Akten un' 15 Bilder. Warsaw, 1891. 8vo, 64 pp.

Rabbi Joselmann, oder Die Gseeres vun Elsass. Historische Oper in fünf Akten, in 23 Bilder. Lemberg, 1892. 8vo, 68 pp.

Theater vun Koenig Achaschwerusch, oder Koenigin Esther. Biblische Operetten in 5 Akten und 15 Bildern. Lemberg, 1890. 8vo, 56 pp.

Das X. Gebot. Komische Operetten (Zauber-märchen) in 5 Acten, 10 Verwandlungen u. 28 Bildern. Cracow, 1896. 8vo, 76 pp.

Die Opferung Isaak oder Die Zerstörung von Sodom und Gomora. Biblische Operette in 4 Acten und 40 Bildern. Cracow, 1897. 8vo, 70 pp.

Golomb, E. Chad Gadjo un' ein Schreckenes vun hundert Rändlich. Zwēi wunderbare Legenden. Vun Peessach zum Sseeder. Wilna, 1893. 16mo, 32 pp.

Gordin, J. Medea, a historische Tragödie in 4 Akten. Bearbeitet für der jüdischer Bühne für die grösse tragische Schauspielerin Madam K. Lipzin. New York, 1897. 8vo, 47 pp.

Gordon, M. Schiree M. Gordon. Jüdische Lieder. Warsaw, 1889. 8vo, 111 pp.

Gordon, J. L. Ssichas Chulin. Lieder in der Volkssprache. Warsaw, 1886. 16mo, 92 pp.

Gottlober, A. B. Der Decktuch, oder Zwēi Chupes in ēin Nacht. A Komödie in drei Akten. Arausgegeben vun Josef Werblein-ski. Warsaw, 1876. 16mo, 72 pp.

* Dās Lied vun'm Kugel. Parodie auf Schillers Lied von der Glocke. Odessa, 1863. 8vo, 24 pp.

Der Ssēim, oder Die grösse Assife in Wald, wenn die Chajes hāben ausgeklieben dem Loeb far a Meelech, vun A. B. G. Zhitomir, 1869. 16mo, 47 pp.

Der Gilgel, ein humoristische Erzaehlung. Herausgegeben vun dem Gabes Enekel. Warsaw, 1896. 8vo, 74 pp.

Harkavy, A. Washington, der erster President vun die Verēinigte Staaten. Mit Beilage: Die Unabhängigkeitserklährung in Englisch un' Jüdisch. New York, 1892. 8vo, 32 pp.

Columbus, oder Die Entdeckung vun Amerika. 2te Auflage. New York, 1897. 8vo, 32 pp.

Geschichte vun Don Quixote vun Miguel Cervantes, übersetzt vun Spanisch un' verglichen mit der englischer un deutscher Übersetzung. (In The Classical Library, 37 numbers.) New York, 1897–98. 8vo, 590 pp.

Hermalin, D. M. Der terkischer Moschiach. A historisch-romantische Schilderung über dem Leben un' Wirken vun Schabsi Zwi. New York, 1898. 8vo, 64 pp.

Jōschua ha-Nozri. Sein Erscheinen, Leben un' Tōdt. Allgemēiner Überblick wegen der Entstēhung vun Christenthum. Entwicklung un' Eindruck vun dieser Religion auf der Menschheit. Geschildert vun a historischen Standpunkt. New York, 1898. 8vo, 64 pp.

Hochbaum, S. Ein Familien-unterhalt vun drei Geschichten. Odessa, 1869. 16mo, 48 pp.

Hornstein, G. O. Slidniewker lebende Photographie, oder A Cholem in Cholem. Eine kritisch-phantastische Erzaehlung. Berdichev, 1891. 8vo, iv and 56 pp.

Kinor Hazwi (Die Harfe). Verschiedene tonisch-metrische Gedichte. Berdichev, 1891. 8vo, 68 pp.

Isabella. Der reicher Vetter. Erzaehlung. Warsaw, 1895. 16mo, 27 pp.

Vun Glück zum Keewer. Erzaehlung. Warsaw, 1895. 16mo, 28 pp.

Kalmus, U. Der Kommissionär Welwele Tareramtschik. Theater in 5 Akten. Warsaw, 1880. 16mo, 112 pp.

Schmerele Trostinezer. Theater in drei Akten. Warsaw, 1883. 16mo, 50 pp.

A Weib' an Arure un' a Mann a Malach. Ein sēhr interessante Begebenheit. St. Petersburg, 1887. 16mo, 24 pp.

Katzenellenbogen, Raschi. Jüdische Melodien oder Volkslieder. Wilna, 1887. 16mo, 86 pp.

Kobrin, L. Jankel Boile. Vun dem jüdischen Fischerleben in Russland un' andere Erzaehlungen. Realistic Library. Issued quarterly. Vol. I. No. 1. New York, 1898. 8vo, 111 pp.

Lefin, M. M. Sseefer Koheles. Odessa, 1873. 8vo, 77 and (3) pp.

Lerner, J. J. Der Vetter Mösche Mendelssohn. A dramatisches Bild in ēin Akt, nāch dem Deutschen far der jüdischer Bühne bearbeitet. Warsaw, 1889. 8vo, 26 pp.

Uriel Akosta. A Tragödie in fünf Akten vun Karl Gutzkow. Far der jüdischer Szene übersetzt un' arrangirt. Zwēite Auflage. Warsaw, 1889. 8vo, 80 pp.

Židowka, Die Jüdin. A Tragödie in fünf Akten. Nāch verschiedene Quellen bearbeitet. Warsaw, 1889. 8vo, 68 pp.

Chanuke. A historische Drama in vier Akten in sieben Bilder. Warsaw, 1889. 8vo, 54 pp.

Rothschild. A Beschreibung . . . Odessa, 1869. 8vo, 34 pp.

Levinsohn, L. Die weibersche Knüpplach, ein Theaterspiel in fünf Akten geschrieben, herausgegeben vun MIWM. Wilna, 1881 (from ed. of 1874). 16mo, 44 pp.

Lew, M. A. Hudel. A Poema in Gedichte. Kishinev, 1888. 8vo, 64 pp.

Lilienblum, M. L. Serubowel, oder Schiwas Siōn. A Drama in fünf Akten. Odessa, 1887. 8vo, 55 pp.

Linetzki, J. J. *Dās pōlische Jüngel, oder A Biographie vun sich allēin. Drinnen is' geschildert akurat der pōlischer Chossid vun Geborenheit ān, sein Erziehung, sein Bocher-leben, sein Chassene un' sein Parnosse mit alle Khols-sachen un' Gemēinde-leben. Odessa, 1875. 132 pp.

Dās chsidische Jüngel. Die Lebensbeschreibung vun a pōlischen Jüden, vun sein Gebōren bis sein Verlōren. Zu der Zeit vun'm Ānfang des jetzigen Jāhrhundert, vun Eli Kozin Hazchakueli. Die zwēite, vollkommen übergearbeitete Ausgabe, vun mein (Pōlischen Jüngel). Wilna, 1897. 8vo, 230 pp.

Der boeser Marschelik. Satirische Volkslieder. Odessa, 1869. 8vo, 96 pp.

The same. (First part.) Warsaw, 1889. 8vo, 48 pp.

*Dās Meschulachas. Kartines vun'm jüdischen Leben. Odessa, 1874. 94 pp.

Der Welt-luach vun'm Jāhr Ein Kessef, oder Die allgemēine Panorame, vun Eli Kozin Hazchakueli, Mechaber vun'm Pōlischen Jüngel. Odessa, 1875. 8vo, 94 pp.

The same. (Zwēite verbesserte Ausgabe.) Odessa, 1883. 8vo, 86 pp.

Linetzki's Ksowim. Dās erste Heft: Die Pritschepe. Dās zwēite Heft: Der Statek. Kritische, satirische un' humoristische Maimorim un' Kartines. Odessa, 1876. 16mo, 127 pp.

Die blutige Nekome, oder Jakow Tirada. In gesauberten jüdischen Žargon. Warsaw, 1883. 8vo, 100 pp.

The same. Warsaw, 1893. 8vo, 100 pp.

Nāssān ha-Chochem. Eine dramatische Unterhandlung über Emune un' Religion, verfasst in Deutschen vun G. E. Lessing. Odessa, 1884. 8vo, 80 pp.

Linetzki's Ksowim. Odessa, 1888. Fol. Der Flederwisch, Der Schōfer, Der Schnorrer, Der Plappler, Der Wicher, Dās Drēhdel, Der Weiser, Der Milgrām, Der Grager, Der Afikōmen, Dās Vōgele, each of 8 pp.

Chag ha-Jōwel. Die Jubilee-feierung am siebzehnten November 1890, welche män hāt gefeiert in Odessa dem berühmten Volksschreiber Jizchok Joel Linetzki zur Ende 25 Jāhr vun seiner literarischer Thätigkeit. Odessa, 1891. 8vo, 48 pp.

Meisach, J. Eesches Chail. Eine historische Erzaehlung in 4 Akten un' 6 Bilder. Warsaw, 1890. 16mo, 80 pp.

Die eifersüchtige Frau, oder Die erste Köchin. A Szene vun a Familienleben. Warsaw, 1893. 16mo, 31 pp.

Der Spiegel für Alle. Ein literarisches Buch. Enthalt verschiedene musterhafte Bilder aus dem jüdischen Leben in Reimen. Warsaw, 1893. 8vo, 32 pp.

Nissim we-Nifloes. (Wunderliche Ssipurim), wās die Babe oleho ha-Scholem hāt erzaehlt. Warsaw, 1893. 16mo, 86 pp.

Perl vun Jam ha-Talmud. Warsaw, 1893. 16mo, 32 pp.

Ssipuree ha-Talmud. Warsaw, 1894. 8vo, 48 pp.

Ssipuree Jeruscholaim. (Dritte Auflage.) Wilna, 1895. 16mo, 72 pp.

A Spazier-schiffel auf dem Jam ha-Talmud. Warsaw, 1895. 16mo, 64 pp.

Die zwēi Wasserträger. A Maisse nōro, wās die Bobe hāt der-zählt ihr Enikel. Äuch a schoene Maisse : A Spei in Ponim. Wilna, 1897. 16mo, 31 pp.

Reb Lemel, oder Der Pariser Bankir. Wilna, 1897. 16mo, 32 pp.

Mordechai ha-Zadik. A Ssipur asō gut wie a Roman, äuch a Maisse-nōro mit dem Kazew in Ganeeden. Wilna, 1897. 16mo, 32 pp.

Der Aschmedai, A schreckliche Maisse, wās hāt amāl getroffen in die Zeiten vun Schlōme ha-Melech. Wilna, 1898. 16mo, 31 pp.

Natansohn, B. Papierene Brück', oder Die hefker Welt. RIBL's Lebensbeschreibung; der Ssod vun Magnetism, äuch wās es thut sich auf jener Welt, etc. . . . Warsaw, 1894. 8vo, 78 pp.

Ostrowski, S. M. Der Maskeradenball. A satirische Poeme in Versen. Warsaw, 1884. 16mo, 135 pp.

Perez, J. L. Poesie. Warsaw, 1892. 16mo, 34 pp.

Poesie. Zwēites Heft. Monisch. Ballada. Warsaw, 1892, 16mo, 40 pp.

Bekannte Bilder. Verfrören gewor'en! (Zwēite Auflage.) War-saw, 1894. 8vo, 22 and 26 and 22 pp.

Klēine Erzaehlungen. Zwēi Bilder. Jōssel Jeschiwe-bocher un' Dās āreme Jüngel. (Ausgabe vun J. Goido.) Wilna, 1894. 16mo, 32 pp.

Perel, M. Die Nacht vun Churban Jeruscholaim. Warsaw, 1892. 8vo, 32 pp.

Pinski, D. Brehm. Die Affen. Bearbeitet vun D. Puls. (J. L. Perez's Ausgaben.) Warsaw, 1894. 12mo, 52 pp.

Reb Schlōme. Erzaehlung. (J. L. Perez's Ausgaben.) Warsaw, 1894. 12mo, 43 pp.

Der grösser Menschenfreund un' Arāb der Joch. Zwēi Bilder. (Goido's Ausgaben.) Wilna, 1894. 16mo, 32 pp.

A Verfallener. Drei Erzaehlungen. (Ausgaben "Zeitgeist.") Warsaw, 1896. 16mo, 65 pp.

Rabinowitsch, S. Supplements of Volksblatt :

    1884, * No. 32–35. Natascha.

        * No. 39–40. Höcher un' Niedriger.

    1886, * No. 1– 6. Die Weltreise.

        * No. 19–22. Kinderspiel.

    1887, No. 20. Kinderspiel. A merkwürdige Liebe vun a gepesteten, a gebaleweten, a reichen jüdischen Benjochid. 4to, 89 pp.

1887, No. 26. A Chossen a Doktor (A Stubsach). 16mo, 18 pp.

No. 27. Lagbōmer (A froehliche Geschichte mit a traurigen Eude. 16mo, 12 pp.

1888, No. 23. Reb Sender Blauk un' sein vullgeschätzte Familie. A Roman ohn' a Liebe. 8vo, 104 pp.

*Schomer's Mischpet.

Dās Messerl. (A narrische, nor a traurige Geschichte vun mein Kindheit.) St. Petersburg, 1887. 16mo, 26 pp.

A Büntel Blumen oder Poesje ohn' Gramen. Berdichev, 1888. 16mo, 45 pp.

Supplements to the Volksbibliothēk:

Steinpenju. A jüdischer Roman. 1888. 8vo, viii and 94 pp.

Jossele Ssolowee. 1889. 8vo, (4) and 180 pp.

Auf Jischuw Erzisroel. A Ssipur ha-Maisse. Kiev, 1890. 16mo, 44 pp.

Kol-mewasser zu der jüdischer Volksbibliothēk. Odessa, 1892. 4to, 40 pp. (80 columns.)

Jaknehos, oder Dās grösse Börsenspiel. A Komödie in vier Akten. Kiev, 1894. 32mo, 172 pp., but p. 32 is repeated 13 times.

Der jüdischer Kongress in Basel. Vorgelesen in alle Kiewer Botee-midroschim nāch dem Referat vun Dr. M. Mandelstamm, bearbeitet in Žargon. Warsaw, 1897. 8vo, 30 pp. (Published by the Zionistic Society Achiassaf.)

Auf wās bedarfen Jüden a Land? Etliche erenste Wörter far'n Volk. Warsaw, 1898. 8vo, 20 pp. (Achiassaf).

Moschiach's Zeiten. A zionistischer Roman. (Verlag Esra.) Berdichev, 1898. 16mo, 51 pp. (unfinished).

Reichersohn, Z. H. Basni Krilow, oder Krilows Fabeln (Mescholim) in neun Ābthēilungen, übersetzt vun Russisch in Jüdisch-deutsch. (2 parts.) Wilna, 1879. 16mo, 156 and 166 pp.

Reingold, I. A Büntel Blumen. Volksgedichte. Chicago, 1895. 16mo, 32 pp.

Der Weltsinger. Prächtige Volkslieder. Chicago, 1894. 8vo, 40 pp.

Rombro, J. Die eiserne Maske, oder der unglücklicher Prinz. Ein historischer Roman aus dem Leben vun dem Koeniglichen Hof

in der Zeit vun Ludwig dem 13ten in Frankreich. Frei übersetzt vun Ph. Krantz. Wilna, 1894. 8vo, 114 pp.

Rosenfeld, M. Poesien un' Lieder. Erster Thēil. Nazionale
Lieder. Gedichte un' Lieder. New York, 1893. 8vo, 46 pp.

Liederbuch. Erster Thēil. New York, 1897. 8vo, 88 pp.

Songs from the Ghetto. With Prose Translation, Glossary, and
Introduction, by Leo Wiener. Boston, Copeland and Day,
1898. 16mo, 115 pp.

Sahik, D. Die Rose zwischen Dörner. Ein Theater in 4 Akten.
Petrokow, 1884. 8vo, 80 pp.

Schafir, B. B. Schire-Bas-Ichuda. Lieder über die Verfolgung
der Juden in Russland und den Antisemitismus in anderen
Ländern, in der Mundart der Juden Galiziens mit hebräischer
Uebersetzung, gesungen von Bajrach Benedikt Schafir aus
Przemyśl [1883]. 16mo, 65 pp.

Freudele die Mame. Lemberg, 1882. Long 16mo, 21 pp.

Melodien aus der Gegend am San. Gedichte und Lieder in
galizisch-jüdischem Dialekte. (2 parts.) Cracow, 1886.
16mo, 75 and 85 pp.

Schaikewitsch, N. M. Der Bal-tschuwe, oder Der falscher
Chossen. Ein höchst interessanter Roman. Wilna. 1880.
8vo, 170 pp.

Der Rewisor. A Komödie in 4 Akten. Umgearbeitet frei vun
der berühmter russischer Komödie "Rewisor." Odessa, 1883.
8vo, 56 pp.

A Patsch vun sein lieben Nāmen. A klēiner Roman. Warsaw,
1889. 8vo, 33 pp.

Schapiro, W. Der Zwuak, oder Der maskirter Reb Zodek. A Roman. (Nāch Mapu's Ait Zowùa.) Odessa, 1896. 8vo, 235 pp.

Schatzkes, M. A. Der jüdischer Var-Peessach, oder Minhag Jisroel. A Ssipur Niflo vun dem Art Leben vun unsere Jüden,
un' bejōsser in der Lito, etc. Warsaw, 1881. 8vo, 180 pp.
Many editions.

Seiffert, M. Bei'm Thür fun Ganeeden, oder A puster Cholem
mit a grōssen Emes. A phantastischer Roman. New York,
1898. 8vo, 64 pp.

Itele un' Gütele. Roman aus dem jüdischen Leben in Lito.
Wilna, 1891. 8vo, 219 pp.

Sharkansky, A. M. Jüdische Nigunim. Poetical Works. New
York, 1895. 8vo, 62 pp.

Sobel, J. Z. Schir Sohow lekowed Jisroel ha-Soken. Übersetzt in Jüdisch-deutsch, Jisroel der Alte. New York, 1877. 16mo, 36 pp.

Sobel, S. Siwugim, oder Die Wikuchim. Zum lustigen Zeitvertreiben. Warsaw, 1874. 16mo, 86 pp.

Spektor, M. * A Roman ohn' a Nāmen. Ein Erzaehlung vun dem jüdischen Leben. Zwēite Auflage mit viel neue Kapitlich un' Verbesserungen. St. Petersburg, 1884. 8vo, 110 pp.

Supplements to the Volksblatt:

    1884, *No. 1–31. Der jüdischer Mužik.

          *No. 41–51. Reb Treitel.

    1885, *No. 1– 9. Reb Treitel.

          No. 9–17. A stummer guter Jüd'. 8vo, 68 pp.

          *No. 18–50. Aniim we-Ewjonim.

          *No. 50–51. Die Krämer in Aleksandria.

    1886, *No. 7–16. Jüdisch.

          *No. 24–42. A Welt mit klēine Weltelech.

Der stummer Guter-Jüd'. Ein Erzaehlung vun der letzter russisch-türkischer Krieg. Wilna, 1889. 8vo, 76 pp.

Scholem Faiwischke die Krämerke. Zwēi Maisses. Warsaw, 1890. 16mo, 26 pp.

The same, under the title: Weiberscher Erewjontew. 1892. 16mo, 26 pp.

Der modner Schuster. Roman. Berdichev, 1891. 16mo, 32 pp.

The same. Warsaw, 1894. 16mo, 32 pp.

A weibersche Neschome. Roman. Berdichev, 1891. 16mo, 32 pp.

The same. Warsaw, 1894. 16mo, 32 pp.

The same, under the title: Schoen un' Mies, oder Zwēi Chawertes. Erzaehlung vun balebatischen Leben. Warsaw, 1895. 16mo. 23 pp.

The same. Russian translation, by M. Chaschkes. Dvě podrugi. Psichologičeskij razskaz. (Reprint of Vilenskij Věstnik.) Wilna, 1895. 16mo, 21 pp.

Chaim Jentes. Erzaehlung. Berdichev, 1892. 16mo, 32 pp.

Der heuntiger jüdischer Mužik. Roman. Berdichev, 1892. 16mo, 32 pp.

Jüdische Studenten un' jüdische Töchter. Roman. 1892. 8vo, 124 pp.

Purim un' Peessach. Bilder un' Erzaehlungen. Berdichev, 1893. 16mo, 36 pp.

Gut gelebt un' schoen gestorben. Erzaehlung. Warsaw, 1894. 16mo, 28 pp.

Supplements to the Hausfreund:

 1895. Reb Treitel. 8vo, 148 pp.

 1896. Drei Parschön. Erzaehlung vun die siebziger un' achziger Jähren. 8vo, 71 pp.

Terr, J. Natur un' Leben. Romanen, Erzaehlungen, Dramen, Skizzen, Anekdoten, Poesie un' Witzen, gesammelte un' originelle. New York, 1898. 8vo.

Winchevsky, M. Lieder un' Gedichte. Poetical Works. Published by the Group "Yehi-Or." New York, 1894. 16mo, 128 pp. (unfinished).

Jehi Ōr. Eine Unterhaltung über die verkehrte Welt. Herausgegeben vun der Newarker Gruppe "Ritter der Freiheit." 2te Herausgabe. Newark, N.J., 1890. 8vo, 24 pp.

Zederbaum, A. Die Gehēimnisse von Berdiczew. Eine Characterschilderung der dortigen jüdischen Gemeinde, als Muster der jüdischen Sitten. Warsaw, 1870. 8vo, 84 and (2) pp.

Zuckermann, M. Der Meschugener in siebeten Himmel, oder A Reise auf dem Luftballon, von Jules Verne. Warsaw, 1896. 8vo, 38 pp.

Zunser, E. Kolrina. Neue acht Lieder. Wilna, 1870. 32mo, 64 pp.

Schirim Chadoschim. Acht neue, grösse, feine Lieder. Wilna, 1871. 32mo, 64 pp.

Der Ssandek. Eydkuhnen, 1872. 32mo, 64 pp.

Hamnageen. Vier neue, herrliche Lieder mit Melodien. Wilna, 1876. 32mo, 31 pp.

Schiree Om. Volkslieder. Drei neue Lieder zu singen mit Melodien. Wilna, 1876. 32mo, 32 pp.

Hamsamer. Neue vier Lieder. Wilna, 1890. 32mo, 31 pp.

Die Eisenbahn mit noch zwēi teuere Lieder. Wilna, 1890. 32mo, 28 pp.

Zunser's verschiedene Volkslieder, welche wer'en gesungen vun'm Volk mit sejere Melodien. Text mit Musik verfasst un' komponirt vun'm Volksdichter Eliokum Zunser, herausgegeben durch David Davidoff. New York, 1891. 8vo, 80 pp.

Zehn jüdische Volkslieder, verfasst mit die Harmonie vun Musikbegleitung. Vierte Auflage. Wilna, 1891. 16mo, 95 pp.

Higojon Bchinor. Neue vier Lieder, wās see seinen gesungen gewor'en mit Begleitung vun Fiedel. Wilna, 1897. 16mo, 60 pp.

Zweifel, B. Z. Tochachas Chaim. Sträfred'. Wilna, 1865. 32mo, 96 pp.

Sseefer Musser Haskel, herausgegeben vun Esriel Epl Weiz. Wilna, 1884. 32mo, 52 pp.

Der glücklicher Maftir. A schoene Maisse, wäs hät getroffen zurück mit ēinige Jāhren; wie a Schneiderjüngel is' durch a Maftir höchst glücklich gewor'en. . . . Warsaw, 1886. 8vo, 46 pp.

FOLKLORE

Sseefer Ssipuree Maisses. Warsaw, 1874. 8vo, 170 pp. There are several editions of it.

Maisse Rambam we-Reb Jōssef dela Reyna. Wilna, 1879. 16mo, 32 pp.

Dem Rambam's Zawoe. Dā werd beschrieben die Lebensgeschichte vun dem grössen hēiligen Mann Rabeenu Mōsche ben Maimon, sēhr schoene interessante Ssipurim, äuch die hēilige Zawoe, wäs er hät geschrieben für seine Kinder, etc. Wilna, 1885. 16mo, 32 pp.

Maisse vun Maharscho, herausgenummen vun Ostrer Pinkes, un' vun Rambam, un' vun Nōda bi-Jehudo. Warsaw, 1879. 16mo, 16 pp.

Maisse Gur Arje. Dā werd derzaehlt a wunderliche Maisse vun dem göttlichen Mann ha-Raw ha-Goen . . . wäs er werd gerufen Gur Arje, etc. Warsaw, 1890. 16mo, 43 pp.

Ssipurim. Erzaehlungen vun Rabi Jizchok Aschkenasi Luria. Versammelt vun Jisroel Bemuhrim ZL. Vol. I. Wilna, 1895. 8vo, 114 pp.

Sseefer Ewen Schlom. Die Beschreibung vun dem Wilner Goen. Sēhr wunderliche Ssipurim vun sein Grösskeit in der Tōre un' in alle Chochmes un' Wissenschaften. Äuch sēhr wunderliche Maisses vun seine berühmte Talmidim. Wilna, 1895. 16mo, 112 pp.

Eine schoene Geschichte vun ha-Raw ha-Goen Haschach und seine Tochter, wäs hät sich passiert in die Gseeres vun Schnas

ThCh. Un' äuch eine schoene Geschichte vun einem pōlischen Koenig, welcher eine grōsse Gseere auf Jüden gegeben hāt, un' wie HSchI seinem Volk geholfen durch ēinen vun die LW Zadikim. Die Maisse is' verschrieben in ein Maisse-buch in Krakau. Vienna, 1863. 32mo, 16 pp.

Sseefer Ssipuree Maisses. (K'hal Chsidim.) In diesen Sseefer werd derzaehlt sēhr viel wunderliche Maisses vun ha-Raw ha-Kōdesch Jisroel Balschemtow, etc. Warsaw, 1881. 4to, 84 pp.

Sseefer Maisse Zadikim. Hier is' wunderliche Maisses vun Kdo-schim, vun dem hēiligen Bescht un' vun Boruch vun Mesibōs un' vun die zwēi Brüder Reb Alimelech un' Reb Susse vun Hanipole un' vun ha-Kōdesch Reb Pinches vun Korez un' vun ha-Kōdesch Reb Mōsche Loeb vun Ssassuw un' vun ha-Kōdesch Reb Jizchok vun Lublin. Cracow, 1889. 16mo, 64 pp.

Sseefer Rosin Kadischin. In dem Sseefer werd gebrengt sēhr schoene un' wunderliche Geschichtes vun sēhr grōsse Leut' Zadikim Jessodee Ōlom. Warsaw, 1890. 8vo, 32 pp.

Ssipurim me-Rabeenu Nissim. Warsaw, 1892. 16mo, 59 pp.

Eine ganz neue Maisse vun dem hēiligen Zadik Reb Schmelke. Lemberg, 1893. 16mo, 16 pp.

Eine ganz neue Maisse vun ha-Raw ha-Zadik Reb Pinches me-Korez. Lemberg, 1893. 16mo, 16 pp.

Eine ganz neue Maisse vun ha-Raw ha-Zadik Reb Jisroel, der Rusi-ner Rebe. Lemberg, 1893. 16mo, 16 pp.

Mefanejach Nelomim ... Jechiel Michel mi-Slatschuw. Warsaw, 1879. 16mo, 22 pp.

Eine ganz neue Geschichte vun dem Sāten, wie er hāt sich verstellt far ein jungen Mann un' hāt gesāgt, as er is' a Row un' hāt gewollt überreden ein Jüd', a Baltschuwe, er soll essen Chomez um Erew Peessach, etc. Lemberg, 1892. 16mo, 16 pp.

Die Gan-eeden-bachurim. Dā werd derzaehlt zwēi schoene Maisses vun zwēi Bochurim Baltschuwes, wie asō see hāben sōche gewe'n zu kummen in lichtigen Gan-eeden, asō ein teuer Ort, wās die grōsste Zadikim können nit ahin kummen. Warsaw, 1885. 16mo, 27 pp.

Die Ssuke in Wald. In diese Geschichte werd derzaehlt, wie Gott helft Alle, wās versichern sich auf ihm. Äuch is' dā zugegeben a Maisse vun a Row mit a Ssar un' ein Geschichte vun Rambam. Wilna, 1891. 16mo, 32 pp.

Maisse me-G Achim. Eine sēhr schoene wunderliche Geschichte vun drei Brüder, grōsse Leut', hanikro Maisse Plies. Warsaw, 1870. 16mo. Large number of editions.

Maisse schnee Chaweerim. A wunderliche Ausschmues mit 22 Maisses. Zhitomir, 1877. 16mo, 76 pp.

Mizwas Mlawe Malke u Maisses Plies mischnee Schutfim. Sēhr a schoene, wunderliche Geschichte vun zwei Schutfim, wās hāben sēhr ehrlich gehalten un' gehüt' die verte Ssude Mizwas Mlawe Malke. Warsaw, 1881. 16mo, 28 pp.

Reb Esriel mit dem Bär. A zwēite Geschichte vun Reb Chaim Baltschuwe un' a dritte vun Reb Sundel Chossid. Wilna, 1896. 16mo, 32 pp.

Die Geschichte vun Bovo. Ein schoen Derzaehlung vun Bovo mit Dresni. Dās is' gemacht auf dem Art vun Tauseud un' Ein Nacht. Warsaw, 1878. 16mo, 72 pp.

There are many editions of the same. In the Harvard Library are the following : Wilna, 1895, and Warsaw, 1889. The latter has for a title : Der Ben Meelach. Dā werd derzaehlt vun a Chossen-kale, viel see hāben gelitten, un' der Ben-meelach, viel Milchomes er hāt eingenummeu, bis es hāt ihm geglückt, as er is' gewor'eu der grösster Kēisser un' sie Kēisserin vun drei Medines.

Eine schoene Geschichte vun Zenture Venture. Dā werd derzaehlt vun ein grössen Ssōcher, wās er is' gewe'n vielmāl in Angst un' Nōt auf dem Jam un' is' gewe'n in die Händ' vun wilde Menschen un' is' nizel gewor'en vun die alle Sachen un' is' gekummen zu sein Haus le-Scholem mit viel Aschires. Wilna, 1895. 16mo, 40 pp. There are many editions of this story.

Ssipuree Haploes, oder Gerühmte Geschichte. Dās Sseefer is' gedruckt gewor'en bischnas ThSH wenikro be-Scheem Maissebuch, etc. Lublin, 1882. 8vo, 68 pp. Very many editions of this book.

A schoene Geschichte, wie a Loeb' hāt ausgehodewet a klēinem Prinz, wās der Loeb' hāt ihm aweggechapt vun sein Mutter, der Koenigin, boees er hāt gesōgen un' hāt ihm asō lang gehalten, bis er is' grōss gewor'en. Vun A. M. Warsaw, 1878. 32mo, 31 pp.

Der lichtiger Gan-eeden. Ein schoene Geschichte vun Reb Schmerel Machnis Ōrach, wie er is' gewe'n in lichtigen Ganeeden, nor er hāt dort kēin ssach nit gewältigt; män hāt ihm bald arausgeworfen. Warsaw, 1878. 16mo, 18 pp.

Ein schoene Geschichte vun ein Bas-malke, wie sie hāt sich verliebt in ein Suhn vun ein Gärtner. Warsaw, 1889. 16mo, 72 pp. There are many editions of this story.

Ein wunderliche Maisse vun dem Bocher Jossenke. Lemberg, 1887. 16mo, 16 pp. ·　　　———————

Anekdoten-buch. Zwēi hundert schoene Witzen, sēhr satirisch zum Lachen, vun M. Kukelstein. Wilna, 1893. 16mo, 96 pp. Many editions.

Reb Herschele Ostrepoler. Beschrieben alle seine süsse Chochmes un' alle seine Wörtlech, wäs er hat übergelāst, etc. Warsaw, 1884. 16mo, 24 pp. Many editions. Second part. Wilna, 1895. 16mo, 24 pp.

Der berühmter Herschel Ostropoler. Zunaufgesammelt vun A. I. Buchbinder. Wilna, 1895. 8vo, 32 pp.

Dās froehliche Herschel Ostropoler oder Der wolweler Theaterstück. Warsaw, 1890. 8vo, 52 pp. Many editions.

Motke Chabad oder Witze über Witze. Herausgegeben vun M. I. Lewitan. Wilna, 1892. 16mo, 32 pp. Many editions.

Schaike Feifer, oder Der weltberühmter Witzling. New York, s. d. 8vo, 32 pp.

Jōssef Loksch vun Drazne (in Pōlen)...; un' vun sein Gabe Akiwe Blas. Wilna, 1895. 16mo, 23 pp.

Der Chelmer Chochem. Dās is' a Geräthenisch vun a Chelmer, wäs er hāt gemēint, as er is' a Chochem, un' män mus lachen, as män lejent die kluge Einfälle vun a Chelmer Chochem. Verfasst vun Hirs Bik. Lemberg, 1887. 16mo, 16 pp.

JUDEO-GERMAN BOOKS WITH GERMAN CHARACTERS

Gnib, I. D. H. Das Chanuke Trenderl, ein antiques Familienstück von Unsere Leut'. In 2 Aufzügen, renovirt. Vienna, 1884. 16mo, 30 pp.

Der Schadchen von Unsere Leut'. Ein rewmatisches Zugstück in drei Aufzügen, zusammengeschlempert. Vienna, 1887. 16mo, 56 pp.

Der Johrmark zu A . . . z. Eine Charakterschilderung von unsere Marktleut'. In 3 Skizzen, aufgenommen. Vienna, 1871. 16mo, 32 pp.

Mendelssohn, L. Intimes aus der Liliengass'. Ein Buchdrama in I. Akt. Berlin, s. a. 16mo, 62 pp.

Rosée, A. Esther und Haman! Ein Purimspiel in einem Aufzuge. Vienna, 1884. 16mo, 24 pp.

S(chwarz) A. Aus längstvergangenen Tagen. Drei alte Goldstückchen nebst einem Anhang. Budapest, s. a. 16mo, 31 pp.

Schwarz, P. Reb Simmel Andrichau. Ein Purimspiel in vier Aufzügen. Vienna, 1878. 16mo, 55 pp.

* Reb Moire Nachrendl. Charaktergemälde in 5 Aufzügen. Eine humoristische Brochure in jüdisch-deutschem Jargon, zur Unterhaltung und Belehrung.

* Reb Jone. Lustspiel zur Unterhaltung und Erheiterung. In fünf Aufzügen.

Wolfsohn. Reb Chanoch der betrogene Bigott, oder Der entlarvte Scheinheilige. Lustspiel in 3 Aufzügen. Pest, s. a. 16mo, 43 pp.

Anonymous. * Der Gütsteher. Travestie nach Schillers Ballade, ' Die Bürgschaft.'

(Reb Leser Scholetsetzer.) Das Lied vom Scholet. Travestie von Schillers ' Lied von der Glocke.' 'n Chosens Kloles. Travestie nach Uhlands ' Des Sängers Fluch.' Vienna, s. a. 16mo, 20 pp.

II. APPENDIX

NAMES OF AUTHORS AND THEIR PSEUDONYMS

The italicized names are those that are better known than the real names of the authors.

AUTHORS	PSEUDONYMS
Abramowitsch, S. J.	*Mendele Möcher Sforim.*
Baranow, M.	Ben Efraim.
Bukanski.	Ben Pōres.
Cahan, Ab.	Bernstein Dāwid, Proletarischker Magid.
Cantor.	Mösche Gläzel, Graf M. I. Kweetl, Welwel Zopzerik.
Dawidowitsch.	Ben Dāwid.
Feigenbaum, B.	Magid vun Ewjenischok, Raüberjüdel, Scha Pesches.
Freid, M.	Fremder, Ssimchessossen.
Frischmann, D.	Goldberg A.
Goido, J.	Hoido J., *Gorin*, Lebensohn A.
Goldberg, I. Ch.	Jaknehuz.
Gurewitsch.	*Libin, Z.*
Katzenellenbogen.	Buki Ben Jogli.
Kobrin, L.	Rafaelowitsch Sch., Genosse Cervera, Witeblanin, L.
Lerner, J. J.	Herdner.
Lewin, I.	Jehalel.
Lewner, J. B.	Nachmen Ben Wowsi.
Linetzki, J. J.	Eli Kozin Hazchakueli.
Meisach, J.	Ssar-schel-Jam.
Perez, J. L.	Ben-tomar, Gam-su, Ha-jossem mi-Nimirow, Finkel L., Lampenputzer, Lez vun der Redakzie, Luziper, Paloi, Dr. Stizer.

Pinski, D.	Dōfek, Dāwid, Puls D.
Rabinowitsch, M. J.	*Ben-Omi.*
Rabinowitsch, S.	Bücherfresser, Essbücher, Esther, Schelumiel, *Scholem Aleechem*, Schulamis.
Rabnizki.	Rebi Kozin.
Rombro, J.	*Krantz Ph.*, Jainkele Chochem.
Samostschin, P.	P. Z., Eli Feelet mi-Sastschin.
Samostschin, Mrs.	Bas-malke.
Schaikewitsch, N. M.	*Schomer.*
Schapiro, E. I.	Isch.
Schatzkes, M. A.	Selikowitsch M.
Selikowitsch.	Litwischer Philosoph, Aus Kapeluschmacher, Sambation, Wachlaklakes.
Spektor, M.	Emes, Lamedwownik.
Spektor, Mrs.	*Isabella.*
Wechsler, M.	Isch Nomi.
Winchevsky, M.	*Ben Nez, Meschugener Philosoph*, Chaim Barburim, Chaim Bolbetun, Der Däsiger, T. E. Debkin, Jankele Traschke.

INDEX

385